JUST TOO

WEIRD

BISHOP ROMNEY
and the
MORMON TAKEOVER of AMERICA:
POLYGAMY, THEOCRACY,
and
SUBVERSION

by Webster Griffin Tarpley, Ph.D.

2012

JUST TOO WEIRD

BISHOP ROMNEY and the MORMON TAKEOVER of AMERICA:
POLYGAMY, THEOCRACY, and SUBVERSION

Copyright 2012 © by Webster Griffin Tarpley, Ph. D.
All Rights Reserved Release Oct. 10, 2012.
Published by *Progressive Press*,
PO Box 12834, Palm Desert, Calif. 92255,
www.ProgressivePress.com.
ISBN 1-61577-724-5, EAN 978-1-61577-724-2
Length: 132,000 words, 278 pages
List Price: $14.95. Format: 240 x 170 mm.
Distribution: Lightning Source.

BISAC Subject Area Codes:
REL046000 RELIGION / Mormonism
BIO010000 BIOGRAPHY / Political
HIS036000 HISTORY / United States

Presidential candidate Mitt Romney's Mormon tradition is revealed as no real religion but a cult invented by a charlatan, a disguise for a subversive ideology opposing all that is best in the American tradition. The British recruited Mormon leaders into their 19th century plot to break up the US, leading to the cult's strategic occupation of Utah territory. Mormonism has never abandoned its secrecy and its enmity to America. Mitt Romney is the hoped-for figure who will fulfill Mormon prophecy and take over the United States. This book provides warning insights into a possible Romney presidency by exploring over 182 years of Latter-day Saints tradition. As Romney is a notorious liar and flip-flopper, it is useless to examine his political positions at any given moment. He attempts to pose as an ultra-patriot, but his family considered the barbaric Mormon practice of polygamy more important than loyalty to the United States. Romney spent years attempting to recruit for the cult, in which black Americans were regarded as inferior. Although Romney demands an aggressive foreign policy, nobody in his family every served this country in uniform – although at least one ancestor fought against the Union in the attempted 1857 Mormon secession of Utah. As president, Romney would rely on and build up the Mormon Mafia in the intelligence community. He might try to carry out Mormon Prophet Joseph Smith's apocalyptic White Horse Prophecy, which calls for a Mormon takeover of the United States, followed by a campaign to conquer the world for their theocracy. Every voter needs to read this book.

TABLE OF CONTENTS

---

[1] Clyde de L. Ryals, "Thomas Carlyle on the Mormons: an Unpublished Essay, *Carlyle Studies Annual* (XV) 1995, pp. 49-54.

PREFACE

"IF I WERE YOU, I'D WONDER WHY ROMNEY HATES AMERICA SO MUCH"

"All writers should be put in a box and thrown in the sea."
– Mormon Prophet Gordon B. Hinckley, 2002.[2]

On Monday, September 17, 2012 American public opinion was shocked by a tape of the cynical remarks made on May 17 by Republican presidential candidate Mitt Romney before a group of wealthy backers at the home of his fellow private equity manager Marc Leder in Boca Raton, Florida. On this occasion Romney, a Bishop of the Mormon Church, made the following remarks before his fund-raising audience:

"There are 47% of the people who will vote for the president no matter what. All right, there are 47% who are with him, who are dependent upon government, who believe that they are victims, who believe the government has a responsibility to care for them, who believe that they are entitled to health care, to food, to housing, to you name it. That's an entitlement. And the government should give it to them. And they will vote for this president no matter what…. These are people who pay no income tax … My job is not to worry about those people. I'll never convince them they should take personal responsibility and care for their lives."[3]

Rarely has a presidential candidate been caught expressing so much contempt for the American people. The premise of the Romney presidential campaign is that this wealthy Mormon businessman is more American than the community organizer Barack Hussein Obama, but Romney's elitist criticism caused even Republicans to doubt that he could govern. A dramatic example came from *Washington Post* columnist E. J. Dionne, who wrote in his column:

"The most incisive reaction to Mitt Romney's disparaging comments about 47% of us came from a conservative friend who e-mailed: 'If I were you, I'd wonder why Romney hates America so much.'"[4]

This book attempts to provide part of the answer, specifically in the tradition of hatred, resentment, and vendetta of the United States of America historically cultivated by the

---

[2] Lawrence Wright, "Lives of the Saints: at a Time When Mormonism Is Booming, the Church Is Struggling with a Troubled Legacy," *New Yorker*, January 21, 2002.
[3] David corn, "Secret Video: Romney Tells Billionaire Donor What He Really Thinks of Obama Voters: When He Doesn't Know a Camera's Rolling, the GOP Candidate Shows His Disdain for Half of America," *Mother Jones*, September 17, 2012.
[4] E. J. Dionne, "At Odds with America," *Washington Post*, September 20, 2012.

Salt Lake City Church of Jesus Christ of Latter-day Saints, commonly known as the Mormons. This is the tradition of Mormon Bishop Willard Mitt Romney, a tradition which goes back to the 1820s in upstate New York. It is a tradition which is insufficiently known to modern-day voters.

THE MORMON TRADITION OF ANTI-AMERICAN RESENTMENT

Bishop Romney's church tradition implies a resentment against all Americans. The great Mormon grievance is that most Americans refused to embrace the mountebank Joseph Smith as their savior, and that an American mob slew the prophet and his brother. Mormon tradition also implies hostility to certain specific groups inside our population. The Mormon Church was founded in polygamy, which we must interpret as an animus against modern women and the rights they have been able to assert. Mormon theology, both in the *Book of Mormon* and the *Book of Mormon*, is explicitly racist in its hostility to people with black or brown skins – the descendents of Ham and the Lamanites.[5] Romney has personally shown contempt for Latinos and Hispanics, demanding that they prepare to "self-deport." Romney's business activities at Bain Capital are a sad catalog of his aggression against American working people of all ethnic backgrounds, with emphasis on asset stripping American factories and shutting them down, or else exporting the jobs to low-wage countries abroad. The Mormon Church has been a reactionary political force in American history over the past century, with hostility to trade unions being combined with vilification of Dr. Martin Luther King and the civil rights movement, plus an eagerness to appease Nazi Germany. Romney has also told us that he hates Russia. For most Americans, Romney's enemies list may already be much too long.

Those who wish to avoid some very unpleasant surprises under a Romney presidency should read on.

Romney's campaign biography this time around is entitled *No Apology: The Case for American Greatness.*[6] Romney argues that Obama is un-American, not sufficiently patriotic, unwilling to accept American exceptionalism, in denial about the greatness of this country, and above all obsessed with apologizing for US superiority. Romney mocks Obama for his "American Apology Tour," which he says has featured the President bad-mouthing the USA in speeches in France, England, Turkey, Cairo, at CIA Headquarters in Langley Virginia, at the National Archives in Washington, DC, and at the United Nations in New York City.[7]

The Romney camp also hopes to benefit from the widespread impression that Obama is secretly a Moslem, and this is perhaps the reason why Obama drinks so much beer in

---

[5] According to Joseph Smith's *Book of Mormon*, the Lamanites were dark-skinned American Indians who descended from one of the tribes of Israel. Their skin was darkened in punishment for their refusal to support the Mormon Jesus in his conflict with Lucifer over the fate of the planet earth.
[6] Mitt Romney, *No Apology: the Case for American Greatness* (New York: St. Martin's Press, 2010).
[7] Ibid., pp. 25-26.

public and chows down in the daytime during Ramadan. But, if this question is relevant for Obama, then it is certainly relevant for Romney. Of all the world religions, the one most explicitly hostile to the United States over the past two centuries is arguably the Mormons.

In a campaign appearance on August 24, 2012, Romney famously quipped that it was public knowledge he had been born in Michigan, and no one had ever asked to see his birth certificate. The reference to Obama's problems in documenting his own past is clear enough. But equally clear is Romney's unspoken premise: that Romney and his wife Ann too are *prima facie* Americans, who do not need to prove anything, and whose loyalty can be taken for granted.

At the same time, a new movie entitled *2016: Obama's America* was playing in theaters. This movie was based on a book by the discredited reactionary writer Dinesh D'Souza, and was produced by Rocky Mountain Films, a production company based in the Mormon stronghold of Utah – in Romney country. D'Souza's argument was that Obama had imbibed the radical anti-colonial project of his late Nigerian father, and that the purpose of the current administration is to reduce the influence and power of the United States so as to make American exceptionalism a dead letter. In reality, Obama's anti-colonialism is nonexistent, as we have seen in his escalation of the Afghan war against Pakistan in his West Point speech of December 2009, and the bombing of Libya in 2011, but this does not prevent D'Souza from attempting to build up a contradiction between Obama's strategy and D'Souza's Chamber of Commerce platitudes about the American tradition.

DINESH D'SOUZA: PROBE OBAMA'S FATHER

Oligarchy seems to be D'Souza's religion, and he made matters worse for himself by joining a very nasty reactionary clique operating at Dartmouth College in the early 1980s under the influence of that elderly degenerate, William F. Buckley. In a recent C-SPAN lecture, D'Souza recounted an exchange he had with Jonathan Alter of *Newsweek*. Alter objected to D'Souza's method of using the ideology of Obama's father to discover the hidden belief structure of the current tenant of the White House. Ronald Reagan's father was an alcoholic, Alter pointed out, but this was not a staple of Democratic Party propaganda in the same way that D'Souza was trying to use the anti-imperialism of Obama *père*. D'Souza conceded that this was true, but added that Reagan had never written a book entitled *Dreams from My Father*. D'Souza therefore felt justified in using the career and views of Obama's father, whom he hardly knew, as a gloss on today's president.

TARPLEY: DONE THAT, PROBE ROMNEYS BACK TO PARLEY PRATT

We can concede this point to D'Souza, having done this job in two books four years ago. But what is sauce for the goose (Obama) is sauce for the gander (Romney). As the first non-Christian president, coming from what in practice is a separate nation, and as a person belonging to an embittered, secretive, totalitarian sect with a history of violent hostility to and hereditary grievances against the United States, Romney merits the most thorough scrutiny, lest he use his presidency to settle old scores with the United States in precisely the way D'Souza attributes to Obama.

Voters are by now familiar with these charges, and will become more familiar with them thanks to the exertions of the Republican Super PACs, funded by wealthy reactionaries at home and abroad.

Nor will it be enough to limit this examination to the life and career of Michigan governor and Nixon cabinet official George Romney, the father of the current candidate. We will need to go all the way back to Joseph Smith and the foundation of Mormonism in the years around 1830. The need to do this is documented by Romney himself, who has portrayed Mormonism as a multi-generational tradition which binds him to certain beliefs today:

> "I believe in my Mormon faith, and I endeavor to live by it. My faith is the Faith of my fathers. I will be true to them and to my beliefs,"

said Romney during the 2008 campaign.[8]

Barack Obama the elder may have been an anti-imperialist of some note in Kenya, but he was hardly a Ho Chi Minh or a Che Guevara. But Romney's great-great-grandfather Parley Parker Pratt was a figure of far greater magnitude in the world of Mormonism. Parley Pratt is now celebrated as the St. Peter and St. Paul of the new faith. Therefore, you need to probe several generations of Romney's background and tradition all the more urgently. D'Souza apparently has plenty of money from wealthy reactionaries for his research fund and even to make it into a movie. This book tries to account for Romney on a somewhat more limited budget.

MORMONS: LOVE THEM OR HATE THEM, YOU DON'T KNOW THEM

If D'Souza can argue that Obama's *Dreams From My Father* contradicts the American dream, then voters have a right to know about the Mormon Oath of Vengeance, which is nothing less than a pledge to God to carry out an implacable hereditary vendetta of blood atonement against the United States of America and its people to avenge the slaying of the Mormon Prophet Joseph Smith in 1844. If D'Souza can argue that Obama rejects American exceptionalism, voters need to be informed about the Mormon claim to represent God's chosen people – a claim which excludes Gentile Americans, meaning everyone except the Mormon Saints.

It does not appear that Obama has anyone in his family tree who waged war against the United States. But Mitt Romney certainly does – one of his ancestors, George Romney, manned the 1857-58 Mormon-held trenches in Echo Canyon, Utah to prevent the passage of United States troops acting under presidential orders through our own national territory during the Mormon Rebellion, America's first civil war. Romney's great-grandfather, Miles Park Romney, was a domestic employee of the infamous Brigham

---

[8] Kranish and Helman, p. 31.

Young, who ordered the massacre of 140 peaceful Arkansas pioneers at the Mountain Meadows Massacre of 1857 – a massacre which Romney's great-great-grandfather, Parley Pratt, contributed to causing through one of his polygamous escapades.

And if D'Souza thinks that Obama swore an oath against the United States while weeping on his father's grave, he should compare that to Joseph Smith's White Horse Prophecy, an apocalyptic prediction of the collapse of the United States followed by a Mormon theocratic seizure of power in the United States and in the entire world, for which Mitch Romney has been touted as the executor since his days at Brigham Young University.

Many in the Republican Party also believe that Obama is a secret Moslem. That allegation must be compared to Romney's emphatic public profession of a religion which includes a polytheistic paradise, in which faithful Mormons become gods ruling over other planets in polygamous harems with the help of Freemasonic underwear, symbols, passwords, secret names, and handshakes. We do not know what Obama's creed is, but we know that Romney's creed includes the proposition "As man is, God once was; as God is, man may become." If Romney believes that Jesus Christ and Lucifer are brothers (as Reverend Huckabee once pointed out), that there is no Trinity, and that God is a material being, he cannot claim to be a Christian.

TIME MAGAZINE: ROMNEY A TYPICAL MORMON "PRAGMATIST"

Five weeks before the 2012 election, Jon Meacham of *Time* magazine attempted to gain insight into what a future Romney presidency might look like by examining "The Mormon Identity" in a cover story. Meacham remarked that "observers have long sought clues to Romney's character and worldview in his Mormonism.... Viewing Romney through the lens of the Mormon understanding of history helps explain his ambition, his devotion to personal liberty and his comfort with expediency." This is the approach followed here, and Meacham is right to use it. But Meacham's analysis is limited to the most fragmentary and superficial account of Mormonism, from which the main political and theological issues have disappeared. Mormon notions of white supremacy do not appear. Mormon communism, which they find embarrassing because of their current reactionary profile, is glossed over. Celestial marriage cannot be avoided, but we are asked to believe that "polygamy, the most notorious of Mormon practices, was linked to practical concerns; the church needed new members." This is the standard LDS cover story for polygamy, spouted by Romney to defend the harem of his great-grandfather Miles P. Romney, portraying this practice as a purely pragmatic measure designed to overcome the demographic crisis caused by the mob murders of Mormons. In reality, Salt Lake City at least generally had more men than women, meaning that a class of permanent bachelors was created in order to provide harems for the Mormon hierarchy – not what a serious policy of natalism would have required.

Using this tissue of clichés, Meacham can celebrate as Mormon pragmatism the systematic alteration of the most basic articles of faith, based on mere expediency – what some might consider unprincipled opportunism. This allows Romney to be explained as a pragmatist devoted solely to expediency, accounting for his flip-flops and also reassuring the *Time* readership that Romney is normal enough to be president.

But Mormon theocracy and secessionism also have to be whitewashed to preserve this result. Meacham follows Kranish and Helman of the Boston Globe in arguing that Lincoln did not crush Brigham Young's dictatorship during the Civil War because the Union needed the Mormons to "stay out of the conflict." But that goal was so minimal because the Mormons themselves were always threatening to secede, and never lifted a finger to save the Union. Meacham thinks that the Mormons "had their own concerns and did not need to invite a war with the Union." But, as the reports of General Connor cited below demonstrate, the Mormons were only waiting for an Anglo-French intervention or a collapse of the Union armies to stab the United States in the back.

Meacham is aware of Joseph Smith's apocalyptic White Horse Prophecy, but fails to understand its hideous implications. He quotes Marion G. Romney, a relative of the current candidate, in a 1976 speech speaking of America's "final great and glorious destiny, Here Zion is to be established and the New Jerusalem is to be built. From here the law of God shall go forth to all nations." This is a frightening call for theocratic world conquest going far beyond the fragmentary horrors of George W. Bush, but Meacham cannot grasp the meaning.[9]

MORMON GLENN BECK TOUCHY ABOUT MAGIC UNDERWEAR

Backers of the Romney candidacy fear an extensive discussion of some of these issues. Glenn Beck continues the Mormon reactionary tradition of witch-hunting ideologues like John Birch Society guru Cleon Skousen. In early September 2012, Beck falsified history on his television program by trying to explain Mormon polygamy as a mere pragmatic response to the heavy casualties the Saints had suffered in their conflicts with their neighbors. He also referred to the Mormon temple garments or magic underwear, complaining that they were uncomfortably warm in the summer. But he did not show his viewers even a peak of his own undershirt. And he warned that any satiric references to these garments would be considered hurtful. But if the President of the United States is going to be wearing magic underwear in the Oval Office, the American public has a right to know. Surely Romney's underwear is just as important as Obama's Blackberry.

What voters may not know is that Brigham Young, revered by the Mormon Church as apostle, second prophet, and American Moses was in fact a hardened traitor – worthy of being included with Benedict Arnold, Aaron Burr, and Jefferson Davis in a quadrumvirate of everlasting infamy. And by the way – as Romney, perhaps influenced by Richard Nixon, whom he resembles, is fond of saying – Romney, his wife, and his five sons are all devoted alumni of Brigham Young University, named after this same traitor.

Do Obama and liberals indulge in a cult of victimhood? They could hardly do so more pathetically than Joseph Smith, Brigham Young, and other leading Mormons who are the architects of the tradition which Mitt Romney claims to revere.

---

[9] Jon Meacham, "The Mormon in Mitt," *Time*, October 8, 2012.

If Romney is so hyper-American, why did the religious establishment to which he belongs hate and revile great American nationalists like Henry Clay, Abraham Lincoln, Justin Morrill, and Ulysses S. Grant?

MORMONISM SEPARATE FROM CHRISTIANITY

Romney has said repeatedly that he is a loyal Mormon. If this is so, then he can in no way be considered a Christian. The Mormon faith, whatever its merits or demerits, is separate and distinct from Judaism, Christianity, and Islam, all of which Mormons condemn. It is *sui generis* – in a class by itself. And it is not only a separate faith; it represents a separate nation, historically distinct from the United States over many decades. In many ways, Mormonism lies outside of Western or Judeo-Christian civilization.

Four years ago, the present writer was concerned enough about the dangers of an Obama presidency to dedicate not one but two books to warning the American public in a timely fashion of what a Wall Street Democrat like Obama might represent, while urging them to find a candidate who could realize the tremendous political potential deriving from the reactionary Republican collapse of 2008.[10] This book in no way reflects a partisan commitment to Obama.

There is indeed an element of contempt for working people which can be observed in Obama's behavior, and this has unquestionably been a factor in his disastrous performance as president. In the spring of 2008, Obama told some of his own moneybags in San Francisco:

> "... In a lot of these communities in big industrial states like Ohio and Pennsylvania, people have been beaten down so long, and they feel so betrayed by government, and when they hear a pitch that is premised on not being cynical about government, then a part of them just doesn't buy it. You go into some of these small towns in Pennsylvania, and like a lot of small towns in the Midwest, the jobs have been gone now for 25 years and nothing was replaced them.... So it's not surprising then that they get bitter, they cling to guns or religion or antipathy to people who aren't like them or anti-immigrant sentiment or anti-trade sentiment as a way to explain their frustrations."[11]

This is the same Obama who says that he is "eager" to reach a grand bargain with the reactionary Republicans during the December 2012 lame-duck session of Congress, where he is likely – under the shadow of the GOP's "fiscal cliff" propaganda hysteria – to consent to catastrophic cuts in the New Deal, New Frontier, and Great Society social safety net programs which represent the inalienable economic rights of the American people, and must not be tampered with under any circumstances.

---

[10] Webster G. Tarpley, *Obama: the Postmodern Coup, the Making of a Manchurian Candidate*; and Webster G. Tarpley, *Barack H. Obama: The Unauthorized Biography* (Joshua Tree CA: Progressive Press, 2008).
[11] Mayhill Fowler, "Obama: No Surprise That Hard-Pressed Pennsylvanians Turned Bitter," *Huffington Post*, April 11, 2008.

Even so, Obama's resentment of the American people may still be somewhat milder than Bishop Romney's. And, as of the late summer of 2012, Obama is the devil we know. What of Romney, the devil we hardly know? One salient fact about Romney is his lifelong devotion to the Mormon Church, The Church of Jesus Christ of Latter-day Saints. Romney's biography leaves no doubt about his ironclad loyalty to this institution. But at the same time, Romney as a candidate shows himself to be extremely reluctant to mention the Mormon Church in any way. Romney is a lifetime Mormon, having worked for the LDS as a missionary in France, as a bishop in Cambridge, Massachusetts, and as a "stake president" in the New England area.[12]

The Mormon Church is not just any church. It is certainly one of the most remarkable and singular religious organizations in the world. Some religious organizations can be considered sedate, mainstream, sated, and complacent. They have come to terms with the world as it exists, and they are factionalized according to the political divisions in the rest of society around them. These might include the mainline Protestants and Roman Catholics, and the reformed Jews. Another kind of religious organization might be regarded as sectarian, activist, aggressive, and perhaps nursing a catalog of bitter grievances. Here the primary unit cohesion of the religious denomination is much stronger than the factional splits that divide the outside world. Marriage outside the faith is vigorously ostracized. It can be argued that the Mormon Church is closer to this second category than to the first.

There has never been a US president who professed the Mormon faith. Romney would therefore represent a significant first in American history.

MORMON THEOCRACY FAIR GAME AS A POLITICAL PROJECT

Perhaps, therefore, it is time to examine Mormonism from a primarily political point of view, to see what a Mormon might do in the top US political office of the presidency. The finding here is that the Mormons or Latter-day Saints represent a religious denomination which, perhaps more than any other, is characterized by a long history of aggressive animus and outspoken hostility against the United States of America. This hostility is rooted in the tragic history of the Mormons during their first decades in New York, Ohio, Missouri, Illinois, and Utah – especially in the 1844 assassination of Joseph Smith and his brother Hyrum Smith in Illinois. During this time, the Mormons developed a catalog of grievances, some doubtless very real, but some others imaginary and hypocritical, for which they wanted revenge from the United States.

Professor Stanley P. Hirshson of Queens College in New York City, a distinguished biographer of Brigham Young, pointed out in his 1969 book that "Mormonism continues to grow in power and influence ... because neither Gentile nor Saint has studied much of

---

[12] In Mormon terminology, a bishop is the equivalent of a parish priest or minister in Christianity. A Mormon stake president more closely approximates a Christian bishop. Romney thus qualifies as a bishop both in terms of his title, and in terms of his functions.

its history."[13] This book is an attempt to change that. We can do it all the more readily because the Mormon Church has been a political movement from its very beginnings, with the quest for theocratic power here on earth always being at least as important as the quest to become a god ruling a planet with a harem in the afterlife.

Having experienced the negative consequences of Obama's resentment against the United States, we ought to be all the more concerned about a presidential candidate professing a theocratic religion in which the tradition of anti-American thought and action is, if anything, more vehement and more vindictive than in the case of Obama.

MORMON BAGGAGE OF POLYGAMY, INSURRECTION, EXPATRIATION

To be sure, Obama carries heavy baggage, containing such figures as the Weatherpeople Bill Ayers and Bernardine Dohrn, and much more. But Romney's baggage includes his transition director and likely White House Chief of Staff, former Republican Utah Governor Mike Leavitt, a leading Mormon activist who said in 1998 that it was quite possible that polygamy was legal in the United States under the First Amendment provision for religious freedom. It also turns out that Mike Leavitt covered up in recent years for the Mormon role in the Mountain Meadows Massacre of 1857, in which one of his direct ancestors was a participant in the butchery. And further: since Romney wants to show off his family, we are more than justified in asking about his great-grandfather, Miles P. Romney, a polygamist who chose to leave the United States and settled in Mexico, rather than give up a practice which the Republican Party once considered along with slavery as a "relic of barbarism."

INSIDE THE "MORMON MOMENT"

Leavitt can already be seen as the harbinger of an unprecedented wave of Mormon nepotism in the upper reaches of the US federal government, especially in domestic and economic affairs. Mormons have a positive duty to get each other promoted, and the solidarity runs deep. Another effect of a Romney administration would be a huge increase in the number of polygamous households in the United States, with all of the terrible problems this will create for the young women who are victims of this system. We can already see from Mormon politicians like Orrin Hatch, Mike Lee, and Mike Leavitt, that mainstream Mormons will never lift a finger to combat polygamy so blatantly practiced by their cousins, the Fundamentalist Latter-day Saints (FLDS), whose most famous living representative is currently the convicted felon Warren Jeffs. This is the real content of the "Mormon Moment" hoped for by so many Saints.

For foreign policy, Romney has already surrounded himself with neocons to vindicate the honor of faction through new wars in the Middle East. These figures include John Bolton, Robert Kagan, Eliot Cohen, Robert Joseph, and Dan Senor. Romney himself has been a close personal friend of Israeli Prime Minister Benjamin Netanyahu since 1976. There is every reason to believe that a newly inaugurated Romney administration would be likely to attack Syria in early 2013 if they saw an opportunity to do so.

---

[13] Hirshson, *Lion of the Lord* (New York: Knopf, 1969), p. 326.

IS ROMNEY STILL BOUND BY THE OATH OF VENGEANCE
AGAINST THE US?

Digging a little deeper into Romney's Mormon baggage we find Brigham Young's "Oath of Vengeance," which demands an eternal blood vendetta against the United States of America, and which was included in the official Mormon temple liturgy until just two decades before Mitt Romney was born. Digging still deeper, we find Joseph Smith's White Horse Prophecy, which speaks of a Mormon seizure of power in the United States. We find that in 1857-58, the Mormons were responsible for the first episode of secession and civil war in US history. We find that the Mormons stubbornly refused to assist Abraham Lincoln in his struggle to save the Union. We find that the first time that an American president ever referred to terrorism, it was James Buchanan talking about the Mormon theocratic dictatorship which was ruling over Utah and beyond.

Because of all this, it is imperative that American voters acquire a basic familiarity with the political tenets of Mormonism, and be able to locate these in the historical context over the past two centuries.

The Hobson's choice between Romney and Obama ought finally to lead politically conscious Americans to the urgent need for a new political direction capable of solving the problems of economic depression with an economic recovery, while promoting a positive conception of the United States in the world – all in the tradition of the New Deal, the Good Neighbor Policy, and the Bretton Woods system of President Franklin D. Roosevelt.

A NOTE ON SOURCES

Mormon history has traditionally been divided into two camps – the hagiographers and the demonizers. The first see only Mormon Saints, and the second see only Mormon devils. But we can learn more from the second than the first. These two approaches cannot be put on the same level, since the hagiographers in their quest to maintain a respectable façade for the Mormons have had to deny and obliterate a vast mass of empirical material embarrassing to the Saints. In the case of the demonizers, embarrassing material which is historically true is mixed together with inventions, fabrications, and exaggerations.

Fawn Brodie attempted to strike a balance with her landmark biography of Joseph Smith, and was excommunicated and vilified by the LDS for her pains. Juanita Brooks tried to tell the true story of the Mountain Meadows Massacre, but she veered away from acknowledging that Brigham Young had ordered the killing.

The New Mormon History which has developed since the time of Fawn Brodie and Juanita Brooks is billed as an attempt to reach an objective synthesis on these highly controversial events. Results have been mixed. A problem with the New Mormon History is that it has been pulled very far in the trendy direction of social history and cultural history. It is therefore hardly capable of total history (*Gesamtgeschichte*). In particular, the covert operations, intrigues, and machinations of figures like Joseph Smith and Brigham Young are much neglected. The New Mormon History also tries to steer clear of any notion of preconcert or conspiracy, and shows very little interest for the inner workings of organisms like the Council of Fifty, Joseph Smith's vehicle for attaining political power.

The most salient point at which this study differs from virtually everything published on the subject of Mormonism so far is the emphasis placed here on the political and later geopolitical function of Joseph Smith's political agitation against Henry Clay in 1844, and then of Brigham Young's empire of Deseret, as gambits of British imperial policy against the United States. The Mormons were certainly promoted by John Stuart Mill, Thomas Carlyle, and the intelligence division of the British East India Company in London.

There has never been any secret about the cordial support extended to the Confederate States of America by the British Foreign Office. There is now a growing awareness that Confederate secessionism was mightily stimulated by the Southern Jurisdiction of the Scottish Rite Freemasons, who were ultimately a satellite of London. It is time to recognize that Mormon theocracy and Mormon secessionism were just as desirable from the British point of view as the creation of the Confederate state.

Just Too Weird is a common response to Mormon theology and church practices.[14]

This book has attempted to glean a kind of meta-history from the vast secondary literature on Mormonism. In doing so, we are pleased to acknowledge profound indebtedness to trailblazing studies like those of Fawn Hall, which can now be supplemented by the work of the pro-Mormon scholar Richard Lyman Bushman. The best biography of Brigham Young is still Stanley P. Hirshson's *The Lion of the Lord.* The greatest recent achievement of Mormon historiography is unquestionably *The Mormon Rebellion* by David L. Bigler and Will Bagley, a *tour de force* on the Utah War of 1857-58. Will Bagley has also contributed *Blood of the Prophets*, an exhaustive examination of the Mountain Meadows Massacre of 1857 which goes beyond anything hitherto produced on this subject. Our indebtedness to Bigler and Bagley will be evident. And, since Brigham Young's machinations cannot be understood apart from British imperial strategy before and during the American Civil War, E. B. Long's *The Saints and the Union* also deserves attention.

Webster Griffin Tarpley, Ph.D.
Washington DC,
September 20, 2012

---

[14] The phrase "just too weird" appears on the internet in relation to Mormonism in some 323,000 instances.

CHAPTER I

"I LOVE MY FAITH": BISHOP ROMNEY AND THE MORMON TRADITION

> "Indeed, such is believed to be the condition to which a strange system of terrorism has brought the inhabitants of that region that no one among them could express an opinion favorable to this Government, or even propose to obey its laws, without exposing his life and property to peril." — President James Buchanan, April, 1858 [15]

If Mitt Romney is really the orthodox Mormon he claims to be, his goal in life is to become a god ruling over a planet, probably not our earth, together with a harem of celestial spirit wives, engendering progeny in the hope that they, too, can rule over planets. In order to attain this status, he will expect to appear before a three-judge (oligarchical) heavenly tribunal composed of Elohim (the Mormon Jehovah), the convicted con man Joseph Smith, and the Mormon Jesus, who happens to be Lucifer's brother. In order to increase his chances of entering paradise, Mitt Romney will go to the Oval Office each day wearing special underwear – the so-called "temple garments" – covered with freemasonic symbols and hex signs designed to ward off the evil eye. Romney presumably believes that his late father George Romney, the former governor of Michigan and member of the Nixon Cabinet, is already ruling over a planet in this way.

But beyond these peculiarities, the main objections to a Mormon presidency are political. Mormonism has always considered itself not just as a faith, but also as a political faction and as a system of government with boundless ambitions to take power in the United States and in the world. Mormons control Utah and have decisive influence in nearby states, including the Las Vegas gambling interests. Mormons represent formidable factions in the CIA, the FBI, the Pentagon, the US intelligence community and in the Federal Government generally. They are a power bloc. They have a huge financial and business empire, a fact not unrelated to the success of Romney's Bain Capital. They display strong elements of institutionalized racism and anti-woman and anti-labor ideology. Mormons tend to be authoritarian, and often vote as a bloc to maximize their impact on elections. Organized Mormonism unmistakably takes its place as one of the most reactionary components of the modern-day Republican Party: Mormons were an important part of the Bush-Cheney regime, and supported its signature policies. A special administrative apparatus inside the Mormon Church attempts to enforce ideological uniformity on its members, generally in a reactionary direction.

Willard "Mitt" Romney is a bishop of the Church of Jesus Christ of the Latter-day Saints (LDS), commonly known as the Mormons. For seven generations, Romney's family has been part of a small group of allied families, sometimes referred to by insiders as "The Compound," which dominate the Mormon Church. Parley Parker Pratt, Romney's great-

---

[15] James Buchanan: "Proclamation—Rebellion in the Territory of Utah," April 6, 1858. Online by Gerhard Peters and John T. Woolley, The American Presidency Project. http://www.presidency.ucsb.edu/ws/?pid=68308.

great-grandfather, was one of the founding twelve apostles of the Mormon or Latter-day Saints Church. Mitt Romney does not like to talk about his Mormonism, and habitually dodges questions about this topic with his standard statements, "I love my faith." If Romney is elected, it will mark, so far as is known, the first time that a bishop of any church has ever become President of the United States. This fact alone justifies an examination of Mormon tradition with a view to seeing how it might impact a possible Romney presidency. A Romney presidency would also be the first time a non-Christian has entered the White House.

MORMONISM: 150-YEAR OLD SCIENTOLOGY?

Mormon theology is also fair game, if only because Romney defends it. When journalist Bret Stephens observed: "It's out there that it's a 150-year-old version of Scientology," Mitt Romney answered: "It's not."[16]

In his public statements, Romney is always adamant that he is a completely orthodox Mormon believer. "I believe my faith" he said on one recent occasion. "I love my faith, and I would in no way, shape, or form try to distance myself from my faith or the fundamental beliefs of my faith."[17] On another occasion, Romney told his fawning biographer Hugh Hewitt, "I love my faith. I am proud of my church."[18] Just what he is proud of is also a political question, which must be examined here.

Romney has five sons – Tagg, Matt, Josh, Dan, and Craig. Each one attended Brigham Young University. Every one of the five has served abroad as a missionary for the Mormon Church. Each one of them has chosen to marry a Mormon wife in a ceremony carried out in the Mormon Temple.[19]

Before becoming a bishop responsible for a district or ward of the Mormon Church, Romney had to advance from the status of the Elder, or priest in the Aaronic priesthood, to the status of High Priest, or holder of the Melchizedek priesthood. Melchizedek status was also necessary before Romney could become stake president, presiding over several Mormon congregations in Belmont Massachusetts, in the Boston suburbs.

On New Year's Day 1982, Romney was awarded the Keys of the Priesthood, conferring on him the title of Bishop and with it the ability to lead the flock: "Mormons believe the resurrected apostles Peter, James and John gave the religion's founder, Joseph Smith, the long-lost keys to God's kingdom in 1829. (The Mormon theory is that Christendom had become degenerate in 570 AD, because of the activities of Pope Gregory the Great.) A century later, the Church president, Joseph Fielding Smith, declared that "those who hold the keys" have the "power and authority to govern and direct all of the Lord's affairs on

---

[16] Hewitt, p. 7.
[17] Hewitt, p. 208.
[18] Hewitt, p. 209.
[19] Hewitt, p. 209.

earth." Romney soon received the keys of one of Mormons' flagship congregations, the Longfellow Park Chapel on Brattle Street in Cambridge, Massachusetts.[20]

In the fall of 1986, Romney was chosen by the Mormon hierarchy in Salt Lake City to be promoted to the post of stake president for the New England region of the Latter-day Saints, with headquarters in Belmont, Massachusetts. Romney served as stake president until 1994, when he ran unsuccessfully for United States Senate against Teddy Kennedy. The "stake" refers to the idea that each Mormon regional organization can be considered a "stake in the tent of Zion," or a component of the New Jerusalem, according to the rhetoric of Joseph Smith.

We must also assume that Romney constantly wears the traditional Mormon undergarments or "magic underwear." Some photographs of the candidate allow the outline of the characteristic magic undershirt to be visible. An enterprising reporter needs to ask him about this. When asked by correspondent Sridhar Pappu, "Do you wear temple garments?" Romney was evasive: "I'll just say those sorts of things I'll keep private."[21]

When Mitt Romney was president of the elite, lily-white, and plutocratic Cougar Club at Brigham Young University, he attended monthly "fireside testimonies" or sacramental meetings, at which each young Saint was expected to recount how he had lived in heaven as an unborn spirit before being born on earth into an elite Mormon family. Members were further expected to state their beliefs in the imminence of the last days, and to put all faith in the Prophet Joseph Smith, in the *Book of Mormon* as the revealed word of God, and in the Mormon Church as the sole path to salvation.[22]

In estimating the role which religion might play if a certain politician becomes president, we need to decide whether the religious denomination in question is an older, established, mainline, and generally sated church, or whether it is a bitter, sectarian, cultist, tightly-knit, extremist formation with a catalogue of grievances and a belief structure in sharp conflict with natural theology and natural law, and with the established political order. If we can agree that the Roman Catholics and mainline Protestants belong in the first category, we must also observe that the Mormon or LDS Church has during long periods of its history veered into the latter category.

POLYTHEISM, NOT CHRISTIANITY

Because the Mormons are a very aggressive sect, sending young male missionaries in pairs around the country and around the world to recruit new members, it is assumed by many that they are simply another entry in the squabbling world of Protestant denominations. This is a mistake. Mormonism is not a form of Protestantism, nor is it a

---

[20] Jason Horowitz, "Mitt Romney, as a leader in Mormon church, became a master of many keys." *Washington Post*, August 20, 2012.
[21] Sridhar Pappu, "The Holy Cow! Candidate," *Atlantic Monthly*, September 2005.
[22] Sally Denton, "Romney and the White Horse Prophecy: a close look at the roots of Romney's – and the Mormon church's – political ambitions" (Salon.com, January 29, 2012).

form of Christianity. It is an entirely new religion designed to subsume and surpass all existing faiths, including Christianity, Islam, and Judaism. Much evidence suggests that Mormonism aims or has aimed at world domination. As part of this commitment, Mormonism in its heart of hearts regards the existence of the United States as an aberration which must be remedied, somewhat in the way that Al Qaeda is said to regard all existing governments as illegitimate because they are not the caliphate.

Mormonism represents in many ways the most extreme denomination among those originating in America. Jehovah's Witnesses, Seventh-day Adventists, Christian Scientists, and Charismatic Pentecostalists each have their peculiarities, but these are dwarfed by the historical and doctrinal Mormon commitment to racism, polygamy, theocracy, secret police, blood atonement, secessionism, and ultimate seizure of political power in the United States and in the world. For example, the Seventh-day Adventists – founded just a few miles away from Joseph Smith's home in upstate New York, and currently the fastest growing Christian denomination worldwide – were once criticized because of their legalism, and because they claimed to predict when the end of the world would occur, and later because of their emphasis on a healthy diet. But these issues shrink into triviality when compared with the Mormons' theocracy, polygamy, Danites, secessionism, and insurrection. And the Seventh-day Adventists have generally practiced racial integration, even at times when that was not the rule: the young Malcolm X., for example, grew up as a Seventh-day Adventist.

From the point of view of a Roman Catholic, Mormonism would be regarded as a heresy. The Southern Baptist convention has officially labeled Mormonism as a cult, and a number of Baptist ministers spoke out against Romney during the 2012 Republican primaries. Public opinion polling also shows that the US electorate in general has doubts about Mormonism, which is probably why Romney attempts to dodge this topic. About half of US voters say that they know little or nothing about Mormonism, but about one third classified Mormonism as outside of Christianity. Fully 42% express that they would feel "somewhat or very uncomfortable" with a Mormon president. About two thirds of those polled said that "Mormonism is very different" from their own religion. 18% said that the connotations of Mormonism were positive, being described as good, dedicated, honest, and friendly, while 24% said that the associations of Mormonism were negative, with key words like cult, polygamy, restrictive, and strange. Some 30% had no opinion. About half of registered voters polled knew that Romney is a Mormon.[23]

A 2011 American Values Survey poll revealed that 50% of Democratic voters, 36% of Republican voters, and 38% of independent voters were at least somewhat uncomfortable with the notion of a Mormon in the White House. Among millennial voters aged 18 to 29, 54% would be at least somewhat uncomfortable with a Mormon president. Among senior citizens, 39% would be at least somewhat uncomfortable. About 36% of registered voters do not believe that Mormonism is part of Christianity; about half think

---

[23] "Romney's Mormon Faith Likely a Factor in Primaries, Not in a General Election," The Pew Forum on Religion and Public Life, November 23, 2011, at pewforum.org.

that it is. Among white evangelical Protestant voters, 49% see Mormonism as outside of Christianity.[24]

Back in 1999, 17% of those polled told Gallup that they would not vote for a Mormon. In mid-2006, a Los Angeles Times-Bloomberg poll concluded that 37% of those responding would not vote for a Mormon in the presidential election. In September 2006, Gallup reported that 66% of those questioned thought that the United States is not ready for a Mormon president. In November 2006, a Rasmussen poll found that 43% would not consider voting for a Mormon.[25] In other words, public suspicion of Mormonism grew during the first decade of the current century, perhaps because Romney has posed the question of a Mormon president for the first time in recent memory.

Those who have studied his political career have no doubt that Romney's policies have been deeply influenced by his Mormonism. As Sally Denton observes, "the influence that Mormonism has had on him has dominated every step of the way. The seeds of Romney's unique brand of conservatism, often regarded with intense suspicion by most non-Mormon conservatives, were sown in the secretive, acquisitive, patriarchal, authoritarian religious empire run by 'quorums' of men under an umbrella consortium called the General Authorities. A creed unlike any other in the United States, from its inception of Mormonism encouraged material prosperity and abundance as a measure of holy worth, and its strict system of tithing 10% of individual wealth has made the church one of the world's richest institutions."[26] Moreover, at the beginning, the Mormon Church was a thoroughly collectivist and communal economic system ("the Order of Enoch"), a form of primitive communism. The right-wing, market-fetishist, Mormon apostles of today are thoroughly embarrassed by any reference to the communistic phase of their faith.

Apologists for Mormonism complain that singling their church out for such negative attention is unfair, and amounts to bigotry. As one Mormon apologist wrote in the *New York Times* after Romney had secured the Republican nomination, "Making Mormons look bad helps others feel good. Imagining Mormons as intolerant rubes, or as mental deviants, Americans from left and right can imagine they are, by contrast, tolerant, rational, and truly Christian. Mitt Romney's candidacy is only the latest opportunity for such stereotypes to be aired."[27] Unfortunately, this does not answer any specific charges, of which there have been plenty, from Joseph Smith down to Warren Jeffs. Moreover, we must distinguish between theological questions, which can also be legitimately discussed, and the political reality of Mormonism, which has often striven for political, and indeed theocratic power, and which operates as a political cabal or combine today.

HAROLD BLOOM: MORMON THEOLOGY IS KEPT SECRET

---

[24] 2011 American Values Survey, Public Religion Research Institute, November 8, 2011.
[25] Hewitt, p. 220.
[26] Sally Denton, "Romney and the White Horse Prophecy: a close look at the roots of Romney's – and the Mormon church's – political ambitions" (Salon.com, January 29, 2012).
[27] J. Spencer Fluhman, "Why We Fear Mormons," *New York Times*, June 3, 2012.

The Yale English professor Harold Bloom has voiced the deep suspicion of Mormonism among establishment intellectuals. Mormons, he argued, are set apart from Christianity and Judaism by their system of many gods, known as polytheism, which is still kept as an esoteric or "shelf" doctrine: "The accurate critique of Mormonism is that Smith's religion is not even monotheistic, let alone democratic. Though the Church of Jesus Christ of Latter-day Saints no longer openly describes their innermost beliefs, they clearly hold on to the notion of a plurality of gods. Indeed, they themselves expect to become gods, following the path of Joseph Smith. There are other secrets also, not tellable by the Mormon Church to those it calls 'Gentiles,' oddly including Jews. That aspects of the religion of a devout president of the United States should be concealed from all but 2% of us may be a legitimate question that merits pondering."[28]

Bloom was much criticized by reactionaries because of these views, but he is on firm ground when he expresses alarm over political implications of a Mormon in the Oval Office. How, for example, could Romney ever be the president of all the people? Bloom doubts it: "Mormons earn godhead through their own efforts, hoping to join the plurality of gods, even as they insist they are not polytheists…. The Mormon patriarch, secure in his marriage and large family, is promised by his faith a final ascension to godhead, with a planet all his own separate from the earth and the nation where he now dwells. From the perspective of the White House, how would the nation and the world appear to President Romney? How would he represent the other 98% of his citizens?"[29]

POLYGAMY, PLURAL WIVES, SPIRITUAL WIVES

The public has the right to know that Joseph Smith, the Prophet and founder of Mormonism, was a practitioner of polygamy, the form of marriage in which one man has many wives. It is sometimes referred to as "plural marriage," and its female victims as "spiritual wives." (In the way that Joseph Smith practiced polygamy, it often translated also into polyandry from the point of view of the women involved, since many of them were married women who ended up with two husbands when they received the "celestial" attentions of the Prophet.)

Writers favorable to the Mormon point of view have been forced to concede that Joseph Smith was just as much a polygamist as is Mormon traditionalist Warren Jeffs in our own time. Joseph Smith's wives included one 14-year old girl. Jeffs' youngest wife was twelve. Apologists for the Mormons list 33 women among Joseph Smith's plural wives, plus another seven who may have been inducted into the Prophet's celestial harem while he was still alive.[30] An additional seven women are listed by these sources as posthumous marriages, in which the women involved were married with (or "sealed to") Joseph Smith after his death, thus ruling out the possibility of consummation. Even so,

---

[28] Harold Bloom, "Will This Election Be the Mormon Breakthrough?" *New York Times*, November 12, 2011.

[29] Ibid.

[30] Todd Compton, "Fawn Brodie on Joseph Smith's Plural Wives and Polygamy: a Critical View," in Newell G. Bringhurst (ed), *Reconsidering No Man Knows My History* (Logan, Utah: Utah State University press, 1996), pp. 175-187.

Mormon doctrine would still maintain that such women, and many others who have followed, are indeed among the founder's heavenly concubines.

Fawn M. Brodie, the 20th century's leading expert on Joseph Smith, set the number of Joseph Smith's wives at 48. She notes that Jerald and Sandra Tanner, the authors of *Joseph Smith and Polygamy* (Salt Lake City, 1969), estimate that the Prophet had no fewer than 84 "spiritual wives."[31] In theory, the Mormon Church stopped practicing polygamy as a condition for statehood in the mid-1890s. But many Mormon families, including the Romneys, continued to practice polygamy for a long time after that. The Romney family's commitment to polygamy was so great that it trumped any loyalty to the United States they may have had, leading them to expatriate to Mexico in order to remain faithful to Joseph Smith's signature practice. The Romney camp claims today that Romney's father and grandfather no longer practiced polygamy, but it is evident that earlier generations certainly did.

As for Joseph Smith's successor, Brigham Young, who led the Saints to Salt Lake City, he practiced polygamy openly, calling it the Order of Jacob. Brigham Young is estimated to have had 55 wives. He married one of these when she was 15, and three others when they were 16, according to published accounts. Ann Eliza Webb was forced to marry Brigham Young in April 1868 when she was a 24 year-old divorcee and he was 66. Ann Eliza Young was then able to secure a divorce from the Prophet in 1875, after which she devoted herself to writing and speaking against the horrors of polygamy. Her autobiography, *Wife No. 19*, is an entertaining and shocking account of the dismal lives of polygamous wives. This book is the basis of Irving Wallace's 1961 biography, *The Twenty-Seventh Wife* (1961), and of David Ebersdorff's novel, *The Nineteenth Wife* (2008), which has been made into a movie for the Lifetime Movie Network. In reality, Ann Eliza Webb underestimated the depravity of Brigham Young: she was in fact his wife number 52.

Polygamy was one of the biggest factors which made it impossible for Mormons to coexist peacefully with other Americans, since their neighbors were always concerned that their wives and daughters might be carried off to a Mormon harem. Indeed, the inner instability of Mormonism, especially during its early decades, was due in large part to quarrels which started when Joseph Smith directed his celestial attentions at the wives and daughters of his principal lieutenants; one of these incidents set the stage for Joseph Smith's assassination in 1844.

At the foundation of the modern Republican Party in Philadelphia in 1856, the platform stated: "It is the duty of Congress to prohibit in the territories those twin relics of barbarism, polygamy and slavery." The first of these points was explicitly aimed at the Mormons. Now, in 2012, the GOP has come full circle, and has a Mormon candidate.

The founder of the Anglican or Episcopal Church was the 16th-century King Henry VIII of England, who had six wives, but not simultaneously, according to the official record.

---

[31] Fawn M. Brodie, *No Man Knows My History: the Life of Joseph Smith, the Mormon Prophet* (New York: Knopf, 1971), second edition, p. xi.

There have been a number of Episcopal presidents. But what can American women expect from a president who subscribes to a religious doctrine founded by a man who had between 33 and 48 wives?

BOOK OF MORMON AND BOOK OF ABRAHAM: ANTI-BLACK RACISM

The public also has a right to know that the *Book of Mormon*, the founding text of the sect, explains dark skin as the heritage of permanent inferiority. It was inflicted on the descendents of certain angels who remained neutral in the struggle between the Mormon Christ and the Mormon Lucifer, in their struggle on Elohim's planet Kolob to determine the fate of this world. Except for momentary reasons of political opportunism, as for example when Joseph Smith wanted to run for president in 1844, blacks were excluded from priesthood, meaning they could not be confirmed in the Mormon Church. Visitors to Salt Lake City even today are often struck by the fact that it is probably the most lily-white major city anywhere in the Western Hemisphere, and perhaps on the entire planet.

This built-in doctrinal racism of the Mormon Church contrasts sharply with the universalism of the Biblical Jesus Christ, who told his disciples to preach the gospel unto all nations, without exception. The Roman Catholic Church had explicitly black African Saints in the 15th century, and these were soon joined by dark-skinned saints in Latin America. This feature of Mormonism made the church attractive over many decades, especially after the 1964 Civil Rights Act, to reactionaries and racists who wanted a racially segregated denomination. This racist principle of selection has contributed much to the demographic makeup of the Mormon Church today, and has certainly not been transformed by the superficial changes of the past three decades.

Fawn Brodie called attention to this phenomenon in 1971, writing in the second edition of her classic study that "if the Mormon Church does not modify its racist practices, it seems likely that its future converts in large part will continue to come, as they have in recent years, from right wing groups who are hostile to black people under any circumstances."[32] These right wingers and racists were Mitt Romney's partners in fellowship for the first three decades of his life, and it is impossible to believe that this has not influenced his outlook on many issues.

Today, Mitt Romney makes much of his enthusiasm for the 1978 decision of the Mormon hierarchy to declare blacks eligible for the Mormon priesthood, thus supposedly opening the church to them. (Black faces are still impossible to find among the First Presidency and Quorum of Twelve, the highest administrative bodies of the LDS.) But it must be pointed out that the partial rehabilitation of African-Americans took place only at the level of church regulations, and not in the Mormon holy writ. The *Book of Mormon* continues to brand blacks as ineligible for the priesthood (confirmation), even if the Mormon Church finds it expedient to disregard this disqualification in its day-to-day operations.

---

[32] Brodie, p. 425.

THEOCRACY

Historically, Mormon doctrine has been adamant that political power and religious power (or temporal and spiritual power, as they are sometimes called) belong in the same hands. This is a Byzantine principle which is utterly alien to the civilization of Western Europe and the Western Hemisphere. For Joseph Smith, the only acceptable form of rule is theocracy, which he attempted to make more palatable to American audiences by calling it "theodemocracy." All power was to be concentrated in the hands of the high priest of the mystery religion, who was obviously Joseph Smith.

The Mormon project was to create the Kingdom of God on earth, with Joseph Smith as its ruler. After Smith had founded the faith near Palmyra, New York in 1830, the center of gravity of Mormon recruitment shifted to Kirtland, Ohio, where Sydney Rigdon, an established sectarian leader, had been recruited. When Andrew Jackson's Specie Circular of 1836 exploded the frontier real estate bubble in the panic of 1837 (a distant mirror for Romney's financial speculation, as we will show), the bankrupt Saints were driven out of Ohio and took refuge in northern Missouri. Here, they entered into conflict with the local population when Joseph Smith announced to the rest of Missouri that they could choose between allegiance to him or death: "… if they come on us to molest us, we will establish our religion by the sword. We will trample down our enemies and make it one gore of blood from the Rocky Mountains to the Atlantic Ocean….Joseph Smith or the Sword!"[33]

After the Mormons had been driven out of Missouri by armed mobs, they took refuge along the Mississippi River in Illinois, where they founded their holy city of Nauvoo, which soon became almost as big as Chicago, as Mormons from Missouri and Great Britain emigrated there. Here Joseph Smith was made the mayor, the head of the city council, the chief judge, and the lieutenant general of a local militia so numerous that it was almost half as big as the entire U.S. Army. On the bluffs of Nauvoo, Joseph Smith and his advisers planned to create one of the world's most powerful fortresses to control the traffic on the Mississippi River, in much the same way that the Confederates used Vicksburg two decades later. Here Joseph Smith was declared King of the Kingdom of God, or in other words the political ruler of the world. The Prophet's boundless megalomania was cut off in June 1844 when he and his brother Hyrum Smith were slain by a mob.

Mormon leadership passed into the hands of Brigham Young, who actually implemented some of Joseph Smith's most daring plans. Following a brief period of regroupment after the slaying of the Prophet, Brigham Young led the Mormons in 1847 to Salt Lake City. At this time, Salt Lake City and the entire Great Basin were part of Mexico. Brigham Young set to work creating an independent country hostile to the United States, and generally oriented in favor of the British Empire. This was the Mormon state of Deseret, a name drawn from the Hebrew word for the honeybee. Deseret was admirably situated to cut the eastern United States off from California, the Oregon Territory, and the Pacific Ocean. Here once again all power – religious, political, military, economic, and judicial

---

[33] Brodie, pp. 230-231.

– was concentrated in the hands of the Mormon supremo, now Brigham Young. Brigham Young was the de facto commander of the military forces. For many years he was governor of the territory, having been appointed by Millard Fillmore. When he was ousted as governor by Buchanan, he fell back on his control of the judiciary, including the judges and juries in the territorial probate courts, which had arrogated to themselves original jurisdiction in all state and federal cases.

When Salt Lake City and the rest of the Great Basin were ceded by Mexico to the United States of America as a result of the treaty ending the Mexican War, and when Americans began crossing the Great Basin on their way to California in the Gold Rush after 1848, Mormon hostility to the United States only increased.

Brigham Young's personal ties to the British Empire included a sojourn of a number of years in England, where he had been sent by Joseph Smith to recruit new members for the church. The fact that this activity was not suppressed by the British government provides an unmistakable indication of British sponsorship, at least in part, for the Mormon project. Mormonism collected defenders, including Thomas Carlyle, John Stuart Mill, and Charles Dickens – the first two with British intelligence pedigrees. Converts from England, Scotland, and Wales probably constituted the majority of the Mormon Church in the middle of the 19th century.

Today, as Harold Bloom points out, Mormons "help stock the CIA, the FBI, the military…. A Mormon presidency is not quite the same as an ostensibly Catholic or Protestant one, since the Church of Jesus Christ of Latter-day Saints insists on the religious sanction for its moralistic platitudes. The 19th-century Mormon theologian Orson Pratt [Romney's great-great-great uncle], who was close to both Joseph Smith and Brigham Young, stated a principle the Church of Jesus Christ of Latter-day Saints has never repudiated: 'any people attempting to govern themselves by laws of their own making, and by officers of their own appointment, are in direct rebellion against the kingdom of God.'"[34] That represents a direct attack on the US Constitution which Mormons have always claimed to revere.

PRESIDENT BUCHANAN: MORMONISM
A "STRANGE SYSTEM OF TERRORISM"

By 1857, military units controlled by the Utah Mormons were interfering with parties of pioneers on their way to California and Oregon, and there was concern that they might do the same thing with the Pony Express. In that year, Brigham Young issued a provocative statement which declared the independence of Deseret from the United States. This is the first case of fully implemented secessionism in the history of the United States, more than three years before South Carolina attempted to leave the Union in December 1860, thus starting a civil war. Need we add that secessionism inherently represents anarchy and treason?

---

[34] Harold Bloom, "Will This Election Be the Mormon Breakthrough?" *New York Times*, November 12, 2011.

Brigham Young started the first US civil war. President Buchanan, for a complex of reasons, decided to send a significant part of the United States Army to Salt Lake City to restore the authority of the United States government. The Mormon forces avoided direct conflict with the US Army, but massacred about 140 peaceful pioneers from Arkansas who were trying to get to Southern California. This was the infamous Mountain Meadows Massacre of 1857, the greatest act of terrorism between the American Revolution and the Civil War. The record will show that the first American president ever to refer explicitly to terrorism was James Buchanan, and that he did so in a public statement condemning the actions committed by Brigham Young and his Mormons.

President James Buchanan warned that Brigham Young and the Mormons had imposed 'a strange system of terrorism' on the people of Utah Territory."[35]

BRIGHAM YOUNG EMBRACES TERRORISM; HIS SON AGREES

Brigham Young, the Mormon theocratic dictator of Utah, did not shrink from the label of terrorism, but rather embraced it quite openly. He said in his sermon of August 31, 1856 that, starting from its creation, God's Kingdom, meaning the Mormon power, had been "a terror to all nations," he said. Its goal was to "revolutionize the world and bring all under subjection to the law of God, who is our law giver." (*The Mormon Rebellion*, Bigler & Bagley, p. 91)

Brigham's son had to concede privately that his father's methods amounted to terrorism. A few years later, Brigham Young Jr. wrote in his diary entry for December 15, 1862 that the religious revival instituted by his father in 1857 had been a "reign of terror." (*The Mormon Rebellion*, Bigler & Bagley, p. 95)

MORMONS PUSH REACTIONARY THEORY OF US CONSTITUTION

During these years, the Mormons helped to originate the combination of idolizing the U.S. Constitution, while vilifying every policy and every official of the US government established under that Constitution. The Mormons argued that the U.S. Constitution was divinely inspired, possibly because they sought the protection of the laws of the United States for polygamy, although that option began to be closed by the Morrill Act of 1862, which banned polygamy. When this law withstood challenge before the Supreme Court about 15 years later, Mormon chances for perpetuating their peculiar institution were driven underground.

BRIGHAM YOUNG: ABRAHAM LINCOLN A "CURSED SCOUNDREL"

During the Civil War of 1861-1865, Brigham Young confirmed himself as a hardened traitor to the United States, pouring scorn and invective on Abraham Lincoln and his government, and preparing another bid for secession, especially in case of British intervention in the wake of some landmark Union defeat. President Lincoln, raved

---

[35] Bigler & Bagley, *The Mormon Rebellion*, p. xi.

Brigham Young, was a "cursed scoundrel."[36] At other times, the Mormon boss stated that Lincoln was "wicked,"[37] "subject to the influence of a wicked spirit,"[38] and "fully adrift on the current of radical fanaticism."[39]

The Utah Territory, as it was by then, was the only part of the United States which took no part in the great conflict between freedom and slavery. The Mormons, still nursing their grievances of their slain Prophet, refused to mobilize for the Union. They did not respond to the call for volunteers in April 1861 after the firing on Fort Sumter, and they prevented conscription into the Union Army under the draft law of 1863. If the Mormons really believed that the U.S. Constitution was divinely inspired, then their refusal to choose sides in the struggle for the Union made them, in their own terms, a kind of political Lamanites.

BLOOD ATONEMENT: HUMAN SACRIFICE

The standard Christian argument, starting with the treatise of St. Anselm of Canterbury about why God had to become man in order to save humanity, is that the sacrifice on the cross of Jesus Christ, Son of God and at the same time a human being who had never sinned, satisfied the demands of divine justice by atoning for the sins of the world. In Brigham Young's view, this was not the case. Brigham Young argued that certain sins, which often turned out to be offenses against Mormondom, were so heinous that they required the sinner to be killed on the spot. This was Brigham Young's infamous doctrine of blood atonement, which was applied in practice to the 140 peaceful Arkansas pioneers, including many women and children, who died at the Mountain Meadows Massacre of 1857. In reality, of course, Brigham Young was attempting to intimidate the notoriously weak Buchanan and prospective Western settlers in general by showing his ability to interdict the passage of Americans through their own territory in the Great Basin. But he was also motivated by a desire to avenge the death of Mormon apostle Parley Pratt, who had recently been killed in Arkansas by the outraged husband of a woman with whom he had initiated celestial relations, with a view to installing her in his harem. There were also suggestions that some of the Arkansans had links to the Joseph Smith assassination in Illinois in 1844.

In the history of the United States, many ethnic and religious groups have acted as a bloc over long periods of time, but no Christian denomination has maintained the relentless consistency of goals as the Mormons. When Mormons arrived in Ohio, or Missouri, or Illinois, or anywhere else, they often frightened the inhabitants by their bloc voting and across-the-board political lockstep. Their goal was always to seize all available power. The notion of checks and balances or separation of powers is utterly foreign to Mormon political thinking.

---

[36] *Saints and the Union*, p. 50.
[37] Ibid., p. 67.
[38] Ibid., p. 37.
[39] Ibid., p. 106.

The Mormons also possessed and evidently still possess a political secret police, the Sons of Dan or Danites. The Danites started out as the bodyguards of Joseph Smith. They then expanded to include the Mormon private army. Today, the Mormons represent powerful factions of the Central Intelligence Agency, the Federal Bureau of Investigation, and the US federal government in general. These may be thought of as the modern Danites. In this context, we should also mention the considerable Mormon political intelligence capability around Cleon Skousen and similar figures. Cleon Skousen is rumored to have originated the profoundly disorienting slogan of "The New World Order," which has been misleading low-information right wingers and libertarians ever since. Mormons have contributed a great deal to the Ron Paul counterinsurgency program of the last several years, as we will show in detail. Suffice it at this point to say that theocracy enforced by Danites can be ranked second only to polygamy as causes of friction between the Mormons and surrounding populations during the 19th century.

SECESSIONISM AND ANTI-AMERICANISM

Brigham Young thus ranks as a leading secessionist who beat Jefferson Davis and the other Confederate leaders to the punch by more than three years when it came to the attempt to break up the United States of America. The curious case of a certain James Strang, who proclaimed himself the independent Mormon King of Beaver Island, Michigan, can serve to show that Mormon secessionism was not a matter of the individual psychology of Brigham Young, but was deeply rooted in the doctrine of Joseph Smith and thus in the entire religion. The Utah War or Mormon War of 1857-1858 was America's first civil war, started at the initiative of the Mormon Saints.

For Joseph Smith and Brigham Young, "American" was a dirty word. For Joseph Smith, Americans were "the Gentiles," an inferior population to be regarded with total contempt. Mormons referred to those "Damned Americans." This feeling was reciprocated: when the U.S. Army finally arrived in Salt Lake City in 1858, Colonel C. F. Smith blurted out that, as far as the US Army was concerned, it "would like to see every damned Mormon hung by the neck." (*The Mormon Rebellion*, Bigler & Bagley, p. 324)

Down to the present day, several sources report, Independence Day is not the biggest holiday in the month of July in the Mormon Mecca of Utah. That honor is reserved for Pioneer Day, which takes place on July 24. In Salt Lake City, the Fourth of July comes in as a distant second: "Normally the Fourth of July was yawned at in Utah Territory— as it still is in today's state— while all of the excitement was reserved for Pioneer Day, twenty days later, which celebrates the anniversary of Brigham Young's arrival in Salt Lake Valley." (*The Mormon Rebellion*, Bigler & Bagley, p. 86)

PRESIDENTIAL CANDIDATES CAN HAVE NO SECRETS

The standpoint of this book is that the American public has a right and indeed the duty to learn and know everything, without any exceptions, from the individuals who are asking for their votes in order to be elected president. Ever since the emergence of nuclear weapons, the powers of the presidency have been practically absolute. Presidents have access to the nuclear launch codes which can unleash World War III, which might well spell death for vast numbers of the population at home and abroad. If you want to get your hands on the nuclear button, we need to know everything about you. There can be no secrets. Another reason for this is that presidents who do keep secrets can then be blackmailed by intelligence agencies and other forces to get what they want – a phenomenon which may have contributed to Obama's disappointing performance.

We argued for this standard in regard to Obama, demanding to know the exact circumstances of his birth, his college transcripts, what he was doing during certain lost years of his biography, and other pertinent facts. These inquiries are contained in *Obama the Postmodern Coup* (published April, 2008) and in *Barack H. Obama: the Unauthorized Biography* (published August, 2008).

Now we want to know about Romney: we want to see his tax returns back to the early 1980s, covering the entire time he worked as a predatory asset stripper at Bain Capital. We want to know everything about his relation to his close friend, Israeli Prime Minister Biniamin Netanyahu. We demand that Bain Capital release the full particulars of what happened to the American companies that they bought up and looted, sometimes driving them into bankruptcy.

BAIN CAPITAL A SATELLITE OF THE MORMON CHURCH?

Recent research suggests that Bain Capital enjoyed a special relation with the Mormon Church of Latter-day Saints. According to reporter Jason Horowitz, "the Church Hierarchy in Salt Lake City … sometimes called on the Mormons at Bain for informal consultation." Along with Romney, there was Bob Gay, "a Bain colleague who once sat with Romney on the Church's High Council." As president of the Boston stake or diocese of the Mormon Church, "Romney appointed his Bain colleague, Darrell Rigby, to teach an alternate tradition class" to Mormons. By now, the brutal exploitation of working people by the asset strippers at Bain has become well known. What deserves to be better known is that these methods apparently reflect the corporate culture of Mormonism.[40]

DENIGRATING THE HOST: "THOSE DAMNED AMERICANS"

While campaigning for the Pennsylvania primary, Romney attempted to humanize himself by sitting at a picnic table with some Republican voters. The hostess served some cookies. Romney responded by complaining about the quality of the cookies, suggesting that they had come from the local Seven-Eleven, and were of inferior quality. It was incredibly rude and boorish, but it is also part of a pattern which characterizes Romney.

On the eve of his visit to London for the opening of the Olympics in late July 2012, Romney was asked by Brian Williams whether he thought the London Olympics would be a success. Romney started out by saying that he was troubled by some of the

---

[40] Jason Horowitz, "In Church, Romney Mastered Many Keys: As a Mormon Church Leader, Romney Was Methodical, Deeply Spiritual," *Washington Post*, August 20, 2012.

organizing problems that had emerged. He also expressed doubt as to whether Londoners and the British people in general were really ready to host the games. It was another incredible gaffe, insulting his hosts and benefactors in advance. British Prime Minister Cameron commented that it was easy to organize Olympics "out in the middle of nowhere" – meaning Salt Lake City. Boris Johnson, the Mayor of London mocked Romney before an audience of 60,000 people. Romney was promptly dubbed as "Mitt the Twit" by the London tabloids. Even European right wingers find Romney "bizarroïde" – beyond bizarre.

These attitudes can be compared to the Mormons of 1857-58, one of whom asked a co-religionist if he had American guests in his home, wanting to know what he was doing with "those damned Americans about his house.'" (*The Mormon Rebellion*, Bigler & Bagley, p. 72)

A FLIP-FLOPPER FROM AN ETCH-A-SKETCH DENOMINATION?

By now, Romney is so notorious as a flip-flopper who has supported both sides of virtually every important issue that examples are hardly necessary. Romney has been for and against gay marriage, for and against an individual mandate in healthcare, for and against gun control, and so forth. Remarkably, Romney flip-flops with absolute impudence, seldom offering a reason with these changes, often arguing that no change has taken place. But can Romney's flip-flops also be rooted in the traditions of Mormonism?

At any given time, the Church of Latter-day Saints has claimed to be in possession of absolute truth, as revealed to Joseph Smith. But at the same time, Mormon views on many fundamental issues have changed from one thing to its diametrical opposite. If we take the example of polygamy, we find that the *Book of Mormon* expressly forbids it, saying: "Hearken to the word of the Lord: for there shall not any man among you have save it be one wife; and concubines he shall have none...."[41] This represents a blanket ban on polygamy as of 1830.

But, impelled by his celestial urges, we find Joseph Smith and his top lieutenants practicing polygamy, while loudly denying that they were doing so. Then, under Brigham Young, the Mormon Church in 1852 openly proclaimed the "Order of Jacob," meaning the absolute imperative of plural marriage for men who wanted to avoid menial status in the afterlife. Then, around 1895, the Mormon Church officially prohibited polygamy, but it was continued by certain doctrinaire diehards like the Romney family, and also surreptitiously by some of the top leaders, which may again include the Romney family. This is a record of flip-flops worthy of Romney himself.

The official explanation offered by the Mormon Church for these drastic reversals came from Prophet Gordon G. Hinckley in 2002, who said: "Polygamy came by revelation, and it left by revelation." Outsiders may be forgiven for wondering about the relation of such revelations with pure political expediency and opportunism.

---

[41] *Book of Mormon*, Jacob, 2, 27.

Concerning the status of black people, the *Book of Mormon*, as already noted, makes dark skin the sign of those spirits who refused to take sides in the struggle between the Mormon Jesus and the Mormon Lucifer. But when Joseph Smith wanted to run for president in 1844, he was at least willing to grant black slaves the hope of being freed, while paying compensation to their owners out of the sale of US public lands in the West. Then, during the Brigham Young era, black people were once again the objects of abuse and discrimination. Then, in 1978, the Mormon Church proclaimed that it no longer discriminated against blacks, based on a new revelation. Again, the doctrinal flip-flops of the Mormon Church can only remind us of the flip-flops of the current Republican candidate, Romney.

For many people, and even for many politicians, such a consistent, pervasive, and outrageous pattern of flip-flops would impose a tremendous psychological burden. Such a flip-flopper might come to feel like a total buffoon, destined to never be taken seriously again by anybody, Much less be elected president of the United States. But Romney does not seem to be afflicted by these psychological difficulties. He flip-flops with reckless abandon. In doing this, he resembles the Mormon Church, which always claims absolute authority compared to the abomination of all the Christian churches, but at the same time feels free to make changes in its absolute belief structure, obviously according to the needs of political expediency. Romney is never more of a true Mormon than when he flip-flops, even as he demands that the voters put him in the White House.

RETROACTIVE RETIREMENT AND POSTHUMOUS BAPTISM

Mormons are known to practice posthumous baptism, inducting departed spirits into the true faith with no way of ascertaining the wishes of the interested parties, or even their families. It is estimated that some 200 million departed souls have been given this treatment, including numerous world leaders and the nominally Roman Catholic members of Paul Ryan's immediate family. Posthumous baptism got the Mormons into trouble when they began applying it to the Jewish victims of the Nazi Holocaust, and they have now promised to back off in this regard. Posthumous baptism is yet another radical divergence between Mormonism and Christianity, since the latter regards only thoughts and deeds of this mortal life as the basis of salvation.

During the 2012 campaign, the issue arose as to whether Romney had indeed continued to work at Bain Capital between 1999 and 2003. He had sworn to the Securities and Exchange Commission in a series of SEC filings that he was indeed a top official of Bain through 2003. He also swore, in a series of filings presented to the Federal Elections Commission, that he had no longer worked for Bain after 1999, and that he left to work on the Salt Lake City Winter Olympics. We note in passing that swearing one thing to the SEC and something contradictory to the FEC would normally constitute a premeditated case of perjury in one or the other of these sworn statements.

But Romney thought of a way to get out of this difficulty. The Romney camp sent out the veteran political hack Ed Gillespie to make the case that Romney had "retired retroactively to 1999." This was a novel concept: how could anybody retire retroactively? This appeared an argument redolent of Mormonism, in which not just individual actions, but one's whole life can be altered in retrospect with a ceremony and the stroke of a pen, *nunc pro tunc*.

OBSESSIVE SECRECY

One aspect of the Romney campaign which has attracted sustained and negative attention is the secrecy of the candidate. Romney has refused to make public more than two years of his federal income tax returns, and one of those years will be available only in outline form. Romney has refused to provide details about his offshore tax shelters and how they work. Even though he claims the presidency on the basis of his supposed track record as a successful businessman, he refuses to provide details about his role at Bain Capital and his participation in certain deals which led to plant closings, layoffs, and the massive transfer of pension liabilities to the federal government. Romney has also not made public his medical records.

Instead, Romney and his wife have become indignant when pressed for these details. Even when their secrecy has exacted a considerable political price, Mitt and Ann have insisted on stonewalling, a tactic which almost never works in modern American politics.

In his late July speech to the Veterans of Foreign Wars in Reno, Nevada, Romney repeated his usual line that Obama is unpatriotic and apologizes for the greatness of American exceptionalism. Romney demanded to know more about leaks of national security information coming from the Obama White House, an issue being raised by a group of reactionary Swift Boaters, veterans working to get Romney elected. "The time for stonewalling is over," and "Americans are entitled to know" so they can receive "a full and prompt accounting of the facts," claimed Romney. The Romney campaign relies almost exclusively on Bush-Cheney neocons when it comes to foreign policy and national security, but it was still grotesque that the campaign sent out Eric Edelman to put some extra spin on these remarks for the press. Edelman had been implicated in an exhaustively documented case of leaking when he worked for Scooter Libby in Cheney's office during the years of Bush the younger. Libby was found guilty in federal court of divulging the identity of CIA agent Valerie Plame to journalist Robert Novak.

When Romney was called in to cover up the role of the Mormon hierarchy and leading Mormons in $1 million in corrupt payments to the International Olympic Committee, in connection to the 2002 Salt Lake City Winter Olympics, he initially promised "complete transparency." But then his operation became totally secret. He refused to tell the Utah state officials supervising the Olympics what his budget was. Most of the key documents about the 2002 Winter Games were destroyed a few days after the event ended. The records of Romney's operation are stored at the (Mormon-controlled) University of Utah, where they are still not open to the public.

The Romney campaign claims that the records were destroyed by Romney crony Fraser Bullock of Bain Capital, who took over the Salt Lake City Olympic Committee when Romney left to run for governor of Massachusetts.

At the end of his term as governor of the state of Massachusetts, Romney spent $100,000 of Massachusetts taxpayers' money to replace computers in his offices. Mark Hosenball of Reuters has described this sanitizing effort as "part of an unprecedented effort to keep his records secret." According to Hosenball, 11 top Romney aides "bought the hard drives of these state-issued computers to keep for themselves." Romney's staff also made sure that e-mails and other electronic communications generated during the Romney administration were deleted from the Massachusetts state's servers. "Those actions erased much of the internal documentation of Romney's four-year tenure as governor," says Hosenball.[42]

Romney is deeply convinced that central questions of public policy should be handled in secret. He has said that controversial issues like income inequality should be discussed in "quiet rooms," presumably meaning in the board rooms of zombie banks. He has also suggested that the illegal Israeli settlements on Palestinian territory should be considered behind closed doors. These attitudes are bound to generate negative attention in an age which elevates transparency to the status of an end in itself.

Thus, the salient features of Romney's life – his time at Bain, his records as governor of Massachusetts, and his administration of his quarter billion dollar personal fortune – are all top secret for the public. Why would Romney choose such a strange public profile? Does he really believe that he can be so secretive, with impunity? Perhaps the answer here is once again to be found in his Mormon background.

The Mormon Church has also practiced this secrecy from the very beginning. Polygamy was at first a secret practice. Even today, the interior of every Mormon Temple is secret, held strictly off-limits to outsiders, and even to Mormons who do not have a certification that they are members in good standing, called a "temple recommend." The liturgy used in divine services in these temples, called the "temple endowment," is also a secret. Mormon theology, as we have seen, is also largely secret. Until little more than two decades ago, individual Mormons swore an oath that they would willingly be deprived of their lives by having their throats cut or by disembowelment if they were to divulge certain of these secrets.

The archives of the Latter-day Saints in Salt Lake City, Utah and elsewhere are far more secret than the Vatican Secret Archive in Rome. The common complaint of researchers who have attempted to consult these closely-held Mormon records is that they have received no cooperation, and sometimes that they have received discouragement.

MORMON ANTINOMIANISM – THE REJECTION OF MORAL LAW

Mormonism, as the words "Latter-day" in its official title suggests, is a religion which expects the second coming of the Messiah and the end of the world as we have known it to occur soon. In other words, Mormons agree that we are currently living in the End Time. Any sect making this claim runs at least one obvious danger: antinomianism. In this context, antinomianism would be the belief that, since the second coming of the

---

[42] Maureen Dowd, "Hiding in Plain Sight," *Falls Church News-Press*, July 26–August 1, 2012.

Savior is at hand, the moral law is suspended, at least for the elect (the "Saints"). Another path to antinomianism comes from the belief that the individual has a direct line to God by way of some sort of extra scriptural revelation, be this through mysticism, or because one has attained the status of a prophet, as Joseph Smith claimed he had. This belief has been observed frequently in Christianity, but it is by no means limited to this faith, since we have had examples of antinomianism in Judaism as well, to go no further than this.

The early phase of Quakerism displayed unmistakable antinomian tendencies. If an individual Quaker were told by his or her inner light that some activity was not a sin, then all the Law and the Prophets were rendered inoperative for that person. George Fox and other Quaker leaders took measures to subordinate the inner light for the "sense of the meeting," but – in a tightly knit denomination like the Quakers – examples of antinomianism have continued to occur centuries later. Richard Nixon and Lyndon LaRouche are examples, since both were raised as Quakers, and as leaders veered into antinomianism.

In the case of Judaism, antinomianism is associated with false messiahs like Sabbatai Zevi (Shabtai Zvi) around 1666, and with the movement around Jacob Frank in the following century. If the Messiah had indeed returned, then the Mosaic Law was suspended, they argued.

The Mormons exhibit a very strong tendency towards antinomianism, first of all because of their core belief that the second coming of the Messiah is at hand, and secondly because they maintain that oracles, prophecies, and revelations have not ceased, but continue to be generated down to the present day, above all by the "Prophets" in command of the Church of Latter-day Saints.

Any account of the history of the Mormons would have to include fraud, counterfeiting, theft, perjury, adultery, and murder. Joseph Smith on one occasion said he would authorize everything but murder, and there is plenty of evidence that his successor Brigham Young removed that exception and was willing to authorize any actions whatsoever in the name of the Mormon Church.

IS ROMNEY BOUND BY THE MORMON OATH OF VENGEANCE AGAINST THE UNITED STATES?

The killing of Joseph Smith and Hyrum Smith in Carthage, Illinois, in 1844 was seen by Brigham Young and other Mormon leaders as the central event of human history and the starting point in a blood feud or vendetta between the Mormon Saints and the United States of America, including all government institutions and the entire American people. Brigham Young, acting in this spirit, succeeded in getting an oath of vengeance inserted into the Nauvoo Endowment, meaning that it became part of the official liturgy for divine services at the most prestigious place of worship of the entire Mormon denomination.

A reasonably reliable version of the Oath of Vengeance reads as follows:

"You and each of you do covenant and promise that you will pray and never cease to pray to Almighty God to avenge the blood of the prophets [Joseph Smith and Hyrum Smith] upon this nation [The United States of America], and that you will teach the same to your children and to your children's children unto the third and fourth generation."[43]

This Mormon obsession with bloody revenge is absolutely anathema to Christianity. This was not a metaphor or plea to God, but rather a pledge of armed struggle for the violent overthrow of the United States. In 1849, William Smith, the surviving brother of the slain Prophet, warned President Zachary Taylor about Mormon activities out in Deseret. He pointed out that Brigham Young had led 1500 Mormon Saints in swearing "to avenge the blood of Joseph Smith on this nation," to "carry out hostilities against the nation, and to keep the same intent a profound secret, now and forever."[44]

Increase and Maria van Deusen, two ex-Mormons who became indefatigable propagandists against the Saints, told of an oath of vengeance being administered as part of the Nauvoo Temple endowment in January, 1846: "We are required to kneel at this altar, where we have an oath administered to us to this effect; that we will avenge the blood of Joseph Smith on this Nation, and teach our children the same. They tell us that the nation has winked at the abuse and persecution of the Mormons, and the murder of the Prophet in particular. Therefore the Lord is displeased with the nation, and means to destroy it, and this is the excuse for forming this leak or conspiracy."[45]

Parley Parker Pratt, the ancestor of Mitt Romney, was personally associated with this treasonous oath. In 1854, John Hyde described a Mormon temple endowment or ceremony in February 1854 in the Salt Lake City Council House. According to Hyde's description, he was awarded his celestial name of Enoch by none other than Parley Pratt. When Hyde was inducted into the first and then the second degrees of the Melchizedek priesthood, the Oath of Vengeance was sworn: "For allowing persecutions of the Saints and not avenging Joseph Smith's murder, those present vowed everlasting enmity toward the United States and promised to inspire their children with this spirit."[46]

Ann Eliza Young, who had successfully sued Brigham Young for divorce, and then gone on to write a lively book about her experiences under Mormondom, recounts her experiences in the Salt Lake City Temple in detail. As part of the temple endowment, she reports that the congregation "swore also to entertain an everlasting enmity to the United States government, and to disregard its laws so far as possible; we swore that we would use every exertion to avenge the deaths of our Prophet Joseph Smith and his brother Hyrum upon the Gentile race, by whose means they were brought to their

---

[43] David John Buerger, *The Mysteries of Godliness: a History of Mormon Temple Worship* (San Francisco, 1994), p. 133.
[44] Hirshson, p. 102.
[45] Increase and Maria Van Deusen, *The Mormon Endowment; a Secret Drama, or Conspiracy, in the Nauvoo Temple, in 1846* (Syracuse, New York: N. M. D. Lathrop, 1847).
[46] John Hyde Jr., *Mormonism, Its Leaders and Designs* (New York: W. P. Fetidge & Co., 1857); Hirshson, p. 136.

unhappy fate, and to teach our children to foster this spirit of revenge also; and last of all, we swore never to reveal the mysteries of the Endowment House."[47]

Evidence of the Mormon Oath of Vengeance against the United States can also be found in the court records of the day. "During an 1889 trial in which the denial of citizenship to an alien who had taken his vows was upheld, Andrew Cahoon, a Saint for forty years and a bishop for eighteen, and Franklin D. Richards, the church historian, both admitted that the endowment preached revenge for the murders of Joseph and Hyrum. Richards further revealed that his arm had been anointed to avenge their blood. Bloodthirsty oaths and polygamy for the masses became Young's legacy to his people."[48]

After Utah had finally been admitted to the Union, Senator Reed Smoot, a Mormon, was chosen as Senator by the Utah Legislature in 1903. Many senators wanted to deny Smoot his seat. They accused him of being a member of the Quorum of the Twelve, the ruling body of Mormonism, and therefore responsible for the continued practice of polygamy, especially in Canada and Mexico, where the Romney family, among others, was continuing to live according to Joseph Smith's Order of Jacob mandating plural marriage. Smoot was also held responsible for the Mormon opinion that church revelation was superior to the Constitution and laws of the United States for Mormon theocracy, and other abuses. The illegal activities of the Danites, the Mormon political Gestapo, were cited, along with the Mountain Meadows Massacre. The resulting Senate hearings lasted from 1904 to 1907, and attracted tremendous public attention. During that time, more than 100 witnesses gave 3,500 pages of testimony. When the Senate finally voted as to whether or not to expel Smoot, the motion to oust him fell short of the required two-thirds vote. With a view to keeping Smoot in the Senate, Mormon president Joseph F. Smith had reaffirmed the ban on polygamy in a special statement in April, 1904, which stated that Mormon officials anywhere in the world, as well as the participants, would be excommunicated if they contracted a polygamist marriage.

DOES ROMNEY'S OATH OF OBEDIENCE TO TODAY'S LDS PROPHET AND APOSTLES VIOLATE THE PRESIDENTIAL OATH?

One of the issues raised in these Smoot hearings more than a century ago was whether the binding Mormon oath of obedience to ecclesiastical authority included actions by the individual Saint in his capacity as an official of the United States government. As David John Buerger writes, "one of the most painful events in 20th century LDS history was the hearings of the United States Senate subcommittee to determine whether elected Utah Senator and apostle Reed Smoot should be allowed to serve in the Senate. Among the many issues the committee heard testimony on were the 'secret oaths' of the temple endowment ceremony. The committee's concern was whether the Mormon covenant of obedience to ecclesiastical authority conflicted with the Senator's oath of loyalty to the

---

[47] Ann Eliza Young, *Wife No. 19, the Story of a Life in Bondage, Being a Complete Exposé of Mormonism and Revealing the Sorrows, Sacrifices and Sufferings of Women in Polygamy* (and Hartford, Connecticut: Dustin, Gilman and Co.), p. 368. online at openlibrary.org.
[48] Hirshson, p. 136.

Constitution. Not surprisingly, in the course of these hearings the oath or prayer of vengeance attracted the committee's sustained interest."[49]

One of the principal accusations against the LDS was that Mormons were compelled to swear oaths pledging to seek revenge against the United States. The transcripts of Senate hearings from 1904 contain the testimony of a number of witnesses who told the Senate about the Mormon Oath of Vengeance. One J. H. Wallis said he had been told to swear "that you and each of you will never cease to importune High Heaven for vengeance upon this nation for the blood of the prophets who have been slain." August W. Lundstrum recounted that in an endowment he attended, "We and each of us solemnly covenant and promise that we shall ask God to avenge the blood of Joseph Smith upon this nation. There is something more added, but that is all I can remember verbatim. That is the essential part.... It was in regard to teaching our children and children's children to the last generation to the same effect." Mrs. Annie Elliott recalled: "One, I remember, they told me to pray and never cease to pray to get revenge on the blood of the prophets on this nation, and also teach it to my children and children's children.."

MORMON GOOD NEIGHBOR POLICY CAMOUFLAGES OATHS

In 1919, the First Presidency of the Latter-day Saints under Heber J. Grant decided to revise the Mormon liturgy, and appointed a committee to carry out this task. The revision was led by Apostle George F. Richards, and was carried out between 1921 and 1927. Richardson informed the presidents of the six Mormon temples functioning at that time that "all reference to retribution" was purged from the endowment ceremony, and that there should be no more talk of "avenging the blood of the prophets." A few years later, when President Franklin D. Roosevelt launched his Good Neighbor Policy towards the nations of Latin America, Mormon publicists began calling the abolition of the Oath of Vengeance the Mormon Good Neighbor Policy. But how sincere were the changes?

There remains the very real possibility that the Oath of Vengeance has been maintained as a shelf doctrine, no longer imparted to the mass of the faithful, but carefully cultivated among the inner elite. The liturgical changes of 1927 might have no more value than the repeated assurances of Joseph Smith up to the day he was killed that he never practiced polygamy.

Michigan Governor George Romney, the father of the current Republican contender, was born in Colonia Dublán, Galeana, Chihuahua, Mexico in 1907. Since the Romneys were devoted Mormons who had fled the United States in order to continue the practice of polygamy, Mitt Romney's father George spent the first 20 years of his life in a church where hatred of the United States was a compulsory article of the faith. We notice that the liturgical changes of 1927 do not seem to include the abjuration of the Oath of Vengeance by those who had already taken it, and this necessarily would have included George Romney.

[49] Buerger, p. 133,

Since some versions of the Oath of Vengeance prescribed that the Mormon vendetta against the United States of America has to be carried on for four generations, we can therefore say that the Oath of Vengeance sworn by George Romney would bind not only Mitt Romney and his generation, but also the generation of Romney's five sons, and also the generation of Mitt Romney's grandchildren.

If George Romney ever repudiated his Oath of Vengeance against the United States, candidate Romney has a responsibility to tell the voters. Otherwise, we must assume that Mitt Romney continues to be bound by this pledge of eternal hostility against this country.

The Oath of Vengeance should not be confused with a better known oath which, according to some reports, was part of the Mormon liturgy until it was removed around 1990. This was a pledge of secrecy in which the adept promises never to tell the secrets of the Temple on pain of death. It also is punctuated by two vigorous slashing gestures, one across one's own throat, and one across the abdomen. These are supposed to signify readiness to have one's throat or belly cut in case a violation of the oath. A 2012 BBC documentary entitled *The Mormon Candidate* and produced by John Sweeney contains confirmation from former Mormons about some details of his oath. The former Mormons interviewed were convinced that Mitt Romney had sworn this oath on numerous occasions, and therefore continued to be bound by it. The Mormon Church was upset enough about this documentary to send two representatives from the public relations and lobbying firm APCO Worldwide to hand deliver a protest note to the BBC Media Center at White City in London.[50]

The question before the American voter is therefore whether it is advisable to choose Mitt Romney for president, even while knowing that he is a member of a cohesive and authoritarian religious organization, some of whose most emphatic doctrines have included, even within the last hundred years, the imperative of exacting revenge from the United States of America and from the American people. Surely there is a strong *prima facie* case that Romney is thus disqualified from holding nationwide federal elective office.

To pronounce a final verdict on this question, it will be necessary to discuss the history and traditions of Mormonism, especially in regard to its connection to British intelligence, and especially in the 19th century. Within that framework, the story of the sometimes polygamous Romney family can be situated. It will finally be necessary to judge whether these elements of tradition, history and biography allow us to forecast, at least to some extent, the future destiny of a possible Romney administration.

---

[50] Ben Dowell, BBC Employee Criticized after PRs Hand Deliver Mormon Documentary Complaint: PR and Lobbying Firm APCO's Representatives Enter BBC Building to Complain about John Sweeney Documentary," *Guardian*, March 27, 2012.

CHAPTER II

JOSEPH SMITH: POLYTHEISM, POLYGAMY, AND THE QUEST FOR THEOCRATIC POWER BEYOND CHRISTIANITY

> "I have more to boast of than ever any man had. I am the only man that has ever been able to keep a whole church together since the days of Adam.... Neither Paul, John, Peter, nor Jesus ever did it. I boast that no man ever did such work as I." Joseph Smith, *History of the Church*, 6:408-409.

Joseph Smith was the founder and principal prophet of the Mormon or LDS religion. Through a burst of activity in the 20 years before his death in 1844, Joseph Smith founded a religion which is separate and distinct from Judaism, Christianity, and Islam. He may have started off in his own mind with the goal of completing and fulfilling Christianity in the same way that Christianity had attempted to fulfill the Old Testament, but the outcome has been unquestionably an entirely new faith. Attempts by the Mormon hierarchy to disguise this fact, such as their decision around 1981 to begin subtitling the *Book of Mormon* as "Another Testament of Jesus Christ," should not be allowed to obscure this central fact.

Joseph Smith considered himself a god, and perhaps even as God Almighty Himself. The New Testament warns against assuming that salvation can be obtained exclusively through merit and good works, and adds "lest anyone should boast" as a warning against the sin of pride, always the most dangerous of the seven deadly sins, because ranking oneself above God leads to all the of the deadly sins. Joseph Smith boasted that he and he alone held the keys to heaven. According to some versions of Mormon theology, every soul will stand in judgment before an oligarchical heavenly tribunal composed, not of the Christian Trinity, but rather of Elohim, the Mormon Jesus, and Joseph Smith. Joseph Smith himself left no doubt that he personally had eclipsed Jesus Christ and the twelve apostles when he stated:

> "I have more to boast of than ever any man had. I am the only man that has ever been able to keep a whole church together since the days of Adam.... Neither Paul, John, Peter, nor Jesus ever did it. I boast that no man ever did such work as I. The followers of Jesus ran away from him, but the Latter-day Saints never ran away from me yet." Joseph Smith, *History of the Church*, 6:408-409.

But Joseph Smith's cosmic ambitions were not limited to the spiritual realm alone. They also aimed unmistakably at a totalitarian and dictatorial power over the affairs of this world. If modern Wahabites proclaim that all Moslem governments are illegitimate because they do not represent the caliphate prescribed by Mohammed, Joseph Smith and his lieutenants similarly argued that all the governments of the earth are intolerable because they do not represent the Kingdom of God. Joseph Smith proclaimed that he would soon provide a military solution to this problem, and thus set the stage for the Apocalypse. In this sense, a religion like Mormonism can be seen as a universal destabilization of all the existing systems of politics and government. Coming as it did at the zenith of the British Empire, it is not hard to imagine who would benefit from the spread of such a doctrine, and this issue will be addressed.

These were the ambitions nurtured by a poor farm boy from Vermont growing up in the backwash of the great awakening of the 18th century, who lived in the shadow of economic crisis from the reckless and irresponsible Jefferson embargo to the Andrew Jackson/Van Buren panic of 1837. Joseph Smith's family background is dominated by antinomianism, the belief that under certain circumstances the moral law may be suspended for the elect, who are therefore authorized to run wild – a note which has always accompanied Mormonism. Joseph Smith in his early youth was considered a mountebank, a charlatan, a con artist. He played the role of the village necromancer, magus, and diviner, taking advantage of the gullibility of ignorant marginal farmers. Just before the Angel Moroni guided him to the fabulous golden plates on the hill of Cumorah near Palmyra, New York, Joseph Smith had been convicted in a New York state court of swindling one of his gulls. Within a few years, Joseph Smith was the charismatic dictator of a sect which managed to attract the attention of much of the United States and far beyond.

It is impossible to understand Joseph Smith without understanding the historical stage on which he played his gesticulating and histrionic role. This means that one must bear in mind the situation of organized religion in the United States in the first half of the 19th century. But it also requires attention to the world geopolitical stage on which the political exertions of the Mormon Saints were unfolding. If the first of these has been neglected, the second has been passed over in almost total silence and incomprehension.

Since Joseph Smith did not hesitate to compare himself quite favorably to Jesus Christ, we can carry the comparison a little bit further in terms of two key components of the life of Christ. First, were there any religious movements that foreshadowed the coming of the Mormons? Secondly, were there any remarkable individuals who prepared the way for the Mormon Prophet?

JOSEPH SMITH'S ESSENES: THE DORRILITES AND THE WOOD SCRAPE

In the case of Jesus Christ, the precursors have often been identified as the Essenes, the third grouping in Judaism at that time, which was distinct from the Pharisees and the Sadducees. In the case of Joseph Smith, we must address the issue of the burned-over area of the northeastern United States, an area which had seen many religious revivals followed by a relapse into indifferentism, skepticism, and cynicism. Many people had been converted and born again several times, and then relapsed. A frenzy of activity was often followed by spiritual torpor. The evangelist Charles G. Finney deplored that the post-enthusiastic hangover convinced many jaded souls "that religion was a mere delusion." (Brodie, p. 15) This would become the initial recruiting ground for Mormonism.

The burned-over area is generally equated with the western part of upstate New York, but the concept needs to be seen more broadly. The Connecticut River Valley between New Hampshire and Vermont was a burned-over area in its own right, owing to the long hangover which followed the vindictive Calvinist rantings of the fire and brimstone demagogue Jonathan Edwards, the key founding figure of the Edwards-Aaron Burr family which has played such an overwhelmingly negative role in American history. Mormonism can be thought of as an abreaction to the excesses of the Jonathan Edwards-George Whitefield "Great Awakening" of 1737-1743, arising among persons still stunted by the horrors of Edwards' infamous sermon, "Sinners in the Hands of an Angry God." The Calvinism of Edwards knew no charity; nor did Mormonism.

THE DORRILITES

The Prophet Joseph Smith was born in eastern Vermont, in the valley of the White River. During the 1790s there appeared in this state, not far from the Massachusetts border, a utopian and collectivist community of about 40 persons known as the Dorrilites, named after their founder, who, appropriately enough, was a retired redcoat officer from the British Army. Was this Dorril a stay-behind operation of the British Empire? The importance of the Dorrilites is that they offer a substantial repertoire of those organizational and doctrinal features which will later characterize Mormonism. Like the Mormons, the Dorrilites had communist property relations, but no political democracy, since the Britisher Dorril demanded total submission to his divinely inspired commands. He imposed a rigorous regime of vegetarianism, banning even leather shoes. The Dorrilites were accused by local ministers not just of doctrinal deviations, but also of holding bacchanalian orgies. The Dorrilites collapsed when their leader was unable to deliver on his revelation that "no arm can hurt my flesh," meaning that he and his followers were immune from pain. But Dorril showed pain when he was physically assaulted by a skeptic, and his hypnotic hold over his congregation waned. This phenomenon, coming as it did in the decades after the Great Awakening and the Revolutionary War, left a pervasive hangover in the valleys of Western Vermont.[51]

THE WOOD SCRAPE

Another candidate for the role of the Essenes in relation to Joseph Smith are the New Israelites, founded in Middletown, Vermont by Nathaniel Wood in the 1790s. This charismatic cult leader gave his name to the Wood Scrape, which occurred when the local militia were called in to maintain public order on the day for which Wood had foreseen the arrival of the "destroying Angel," and thus of the Apocalypse. Here even more explicit Mormon motifs are on display. The New Israelites of Vermont claimed to be one of the 10 Lost Tribes of Israel, a major theme of the *Book of Mormon*. Wood preached immortalism, a doctrine perhaps not very different in the eyes of the average person from Joseph Smith's eternal progression understood as the possibility of becoming a god. The followers of Wood, like the later followers of Joseph Smith,

---

[51] Daniel M. Ludlum, *Social Ferment in Vermont 1791-1850* (New York: Columbia University Press, 1939), pp. 238-244, online at olivercowdry.com

practiced spiritual wifery and polygamy. Both groups engaged in divination. Both groups thought it was important to begin building an edifice for worship which they called a temple. Behind the scenes, both groups were notorious for counterfeiting bank notes.

According to some accounts, the New Israelite movement may have included Joseph Smith Sr., who was later to become the father of the Mormon Prophet. Joseph Smith the elder apparently got his introduction to money digging during his time with Wood. Money digging generally meant the hunt for buried treasure, usually practiced at the expense of a debt-strapped and desperate farmer who could be conned into believing that there were vast riches hidden on his land. Here, as in the later history of the Mormons, the need and desire to be duped plays perhaps an even greater role than the bravura of the con artist.

JOSEPH SMITH'S ST. JOHN THE BAPTISTS: WALTERS AND WINCHELL

Another member of the New Israelites was probably William Cowdery, the later father of Oliver Cowdery, the expert with a divining rod who was part of Joseph Smith's circle of friends at the time that the *Book of Mormon* was being prepared. Another Wood veteran who found his way to the Palmyra, New York region was a certain Justus Winchell, a counterfeiter and treasure hunter. According to Professor Daniel Ludlum, "Winchell and Oliver Cowdery, subsequently moved from Middletown [Vermont] to Palmyra in New York State, and there became acquainted with another transplanted Vermont rodsman, Joseph Smith, the founder of Mormonism."[52]

If these were Joseph Smith's possible Essenes, is there also a candidate for the role of St. John the Baptist preparing the way for the Mormon Prophet, and also coming into immediate personal contact with him? One individual who might fill this bill is, according to the work of the trailblazing scholar Fawn Brodie, a certain Walters. Brodie calls our attention to a "'vagabond fortune-teller" named Walters, who so won the confidence of several farmers that for some months they paid him three dollars a day to hunt for buried money on their property. Walters had crystals, stuffed toads, divining rods, and the "scryer's usual paraphernalia." But he also claimed to have an ancient Indian manuscript which specified the location of hidden treasure hordes, which he would read aloud to the illiterate farmers. According to a reporter, this was actually the Latin text of Caesar, or perhaps Cicero's *Orations*. According to a press account, when Walters had to get out of town, Joseph Smith did everything to take over his niche. (Brodie, p. 19)

The atmosphere in Joseph Smith's family was redolent of antinomianism. We have just seen his father's background. Joseph Smith's mother was Lucy, the essence of whose religious convictions was "simply the core of Antinomianism – the inner life is a law unto itself; freedom and integrity of religious experience must at all costs be

---

[52] Daniel M. Ludlum, *Social Ferment in Vermont 1791-1850* (New York: Columbia University Press, 1939), pp. 238-244, online at olivercowdery.com

preserved."[53] Lucy was not bound by any specific confession, but was "devoted to the mysticism so often found among those suddenly released from the domination and discipline of a church." (Brodie, p. 5) Joseph and Lucy Smith reflected an antinomian abreaction against the crushing burden of the law in Calvinism as preached by Jonathan Edwards. (Brodie, p. 4) In Joseph Smith, this abreaction would go all the way to hedonism.

Vermont was in economic depression because of Jefferson's embargo on all foreign trade, and also because of the dislocations caused by the War of 1812. Lake Champlain was still a hotbed of smugglers and counterfeiters, who liked this area since they could always flee to Canada if things got too hot. (Brodie, p. 7)

Joseph Smith later became famous for his cultivation of spirituality, but the adolescent Joseph Smith seems to have shown little interest in the needs of the soul. After reviewing development sources, Fawn Brodie concluded that Joseph Smith had not projected the image "of an adolescent mystic brooding over visions, but of a likable ne'er-do-well who was notorious for tall tales and necromantic arts and who spent his leisure leading a band of idlers in digging for buried treasure." (Brodie, p. 16)

NEW YORK COURT BRANDS JOSEPH SMITH AS "A DISORDERLY PERSON AND AN IMPOSTER"

Joseph Smith later claimed that God the Father accompanied by Jesus Christ had appeared to him around 1820, and warned him not to join any existing religious denomination, because all of them had become lost in the wilderness. In March 1826, when Joseph Smith had reached 21 and had therefore come into his majority, he was convicted of disturbing the peace at a New York state court in the town of Bainbridge, New York on charges that he was "a disorderly person and an imposter." Here Joseph Smith confessed to practicing magic and money digging in quest of buried gold. (Brodie, p. 16)

Joseph Smith claimed that certain rocks have magic powers and could help to find a buried treasure. These were called "seer stones" or "peep stones." They were used by putting them in the crown of a hat, and then covering one's face with the hat. In the resulting darkness, the stones were said to come alive and show visions of the desired treasure troves.

There is an abundant literature on the barren and misspent youth of Joseph Smith, mitigated by very little in the way of exculpatory evidence. When Joseph Smith had published a *Book of Mormon*, the editor of the *Palmyra Reflector*, the local paper, published a series of muckraking articles about the Prophet as a young man. These appeared under the nom de guerre of Obadiah Dogberry in 1830 and 1831. (Brodie, pp. 16-17)

---

[53] Brodie, p. 5.

FIFTY-ONE NEIGHBORS CALL THE PROPHET
"DESTITUTE OF MORAL CHARACTER AND ADDICTED TO VICIOUS HABITS"

Later, in 1833, when the Mormon Church was absorbing large numbers of new converts, a disillusioned refugee from Mormonism named Hurlbut collected affidavits from more than a hundred persons who claimed to have known the pre-prophetic Joseph Smith. These testimonies were overwhelmingly negative, and in 1834 appeared in book form edited by Eber D. Howe under the title *Mormonism Unvailed. [sic]* For example, fifty-one of Joseph's former neighbors testified that he had been "destitute of moral character and addicted to vicious habits." (Brodie, p. 18)

Because of the animus against Joseph Smith displayed by many of those interviewed, Mormon historians have later tried to argue that Hurlbut had collected a self-prejudicing sample. (Brodie, p. 17) But recent scholarship has tended to validate the essential facts cited by the Hurlbut affidavits, which together with the court record and the Dogberry editorials constitute a strong *prima facie* case against young Joseph Smith.[54]

Elmira, New York was in the middle of the Erie Canal boom country. Joseph Smith was so poor that he had to find sponsors to travel out of town to court his future wife, Emma. Between 1826 and 1830, Joseph Smith, who had little to no formal education, produced the *Book of Mormon* and then used that text to found a new religious sect.

The story is well known: Joseph Smith reported that he had been approached by the Angel Moroni, and had been shown the location of gold plates buried in the ground on a hill Moroni called Cumorah. Various apocryphal traditions place either a toad or a white salamander on top of the plates as their guardian. His gold plates had allegedly told the story of the Nephites, the now extinct white people who had dominated the New World until they were defeated at the hands of the Lamanites, the ancestors of 19th century Indians. Both groups were considered to be lost tribes of Israel, a view which had been espoused by Ethan Smith (no relation) in his book *View of the Hebrews* in 1823, a work which may have inspired the Mormon Prophet. Mormon had been the last great leader of the Nephites before they were wiped out.

Joseph Smith claimed that these plates were written in "Reformed Egyptian Hiero-glyphics." No person other than Joseph Smith ever saw the gold plates, and when the translation into English and transcription of the *Book of Mormon* was complete, Moroni took the plates to heaven for safekeeping. Since it would have been instant death for anybody but the anointed Joseph Smith to see the gold plates, Joseph Smith would work on them behind a curtain. But it later transpired that Joseph Smith did not work directly from the gold plates, but rather employed two seer stones, Urim and Thummim, sometimes presented as a pair of celestial goggles. When used together with Joseph Smith's hat to create the necessary darkness, these two seer stones would present the correct English expression for the "reformed Egyptian hieroglyph" that was to be translated.

---

[54] Rodger I. Anderson, *Joseph Smith's New York Reputation Re-Examined* (Salt Lake City: Signature Books, 1990), for example, argues that many of those interviewed by Hurlbut were eyewitnesses to and participants in the escapades described.

In transcribing the contents of the golden plates, Joseph Smith got help from his wife, from Oliver Cowdery, and from neighbors. Joseph Smith was able to convince a prosperous neighboring farmer named Martin Harris to mortgage his property to get the money to publish the manuscript. Harris' wife was indignant about her husband's gullibility, and tried to sabotage the project by destroying the first 116 pages of the translation, which Joseph Smith had unwisely agreed to lend to Harris. Mrs. Harris said that, if the plates were real, Joseph Smith would be able to translate them again. Faced with the exposure of his entire complicated imposture, Joseph Smith announced a revelation giving him the plates of Nephi, the story of the same events written from a slightly different point of view.

The first edition of the *Book of Mormon* was published with the help of Harris's money by Egbert B. Grandin of Palmyra, New York in 1830. Proclaiming that this constituted a new revelation supplementing the Christian Bible, Joseph Smith immediately proceeded to found the Church of Christ on Tuesday, April 6, 1830, with a total of six members. One month later, the congregation had grown to forty. (Brodie, p. 87) Baptism was by total immersion, and involved acknowledging Joseph Smith as "Seer, a Translator, a Prophet, An Apostle of Jesus Christ, an Elder of the Church, through the Will of God the Father, and the Grace of Your Lord Jesus Christ."[55]

The *Book of Mormon* was a clever pastiche, with heavy borrowing from the King James Bible in both style and content. The principal novelty was that Jesus Christ had returned to the earth after his ascension and had preached to the inhabitants of the New World. It therefore could trade on being unmistakably American. As Brodie points out, Joseph Smith was a glib and clever writer with great sensitivity for the intellectual trends and unspoken needs of people in his time, but he was also incapable of grasping the principal issues at stake in theology. As for readability, Mark Twain once quipped that the *Book of Mormon* was "chloroform in print."

The book also provided explanations of the origins of the Indian tribes, as well as of the burial mounds found in New York State and elsewhere. These issues were the objects of lively debate at the time. Many of the place names appear to be borrowed from localities in the northeastern United States. No archaeological evidence of the flourishing Nephite civilization has ever been found, nor have tombs or inscriptions confirmed the existence of the main *dramatis personæ* of the *Book of Mormon*. As for the American Indians, DNA analysis suggests that their origin is to be sought in Asia, and not among the Israelites.

BOOK OF MORMON FORBIDS POLYGAMY, DESPITE LATER FLIP-FLOPS

Many aspects of the *Book of Mormon* were later repudiated by the Latter-day Saints in theory and practice. Polygamy was expressly forbidden by the *Book of Mormon*. Joseph Smith had backed up this canonical prohibition with a revelation of February 1831 which stated: "that shalt love thy wife with all my heart, and shall cleave unto her and none

---

[55] Ahlstrom, p. 505.

else."[56] But it was not long before Joseph Smith and others began cultivating this forbidden practice on a grand scale.

In line with the anti-Masonic political movement of 1828 to 1838, the *Book of Mormon* promises destruction for those in league with the Freemasons. By the time Joseph Smith reached Nauvoo, Illinois a decade later, Mormonism was pervaded by Freemasonic forms, signals, handshakes, and other practices. This is the peculiarity of Mormonism, which claims to have absolute truth in any given moment, but has a hard time accounting for why absolute truth is constantly changing. This tendency notoriously lives on in the Romney campaign.

ROMNEY ANCESTOR PARLEY PARKER PRATT AMONG THE FIRST RECRUITS

One of the first new recruits to be attracted by the new *Book of Mormon* was Parley Parker Pratt, Mitt Romney's great-great-grandfather, and one of the central figures of the early decades of Mormonism. Pratt borrowed a copy of the *Book of Mormon* from a Baptist deacon, and then proceeded immediately to Palmyra, New York in the hopes of meeting Joseph Smith. Parley Pratt soon became a convert to Mormonism, and he proceeded to recruit Sidney Rigdon of Ohio, an established minister of some note. Parley Pratt soon became the author of *A Voice of Warning*, the most effective Mormon tract of the 19th century.

In Palmyra, Joseph Smith and his growing band of followers were subjected to constant harassment by groups of neighbors that were behaving increasingly like mobs. He was also chased from county to county by constables. Joseph was arrested as a debtor. He tried to clean up his act by jettisoning his seer stones and divining rods, or at least announcing that he had. One of Joseph Smith's revelations of 1830 specified that the purpose of the new religious movement was to build the City of Zion somewhere out west, on the border with the Lamanites, or Indians.[57] Like many other Americans, the Mormon Prophet and his followers wanted to move west and seek success on the frontier. Joseph Smith and Sidney Rigdon decided to get the Mormons out of Palmyra and take them towards two destinations farther west. These were Kirtland, Ohio, today an exurb of Cleveland, and Independence, Missouri, where the Mormons thought that the Garden of Eden had been located. In general, the poor Mormons went to the holier site in Missouri, while the wealthier ones preferred the unconsecrated but more built-up Kirtland, called Zion's Camp. Joseph Smith gravitated to the latter group.

CHRISTMAS 1832: JOSEPH SMITH PROPHESIES CIVIL WAR, BRITISH INTERVENTION

The choice of Missouri was self-destructive in the extreme, and seems to reflect a desire on the part of somebody to cause trouble. A more rational choice would have been some location in the upper Midwest not inflamed by slavery and sectional resentment. Local

[56] Brodie, p. 187.
[57] Brodie, p. 93.

potentates feared the influx of new settlers with no vested interest in slavery. This salaam was magnified by the Mormon habit of monolithic bloc voting, which seemed to others to represent a naked power grab. But there were problems in Kirtland as well. On one occasion, a mob surrounded Joseph in his house and proceeded to tar and feather him.

In the midst of these events, and under the influence of the nullification crisis between President Jackson and the state of South Carolina, Joseph Smith issued his infamous Civil War Prophecy on December 25, 1832. A civil war, starting with the rebellion in South Carolina, was imminent, he intoned, and the secessionists would soon seek the help of Great Britain.

By now he was calling himself "Joseph Smith The Prophet." In Kirtland, the Saints began practicing primitive communism, according to that passage of the Acts of the Apostles which specifies that the early Christians "had all things in common; and sold their possessions and goods, and parted them to all men as every man had need." The vehicle for this collectivism was called the United Order of Enoch, with center of gravity in Kirtland. A Mormon temple was soon under construction, but the settlement in Missouri grew even faster, thanks to the management skills of Edward Partridge.

Trouble emerged first in Missouri, where slaveholders were heavily represented among the older settlers. The Mormons, by contrast, were overwhelmingly Yankees without slaves. At one point a Mormon publication discussed the advisability of bringing free black converts to Missouri, which filled the slaveholders with the fear of an uprising fomented by these more knowledgeable outsiders. The Mormons also seemed to do everything humanly possible to antagonize the existing population. The established Missourians were told that their religion was an abomination, and that the Mormons would soon inherit all of their property. One of the old settlers complained: "We are daily told... that we, [the Gentiles], of this county are to be cut off, and our lands appropriated by them [the Mormons] for inheritances. Whether this is to be accomplished by the hand of the destroying angel, the judgments of God, or the arm of power, they are not fully agreed among themselves.'" (Brodie, p. 131) The Mormon Saints were driven out of certain locations in Missouri, and had to take refuge in other counties north of the Missouri River. Established settlers disarmed the Mormon gangs, which they called militia. Joseph Smith responded by accentuating his tendencies towards a theocracy in arms. He began raising what he hoped would be a Mormon militia of 500 men between Kirtland and Missouri.

BRITISH ESTABLISHMENT CONTACTS THE MORMONS

In June 1835, the British oligarchy established what looks like their first significant contact with the Mormons, with the arrival of Rev. John Hewitt. Hewitt had been dispatched for contact talks by a congregation of charismatic Pentecostalist Christians in Barnsley, England. Their interest had been attracted by a Mormon publication, and the English faithful hailed them as "kindred spirits." The Barnsley group was affiliated with the Catholic Apostolic Church, which enjoyed the support of Foreign Secretary George Canning, and the interest of the famous Victorian man of letters Thomas Carlyle, who was also an admirer of the Mormons. Hewitt's visit raised the question of affiliations and alliances with other religious movements in the 1830s." (Bushman, pp. 270-71) Subsequently, Joseph Smith would order two of his top lieutenants to Britain in 1837, followed by the entire top leadership in 1839-40. From that time on, Great Britain – and not the United States – would become the principal source of new converts for the Mormon Saints. The Mormons would become increasingly British in composition and mentality.

THE PROPHET DISCOVERS THE PLANET KOLOB

In 1835, Joseph Smith was visited by an itinerant exhibitor who was touring with a show featuring four Egyptian mummies and several papyri. Joseph purchased an Egyptian papyrus showing mortuary practices and depicting the Egyptian deity Osiris. Since he had a reputation as a skilled translator of Egyptian hieroglyphics, he had to proceed to produce a translation, which he called the *Book of Abraham* (no such book is in the Bible). Naturally, the resulting text in no way represents a faithful translation of the original Egyptian document, but rather must be seen as invented out of whole cloth by the Prophet. Here we learn from Abraham that the center of the universe is constituted by the star (or planet) Kolob, which is situated close to the throne of God. Kolob and other celestial bodies are inhabited by numerous eternal deities. Among these deities there is a rank order of intelligence, just as there are differences in magnitudes among the stars. This talk of intelligences and of the plurality of worlds is a reflection of the doctrines of Emmanuel Swedenborg and of a 17th century Italian, Giordano Bruno, both favorites of European freemasonic circles.

THE BOOK OF ABRAHAM, A HOAX USED TO PROMOTE WHITE SUPREMACY AND JIM CROW

The *Book of Abraham* also represents a decidedly pragmatic turn towards racism. Joseph Smith was aware that he now had converts in the slave states, and he wanted to increase his recruiting operations there. Here is another example of Mormon behavior, dictated in reality by pure expediency, which is nevertheless portrayed for the credulous as the outcome of the Divine Revelation. The *Book of Abraham* furnishes the theological basis for the anti-black racial segregation policy of the Mormon Saints, which was officially in force until 1978. In Joseph Smith's garbled text, we read that Abraham had considered the Pharaohs of Egypt as not entitled to "the priesthood," since they "sprang from the loins of Ham and Egyptus."[58] (Brodie, p. 423) Out of this obvious forgery, Joseph Smith and subsequent Mormon theologians manufactured the Jim Crow ban on blacks in the priesthood. In reality, it was an opportunistic concession to the growing Slave Power. Joseph Smith, as we can see, was a doughface in theology.

---

[58] The relevant section reads: "The land of Egypt being first discovered by a woman, who was the daughter of Ham, and the daughter of Egyptus, which in the Chaldean signifies Egypt, which signifies that which is forbidden. When this woman discovered the land it was under water, who afterward settled her sons in it; and thus, from Ham, sprang that race which preserved the curse in the land.... Now, Pharaoh being of that lineage by which he could not have the right of Priesthood, notwithstanding the Pharaohs would fain claim it from Noah, through Ham...." The point of all this is that Ham was supposedly black. (Brodie, p. 424)

1832: FIRST REPORTS OF PROPHETIC POLYGAMY

As early as 1832, rumors had been circulating that the handsome and magnetic Mormon Prophet had been indulging in the sins of the flesh. Joseph Smith, always anxious for learning and respectability, had procured a grammar tutor, one C. G. Webb. This tutor later recorded that some time in 1835 a teenage orphan girl living in Joseph Smith's house was no longer able to "conceal the consequences of her celestial relation with the Prophet," and was expelled from the Smith home by Emma Smith. (Brodie, p. 181)

1835: POLYGAMY VEHEMENTLY DENIED

As a result of this and other scandals swirling around the Mormon Prophet, the sect in August 1835 issued its first formal denial that polygamy was being carried on. The Church conference of that months announced: "Inasmuch as this Church has been reproached with the crime of fornication and polygamy, we declare that we believe that one man should have one wife, and one woman but one husband, except in the case of death, when either is at liberty to marry again." (Brodie, p. 185) By 1852, this and other denials were declared inoperative. We can see that Romney's flip-flops are deeply rooted in the history of the Church to which he is so devoted.

In 1836, Aaron Burr's close associate Andrew Jackson successfully attacked the Second Bank of the United States, which had provided this country with the financial stability necessary for economic development for two decades. After that, the United States witnessed the rise of the state chartered pet banks, which began receiving US government funds in 1833. Easy money and nonexistent regulation soon lead to a Western land boom in the form of a classic speculative bubble.

MORMONS JOIN JACKSON-VAN BUREN SPECULATIVE BUBBLE

Joseph Smith, although he was supposedly a prophet, had never stopped being an unscrupulous businessman, so he joined in this orgy of speculation with great gusto. The Saints soon decided to create a bank of their own, which was to be called the Kirtland Safety Society Bank. Unfortunately, just as they were preparing to issue their first bank notes, word arrived that the Ohio State Legislature had refused to authorize this new venture. The banknotes had already been printed, so the Saints decided to recycle them by stamping them with an "Anti' before the "Bank," and an "ing Co." at the end, yielding "The Kirtland Safety Society Anti-Banking Company." Some were fooled, but not for long.

MORMON BANK FRAUD OF 1837

This dubious entity never had the reserves prescribed for the amount of bank notes it tried to float. Inside the bank vaults were numerous boxes, each marked as containing $1,000 in specie (gold and silver). But the boxes actually contained sand, lead, scrap iron, stone, and coal, covered by a thin layer of fifty cent coins. Customers who were skeptical about the bank reserves were invited to view these boxes. (Brodie, pp. 196-97)

But then came Jackson's 1836 specie circular, which specified that only gold and silver would henceforth be acceptable in payment for public lands. Combined with events in Europe, this immediately unleashed a banking panic in which the state-chartered pet banks were among the first to fail. The pro-deflationary faction of the Democratic Party, also known as the Locofocos, had the upper hand and proceeded to wipe out the wildcat banks which had stoked the inflationary land bubble. (Brodie, p. 196)

JOSEPH SMITH, DEAD BEAT DEBTOR, IN INTERSTATE FLIGHT

Joseph Smith had not shown himself a very competent prophet on this occasion. He was caught in disastrous long speculative positions as the bottom fell out of the real estate market. During the inflationary bubble, he had also contracted a crushing burden of debt. A census of Joseph Smith's indebtedness showed "outstanding Kirtland loans, "which amounted to more than $33,000," plus two large loans of $30,000 and $60,000 borrowed in New York and Buffalo in 1836." In aggregate, "the Mormon leaders owed to non-Mormon individuals and firms well over $150,000." (Brodie, pp. 201-02) Joseph Smith's sharp business practices live on in the asset stripping vulture capitalism of his ideological descendent, Mitt Romney.

All over the Mormon world, distressed merchandise sales were the order of the day. Zion's Camp in Kirtland was soon in chaos. There, the temple, a structure worth $40,000, was auctioned off for $150 to pay a financial judgment. The local sheriff was about to confiscate the Mormon printing plant to make good a $2,000 judgment which had been entered against Smith and Rigdon for floating very illegal banknotes, but the building mysteriously burned to the ground. Early on December 22, 1837, Brigham Young, already an important Mormon official, fled the town. The Mormon account of this embarrassing exit is that the Lion of the Lord decamped "in consequence of the fury of the mob spirit that prevailed in the apostates," but the reality is that he was trying to stay two steps ahead of his creditors. Joseph Smith and Sidney Rigdon held on a little longer, but in the dark night of January 12, 1838, they absconded in the direction of Missouri, hounded over 200 miles by an angry mob of "human blood-hounds, armed and thirsty for their lives." (Hirshson, pp. 26-27)

In fact, the flight of the two Mormon chieftains represented interstate flight to avoid prosecution for white-collar crime. Joseph had finally decided to flee "when word came that Grandison Newell had secured a warrant for his arrest on a charge of banking fraud...." (Brodie, p. 207)

INTERNAL OPPOSITION AGAINST THE PROPHET. 1836-7

During this phase, Joseph Smith's charismatic leadership underwent a number of challenges. One came in the autumn of 1836, when "several of the Twelve, the three witnesses to *The Book of Mormon*, and some other church leaders tried to make [David] Whitmer the head of the church, Young, Father Smith, and Kimball opposed the scheme." (Hirshson, p. 23)

After the indecorous exit from Kirtland, these tensions increased. By now, half of the Quorum of the Twelve Apostles were arrayed against the Prophet. Even Mitt Romney's great-great-grandfather was in polemic with Joseph Smith. On May 23, 1837, Parley Pratt admonished Joseph to pay up:

> "And now dear brother, if you are still determined to pursue this wicked course, until yourself and the church shall sink down to hell, I beseech you at least, to have mercy on me and my family, and others who are bound with me for those three lots (of land) which you sold to me at the extortionary price of 2,000 dollars, which never cost you 100 dollars." (Pratt to Smith, May 23, 1837, online at josephsmithpapers.org)

Here Joseph Smith sounds as predatory as a Mitt Romney of the Jacksonian era. In retaliation, Joseph said he would excommunicate any Saint who sued a fellow Mormon, and tried to put Pratt on trial. But the council was split and the trial never happened, saving Mitt Romney's current position as Mormon royalty. (Brodie, p. 203)

Joseph Smith now refurbished the earlier Mormon theory that Independence, Missouri was the original location of the Garden of Eden. He now embroidered this idea, saying that the town of Adam-ondi-Ahman (Adam of the Ancient Days), somewhat to the East of Eden, had been the home of Adam after the expulsion from the garden. The town of Far West was identified as a place where Cain slew Abel. (Brodie, p. 211)

CREATION OF THE SONS OF DAN OR DANITES,
THE MORMON MILITIA AND SECRET POLICE

Joseph Smith also embarked on the foolhardy venture of trying to oppose the Missouri mobs and militia with an armed force of his own. This is the origin of the infamous Mormon *soldatesca* known as the Danites. Founded around mid-June 1838, this secret society was variously called the Brothers of Gideon, the Daughters of Zion, the sons of Dan, or the Danites. Its first commander was Sampson Avard, who was excommunicated before long and became an inveterate enemy of the Mormons. (Brodie, pp. 213-14)

According to one high-ranking Mormon eyewitness, Avard on one occasion recommended starting a plague among the Gentiles by "by poisoning their corn, fruit &c., and saying it was the work of the Lord; and said Avard advocated lying for the support of their religion, and said it was no harm to lie for the Lord." Here again the note of antinomianism is unmistakable.

Joseph Smith gave de facto encouragements of these designs by assuring the Danites that God would send angels to fight on their side, and that they would be impervious to Gentile bullets. Two Danites, he promised, could defeat 10,000 Gentiles in pitched battle. One Mormon later recalled that he had been convinced by his exhortations to the point that "If Joseph should tell me to kill [President Martin] Van Buren in his presidential chair, I would immediately start and do my best to assassinate him, let the consequences be as they would." (Hirshson, p. 31) This was too much power for one man in a democratic society. Skirmishes and other armed clashes between Mormons and local vigilantes now became increasingly common.

Joseph Smith was guilty of financial corruption, because he allowed his revelations on the conduct of the Church to be colored by his own economic needs. After ousting an opposition faction, he attempted to revivify the United Order of Enoch, his primitive communist administration. On July 8, 1838 in Far West, Smith announced a new revelation urging the Saints to transfer the title of all of their property to the Mormon Church. In return, each man would receive a tract of land for his "everlasting inheritance," with the number of acres increasing with the size of his family. (Brodie, p. 220)

Since many had already been skinned in Kirtland, Joseph asked the Saints to lease their property to the Mormon Church "without consideration or interest" for terms varying between 10 and 99 years. What he had in mind was a kind of theocratic corporate state: "The whole church was then to be divided into four huge 'corporations' – farmers, mechanics, shopkeepers, and laborers – which would utilize the land, machinery, and skills of the church members for the common good." (Brodie, p. 221)

In another measure which modern reactionaries would immediately brand as communist, the Mormon corporations would offer jobs and wages of one dollar per day. Any profit realized by the corporation would then be distributed "according to the needs and wants (not according to the property invested) of each family, annually or oftener if needed...." (Brodie, p. 221) The farming corporation was developed more than the others. This was a combine of cooperatives doing business as the "Big Field United Firms." Each of the cooperatives was responsible for the "communal farming" of about 7,000 acres of farmland. Mormon overseers assigned tasks and allotted horses and machinery. (Brodie, pp. 221-22)

THE "SECOND MOHAMMED": "JOSEPH SMITH OR THE SWORD!"

As Sydney E. Ahlstrom has written of the Mormons, "when Joseph went west in 1838, this situation was becoming precarious, and it must be said that he soon made it hopeless. The point of no return was probably passed on July 4, 1838, when Joseph Smith delivered a major speech containing a "spine chilling promise to wreak vengeance on his oppressors.[59] As he reached the peroration of his address, he exploded in a crescendo of violent threats against his Missouri adversaries, but also against the entire American people, declaiming: "If the people will let us alone, we will preach the gospel in peace. But if they come on us to molest us, we will establish our religion by the sword. We will trample down our enemies and make it one gore of blood from the Rocky Mountains to the Atlantic Ocean. I will be to this generation a second Mohammed, whose motto in treating for peace was 'the Alcoran or the Sword.' So shall it eventually be with us – 'Joseph Smith or the Sword.'"(Brodie, pp. 230-31) This flourish was injudicious in the extreme, and left Joseph Smith sharing the responsibility for the tragic outrages that were about to be visited on the Mormons in Missouri. And since the Mormons absolutely

[59] Ahlstrom, p. 506.

lacked the military means for carrying out this retaliation, this must be considered one of the first signs of the Prophet's decline into megalomania and violent fantasies.

MORMONS AND BORDER RUFFIANS

Tensions between the Mormons and their neighbors escalated on August 6, 1838, which was election day in Missouri. The Mormons were practicing their usual policy of monolithic bloc voting, and they came into collision with slaveholding Southerners. When the first Mormon tried to vote in the town of Gallatin, "a grinning settler barred his path. 'Davies County don't allow Mormons to vote no more than n****rs,' he said." (Brodie, p. 225) After this, the sporadic violence became more and more intense.

MISSOURI GOVERNOR ORDERS EXTERMINATION OF MORMONS, 1838

On October 27, 1838 Governor Boggs of Missouri issued a shocking and illegal order that the state militia act ruthlessly against the Mormons, writing: "The Mormons must be treated as enemies and must be exterminated or driven from the state, if necessary, for the public good. Their outrages are beyond all description." (Brodie, pp. 234-235) Even if a strong president had wanted to interfere, there was at that time no Fourteenth Amendment to prevent a state from depriving persons of life, liberty, and property without due process of law.

After more fighting, Joseph Smith, Parley Pratt, and other Mormon leaders were imprisoned in the jail of Liberty, Missouri, where they were confined from December 1838 to April 1839. Smith was accused of "treason, murder, arson, burglary, robbery, larceny, and perjury," and he and the others faced the death penalty,[60]

  While in the Liberty jail, Joseph Smith found time to defend himself against repeated accusations of polygamy. He wrote to the Saints: "Some have reported that we not only dedicated our property, but likewise our families to the Lord, and Satan taking advantage of this has transfigured it into lasciviousness, a community of wives, which things are an abomination in the sight of God.'" (Hirshson, p. 41) But, Joseph Smith had married, among many other women, Helen Mark Kimball, who was the 15-year-old daughter of Heber Kimball. In gratitude for his allowing this marriage, "the Prophet now gratefully promised that Kimball's estate in heaven would adjoin Smith's on the north." (Hirshson, p. 41) Here we see once again the naïve materialism that seems to be an integral part of the Mormon creed.

In April 1839, Joseph Smith – perhaps with the connivance of some of the locals – was able to escape from the Liberty jail and successfully cross the Mississippi River into Illinois. Here the Mormons fleeing from hostile Missouri created new settlements across the river from Keokuk, Iowa. This he called Nauvoo, which he said meant "beautiful plantation" in Hebrew. Nauvoo was situated on bluffs above the Mississippi River, and was surrounded by lowland swamps. Within a short time Nauvoo had 3,000 inhabitants, and had become the second-largest city in Illinois after Chicago.

---

[60] Brodie, p, 243.

In Nauvoo, Joseph Smith insisted on trying to influence political developments. The goal was now to secure some kind of governmental protection for the community of the Saints. Smith and Rigdon went to Washington during the winter of 1839-40 to secure some support from the Democratic President Martin Van Buren, a creature of the Astor banking interests in New York City who had been Andrew Jackson's chief political lieutenant. The Mormons were continually haunted by the fear that the violent Missourians would cross the Mississippi and attempt to enforce the outstanding warrants against Joseph Smith and the other top leaders.

VAN BUREN REFUSES TO HELP MORMONS, 1839

So Joseph Smith and Rigdon asked Van Buren for help. "'Help you!' the President shouted, 'How can I help you? All Missouri would turn against me.' After arguing with his guests for several minutes, Van Buren rose, left the room, and did not return." But with his usual diplomatic finesse, Joseph Smith told a newspaper reporter that Van Buren was *"not as fit as my dog for the chair of state*, for my dog will make an effort to protect his abused and insulted master, while the present chief magistrate will not so much as lift his finger to relieve an oppressed and persecuted community of freemen, whose glory it has been that they were citizens of the United States." Although he was a supplicant, the Mormon chief was also unable to refrain from ill-timed threats. Van Buren was visibly putting on weight, so Joseph Smith said he "hoped he would continue to grow fat, and swell, and before the next election burst!" (Hirshson, pp. 38-39) Irenic and conciliatory our Mormon Prophet was not.

In addition to reaching out for political support, Joseph Smith also looked for ways to enhance Mormon recruiting abroad, specifically in Great Britain. In 1837, the Prophet had sent Kimball and Hyde to seek converts in England. In 1839, he ordered the entire Quorum of the Twelve Apostles to go to Britain and establish a recruiting mission there. Brigham Young, Heber Kimball, Romney's ancestor Parley Pratt, Orson Hyde, Willard Richards, John Taylor, William Smith, Wilford Woodruff, George A. Smith, Orson Pratt, John E. Page, and Lyman Wight were all impacted by this deployment, and thus the entire top leadership was Anglicized.

Now Mormondom began to attract as converts licentious men who were specifically interested in the pleasures of polygamy. One of the most fateful of these was John C. Bennett, an Ohio medical doctor who joined the Saints in late 1840. Bennett was an admitted religious cynic, but he soon became Joseph Smith's great favorite. Bennett was more skilled as a political operator than the irascible Joseph Smith. He went to the Illinois State Capitol at Springfield and made a deal with Democratic Judge Stephen A. Douglas. Douglas got the Illinois State Legislature to issue three charters. One made the city of Nauvoo practically a self-governing entity. A second charter established the University of the City of Nauvoo. The third set up a militia called the Nauvoo Legion, with Joseph Smith as the lieutenant general in command, and Bennett as major general. Joseph Smith now outranked all the generals in the United States Army. He ordered the Mormons to vote Democratic. In 1842, Joseph Smith, showing that pride which ever goes before a fall, boasted to the *New York Herald* that he could "already dictate to the State of Illinois." (Hirshson, p. 39)

In Nauvoo, Joseph Smith continued the career of spiritual profiteer which he had begun in Kirtland and continued in Missouri. In addition to all of his titles and offices, he also had dominant economic interests in the town. He had a hotel where liquor was served. He owned a store. The Mormon leaders were back to land speculation, since they felt they could count on a continuous flow of Mormon converts coming into town. "At Nauvoo, he, Young, and the Twelve speculated in land." Showing that his kingdom was most emphatically of this world, Joseph Smith demanded cash payment for the real estate he was offering for sale. A new convert came to him one day while he was being interviewed and said, "I wish to buy a piece of land for which I will pay trade of various kinds to the amount of $500, will you sell me some?" Joseph gave the man a hardhearted answer worthy of his contemporary Ebenezer Scrooge, saying: "My lands are all good titles, and I must have the money for them." (Hirshson, pp. 39-40)

In Joseph Smith's general store, the invariable rule was cash on the barrelhead, and no credit whatsoever, not even for Saints. Some of the faithful became disgruntled when they saw that even Gentile merchants were willing to put some purchases on the tab. The rule of tithing was enforced, meaning that the Mormon Saints had either to deposit 10% of their earnings, or else to spend one day out of 10 quarrying rock for the expansive temple Joseph Smith wanted to erect. Already, the Mormon Prophet was acquiring a deserved reputation for greed. It is also notable that while antinomianism pervaded all things, it was not allowed to interfere with Joseph's demands for cash payment. (Hirshson, p. 40)

Fawn Brodie, referring to the work of psychiatrist Phyllis Greenacre, has argued that Joseph Smith should not be considered exclusively as a conscious fraud, but ought rather to be classified as an imposter in psychoanalytic terms. The present writer would argue, based on first-hand experience of charismatic leaders, that Joseph Smith probably relied on a form of mental self-management which can be labeled as "multiple personality order."[61] Significant parts of his psyche remained those of a failed village necromancer, but these coexisted with the personality of the charismatic Prophet of God assigned to conquer the world. Certain aspects of Joseph Smith's behavior indicate that he was able to control which of these personalities was on display. An important piece of evidence in this regard comes from the documented moments of self-awareness, in which Joseph Smith momentarily, and not without self-deprecating humor, revealed some interior distance between his apocalyptic and megalomaniac outward pretensions, and how he actually felt about himself.

Multiple personalities would be coherent with so much about Joseph Smith. In cosmology, he asserted the infinite plurality of worlds. In theology, he was an aggressive polytheist. In his personal life, he was polygamous. Many worlds, many gods, many wives, many personalities.

---

[61] See the appendix for a discussion of Joseph Smith and other cult leaders in terms of "multiple personality order."

Asked about how he could exercise so much power, Joseph slyly replied: "In your hands or that of any other man, so much power would, no doubt, be dangerous. I am the only man in the world whom it would be safe to trust it with. Remember, I am a prophet!" The remarkable thing was that this last sentence was delivered "in a 'rich, comical aside, as if in hearty recognition of the ridiculous sound they might have in the ears of a Gentile."[62]

On another occasion, the Prophet was visited by the significant British agent, Edwin de Leon, who went on to become a mainstay of the Confederate foreign service. De Leon asked Joseph about the attractive females he observed going in and out of the Prophet's dwelling. Joseph said that these were his nieces. De Leon expressed some skepticism. Then, "There was a slight twinkle in the prophetic eye, as he poked me in the ribs with his forefinger, and rebuked me, exclaiming, 'Oh, the carnal mind, the carnal mind!' and I thought it discreet not to press the subject."[63] (Hirshson, pp. 44-45) On another occasion, the Prophet confessed to an associate, "Whenever I see a pretty woman, I have to pray for grace."

This cynical self-awareness also extended to the dialectical relationship between the Prophet and his cult following. At a Mormon gathering where Joseph Smith was introducing the Whig politician Cyrus Walker, Joseph commented to him: "These are the greatest dupes, as a body of people, that ever lived, or I am not so big a rogue as I am reported to be."[64]

But now, in the last several years of the Mormon Pompeii in Illinois, the results of polygamy were coming home to roost. At the April 1842 church conference, both Joseph and his brother Hyrum had to issue another denial of polygamy. Responding to charges that top Mormons had tried to convince a girl to become a plural wife, the Prophet declared that "no person that is acquainted with our principles would believe such lies." When Joseph was asked similar questions by influential Mormon leaders, he had to admit that the charges were true. But he claimed that he had heard bad things about the girl, and was testing her virtue. (Hirshson, p. 44)

Joseph Smith received decisive help from Brigham Young in convincing the Mormon Saints that polygamy was divinely ordained. Brigham Young asserted that Adam was Elohim, the Mormon Jehovah, and that humanity had been divinely commanded to live under seven dispensations or divine plans for human affairs. The final dispensation was the one borne by Joseph Smith. According to Brigham Young, Joseph Smith's publication of the *Book of Mormon* in 1830 was a sign of the end time, in part because it came 1,260 years after the Roman Catholic Church had become degenerate in 570 AD. Mormons associate this state with the centralizing activity of St. Gregory the Great, who extended a church administration over much of Christendom. The Catholic Church, needless to say, Brigham reviled as the Whore of Babylon. The year 570 AD also marks

---

[62] Online at brainyquote.com, Joseph Smith Jr. quotes.
[63] De Leon, online at ebooksread.com.
[64] *Journal of Discourses*, 2:30.

the birth of the Prophet Mohammed. In addition, the Mormons assert that at this time the Holy Grail was definitively lost. But the resulting corruption of God's Word in a universe where God's priesthood had become extinct had now ended, and the time was now right for the second coming of Christ. The beginning of the final dispensation brought with it fundamental changes, including the imperative of polygamy. In addition, the Mormons stressed the doctrine that God/Elohim/Jehovah/Adam had once been human, but had advanced to the level of divinity with the help of his faithful wife Eve. (Hirshson, p. 46)

Heaven was therefore imagined by the Mormons as a community centering on a complex of allied oligarchical families whose leaders were carrying on polygamy. Durkheim and Feuerbach might easily see in this a religious concept which in fact involves the naïve projection of human social relations onto the plane of the divine. The Mormon heaven was a kind of Olympian pantheon based on polygamy, understood as the highest expression of oligarchical and patriarchal power. It was polylatrism[65] and polytheism. And polytheism, when it arises in the context of Western civilization, must be seen as paganism.

The Mormon leader Lorenzo Young summed up this proposition with a pithy aphorism: "As man is, God once was; and as God is, man may become." This went beyond notions of theosis, divination, or deification. It went beyond the mystics' quest for direct communion with the divine. If Horatio Alger had become rich and powerful on earth based on a philosophy of ceaseless striving onward and upward, what could such a greedy, carnal radical subjectivist hope for in the other world? He obviously could hope to become a god, or even to become the God. His ambition might include the ability to rule over larger and larger planets, and to cavort with a more and more numerous harem of goddess wives, engendering infinite numbers of divine offspring who could themselves rule over new planetary empires. People who thought that the religious opinions of George W. Bush were disturbing may soon be confronted by a reality of a far greater order of magnitude.

Under Joseph Smith, polygamy tended to be reserved for the top leaders. The women were told that these celestial relations were a sure ticket to paradise for them. (Brodie, p. 297)

"Neque nubent," said St. Paul according to the Latin Vulgate—the souls in heaven do not marry.[66] This was not good enough for Joseph Smith, who thus demonstrated once again that his doctrine was alien to Christianity. In the words of Mitt Romney's ancestor Parley Pratt, "'the result of our endless union would be offspring as numerous as were the stars of heaven, or the sands of the seashore.'"[67] (Brodie, pp. 299-300) The Romney family tradition is thus polytheism with a vengeance.

---

[65] Polylatrism is a form of polytheism in which some gods are actively worshipped, while other gods are thought to exist but can be ignored.
[66] Matthew xxii, verse 30.
[67] Parley P. Pratt, *Autobiography*, p. 329, online at books.google.com.

On the other hand, those who failed to yield to the polygamous imperative would not fare well. A man who was sealed (Mormon-speak for married) to only a single wife would be separated from her in heaven as she was given to a polygamist as a reward. The man would be doomed to spend eternity as a ministering angel, a kind of heavenly flunky, forced to carry out the orders of the true polygamous elect. (Brodie, p. 300)

In one of his celestial courtships which started in 1834, Joseph Smith was able to convince a woman to become his polygamous bride based on his fanciful allegation that an angel was threatening his life in case the union were not consummated. Joseph said he was terrified, because the angel had visited him three times, and the last time with an unsheathed sword. (Brodie, p. 303) In another case, Joseph Smith informed the object of his affections that, if she did not yield to him immediately, the door of paradise would forever slam shut in her face. He also threatened Emma with the divine revelation that, if she did not cooperate with this celestial hanky-panky, she would be "destroyed."

Since it was the Victorian age, resistance to polygamy came from many quarters. Joseph Smith was on bad terms with his brothers, and one of them, Don Carlos Smith, vigorously opposed polygamy. In 1841, he stated his conviction that "Any man who will preach and practice spiritual wifery will go to hell, no matter if it is my brother Joseph."[68]

Joseph tried to seduce Sarah M. Kimball, the wife of his top lieutenant Heber Kimball, in 1842, but she rebuffed him, telling him to teach the concept to somebody else. However, she kept his unwelcome celestial advances a secret from the Welfare Society, the principal Mormon ladies auxiliary. He made an attempt on Mrs. Orson Pratt, who also declined, and did tell a few friends.

A watershed case was that of an intelligent eighteen-year-old English girl, Martha Brotherton, whom Joseph Smith and Brigham Young lured into a room above Joseph's general store and then tried to browbeat into becoming the celestial spouse of Brother Brigham. If she accepted, Brigham Young promised her a passport to paradise, adding that the union could be consummated immediately and she could go home, so that her parents need know nothing of this celestial liaison. (Brodie, p. 306-07)

Martha Brotherton said she needed to go home and pray, but when she had escaped the clutches of the two holy satyrs, she informed her parents and proceeded to write an account of the attempted celestial seduction. She escaped with her father and mother via steam boat to St. Louis, where Martha's account was published in the *St. Louis Bulletin* of July 15, 1842, and was soon widely copied by the national press. (Brodie, p. 307) Kimball and Brigham Young issued denials in defense of Joseph. Martha had two sisters who were induced by the Saints to swear in public that Martha was a liar and a harlot.

Interestingly for us today, one of these two cruel sisters, Elizabeth Brotherton, soon married Parley Parker Pratt, Mitt Romney's great-great grandfather. In one of her love letters to Parley, Elizabeth Brotherton wrote on April 20, 1842 that her own faith was intact, but that her sister Martha had been spreading "falsehoods of the basest kind." In a

---

[68] Shook, *True Origins of Mormon Polygamy*, p. 63, online at books.google.com.

transparent celestial proposition of her own, Elizabeth Brotherton told Parley " I believe it is your privilege" to see how sincere our faith really was. She added: "Oh! How I long to see you and enjoy your society, and unbosom all my care to you."[69] After Martha had died in 1886, Elizabeth caused Martha's children, who had predeceased her, to be sealed to the departed Brigham Young. Martha had courageously resisted Brigham's theocratic bullying, yet this did not prevent her sister from giving the Mormon Moses custody of Martha's children. This is another instructive example of Romney family values.

MORMON ABORTIONS

In the meantime, John C. Bennett had been using the celestial marriage argument to seduce large numbers of young women. Bennett had also been promising abortions on demand to the women he approached. "Zeruiah N. Goddard, repeating the gossip of Sarah Pratt, reported that 'Dr. Bennett told her he could cause abortion with perfect safety to the mother at any stage of pregnancy, and that he had frequently destroyed and removed infants before their time to prevent exposure of the parties and that he had instruments for that purpose.'"[70] (Brodie, p. 311-12)

The beginning of the end for Joseph Smith came when he clashed with Bennett, who had become his rival for the affections of the attractive nineteen-year-old girl Nancy Rigdon, the daughter of Sidney Rigdon, the Mormon second-in-command. (Brodie, p. 310) Joseph alleged that Bennett was trying to get him accidentally shot while he was attending target practice with the Nauvoo Legion.

DEATH THREATS FROM JOSEPH SMITH

Bennett later alleged that when he came to see the Prophet in his office, Joseph had locked the door, pocketed the key, and pulled out a pistol. The Prophet then declared:

> "The peace of my family requires that you should sign an affidavit, and make a statement before the next City Council, exonerating me from all participation whatever, whether directly or indirectly, in word or deed, in the spiritual wife doctrine, or private intercourse with females in general, and if you do not do it with apparent cheerfulness, I will make catfish bait of you, or deliver you to the Danites for execution tonight—for my dignity and purity must and shall be maintained before the public."[71]

Bennett was soon expelled from the community of Saints. He retaliated by writing a lurid but partly factual account of his experiences in Mormondom, which was serialized in major newspapers, and then published as a widely read book, *The History of the Saints* (Boston, 1842). The *New York Herald* printed the installments of Bennett's *The History*

[69] R. Steven Pratt, "The Family Life of Parley P. Pratt: A Case Study of Mormon Plural Marriage," in Armstrong, Grow, and Siler, eds., *Parley P. Pratt and the Making of Mormonism* (Norman OK: author H. Clark Co., 2011), pp. 53-54.
[70] Online at FAIRMormon.org, 1839-1844.
[71] Bennett, *History of the Saints*, p. 287, online at books.google.com.

of the Saints, and also censured them as 'obscene and licentious in the highest degree.'" (Brodie, p. 317)[72]

THE MORMON PLAN FOR A WESTERN EMPIRE EXPOSED, 1842

One of Bennett's most important charges against Joseph Smith was that the Mormons intended to create a secessionist Confederation of Western states and territories, over which Joseph Smith would rule as the King. This puts the Mormon Prophet squarely in the tradition of the arch-traitor Aaron Burr, who had attempted to create his own breakaway Western Empire between 1804 and 1806, taking advantage of the weakness of the Thomas Jefferson administration and of the collusion of Burr's cousin Albert Gallatin, the Secretary of the Treasury. This conspiracy had been sponsored by the British, who would also have been the beneficiaries of Joseph Smith's evolving Western plans. Bennett alleged that the Nauvoo Legion had already acquired 30 cannon and large quantities of small arms at the expense of the state of Illinois. (Brodie, p. 314) With 30 guns mounted in fortified emplacements on the bluffs at Nauvoo, the Mormons would have been able to block traffic on the Mississippi River in something of the way that the Confederates were later to do using the fortress of Vicksburg.

The Nauvoo Legion, said Bennett, had sworn the Danites oath and would obey the commands of the Prophet without question, no matter how illegal they were. Bennett also spoke of a super-secret inner elite within the Danites. These were the Destroying Angels, representing a kind of palace guard with the intelligence function of spying on the adversaries of the Prophet and murdering them, preferably at midnight, while wearing white robes and a red sash. (Brodie, p. 314-15)

JOSEPH SMITH'S REPUTATION IN RUINS

Owing to Bennett's shocking revelations, coming as they did from a recognized top-level insider in the Mormon sect, the genie was now out of the bottle as far as Mormon abuses were concerned. The reputations of Joseph Smith and of the Mormons in general had now been irreparably damaged.

---

[72] Bennett compared the Saints to the Anabaptists in Germany during the Peasant War of the 1520s. Under the prophet Thomas Müntzer, the Anabaptists tried to destroy all earthly authority and create the kingdom of God on earth. Like the Mormons, they practiced primitive communism. Bennett wrote that the Anabaptists "appeared in the year 1525, in Germany, during the religious excitement and confusion produced by the attempts of Luther and his coadjutors to reform the papacy. They so remarkably resemble the Mormons, that it is quite evident the latter have taken them for models, and have copied their doings with as much accuracy as the spirit of the age would permit. The first leader of the Anabaptists was a low, ignorant fellow, named Thomas Munster, who, like Joe Smith, was at the same time their Prophet and military commander. They, precisely again like the Mormons, gave themselves out for 'Latter-day Saints,' and profess to be chosen by the Almighty as instruments to produce the promised millennium reign of Christ on earth. They believed, likewise, that they were especial favorites of heaven in every respect, and that they were, when they wished it, favored with familiar personal intercourse with the deity, and from him constantly received revelations and instructions." (Bennett, p. 304)

To make matters worse, during the summer of 1842, Joseph Smith was forced to evade capture on charges that he had been part of a recent attempt to assassinate former Governor Boggs of Missouri, the man who had issued the infamous extermination order against the Mormons. (Bushman, p. 468)

During the entire period from 1835 to 1852, Joseph Smith and the Mormons had vehemently denied the practice of polygamy, even as they systematically indulged themselves. The specious basis for these denials was in many cases a mere quibble: when they were asked about spiritual wives, plural marriage, or polygamy, the Mormons were able to lie convincingly because they told themselves that celestial marriage according to the ancient Order of Jacob was worlds apart from the vulgar practices about which they were being questioned. This was because the initiation of celestial relations was always supposed to be preceded by a solemn ceremony of sealing the bride, be it limited for time in this world, or be it extended to all eternity.

JOSEPH SMITH PREACHES HEDONISM

Joseph Smith always argued a hedonistic theory of the world: the purpose of human existence, according to him, is the pleasure principle. As Fawn Brodie notes, the maxim that "Man is that he might have joy" represents one of the first "significant pronounce-ments in the *Book of Mormon*...." Joseph Smith was working towards the polar opposite of the Calvinism of Jonathan Edwards, but on the same empiricist and subjectivist plane. The result was an eclectic mix of science fiction, occultism, and materialism, promising a hedonistic heaven filled with eternal pride, power, money, and sex."[73]

As noted, in the spring of 1842, Joseph Smith became the rival of John C. Bennett for the favors of Nancy Rigdon, the daughter of Sydney Rigdon, who was theoretically the second ranking Mormon leader. Nancy had been warned by his rival that Joseph Smith was coming her way, so she burst into tears and threatened to scream unless Joseph Smith agreed to leave her alone. After Nancy Rigdon had rebuffed the celestial advances of Joseph Smith, the Prophet imprudently dictated a letter to her in which he expounded his hedonistic theory of the purpose of human existence: "happiness is the object and design of our existence; and will be the end thereof, if we pursue the path that leads to it...."[74] Christianity, in contrast, has traditionally argued that the purpose of human existence is to carry out the will of God and to work for the greater glory of God. "*Ad Maiorem gloriam dei*" has been a favorite slogan of numerous Christian factions, and expresses the idea that the happiness of the individual is subordinated to the working out of God's plan of salvation. Mormonism is not Christian.

MORMONISM GOES FREEMASONIC

It was during the time in Nauvoo that the already implicitly Masonic character of Mormonism became heavily accentuated. The temple endowment, or liturgy for divine

---

[73] Online at exmormon.org.
[74] Online at exmormon.org.

services in the temple, was heavily larded with freemasonic symbols, gestures, secret oaths, handshakes, secret names, and the like. The famous temple garments or magic underwear are evidently related to the freemasonic apron, and the garments carry symbols and hex signs designed to facilitate the ingress of the wearer to Paradise. The Nauvoo Temple was also heavily festooned with freemasonic symbols and artifacts. At the time of his assassination in the Carthage jail in 1844, Joseph Smith attempted to secure help from freemasons on the scene by raising his extended arms above his head and reciting the freemasonic SOS of "Oh Lord my God, is there no help for the widow's son?" Joseph Smith was said to have been simultaneously promoted through all thirty-three degrees of the freemasonic hierarchy, evidently thanks to the fact that Mormons had seized control of the Illinois freemasonic lodges. Later, other freemasons are said to have put the Illinois lodges into receivership and replaced them with their own appointees. Joseph Smith was said to carry with him at all times the so-called "Jupiter Talisman," a kind of amulet to which he attributed supernatural powers. All of these elements point unmistakably to the fact that Mormonism had long since become a separate religion, not to be confused with Judaism, Christianity, or Islam. And we should bear in mind that the mother lodges of freemasonry were located in London.

THE KING FOLLETT FUNERAL SERMON

On April 7, 1844 Joseph Smith addressed the conference of the Mormon Church and in his speech recalled the recent death of a Mormon stalwart by the name of King Follett, who had been killed in a construction accident. This sermon represents one of the most important statements of Joseph Smith's theology during the last days of his life.[75] The theme was the nature of God, and how God came to be God. Posing the question "what kind of being is God? Does any man or woman know?" Joseph Smith answered that "God himself was once as we are now, and he is an exalted man, and sits enthroned in yonder heavens! That is the great secret. If the veil were rent today, and the great God who holds this world in its orbit, and who upholds all worlds and all things by his power, was to make himself visible – I say, if you were to see him today you would see him like a man in form – like yourselves in all the person, image, and very form as a man." Many religions have obvious anthropomorphic elements, but few so explicitly as this.

The central point of the sermon was this: "in order to understand the subject of the dead, for consolation of those who mourn for the loss of their friends, it is necessary we should understand the character and being of God and how he came to be so; for I am going to tell you how God came to be God. We have imagined and supposed that God was God from all eternity. I will refute that idea, and take away the veil, so that you may see... it is the first principle of the Gospel to know for a certainty the character of God, and to know that we may converse with him as one man converses with another, and that he was once a man like us; yea that God himself, the father of us all, dwelt on earth, the same as Jesus Christ himself did, and I will show it from the Bible."

---

[75] Robert L. Millet, ed., *Joseph Smith: Selected Sermons and Writings* (New York: Paulist Press, 1989), pp. 128-144.

Joseph Smith's ontology, moreover, was explicitly polytheistic. He preached that "the head God called together the Gods and sat in grand council to bring forth the world. The grand counselors sat at the head in yonder heavens and contemplated the creation of the worlds which were created at that time." And again: "in the beginning, the head of the Gods called the Council of the gods; and they came together and concocted a plan to create the world and people it."

Joseph Smith's method was therefore to start from the beliefs and prejudices of his own mind, of his associates, and of his age, and to project them onto the plane of eternity. America was radically egalitarian, and heaven had to be the same. The Mormons were run by an oligarchy of committees, and heaven had to be the same. Joseph Smith had multiple personalities, and this implied that the universe had to be polytheistic.

For Bushman, the key point was that "God was one of the free intelligences who had learned to become God. The other free intelligences were to take the same path. (Bushman, pp. 534-35) Smith elaborated: "You have got to learn how to make yourselves God, king and priest, by going from a small capacity to a great capacity to the resurrection of the dead to dwelling in everlasting burnings....You have got to learn how to be a god yourself in order to save yourself—to be priests & kings as all Gods have done—by going from a small degree to another—from exaltation to ex[altation]—till they are able to sit in glory as with those who sit enthroned. [Christ said:] I do the things that I saw the father do when worlds came into existence. I saw the father work out a kingdom with fear & trembling & I can do the same & when I get my K[ingdom] work[ed out] I will present [it] to the father & it will exalt his glory and Jesus steps into his tracks to inherit what God did before."[76]

Bushman tries to argue that Joseph Smith has not created a polytheistic pantheon like the world of Greek mythology, because the free intelligences must be in harmony with the overall divine will. He sees a plurality of gods who have formed an infinite alliance, in the kind of idealized version of the Quorum of the Twelve Apostles. (Bushman, p. 535) Mormons generally do not like to be labeled as polytheistic.

Lawrence Wright of the *New Yorker* asked the late Prophet Hinckley whether Mormon theology was a form of polytheism.
"I don't have the remotest idea what you mean," Hinckley said impatiently.
"More than one god."
"Yes, but that's a very loose term," he replied. "We believe in eternal progression." By that he meant that human beings can evolve toward godhood by following the Mormon path. "You want to be a reporter always?" he said. "You want to be a scrub forever, through all eternity? We believe that life, eternal life, is real, that it's purposeful, that it has meaning, that it can be realized. I wouldn't describe us as polytheistic."[77]

---

[76] Andrew F. Ehat and Lyndon W. Cook, eds., *The Words of Joseph Smith* (Provo UT: Religious Studies Center, Brigham Young University, 1980), pp. 344-45, 357-58, 345 (April 7, 1844).
[77] Lawrence Wright, "At a time when Mormonism is booming, the Church is struggling with a troubled legacy," *New Yorker*, January 21, 2002.

Mormonism tries to escape the troubling paradox of free will and divine predestination and the clash between Erasmus and Luther on that score through means which resemble the Pelagian heresy. As Bushman comments, Joseph Smith "made individual persons radically free....Rather than God being the sovereign creator of all things from nothing, He was the most intelligent of the free intelligences. The universe is a school for these free, self-existing intelligences....This discourse envisioned a far different universe than the God-created universe of traditional Christian theology. The universe was composed of a congeries of intelligences and self-existent matter that God organized rather than made. He was bringing order out of chaos rather than making something from nothing." (Bushman, p. 535-6) Here again, the freemasonic influence is evident.

1843: JOSEPH SMITH ASKS CONGRESS FOR AUTONOMOUS MORMON THEOCRACY WITH POWER TO COMMAND FEDERAL TROOPS

The geopolitical designs of the Mormons had long been an object of lively speculation in the press. In 1841 *New York Herald* editor James Gordon Bennett editorialized that "we should not be surprised if Joe Smith were made Governor of a new religious territory in the west, that may rival the Arabians one of these days." The Mormon Empire, thought Bennett, might "one day, control the whole valley of the Mississippi, from the peaks of the Alleghanies to the pinnacles of the Rocky Mountains." (Bushman, p. 518) This was in fact the direction in which Joseph Smith began to tend.

Joseph Smith now began to wander not just west, but into the wild blue yonder of acute megalomania. In December, 1843, he addressed a petition to Congress requesting that the Mormon city state of Nauvoo be made an autonomous Federal territory, something like a state, Commonwealth, or the District of Columbia. He also wanted the Nauvoo Legion to be federalized into the United States Army, with the mayor of Nauvoo [Joseph Smith] being in power to mobilize federal troops whenever he thought it necessary. The implication was that these troops would be fighting the state militia of places like Missouri or Illinois. Fawn Brodie saw this gesture as one of Joseph Smith's gravest political blunders. Under the Constitution, carving up the territory of any state was exceedingly difficult, and there was no way a majority could be found in Congress. In addition, the idea of carving a piece out of Illinois was guaranteed to create a backlash among any residual supporters of Mormondom that might still be found in Springfield. (Brodie, p. 356)

Sometime after April, 1843, Joseph Smith entered into a celestial marriage with Mary Ann Frost Pratt, the wife of Romney's ancestor Parley P. Pratt. On December 7, 1844 Mrs. Parley P. Pratt gave birth to a son named Moroni Pratt. Scholars like Fawn Brodie suggest that Moroni Pratt may have been a biological son of Joseph Smith.[78]

---

[78] Brodie, p. 345.

1844: JOSEPH SMITH CREATES COUNCIL OF FIFTY, INSTRUMENT TO SEIZE POWER IN US AND WORLD

But Joseph Smith's manic political ambition did not stop here. In March 1844, he created a new political vehicle, which he called the Council of Fifty. The Council of Fifty was radically different from all of the governing bodies of the Mormon Church, because the Fifty were designed to include some token non-Mormons alongside the Saints. In other words, the Fifty were distinct from the Saints, and subsumed them. The Prophet was evidently aiming at a united front that would allow him to mobilize forces beyond the bounds of his own church. One thinks of the government of the now extinct German Democratic Republic, which allowed a significant if token presence of so-called "block parties" of liberals and Christian Democrats to be elected to the People's Chamber alongside an overpowering majority of Communists. The idea was to represent and mobilize these broader strata. Research is needed to examine the possible parallels between the Council of Fifty and the ruling body of the contemporary Chinese Taiping.

APRIL 11, 1844: COUNCIL OF FIFTY DECLARES JOSEPH SMITH "KING OF THE KINGDOM OF GOD"

Brodie regards the Council of Fifty as one of the best-kept secrets in the Mormondom. Bushman, certainly no adversary of the LDS, complains that, halfway through the first decade of the 21st century, the "council's original records are not available to researchers." It is known that one of their first actions was the coronation of Joseph Smith as "King of the Kingdom of God". Many of the components of the Fifty were just as imbued with the radical Jacksonian etiology of democracy as the subjects interviewed by de Tocqueville at around this time. And yet, here they were repudiating the bedrock of the American creed in favor of a temporal and celestial monarchy. They were similar to the dupes of Aaron Burr a generation before, but they compounded their crime by pretending that it was pleasing in the sight of God. (Brodie, pp. 356-57)

Apparently, the post of King of the Kingdom of God was an elective monarchy. In that April 11, 1844 meeting, one Mormon recorded, President Joseph "voted our P[rophet] P[riest] and K[ing] with loud Hosannas." According to Bushman, "the office of king came out of temple rituals where other Saints were anointed 'kings and priests....'" Joseph also acquired the title of "King and Ruler over Israel." At the same time, he remained chairman of the Council of Fifty. (Bushman, p. 523) Joseph Smith's theory of kingship appears to have been that of the sacral king rather than that of the absolute monarch known in Western Europe. His approach was closer to the Byzantine concept, and to caesaropapism. (Bushman, p. 524)

ROMNEY ANCESTOR PARLEY PRATT ENDORSES ONE WORLD GOVERNMENT

The Council of Fifty saw itself as the "the summit of all earthly powers." a universal empire. Mitt Romney's ancestor Parley Pratt wrote in April 1844 that the Council of Fifty represented "the most exalted Council with which our earth is at present Dignified" – a one world government if there ever was one. When Joseph Smith declared his candidacy for president shortly after his apotheosis through the Fifty, Lyman Wight said to him, "You are already president pro tem of the world." (Bushman, pp. 520-21) Years later, Parley Pratt had a town in Utah named after him. This was Parley's Park. The name was later changed to Park City. Mitt Romney owns a palatial residence there. In late June 2012, when Romney wanted to gather his own Council of Fifty for a weekend of fundraising and strategizing, he gathered them in Parley's Park. This continuity points once again to the overwhelming importance of Mormon traditions in the way the current GOP candidate operates.

In the view of Hirshson, the Council of Fifty embodied "the earthly Kingdom of God, the organization destined to plan and control the westward migration… the Kingdom was to prepare the world for the coming of God." As King of the Kingdom of God on Earth, Joseph Smith appointed fifty-three princes to assist him. "Unlike the Twelve and the Seventies, the Council of Fifty was an independent organization and theoretically had nothing to do with the Mormon hierarchy." But in reality, its leaders were the same people who controlled the church. The Council of Fifty became Smith's election committee for the 1844 presidential campaign, and also finished building the Nauvoo Temple. (Hirshson, pp. 79-80)

MORMON 1844 COUNCIL OF FIFTY TASKED WITH "OVERTHROW OF THIS NATION"

Bushman stresses that the Council of Fifty had an explicitly political mission, which was directed against existing governments. He argues that "as the council's original records are not available to researchers, its exact nature is hard to determine, but the council may have considered itself the incipient organization for millennial rule, a shadow government awaiting the demise of worldly political authority and the beginning of Christ's earthly reign. In early April 1844, Joseph 'prophesied the entire overthrow of this nation in a few years.'" (Bushman, p. 521)

Nor did the Council of Fifty become extinct with the assassination of Joseph Smith in June 1844. In 1848, Romney's ancestor Orson Pratt said this of the Fifty:

> "It is the only legal government that can exist in any part of the universe. All other governments are illegal and unauthorized. God, having made all beings and worlds, has the supreme right to govern them by His own laws, and by officers of his own appointment. Any people attempting to govern themselves by laws of their own making, and by officers of their own appointment, are in direct rebellion against the Kingdom of God.' For the past thousand years no 'true and legal government' had existed. 'All the emperors, kings, princes, presidents, lords, nobles, and rulers, during that long night of darkness, have acted without authority. Not one of them was called or anointed a king or prince by the God of heaven—not one of them received any communication whatsoever from the rightful sovereign, the Great King."[79]

---

[79] Online at brainyquote.com.

Parallel to these institutional preparations for world domination, the Mormons were conducting a military buildup. The Nauvoo Legion now had almost four thousand men, and an arsenal and a gunpowder factory were in the planning stages. The *New York Sun* pointed with alarm to the huge military dictatorship that was emerging along the Mississippi. (Brodie, p. 357)

The Council of Fifty was acting more and more like a sovereign state, especially by sending Lucian Woodworth as its own ambassador to Texas with instructions to negotiate a treaty – an action barred by Joseph Smith's supposedly beloved Constitution. (Brodie, p. 360)

JOSEPH SMITH DEMANDS CONGRESS MAKE HIM MILITARY DICTATOR OF THE AMERICAN WEST

Now, with the manic phase in full career, the Mormon Prophet escalated his insatiable demands on the US government even further. In March 1844, the Council of Fifty, acting on behalf of Joseph Smith, petitioned Congress to appoint the Prophet as an officer of the United States Army with the power to call up 100,000 volunteers to secure the US Western borders from Oregon to Texas. At this time, the entire United States Army numbered fewer than 15,000 troops. These 100,000 armed volunteers were supposed to maintain order, repel foreign invasions, and protect settlers against Indians, robbers, and criminals. They would not be formally a part of the US Army, although they would carry out military tasks, and were touted as a way to economize by not creating a large standing army for the West.

The spirit of Aaron Burr was once again abroad in the land, but this time with the kind of bombastic theocratic impudence which Burr never possessed. Joseph Smith had demonstrably lost all sense of political reality and proportion. On May 25, 1844, the US House of Representatives rebuffed him by refusing to allow his petition to be read on the floor. (Brodie, p. 360-1, Bushman, p. 519)

JOSEPH SMITH FOR PRESIDENT, 1844: STOP HENRY CLAY'S AMERICAN SYSTEM, ELECT POLK

The Mormons had a history of bouncing back and forth between the pro-Jackson Democrats and the anti-Jackson Whigs, who included an authentic nationalist faction. During the 1830s, the Mormons generally supported Democrats like Jackson and Van Buren, but when Van Buren rejected Joseph Smith's direct appeal for help after the Mormon war in Missouri, the Mormons switched to the Whig William Henry Harrison in 1840. The help the Mormons received from Stephen Douglas in Illinois moved them back into the Democratic column in 1841, but this was reversed when the Democrats supported the expulsion of Joseph Smith to Missouri in 1842, in connection with the shooting of former Governor Boggs, while a Whig judge let him off.

In 1843, Joseph Smith pledged his support to the Whigs. But, at the last minute, Hyrum Smith announced that he had received a revelation that it would be better to vote for the Democrats. The Democrats then won thanks to Mormon votes, and the Whigs, according to some accounts, began thinking of how to get rid of the Mormons. (Bushman, p. 508-9) Here again, the inherent dangers of monolithic bloc voting were presented in sharp relief.

Joseph Smith now wrote letters to all of the prospective presidential candidates for 1844, asking them for assurances that they would help protect the Mormons. As the result of unsatisfactory responses to Joseph Smith's circular letters to the candidates demanding protection for the Mormons, on January 29, 1844 the Twelve Apostles nominated the Prophet for the office of President of the United States. (Bushman, p. 514) Joseph Smith got William Phelps to ghost write a presidential platform, which was duly published under the title of *General Smith's Views of the Powers and Policy of the Government of the United States*. (Bushman, p. 515) "General" was now his favorite title.

Joseph Smith joined the Democrats in supporting the annexation of Texas as a slave state, but also recommended that slavery be abolished in Texas after statehood, with compensation to the slave owners being paid out of the sale of US public lands. The Mormon Prophet expressed what was fundamentally a plan for world conquest in terms of universal harmony, intoning "Come Texas: come Mexico; come Canada; and come all the world—let us be brethren: let us be one great family; and let there be universal peace." Smith supported the reinstitution of a national bank. (Bushman, p. 516) It was a middle position designed to siphon votes away from Clay.

The major party candidates for 1844 turned out to be James Knox Polk for the Democrats, and Henry Clay of Kentucky for the Whigs. Clay was the great patriot of the age, and advanced the classic program of the American System of Political Economy. This included a Hamiltonian National Bank, a protective tariff to promote industrialization, and internal infrastructural improvements paid for by the federal government when they were of national utility, even if they happen to be located in a single state. Clay was also not enthusiastic about the expansion of slavery.

HENRY CLAY'S 1844 CANDIDACY WAS LAST CHANCE TO AVOID CIVIL WAR

From the profile of Joseph Smith's campaign, which partially mimicked the Henry Clay Whig program of the National Bank and the gradual phasing out of slavery, it is possible to discern that the Mormon Prophet's candidacy would in practice have siphoned votes away from the Whigs, to give victory to the Democrat Polk. In the event, Polk's victory depended on another minor party, the abolitionist Liberty Party of James G. Birney. Slave owners and British imperialists united in their support for Polk, who would strengthen the Slave Power by the admission of Texas into the Union. Henry Clay's 1844 presidential bid may be considered as the last best chance for the United States (apart from the later Zachary Taylor presidency) to reestablish a national bank, restart the process of vigorous economic development which had been interrupted under Jackson and Van Buren, diminish the importance of slavery on the national scene, and thus avoid civil war. From this point of view, Joseph Smith's attempt to construct a countergang against Henry Clay emerges as profoundly dangerous for US national survival.

The Mormons immediately launched a robust nation-wide campaign. Their center of gravity was in Nauvoo, but they also had organizations across the United States. They had a newspaper in New York, and one in San Francisco, among others. In April 1844, forty-seven campaign conferences were to be held in 14 states. Some 339 Mormon elders were pressed into service as political operatives. (Bushman, p. 517)

In a manner similar to Mitt Romney's use of the Latter-day Saints Church apparatus and the Mormon-dominated Utah state government bureaucracy, Joseph Smith mobilized the Mormon Saints to help him become the decisive swing factor in the election. The King of the Kingdom of God might not become president, but he would surely be a kingmaker.

The *New York Herald* understood that the Mormons were seeking to gain political power by controlling the outcome of the election, writing on May 23, 1844 that the Saints "claim possession of from two hundred thousand to five hundred thousand votes in Nauvoo and throughout the Union, and with that they calculate that they can hold the balance of power and make whoever they please President. Well, if so, they may be worth looking after…. It seems by this movement that Joe Smith does not expect to be elected President but he still wants to have a finger in the pie, and see whether something can't be made out of it.'" (Brodie, p. 363)

FROM THEOCRATIC TO "THEODEMOCRATIC" DICTATORSHIP

Modern libertarian ranters against Big Government can look back with admiration at Joseph Smith's assault on the modern secular state. "The world is governed too much, and there is not a nation or a dynasty now occupying the earth which acknowledges Almighty God as their lawgiver, and as 'crowns won by blood, by blood must be maintained,' I go emphatically, virtuously, and humanely, for a Theodemocracy, where God and the people hold the power to conduct the affairs of men in righteousness. And where liberty, free trade, and sailor's right, and the protection of life and property shall be maintained inviolate, for the benefit of ALL." (Bushman, p. 522) Joseph Smith's answer to Big Government was to promote Big Theocracy, which turned out to be far more oppressive and destructive. The alternative to the partisan clash of political parties was a one-party state dominated by the Mormon party of God. Notice also that Joseph Smith endorsed British free trade, the hallmark of the anti-national opponents of the American System, as the work of Friedrich List and Henry Carey made clear.

JOSEPH SMITH DEMANDS ARISTARCHY

In practice, theodemocracy meant the usual dictatorship of Joseph Smith as messenger of God. But this time he was dressed up as a kind of guide to democracy, in which the Church authorities would allow self-rule, but intervene if the people went astray. The Mormon Prophet lectured the Nauvoo High Council that theodemocracy was "the principles of democracy that the people's voice should be heard when the voice was just, but when it was not just it was no longer democratic, but if the minority views are more just, then Aristarchy should be the governing principle. i.e. the wisest & best laws should be made." (Bushman, p. 523)

Some politicians could understand that the Mormons were a ticking time bomb, and tried to get rid of them by sending them west as far as possible. One Illinois politician wanted them to go all the way to California. (Bushman, p. 520)

MORMON DISSIDENTS PROTEST THE PROPHET'S ABUSES

But now the final crisis of the Nauvoo theocracy was at hand. Once again, despite repeated purges, a dissident group of marginal Mormons had emerged as a kind of internal opposition to the Prophet. The leader of the malcontents was William Law, who had been excommunicated in the spring of 1844. Once again, the principal grievance cited by the opposition was polygamy, since the Prophet had attempted to initiate celestial relations with Law's wife.

Because of Joseph Smith's notoriously unscrupulous business practices, the Mormon dissidents also had economic grievances. Law alleged that the Prophet was using church funds collected through tithing in order to buy land which he then intended to sell at exorbitant prices to new Mormon converts as they arrived in Nauvoo. (Brodie, p. 368) Some of the dissidents wanted to break out of the autarkic command economy which Joseph Smith had mandated. They bid against him to buy lumber, and began building houses and other structures in Nauvoo. These breakaway entrepreneurs paid their workers in cash, while Joseph Smith offered only goods and payments in kind, supplemented by Nauvoo scrip or local funny money. When workers preferred to sell their labor for actual money, a crisis broke out in the Nauvoo labor market, with Joseph Smith averring that his projects were more important because salvation depended on them. (Brodie, p. 368)

The dissenters chose a course of robust muckraking, but they appear to have regarded Joseph Smith as a fallen prophet rather than a con artist. They still venerated the *Book of Mormon*, and wanted to go back to the early days when spiritual wifery had not been an obvious problem. "What they hated was polygamy, the Kingdom of God, and the 'tyranny' of Joseph Smith." (Bushman, pp. 537-38) Joseph Smith kept denying polygamy until the end. "What a thing it is for a man to be accused of committing adultery, and having seven wives, when I can find only one," he quipped in 1844.

These were the goals of the *Nauvoo Expositor*, the dissident Mormon newspaper which appeared only once, on June 7, 1844. This journal announced its intention to "explode the vicious principles of Joseph Smith, and those who practice the same abominations and whoredomes." It also took exception to Joseph's teaching of polytheism, specifically his authoritarian doctrine "that there are innumerable Gods as much above the God that presides over this universe, as he is above us." (Bushman, p. 539) The dissidents also rejected the idea that Joseph Smith was a King, since this title had to be reserved for Christ alone.

JOSEPH SMITH TRASHES DISSIDENT PRESS, VIOLATES CONSTITUTION HE CLAIMED TO REVERE

Brodie points out that Joseph Smith could have chosen this moment to go on the offensive, confess that divine revelations had long dictated polygamy, and announce the beginning of the great trek towards the Rocky Mountains. But, in her opinion, the Prophet was now crushed under a burden of "secrecy, evasion, and lying" which robbed him of coverage and initiative. His earlier charismatic demagogy deserted him at the most critical moment. (Brodie, p. 376)

So when the paper exposing a catalog of abuses was distributed in the town, Joseph Smith responded by ordering the Danites into action. They proceeded to destroy the printing office, smashed the press, and burn all the copies they could find. On Joseph's orders, the city council had declared the publication libelous. Joseph Smith thus trampled on the First Amendment of the Constitution which he always claimed to be divinely inspired. It was a colossal example of Mormon doublethink.

And then he did more; he called together The Nauvoo Legion, his private Danite Army, and pledged before God "that this people shall have their legal rights, and be protected from mob violence." (Brodie, p. 379) Of course, when it came to the small group of dissidents, the majority Saints were themselves the mob.

THEOCRACY LEADS TO ANARCHY: JOSEPH AND HYRUM SMITH MURDERED BY LAWLESS MILITIA, JUNE 27, 1844

Joseph Smith and his brother Hyrum were now arrested and jailed on the charge of treason, because they had declared martial law and mobilized the Nauvoo Legion to fight off a posse of militia which was coming to arrest the Prophet. Joseph, Hyrum, and some other Mormon leaders were imprisoned in Carthage, Illinois. Concerned to his last day about revenge, Joseph had wanted to save Hyrum so his brother could "avenge" his own death – not a Christian sentiment. Anti-Mormon militias from nearby towns, including the Warsaw militia and the Carthage Grays, massed outside the jail, and then stormed the premises. The Smith brothers defended themselves with firearms, and hit some attackers, but they were overwhelmed and killed. John Taylor and some other top Mormons survived.

Some Mormon historians have attempted to develop a conspiracy theory according to which the militia mob action that killed the Smith brothers in Carthage Jail had been fomented by the leaders of the Illinois Whig party, the friends of Henry Clay.[80] But the case they have made so far fails to convince. It is characteristic of the Mormons that their hostility should be directed over decades against the most positive figures of the American tradition, including Henry Clay, Abraham Lincoln, Justin Morrill, and others.

---

[80] See Robert S. Wicks and Fred R. Foister, *Junius and Joseph: Presidential Politics and the Assassination of the First Mormon Prophet* (Logan UT: Utah State University Press, 2005).

MORMON THEOLOGY

What are the main beliefs of the faith which Joseph Smith founded? The task of answering is difficult because some points of Mormon doctrine are kept secret, while others are obscured. Mormonism, so far as is known, has never announced a Creed, although such a Creed may exist as an esoteric or shelf doctrine. So, we are left with guesswork to some extent. Still, a number of writers who know Mormonism well have attempted to sum up the main Mormon articles of faith. One was the nineteenth-century British publicist William Hepworth Dixon, who wrote a book critical of Mormonism. In it he included the following surmise of the "Mormon Creed":

> "(1) God is a person with the form and flesh of man. (2) Man is a part of the substance of God, and will himself become a god. (3) Man was not created by God, but existed from all eternity, and will never cease to exist. (4) There is no such thing as original or birth sin. (5) The earth is only one of many inhabited spheres. (6) God is president of men made gods, angels, good men, and spirits waiting to receive a tabernacle of flesh. (7) Man's household of wives is his kingdom not for earth only, but also in his future state. (8) Mormonism is the kingdom of God on earth."[81]

A more recent summary of the key tenets of Mormonism was offered by the Associated Press on January 16, 2008, when Romney was competing against McCain in the GOP primaries. Here we read:

> "Nature of God: God once was a mortal who became an eternal being after a great trial.
> Jesus Christ: Christ was God's first-born spirit child, his only earthly child and the only perfect mortal.
> No Trinity: Mormons reject the idea of the Christian Trinity — God, Jesus Christ and the Holy Spirit as one ethereal being. Instead, they believe the three are separate beings joined in a common purpose.
> Pre-existence and the afterlife: Before their mortal birth, humans existed in pre-mortality and were born in the spirit world to heavenly parents. Mormons also believe in the resurrection and teach that most people will receive some measure of salvation and have a place in a three-level eternal kingdom.
> One true church: Mormons say their faith is not Protestant, Catholic or Orthodox but holds a unique place as 'restored New Testament Christianity.' Founder Joseph Smith said God told him none of the existing churches were practicing Christianity as it was intended.

---

[81] William Hepworth Dixon, *New America* (Philadelphia: Lippincott, 1867; reprint Ann Arbor: Scholarly Publishing Office, University of Michigan Library, 2006), i. 24, cited by E. Cobham Brewer, *Dictionary of Phrase and Fable* 1894, online at Mormon Creed — Infoplease.com and bartleby.com.

A living prophet: Mormons believe the head of their church is a living prophet, seer and revelator who can communicate with God."[82]

The late religious broadcaster and author Walter Martin, known for his radio program "The Bible Answer Man," summed up several points which represent the specific personality of Mormonism as a religion:

> "The Bible is the Word of God in so far as it is correctly translated. There are three sacred books in addition to the Bible: *The Book of Mormon, Doctrine and Covenants*, and the *Pearl of Great Price*.
> The Earth is one of several inhabited planets ruled over by gods and goddesses, who were at one time humans on other planets. Mormonism is polytheistic in its core.
> The Trinity consists of three gods born in different times and places; the Father begot the Son and the Holy Ghost through a goddess wife in heaven.[83]
> Humankind is of the same species as God. God begot all humans in heaven as offspring of his wife or wives, who were sent to Earth for their potential exaltation to godhood. Salvation is resurrection, but exaltation to godhood, for eternal life in the celestial heaven, must be earned through self-meriting works."[84]

Martin's evaluation of Mormonism is well-informed and severe. He writes that "Mormonism, with its apostles, priesthood, temples, secret signs, symbols, handshakes, and mysteries, claims to be 'the church of the restoration'; but at its heart, in its doctrine of the Messiah, it is found to be contrary to every major biblical pronouncement."[85]

WALTER MARTIN: MORMONISM A "POLYTHEISTIC NIGHTMARE" AND "NON-CHRISTIAN CULT SYSTEM"

Martin also rejects the Mormon three-tiered heaven with telestial, terrestrial, and celestial levels in ascending order, like first class, business, and economy accommodations on an airliner. He points out that "even in the celestial kingdom godhood is by slow progression, and in the end each who becomes a god will, with his family, rule and populate a separate planet of his own. It is almost superfluous to comment that this entire scheme of the consummation of Mormon salvation is the antithesis of the biblical revelation, which knows nothing of godhood, either constituted or progressive, and which teaches instead that in heaven the destiny of the redeemed will be the special providence of God himself...."[86]

---

[82] Associated Press, January 16, 2008; online at Mormon Coffee.org. AP has scrubbed the original article as of September 2012.

[83] This resembles the Arian heresy, with additions. See Appendix for a comparison of Mormonism to the Nicene-Constantinopolitan Creed.

[84] Walter Martin, *The Kingdom of the Cults* (Minneapolis MN: Bethany House, 2003), p. 192.

[85] Martin, p. 253.

[86] Martin, pp. 256-7.

Martin was also well aware of the esoteric theology of Mormonism (the "shelf doctrines"), which tend to mask what is really professed. He observed that

> "... the Mormon religion utilizes biblical terms and phrases and even adopts Christian doctrines in order to claim allegiance to the Christian faith. Mormons have also come to lay much stress on public relations and take pains to make certain that they do not use language that might reveal the true nature of their theological deviations. We have also seen that the Mormon Church considers itself alone the true church of Christ in our age, and further that they consider all other groups to be Gentiles and apostates from the true Christian religion.... From these facts it is evident that Mormonism strives with great effort to masquerade as the Christian church complete with an exclusive message, infallible prophets, and higher revelations for a new dispensation that the Mormons would have us believe began with Joseph Smith Jr. But it is the verdict of both history and biblical theology that Joseph Smith's religion is a polytheistic nightmare of garbled doctrines draped with the garment of Christian terminology. This fact, if nothing else, brands it as a non-Christian cult system."[87]

Accordingly, Martin directed his efforts to helping his readers avoid or escape "the spiritual maze that is Mormonism."[88]

Mormonism was thus an entirely new religion, radically separate from Christianity. It was also a program to create a new theocratic nation at the expense of the United States.

---

[87] Martin, pp. 258-9.
[88] Martin, p. 259.

CHAPTER III

THE MORMONS AND THE BRITISH EMPIRE
AGAINST THE UNITED STATES

"I don't think the White Horse Prophecy is fair to bring up at all. It's been rejected by every church leader that has talked about it. It has nothing to do with anything." – Mitt Romney

Professor Aly Mazahéri (1914-1991) of the Paris School of Advanced Studies in Social Science and one of the most eminent Iranian intellectuals working in Western Europe, was fond of saying that there had been three miracles of the Victorian age, the mid-nineteenth century high point of British imperial world power.[89] By Mazahéri's count, these three were Karl Marx, the founder of communism; the Bab, the founder of the Bahá'í religion: and Joseph Smith, the founder of Mormonism. These were three prophets whose appearance on the world scene occurred at roughly the same time, and shared one characteristic: all were extraordinarily helpful for maintaining and advancing British world power.

In the case of Karl Marx (1818-1883), the idea that industrial workers should regard industrial entrepreneurs – and not British imperialists, feudal aristocrats or parasitic bankers – as their main enemies was a perfect divide-and-conquer strategy for British power plays against Germany, France, Italy, Russia, and other European nations that were at that time in the process of industrialization.

The Bab (1819-1850) provided a partial solution for the problems encountered by the British in the Moslem parts of the empire, where they found that those professing the Islamic faith refused to become colonial administrators for foreign infidels. The Bab was a merchant of Shiraz in Persia (today's Iran) who in 1844 proclaimed himself the Mahdi, the Muslim equivalent of the Messiah. He promulgated a new system of sharia law which differed from the original one in some important respects. Later, the Bab's teachings were codified into a new religion, the Bahá'í faith, whose supporters turned out to be perfectly willing to take up their posts as British colonial bureaucrats, thus adding to the stability of imperial rule.

THE TAIPING OF CHINA: A DISTANT MIRROR FOR THE MORMON SAINTS

Another name which deserves to be added to this list is that of Hong Xiuquan (1814-1864), a young misfit of the Hakka ethnic group who, after having failed to pass the Confucian examinations to become a civil service official and thus a member of the

---

[89] I got to know the Iranian historian Aly Mazahéri in Paris during the 1980s, when he was teaching at the Ecole des Hautes Etudes en Sciences Sociales. He was the author of many articles and books, notably *La route de la soie* (Paris: S.P.A.G. Papyrus, 1983).

Chinese elite, turned to Christianity and soon declared himself to be the younger brother of Jesus Christ. This made Hong a Chinese Son of the Christian God. Soon a movement of 10,000 to 30,000 followers (comparable to the early Mormon community) had gathered around Hong. This he called the God Worshipers Society. Hong and his movement soon created the Celestial Kingdom of Taiping with Hong as "Heavenly King" – another neat parallel to Joseph Smith, who had been named the King of the Kingdom of God in Nauvoo, Illinois a few years earlier. And the parallels keep coming. The Celestial Kingdom, like Mormondom, was explicitly a theocracy. The Taiping capital was Nanking, and the Celestial Kingdom embraced parts of half a dozen provinces in southeast China. The Taiping Rebellion against the Qing (or Ching) dynasty (1851-1864) followed. The Ching dynasty sent an army to restore imperial authority, which soon met the resistance of between 1 million and 3 million Taiping regular troops. Total war was waged on both sides, especially in regard to the destruction of agricultural production and the mass slaughter of the populations of captured cities. Some 600 cities were reported destroyed. The standard estimate of total military and civilian deaths in the Taiping rebellion is about 20 million, but other estimates go as high as 40 million. From this point of view, the Taiping rebellion is unquestionably the biggest civil war and most likely the biggest military event of any kind of the entire 19th century. It was a way to destroy some of the most advanced and westernized parts of Chinese society, while weakening the country in the midst of the three Opium Wars waged by the British.

BRITISH USE THEOLOGY FOR DESTABILIZATION

The teacher who had started Hong on his career as prophet and martyr was the Baptist Isaachar Jacox Roberts, born in Tennessee, trained at Furman University in the South Carolina cradle of secessionism, long a playground for British intelligence. Hong studied with Roberts for several months at Canton in 1847. Roberts became an advisor to the Taiping foreign minister, but eventually became disaffected and had to flee on a British gunboat. The enormous social dislocation of the Taiping rebellion is a stark illustration of how much damage can be done to an existing society by unleashing a millennial, apocalyptic, theocratic cult. Under slightly different circumstances, the Mormons might have been able to wreak comparable havoc on the United States. And they still may.

Between 1830 and 1870, the British Empire reached the peak of its world power. The London elites intended to use this opportunity to wipe out every independent center that might resist its Imperial dictates. In 1830 and 1848, the British used their Mazzini, Marx, and Bakunin networks to destabilize the continental European powers – France, Prussia, Austria, Spain, and the smaller states of Italy and Germany. As a result of the French destabilization, the British were able to install Napoleon III as Emperor of France, where he served as a geopolitical tool of London, invading Indochina and Mexico, weakening Austria, and joining in Britain's Crimean war against Russia. The British waged three Opium Wars against China. They provoked the Great Mutiny or Sepoy Mutiny in India. They sponsored the Confederate States of America.

But, in addition to these geopolitical and military operations, there was another dimension. The British religious and theological establishment deliberately fomented a worldwide wave of religious irrationalism, taking the form of charismatic prophets and prophecies, speaking in tongues, false Messiahs, predictions of the end of the world, and frenetic enthusiasm. The goal in every case was to weaken the social order and spread mass hysteria. In China, Iran, and the United States, these movements became large and powerful enough to pose serious risks to internal stability and even to national survival. British religious currents like the Darbyites, the British Israelites, and the charismatics were all deployed as part of this effort.

In the 18th and 19th centuries Britain also sponsored the development of Wahhabism or Salafism in Arabia, a form of purism claiming to return to the original doctrine of Islam. This theocratic, reactionary belief system was used to good effect in breaking up the Turkish empire. Today, secular, pluralistic Syria is being destroyed by a kind of Taiping rebellion of Wahhabite fanatics backed by Saudi Arabia, the UK puppet sultanate of Qatar, and the US.

JOSEPH SMITH'S 1832 ANGLOPHILE PROPHECY OF THE AMERICAN CIVIL WAR

In 1832, the state of South Carolina, prefiguring its later role as the official cradle of secessionism, announced its intention to nullify the new federal tariff legislation, which free trade ideologues called the "tariff of abominations." For a while it seemed as if secession and possible civil war might result. After a time, the South Carolina fire eaters decided to back down, and a reprieve of almost three decades on the question of civil war was thus achieved. Joseph Smith responded immediately to these events with his famous Civil War Prophecy of December 25, 1832. Here Joseph Smith forecast:

> Verily, thus saith the Lord, concerning the wars that will shortly come to pass, beginning at the rebellion of South Carolina, which will eventually terminate in the death and misery of many souls; and the time will come that war will be poured out upon all nations, beginning at this place. For behold, the Southern States shall be divided against the Northern States, and the Southern States will call on other nations, even the nation of Great Britain, as it is called, and they shall also call upon other nations, in order to defend themselves against other nations; and then war shall be poured out upon all nations.
>
> And it shall come to pass, after many days, slaves shall rise up against their masters, who shall be marshaled and disciplined for war.... and thus, with the sword and by bloodshed the inhabitants of the earth shall mourn; and with famine, and plague, and earthquake, and the thunder of heaven, and the fierce and vivid lightning also, shall the inhabitants of the earth be made to feel the wrath, and indignation, and chastening hand of an Almighty God, until the consumption decreed hath made a full end of all nations....[90]

The scenario thus developed by the Mormon Prophet substantially corresponds to the strategic intentions of the British Empire in regard to the United States, as displayed

---

[90] Miller, *Joseph Smith*, pp. 172-3.

during 1861-65. These were to foment a rebellion of the slave states against the Union, and then to arrange an intervention by Britain and possibly France and Spain against the United States. In the event, Anglo-French intervention was prevented by a number of factors, notably the strong support given to the United States by the Russian Empire, the world power which London and Paris had good reason to fear. This 1832 revelation prefigures in many essential details the White Horse Prophecy of almost a dozen years later, in which the Mormon White Horse and the British Red Horse unite against the American Pale Horse and defeat it.

1835: CATHOLIC APOSTOLIC CHURCH OF BRITAIN CONTACTS JOSEPH SMITH

The month of June, 1835 marks the first demonstrable official contact between the Mormon leadership around Joseph Smith and a representative of the British theological-intelligence establishment. This contact was established through a visit to Kirtland, Ohio by the British Reverend John Hewitt. Reverend Hewitt had been sent by a charismatic congregation in Barnsley, England. Reverend Hewitt, who came from the Rotherham Independent Seminary, explained that the Barnsley congregation had seen a Mormon-controlled newspaper which had been brought back to England by a merchant who had been in New York City. Based on this newspaper, the Barnsley group had concluded that the Mormons had common ground with them. The Barnsley letter announced that "The Lord hath seen our joy and gladness to hear that He was raising up a people for Himself in that part of the New World, as well as here." (Bushman, pp. 270-71)

Hewitt proposed an alliance between the Mormons and the Barnsley group. He was able to assure Joseph Smith that many members of his congregation were people of means who could be of great assistance. There was also the distinct possibility that many of the English charismatics would want to come to America. The letter from the Barnsley group promised the Mormon Saints that "many will follow, should he approve of the country, etc., who will help the cause, because the Lord hath favored them with this world's goods." This was a timely offer, since the Mormons were at this time in dire financial straits. The letter also indicated that the Barnsley group was not likely to be deterred by mob attacks and harassment: "we understand that persecution had been great among you, or would be, but we were commanded not to fear, for He would be with us."

Pro-Mormon historians argue that this visit did not lead to further contacts, but there is no doubt that the first official Mormon delegation departed for England less than two years after this first contact was made. That was then followed in 1839 by the transfer of the entire Quorum of the Twelve to England for an intensive program of publishing, fundraising, and recruiting work which made British subjects, be they English, Scottish, or Welsh, the majority of the world Mormon movement. Within a few years after this fateful 1835 encounter, Mormonism had been thoroughly Anglicized, and its dominant temper became decidedly Anglophile.

The curiosity of the Barnsley group about the Mormons had been whetted by parallels in the ecclesiastical apparatus of these two sects. Between 1832 and 1835, charismatic leaders in London, having allegedly received revelations, created a group of twelve apostles, just like the Mormons and at more or less the same time. The selection of the English Twelve Apostles had been completed on July 14, 1835. The Barnsley group also called themselves Saints.

The Barnsley group continued the charismatic-irrational religious revival which had been set into motion through the efforts of a famous London preacher of Scottish background, Edward Irving. Irving had preferred the name "congregations gathered under apostles," but eventually this denomination called itself the Catholic Apostolic Church. Edward Irving was a former Scottish Presbyterian who had been expelled by the Kirk in 1822, and who had thereupon set up shop in the Caledonian Chapel in Hatton Garden, London.

Irving quickly attracted the sympathetic attention of the top levels of the ruling British oligarchy. The chapel had seats for about 500 persons, but, for a time at least, Irving was able to draw two to three times that number. The neighborhood streets were blocked by luxurious carriages: "it has been said that, on one occasion at least, the queue of carriages waiting to return the worshipers to their homes was four miles in length."[91]

CHARISMATIC EDWARD IRVING, CHAPLAIN TO THE BRITISH ELITE

Edward Irving was a close friend of the famous British reactionary essayist and man of letters Thomas Carlyle, with whom he had been associated back in Scotland. Carlyle, like James Mill, John Stuart Mill, John Ruskin, and other celebrated British literary figures of the Victorian age, was part of the ideological and cultural control apparatus of the empire. Irving attracted his following in part due to praise he had received during a parliamentary debate in the House of Commons from George Canning, the British Foreign Secretary and future Prime Minister. After Canning had called attention to Irving's church, other members of Parliament, wealthy lawyers and bankers, and clergyman from the English and Scottish established churches flocked to hear the new charismatic message. (Bushman, pp. 271-72)

Support from Canning meant support from the very heart of the British imperial apparatus. George Canning was one of the most powerful British politicians of the Napoleonic era. An associate of William Pitt the younger, he became Undersecretary of State for Foreign Affairs from 1796 to 1799. He then served on the India board between 1799 and 1800. He was in Parliament between 1801 and 1804, when he became Treasurer of the Navy for two years. He was Foreign Secretary between 1807 and 1809, during which time he was associated with the cowardly British sneak attack on the Danish fleet in Copenhagen harbor. After five years in Parliament and two years as British Ambassador to Portugal, he became president of the India Board between 1816 and 1820. After two more years in Parliament, Canning became Foreign Secretary and Leader of the House of Commons, posts which he held from 1822 to 1827. These were the greatest years of Edward Irving's success in London. In 1827, Canning became prime minister, with Lord Lansdowne, the son of the leading oligarch William Petty, the Earl of Shelburne, as a member of his cabinet, but he died suddenly on August 8, 1827.

---

[91] Flegg, p. 47.

IRVING BACKED BY GEORGE CANNING,
BRITISH FOREIGN SECRETARY AND PRIME MINISTER

Along with his rival Castlereagh, Pitt, and the Duke of Wellington, Canning was by any measure one of the leading British oligarchs of the age. His promotion of Edward Irving can be thought of as serving two goals. The first was to increase the degree of religious irrationality in the British ruling class, so as to facilitate the final push for total world domination over the coming few decades. The second aspect was that Canning could see the vast potential of preachers inspired by Irving's brand of charismatic irrationalism for destabilizing and disrupting nations around the world, which otherwise might offer resistance to the triumphant march of the British Empire. The British, in short, promoted Edward Irving for the same reasons that the Venetians promoted Savonarola against Florence and Martin Luther against Germany: to create chaos and conflict, and to weaken strategic rivals to the mother country.

Irving's congregation "was particularly notable for the proportion of professional people that contained lawyers, physicians, actors, artists, diplomats, and men from similar walks of life. They and their fine ladies were drawn in large numbers to his ministry.... England's literary circles were especially well represented."[92]

Frequenters of Irving's Sunday services included famous people like the anti-slavery activist Zachary Macaulay, an associate of Bishop Wilberforce. There was the poet and essayist Charles Lamb, and the philosopher and painter William Hazlitt. In another pew might sit journalist Thomas de Quincy, the author of the sensational *Confessions of an English Opium Eater* (1821). The romantic poet Samuel Taylor Coleridge, who also dabbled with narcotics, was a friend and admirer of Irving. Another worshiper was the future historian and Whig politician, Thomas Babington Macaulay. William Wordsworth, the future poet laureate, was also a visitor, as was Sir Walter Scott, the leading practitioner of the romantic historical novel and a prime asset of British cultural-political operations, as for example in the American South. The young future Prime Minister William Gladstone attended, and laughed to see the headmaster of Eton College in the crush. A wealthy couple, Mr. and Mrs. Basil Montagu, tried to help Irving find a wife. He was originally interested in Jane Welsh, but she married Thomas Carlyle, and then moved on to Mazzini.[93] British intelligence was a small world at the top.

The Barnsley congregation may be thought of as a kind of contact bureau for the Caledonian Chapel and later Catholic Apostolic Church mother ships, a bureau tasked with keeping in touch with charismatic and apocalyptic movements across Britain and across the Atlantic. The followers of Edward Irving allowed various church members to act as prophets and speak in tongues during the worship services as the spirit moved them. But, Joseph Smith reserved the gift of prophecy to himself alone, and this practice was imitated by his successors such as Brigham Young. Despite these differences, large numbers of Catholic Apostolics transferred to the Mormon Saints.

---

[92] Dallimore, pp. 47-48.
[93] Dallimore, p. 49.

THE MORMONS AND THE CATHOLIC APOSTOLIC CHURCH

Columba Graham Flegg, in a recent study of the Catholic Apostolic Church, includes the Mormons among various religious formations which the Irving tradition had helped to shape: "A further possible candidate for Catholic Apostolic influence might be the eschatology of the Mormons, who were also pre-millennialists and practicers of charismatic gifts ... [and] were prepared to publicize prophetic revelations widely in a way which the Catholic Apostolic apostles largely avoided.... Like the Catholic Apostolics, the Mormons believed in the gathering of Israel to 'Zion' (though locating this in the United States), in a personal return of Christ to reign on earth, and in the gathering together of an elect body in preparation for the Second Advent."[94]

Flegg sees Mormonism to some extent as a lower class version of Irving's charismatic preaching: "the Mormon mission in England, for example, had a strong appeal for the lower classes, because it preached a classless society, and had the added incentive of the possibility of immigration to the New World."[95]

Ernest R. Sandeen, in his 1970 *Roots of Fundamentalism*, places the Mormons in the millenarian (i.e. end time) tradition launched in Britain in the first half of the 19th century: "Joseph Smith taught an apocalyptic and pre-millennial eschatology; the Mormon periodical was entitled the *Millennial Star*; and as they gathered for worship, the Latter-day Saints could choose from dozens of hymns... which focused their attention on the daunting glory and the imminent judgment... as their headquarters moved from Ohio into Missouri and then Illinois, the Mormons began to concentrate more upon Zion as a place than upon 1843 or 1844 as a date [for the end of the world].... Their expectations about the future, however, remained curiously mixed. The triumph of the Mormon cause was anticipated through a cataclysmic judgment rather than the gradual conversion of the world; and since natural calamities had been predicted as one of the indications of the nearness of this judgment, reports of fires, wars, and railroad and steamship disasters were regularly reported in the *Millennial Star* under the Heading "Signs of the Times" ... But while the Latter-day Saints waited anxiously for the fulfillment of these signs of the times (including the restoration of the Jews to Palestine), they were also laboring mightily to build the New Jerusalem in Utah."[96]

Many members of the British elite, Carlyle among them, became estranged from Irving's church when it became clear that the Scottish charismatic had not recognized that his brand of revivalism might set off a wave of hysteria in the British capital. The British imperial elite wanted charismatic cults for export to countries targeted for destabilization, not for domestic consumption. But Irving was really convinced that God was raising up a new order of prophets among the British. On November 19, 1831, the London Times reported that Irving's church was being "disturbed by individuals pretending to the miraculous gift of tongues." A certain Miss Hall spoke in tongues with such vigor that she had to retreat to the vestry. One Mr. Taplin violently harangued the congregation "in

[94] Flegg, p. 437.
[95] Flegg, p. 443.
[96] Sandeen, pp. 47-48.

an unknown tongue." Irving, convinced he was witnessing the operation of the Holy Spirit, called for more spiritual gifts with a call on December 31, 1831 to "let prophecies and tongues go forth." The experiment was threatening to get out of hand and boomerang.

In 1832, Irving and his charismatic ban of "gifted" persons in Regent Square were largely abandoned and ostracized by the British upper crust. Carlyle and wife Jane played a key role. In the account of Irving's biographer, "Thomas Carlyle and his wife, both much beloved, not only disagreed, but remonstrated, the former making a vehement protestation against the "Bedlam" and "Chaos" to which his friend's steps were tending, which Irving listened to in silence, covering his face with his hands." The Bedlam and Chaos were supposed to be inflicted on the United States and other nations, not unleashed on London.[97] Irving died in relative obscurity in 1834, but the Catholic Apostolic Church continued.

ELITE BRITISH MEN OF LETTERS SUPPORT MORMONS

Another way to see the support given to the Mormons by the elites of the British aristocracy is to examine the attitudes towards them exhibited by some of the leading Victorian men of letters. Given the inherent prudery and bigotry of the Victorian age, one would normally expect a sect of uncouth polygamists in the wilds of North America to be an object of execration among British literary elitists. But, surprisingly enough, the Mormons had powerful supporters, doubtless for anti-American geopolitical reasons. Some of these writers were notoriously linked to the British intelligence establishment, sometimes through the British East India Company. Writers seeking acceptance after about 1870 by a lower middle-class market, such as Sir Arthur Conan Doyle, could portray the Mormons in a negative light, as in *A Study in Scarlet*, the first of the Sherlock Holmes mysteries. The Mormons also got a bad press in Robert Louis Stevenson's *The Dynamiter*. By this time, London's hopes for a Mormon version of the Taiping rebellion had cooled, and the mainline of British propaganda was simply to denigrate everything American.

But the more elite pre-1870 writers, with greater intellectual and social pretensions, often showed support for the Mormon Saints. Thomas Carlyle, one of the biggest names, was a warm admirer of Mormondom. So was his colleague, John Stuart Mill of the British East India Company. John Stuart Mill was the son of James Mill, who also claimed to be an economist. James Mill (1773-1836), a direct disciple of the satanic Jeremy Bentham, served for 18 years as the Examiner of Correspondence for the East India Company. This is another way of saying that he was one of the top bosses of British intelligence at that time. The elder Mill's job was to develop an intelligence picture based on the reports he received, and to promote policies to maximize profits and power, often with horrendous consequences for the people of India. The East India Company was much concerned with the manipulation of religious institutions, and systematically promoted

---

[97] Margaret Oliphant, *The Life of Edward Irving* (London: Hurst and Blackett, 1864), 3rd edition, pp. 342, 325.

the most backward and self-destructive tendencies in Hinduism and Islam, creating distortions which continue down to the present day. Others working for the British East India Company included the monetarist economist David Ricardo and the ideologue of genocide Thomas Malthus.[98]

After working for the British East India Company for 34 years, John Stuart Mill (1806-1873) took over the post of Examiner of Correspondence. The younger Mill directed a vast program of British cultural warfare, with special attention for the United States, which was seen along with Russia as a threat to the British Empire. He sponsored the career of the Scottish feudalist, neo-pagan, and proto-fascist Thomas Carlyle, who in turn became the main guru for Ralph Waldo Emerson of Harvard, the luminary of the Transcendentalist school. Emerson was famous for his concept of "self-reliance," which later morphed into the "rugged individualism" of Herbert Hoover, and the "you're on your own" doctrine of the current Republican Party.

THOMAS CARLYLE, REACTIONARY ROMANTIC, LIKES BRIGHAM YOUNG

The reactionary essayist Thomas Carlyle represented a younger generation of the British intelligence establishment following in the footsteps of Jeremy Bentham and Thomas Malthus. Carlyle was so reactionary that he opposed the very timid British Reform Bill of 1867. Reacting to Lincoln's victory in the US Civil War, which had captured the imagination of British workers, it finally allowed urban industrial workers the right to vote. Like Dickens, Carlyle was a great hater of the United States. Carlyle was a close friend of the charismatic Pentecostalist and mystic Edward Irving, to whom he devoted an essay of over 200 pages, which appears in his volume of *Reminiscences*.[99]

Carlyle was heavily involved in many important British strategic operations of the mid-19th century. One of the principal British political assets of this era was the Italian revolutionary nationalist firebrand Giuseppe Mazzini, who generally used Great Britain as his base of operations. Mazzini's assignment was to destabilize the Austrian, Russian, and Ottoman empires, while making sure that no powerful independent states could ever emerge from their wreckage. Carlyle worked so closely with the Italian provocateur and wrecker that his wife, Jane Welsh Carlyle, became a mistress of Mazzini. Another of Carlyle's important projects was the American transcendentalist movement, and especially its leading light, Ralph Waldo Emerson. Carlyle must count as one of the largest single influences on the Bostonian Emerson. Carlyle presented himself as an expert in German philosophy, which was considered chic by the British upper classes, who of course could read no German. Carlyle thus became the authoritative interpreter of German thought and literature (especially Goethe) in the British Isles. Carlyle is thus a leading example of epistemological warfare and subversive political operations in the Victorian era. Carlyle's draft essay on the Mormons was written in early January, 1854, but never published in his lifetime. It was discovered in the Beinecke Library at Yale

---

[98] See Anton Chaitkin, *Treason in America* (New York: New Benjamin Franklin House, 1985).
[99] Thomas Carlyle, *Reminiscences*, edited by James Anthony Froude (New York: Charles Scribner's Sons, 1881), pp. 55-267.

and appeared in print for the first time in 1995. It is not known why it was never completed and published, but the essay still speaks for itself. (See appendix C.)

CARLYLE: THE DICTATORSHIP OF BRIGHAM YOUNG AS THE ANTIDOTE TO AMERICAN DEMOCRACY

Carlyle was deeply hostile to the United States and to the system of representative government in general. As a reactionary romanticist, he wanted institutions to evolve "organically," meaning that positive change would be either impossible or excruciatingly slow. Carlyle's fascination with the dictatorial regime of Brigham Young is that it had been created in the midst of the hyper-democratic American society of the Jacksonian era, where free speech and other political freedoms were available to many. Democracy had brought forth tyranny. Mormonism he considered better than other religions because it was openly dictatorial and theocratic, and did not pretend to be a democracy:

> Mormonism is a gross physical form of Calvinism; Gross, physical and in many ways very base; but in this one incommensurably (transcendently) superior to all other forms of religion now extant. That it is believed, that it is practically acted upon from day to day and from hour to hour; taken as a very fact, the neglect or contradiction of which will vitiate and ruin all other facts of the day and of the hour. That is its immeasurable superiority; in virtue of that it has still a root in this feracious [fruitful] Earth, and prospers as we see.[100]

Carlyle harped on the notion that democratic institutions were necessarily slow and inefficient, and not adept at getting things done. He would have applauded Mussolini crushing unions and stripping Italians of their political rights, while famously making the trains run on time. He would have endorsed Mayor Giuliani of New York when he decided to conceal the problems of homelessness and poverty by ordering the police to drive panhandlers off the streets. Carlyle hated the notion of a democratic republic because it was not sufficiently aristocratic, although he had to camouflage his aristocratic prejudices behind a meritocratic façade. He also tried to show that democratic elections generally failed to select the most capable leaders for purposes of governing:

> Mormonism illustrates: 1° The value of sincerity towards one's convictions (as above); 2° it offers a good illustration of the mixture of Despotism and Liberty, – indicates, in dim rude outline, what a perfect Form of Government may be which men are several universally groping after at present. Here, sure enough, is Liberty: all these people are free citizens, to begin with; members

[100] Clyde de L. Ryals, "Thomas Carlyle and the Mormons: an Unpublished Essay," *Carlyle Studies Annual* XIV (1995), pp. 48-55. Ryals comments: " Thomas Carlyle's essay on the Mormons, unpublished during his lifetime, reflects a surprising sympathy with the religious sect that had first come to Britain from the United States in 1837 and had grown to an extent that a decade later one out of every three members of the Latter-day Saints was British. Carlyle was impressed by the sect's hierarchical administration dominated by a strong leader, the earnestness of belief on the part of its adherents, and their total dedication to it, even to the point of death." See Mark Cumming, ed., *The Carlyle Encyclopedia*, article by Ryals on "Mormons."

of the model republic: entitled to the ballot box, caucus, free press, open vestry, open congress, fourth estate and every form of opposition, conceivable by the human mind. – nothing to limit whatever mutiny may be in them except the universal parish-constable, speaking symbolically. 'Hands *not* in each other's pockets; hands off each other's skins!' To this degree of liberty, unsurpassable even by fancy they were all born; to this any time they can appeal, and practically return, with themselves and all their interests.

At the time he wrote this draft essay, he was working on his biography of King Frederick the Great of Prussia, whom he subsumed into his general theory of history based on charismatic heroes and hero worship. Carlyle was also a great admirer of the Puritan dictator Oliver Cromwell, and he must have seen the strong similarities between Cromwell and Brigham Young. Carlyle felt that British society was plagued by hypocrisy and was therefore not producing the true heroic type.

CARLYLE: BRIGHAM YOUNG MORE ABSOLUTE THAN THE CZAR OF RUSSIA

Because of his feudal and oligarchical mentality, Carlyle was violently opposed to industrialism, and to the prestige acquired by industrialists in society, at the expense of the traditional landed aristocrats and their pseudo-paternalistic values. He was obsessed with tearing down the industrialist George Hudson, known as the "Railway King," who built several rail lines before going bankrupt when his speculative investments collapsed. Carlyle used Hudson as an example of the bogus hero of modern times, and contrasted him with the true heroes of previous eras. Carlyle celebrated Brigham Young as a beneficent despot, the prototype of a new form of reactionary dictatorship capable of leading mankind out of the social crisis of the 19th century:

> But the curious point is to see Despotism withal. No Czar of Russia is so absolute as Joseph Smith's successor…. Here then is a 'beneficent Despotism': a thing much in request with some among us, but impossible to discover hitherto by any hustings manipulation, or other constitutional apparatus. The question. How it is got there, is very well worth meditating, and will lead a man's thoughts into many reflections not quite common to the general mind at present.

Carlyle, already thinking in terms of fascism, welcomed the existence of Mormonism as a theocratic dictatorship on the North American continent, implacably opposed to the American democratic republic. It is clear that he hoped that the principle of theocratic dictatorship would overcome and supplant the democratic republic. The Mormons, he argued, have to be a dictatorship because they are constantly under siege, a situation which Carlyle evoked using the terminology of social Darwinism:

> "But alas the Mormons have several advantages in choosing their King, in which we European men are still sadly behind them. First they had the conviction that wisdom is necessary; that it will be a sin, nay the chief fountain of sins, if the Fittest Mormon is not got to the top of Mormonism: sin which God will assuredly punish; – and indeed it is too plain to me that the

very laws of Nature, as we call them, do protest daily and hourly against any other than the Fittest being put to the top in anything what ever, especially in Society which is the summary of things."

Carlyle imagines that Mormonism can attain a harmony of will between the ruler and ruled, which is far from the partisan clash of government and opposition in a parliamentary system. Carlyle wanted charismatic leaders with absolute powers to carry out what he imagined as a conservative revolution in reaction against constitutional democracy and industrial development. Many of his ideas later came to form the basis for European fascism. At various points he gets very close to a fascist *Führerprinzip*, and this is what he thinks he sees in Brigham Young.

> "Being in earnest about this preliminary part is probably the chief secret of the Mormon success in getting their Fittest Man. And a second head of advantage to them, their getting a beneficent despot in their Fittest follows out of this first one, or is almost only the first one over again. The Mormon Government is supreme in Mormon Conviction; what he does and orders is what every good Mormon is longing to see done. That is the secret of just despotism, of a Despotism which can be called beneficent. The few wise are all for it; None but the insincere and unwise are against it – and these are not so given up to their many insincerities and cowardices and unwisdoms as not to be amenable when better is shown to them. Joseph Smith's successor has his Council of Elders, Inspectors, Deacons etc. etc. – an actual Aristocracy sufficient for the nonce. All proceeding from sincerity on the part of his people. A government that fills us with envy."[101]

Another affinity felt by Carlyle for the Mormons could well have been the racism they shared. Carlyle's *Latter-Day Pamphlets* became infamous for their contention that black people in Jamaica and the Caribbean were parasitical: Carlisle saw the British West Indies ("our Black West Indies") as the embodiment of the "lazy refusal to work." Carlyle's "Occasional Discourse on the N****r Question" scandalized even less vehement racists. Carlyle praised "heroic white men" and said he wanted "to abolish the abuses of slavery, and save the precious thing in it."[102]

BRIGHAM YOUNG, PARLEY PRATT, AND THE TWELVE APOSTLES IN ENGLAND

Most historiography about the Mormons concentrates almost exclusively on events in and around Salt Lake City and Utah, but it should always be recalled that Great Britain was in many ways the other leg of Mormonism, indispensable for its recruiting, finance, and world influence. For example, by 1855 the Utah Territory had 60,000 people and Salt Lake City had a population of about 15,000, most of whom were Mormons. But, by

---

[101] Clyde de L. Ryals, "Thomas Carlyle and the Mormons: an Unpublished Essay," *Carlyle Studies Annual* XIV (1995), pp. 48-55.
[102] Paul E. Kerry, "Thomas Carlyle's Draft Essay on the Mormons," *Literature and Belief* 25:1.

July 1853 there were almost 31,000 Mormons in Great Britain, and the Mormon weekly newspaper, the *Millennial Star*, had a press run of over 25,000 copies.[103]

In 1837, two years after having been contacted by Reverend Hewitt, Joseph Smith sent two of his top lieutenants, Heber Kimball and Romney's great-great-great uncle Orson Pratt, to Great Britain. About two years later, soon after Brigham Young had established his family in Nauvoo in 1839, Joseph Smith announced that he had received a revelation from God telling him that it was now imperative to spread the doctrine of Mormonism in Great Britain. Brigham Young, although ill, immediately obeyed the Prophet's order to leave for Britain. As Brigham and other apostles departed, they cheered "Hurrah, hurrah, hurrah for Israel!" Brigham Young left his family behind, and his wives and children were soon destitute. More than legend has it that Brigham and his associates financed their trip to England by fund-raising on the way. Brigham recounted later in life that whenever he traveled in the service of the Faith, he would put his hand in his pocket and always find some money, evidently as a gift of God. One wag suggested that Brigham was not putting his hand into his own pocket, but into somebody else's.[104]

In England, Brigham Young produced a British edition of the *Book of Mormon*. He started a weekly newspaper, *The Millennial Star*, under the editorship of Mitt Romney's ancestor Parley P. Pratt. There was a recruiting meeting virtually every day in some parts of England, with the largest number of new converts coming at the expense of the Methodists, whose clergy lodged complaints which mysteriously went nowhere, suggesting support in high places. Werner writes that "Brigham Young and his associates established branches of Mormonism in most of the large towns and cities, converted 8,000 people, sending 1,000 of them to Nauvoo, and published 5,000 copies of the *Book of Mormon*, 3,000 hymn books, and 50,000 tracts." They also established a travel agency for converts who wanted to emigrate to the New Zion.[105] The main foci of this activity were places like Liverpool and Manchester, in the north of England. London, by contrast, proved to be a difficult place to recruit new members. Before long, the Mormon Church had more members from England, Scotland, and Wales than from the United States. This made it easier for the Mormon Saints to act like the foreign body they were on the borders of the new American Republic.

JOSEPH SMITH'S PLAN TO CONVERT QUEEN VICTORIA

Werner points out that Brigham Young's recruiting machine was during his lifetime "the most extensive source of converts to Mormonism." Before long, Joseph Smith had a megalomaniac vision that he could convert Queen Victoria and Prince Albert to Mormonism. He sent an order to Elder Lorenzo Snow to deliver copies of the *Book of Mormon* to Buckingham Palace. He even thought Victoria and Albert might decide to leave London and make the journey to the rude frontier village of Nauvoo, Illinois. But this went far beyond the tasks which the British establishment had in mind for the Mormon Saints.

---

[103] Hirshson, p, 138.

[104] Werner, *Brigham Young* (New York: Harcourt, Brace, 1925), p. 110.

[105] Werner, p. 111.

But that did not stop Eliza Snow, the resident poetaster of the Mormon Church, from waxing poetic on the perspective of Queen Victoria and the Prince Consort declaring open support for the Latter-day Saints:

> "Oh! Would she now her influence lend –
> The influence of royalty –
> Messiah's kingdom to extend,
> And Zion's nursing mother be,
> Then with the glory of her name
> Inscribed on Zion's lofty spire,
> She'd win a wreath of endless fame,
> To last when other wreaths expire."[106]

Naturally, Queen Victoria, as head of the established Anglican Church of England, never openly embraced Mormonism. But Joseph Smith's idea that he could convert the British royal family, and the propaganda exercises generated by the Mormons around this perspective, give us an idea of how closely the Mormon Saints felt themselves to be allied to the British monarchy – an institution which most Americans of their time held in deserved contempt. For much of the 19th century, the LDS has to be considered as the agency of a hostile, foreign, imperialist power – London. Whereas Americans regarded Great Britain with grave suspicion, the Mormon Saints were enthusiastic about their British alliance.

JOSEPH SMITH, THE BRITISH ISRAELITES, AND LORD PALMERSTON'S POLICY TOWARDS THE OTTOMAN EMPIRE

One book which is often mentioned as a possible source for the *Book of Mormon* is the 1823 *View of the Hebrews* by Ethan Smith (apparently no relation to Joseph Smith). Ethan Smith was from Poultney, Vermont, where he had been the minister in a Congregational church attended by Oliver Cowdery, who was one of the stenographers used by Joseph Smith in compiling the *Book of Mormon*. The thesis of this book lies that the American Indians were the descendents of one of the Ten Lost Tribes of Israel. An alternative view, which was popular in Great Britain at this time, was that the inhabitants of the British Isles were in fact the true descendents of the Ten Lost Tribes of Israel.

Joseph Smith imagined the end of the world as the culmination of a two-pronged process. On the one hand, the Mormons would gather into their New Zion – whatever that happened to be – the remnants of Israel which could be found in the British Isles, northern Europe, and among the Lamanites or American Indians. At the same time, a parallel concentration was supposed to result in the transfer of Jewish populations into Palestine. This latter process was being sponsored by Lord Palmerston and other British colonial strategists as a key part of their destabilization of the Ottoman Empire, which at this time held Jerusalem and the nearby holy places.

---

[106] Werner, p. 113.

In 1840, after most of the Quorum of Twelve had transferred their operations to Britain, Joseph Smith detailed Orson Hyde to travel to Jerusalem and to report on the ingathering of the Jews. Smith asked John Page to accompany Hyde. (Bushman, p. 407) According to Bushman, "Joseph was enthralled with Israel's destiny." He believed that those who assisted the ingathering of the Jews to Palestine would receive a special reward, assuring Hyde and Page that "'those engaged in seeking the outcasts of Israel,' he wrote Hyde and Page, 'cannot fail to enjoy the Spirit of the Lord, and have the choicest blessings of Heaven rest upon them in copious effusions.'" (Bushman, p. 408)

Hyde reached Liverpool in February, 1841 and wrote to Solomon Hirschel, the Grand Rabbi of London, urging him to start the mass migration of Jews to the Holy Land. (Bushman, p. 408) Hyde reached Jerusalem in October 1841, where he found a population of 7,000 Jews. He climbed to the top of the Mount of Olives and composed a prayer "to dedicate and consecrate this land . . . for the gathering together of Judah's scattered remnants." Hyde also prayed to "restore the kingdom unto Israel—raise up Jerusalem as its capital, and constitute her people a distinct nation and government" under a king from the House of David. Hyde assembled a pile of stones on the Mount of Olives and another on Mount Zion to mark the Mormon commitment to Zionism. (Bushman, p. 408)

J. S. MILL: A *CIVILIZADE* AGAINST MORMONDOM WOULD BE TYRANNY

John Stuart Mill of the infamous East India Company family was a direct disciple of Jeremy Bentham, the *de facto* leader of British intelligence during the French Revolution and the Napoleonic wars. Mill showed a decided sympathy for the Mormons. In his famous treatise, *On Liberty* (1859) he deplored the "persecution" of Mormonism.

> "I cannot refrain from adding to these examples of the little account commonly made of human liberty, the language of downright persecution which breaks out from the press of this country, whenever it feels called on to notice the remarkable phenomenon of Mormonism. Much might be said on the unexpected and instructive fact, that an alleged new revelation, and a religion founded on it, the product of a palpable imposture, not even supported by the prestige of extraordinary qualities in its founder, is believed by hundreds of thousands, and has been made the foundation of a society, in the age of newspapers, railways, and the electric telegraph,

> "What here concerns us is, that this religion, like other and better religions, has its martyrs; that its prophet and founder was, for his teaching, put to death by a mob; that others of its adherents lost their lives by the same lawless violence; that they were forcibly expelled, in a body, from the country in which they first grew up; while, now that they have been chased into a solitary recess in the midst of the desert, many in this country openly declare that it would be right (only that it is not convenient) to send an expedition against them, and compel them by force to conform to the opinions of other people. The article of the Mormonite doctrine which is the chief provocative

to the antipathy which thus breaks through the ordinary restraints of religious tolerance, is its sanction of polygamy; which, though permitted to the Mohammedans, and Hindus, and Chinese, seems to excite unquenchable animosity when practiced by persons who speak English, and profess to be a kind of Christians.

"No one has a deeper disapprobation than I have of this Mormon institution; both for other reasons, and because, far from being in any way countenanced by the principle of liberty, it is a direct infraction of that principle, being a mere riveting of the chains of one half of the community, and an emancipation of the other from reciprocity of obligation towards them. Still, it must be remembered that this relation is as much a voluntary [act] on the part of the women concerned in it, who may be deemed the sufferers by it, as is the case with any other form of the marriage institution; and however surprising this fact may appear, it has its explanation in the common ideas and customs of the world, which teaching women to think marriage the one thing needful, make it intelligible that many a woman should prefer being one of several wives, to not being a wife at all. Other countries are not asked to recognize such unions, or release any portion of their inhabitants from their own laws on the score of Mormonite opinions.

"But when the dissentients have conceded to the hostile sentiments of others, far more than could justly be demanded; when they have left the countries to which their doctrines were unacceptable, and established themselves in a remote corner of the earth, which they have been the first to render habitable by human beings; it is difficult to see on what principles but those of tyranny they can be prevented from living there under what laws they please, provided they commit no aggression on other nations, and allow perfect freedom of departure to those who are dissatisfied with their ways.

"A recent writer, in some respects of considerable merit, proposes (to use his own words) not a crusade, but a *civilizade*, against this polygamist community, to put an end to what seems to him a retrograde step in civilization.[107] It also appears so to me, but I am not aware that any community has a right to force another to be civilized. So long as the sufferers by the bad law do not invoke assistance from other communities, I cannot admit that persons entirely unconnected with them ought to step in and require that a condition of things with which all who are directly interested appear to be satisfied, should put an end to it because it is a scandal to persons some thousands of miles distant, who have no part or concern in it. Let them send missionaries, if they please, to preach against it; and let them, by any fair means (of which silencing the teachers is not one), oppose the progress of similar doctrines among their own people.

---

[107] For the *civilizade*, see Thomas Taylor Meadows, *The Chinese and Their Rebellions* and *An Essay on Civilization* (London: Smith, Elder, 1856), p. 544. This work is interesting for its comparison between Mormondom and the Middle Kingdom.

"If civilization has got the better of barbarism when barbarism had the world to itself, it is too much to profess to be afraid lest barbarism, after having been fairly got under, should revive and conquer civilization. A civilization that can thus succumb to its vanquished enemy, must first have become so degenerate, that neither its appointed priests and teachers, nor anybody else, has the capacity, or will take the trouble, to stand up for it. If this be so, the sooner such a civilization receives notice to quit, the better. It can only go on from bad to worse, until destroyed and regenerated (like the Western Empire) by energetic barbarians."

Notice that Mill is arguing that it is better to permit the collapse of civilization than to compel a community of fanatics to give up flagrant abuses. Clearly, in a debate between Saint Augustine and the Donatists, Mill would take the side of the Donatists. But Mill is throwing out the window even his own dubious criteria about when society is justified in interfering with the activities of individuals. According to Mill, interference with individuals is justified only when their behavior causes harm to others. This is clearly the case with polygamy, the issue which Mill here refuses seriously to consider. Mill undoubtedly knew that Deseret was an oppressive dictatorship, enforced by a Danite reign of terror. Lurid tabloid stories of women desperately attempting to escape from the harem of Brigham Young were already circulating widely. He is also not interested in the issue of little girls being forced into marriages with men old enough to be their grandfathers.[108]

Most of all, Mill is utterly contemptuous of the sovereignty of the United States. He seems to think that America is so big that anybody who wants to can carve out a vast area and set up an independent theocracy. Mill clearly acted in bad faith, anxious to foment a Mormon rebellion which only one year earlier had brought the United States to civil war. If the Mormons could cut off US travel and communications to California, Mill would be delighted. Would he say the same thing if the Mormons had decided to take over the county of Northumberland or Scapa Flow and set up the Kingdom of God in an area of strategic importance for the British Empire? Surely not. Mill was, as usual, in bad faith.

CHARLES DICKENS PRAISES MORMONS, DOWNPLAYS POLYGAMY

Charles Dickens, who generally hated everything American, became to some extent a fan of Mormonism – perhaps because Mormonism is so fundamentally anti-American. In an article originally published in his magazine *All the Year Round*, Dickens relates that in June 1863 (one of the moments when the United States and the British Empire were moving towards war over ironclad warships, which the UK's Laird shipyard was building for the Confederacy), the famous writer went to visit the steamer *Amazon* in London Harbor, and got to know its many Mormon passengers who were about to leave for North America. Dickens says that his purpose was "to see what 800 Latter-day Saints were like." He admits that he started with a negative impression of the Mormons, since he

---

[108] See Bruce Baum, "Feminism, Liberalism and Cultural Pluralism: J. S. Mill on Mormon Polygyny," *The Journal of Political Philosophy*, vol. 5, number 3, 1997, pp. 230-253.

"went aboard their ship to bear testimony against them if they deserved it, as I fully believe they would." But instead, he was favorably impressed by the seriousness, calm, literacy, and organizational discipline of the Mormon passengers he found on the boat. His observations thus caused "the rout and overthrow of all my expectations." Far from being inferior, Dickens discovered that the Mormons were, "in their degree" "the pick and flower of England."[109] "I went over the *Amazon*'s side, feeling it impossible to deny that, so far, some remarkable influence had produced a remarkable result which better known influences have often missed."[110] Dickens later reprinted this account in his collection, *The Uncommercial Traveler*.

Dickens also tried to downplay the issue of polygamy among the passengers of the *Amazon*: "that they had any distinct notions of a plurality of husbands and wives, I do not believe. To suppose the family groups of whom the majority of emigrants were composed, polygamically possessed, would be to suppose an absurdity, manifest to any who sought the fathers and mothers."[111]

BRITISH PARLIAMENT FAVORS MORMON SAINTS

Dickens added that he had talked about the Mormons with the well-known essayist Richard Monckton Milnes (Lord Houghton), who had an article of his own about the Mormons in January, 1862, in one of the flagship magazines of the British establishment, *The Edinburgh Review*. This was a review of the description of the Mormons published by Sir Richard Burton, the famous British Orientalist and intelligencer. Milnes was also exceedingly favorable to the Mormons, citing an 1854 report by the House of Commons about the Mormon program for transatlantic migration of new converts. Milnes reported that the British Parliament was also very much on the side of the Mormon Saints. Their report had declared:

> "The Select Committee of the House Of Commons on immigrant ships for 1854 summoned the Mormon agent and passenger broker before it, and came to the conclusion that no ships under the provisions of the "Passengers Act" could be depended on for comfort and security in the same degree as those under his administration.... The Mormon ship is a Family under strong and accepted discipline, with every provision for comfort, decorum and internal peace."[112]

This inquiry reminds us of so many recent whitewashes of outrageous crimes, like the death of weapons expert David Kelley, issued by the British Parliament. Even a cursory reading of the account by Dickens tells the story of a distraught mother who came on board the *Amazon* looking for her daughter, who had "run away with the Mormons." She

---

[109] Paul E. Kerry, "Thomas Carlyle's Draft Essay on the Mormons," *Literature and Belief* 25:1-2, 2005.
[110] Charles Dickens, *The Uncommercial Traveler* (New York: Hurd and Houghton, 1873), p. 326
[111] Dickens, p. 311-312.
[112] Paul E. Kerry, "Thomas Carlyle's Draft Essay on the Mormons," *Literature and Belief* 25:1-2, 2005.

did not find her, and Dickens was forced to concede that "the Saints did not seem to me particularly interested in finding her."[113]

JOSEPH SMITH'S SECOND ANTI-AMERICAN CRISIS PROPHECY – JANUARY 4, 1833

In his book *The Cleansing of America*, a compendium of Mormon apocalyptic thought, the late W. Cleon Skousen stresses that "Joseph Smith knew there would be two great crises in American history." Skousen saw the first as the Civil War, and the second as still located in the future as seen from the early 21st century.

We have already seen Joseph Smith's famous Civil War Prophecy of 1832. Here is what Skousen calls the Second Crisis Prophecy of 1833:

> "...I am prepared to say by the authority of Jesus Christ, that not many years shall pass away before the United States shall present such a scene of bloodshed as has not a parallel in the history of our nation; pestilence, hail, famine, and the earthquake will sweep the wicked of this generation from off the face of the land, to open and prepare the way for the return of the lost tribes of Israel from the North country.... Repent ye, repent ye, and embrace the everlasting covenant, and flee to Zion before the overflowing scourge overtakes you."[114]

Skousen comments: "notice that in the Civil War, the military conflict took upwards of 600,000 lives, but the nation survived. In the subsequent crisis incidental to the cleansing of America, Joseph Smith speaks of an 'overflowing scourge' that will depopulate much of the nation and be accompanied by 'pestilence, hail, famine, and earthquake.' This ominous prophecy remains to be fulfilled sometime in the future."[115]

Cleon Skousen's last work was a warning to "The Gentiles" and a call to prepare the Kingdom of God on earth, much in the tradition of Joseph Smith and Brigham Young. Skousen's program includes "the restoration of the Constitution, the adoption of God's law, the introduction of a Zion Society under the law of consecration with individual stewardship, the great last gathering of Israel, the coming of the ten tribes, and the building of the New Jerusalem."[116]

Apocalyptic fantasies against the United States have always been a staple of the Mormon outlook. As Lukács famously warned, every prediction of the end of the world has a very specific class content. In many of these, the element of gloating or *Schadenfreude* is markedly present. Take for example the vision attributed by Skousen to top Mormon

---

[113] Dickens, p. 313.
[114] *Teachings of the Prophet Joseph Smith*, Section One 1830-1834. Doctrinal History of the Church I: 315, cited by Skousen
[115] W. Cleon Skousen, *The Cleansing of America* (Orem UT: Valor Publishing Group), online preview at books.google.com.
[116] Skousen, Ibid.

leader and Britisher John Taylor, successor to Brigham Young as the First President of the church, which he experienced in the night of December 16, 1877.

MORMONS SEE APOCALYPSE FOR US

In Taylor's vision, most of the houses in America had a badge of mourning on the door. The railroads and the roads had collapsed, but the roads were full of refugees carrying bundles and seeking to make their way to the Intermountain West. In deserted Washington, DC, the halls of Congress and the White House were empty, and everything was in ruins. In downtown Baltimore, "the dead piled up so high as to fill the square." The waters of the Chesapeake Bay stank of the putrefying flesh of dead bodies. Philadelphia was equally abandoned and filled with the stench of death. New York was in ruins. Every city in the United States had been destroyed, and most of the population wiped out. Missouri, Illinois, and part of Iowa were singled out for special punishment, with most human life extirpated. But near Independence, Missouri, Taylor saw twelve men in robes representing the twelve gates of the New Jerusalem. Refugees were arriving to help build the temple. When Taylor awoke from his trance, he was back in Utah.

Another Mormon ideologue was Orson Pratt, who figures in Mitt Romney's family tree. Pratt had a vision that the "great, powerful and populous city of New York… within a few years become a mass of ruins. The people will wonder while gazing on the ruins that cost hundreds of millions to build, what has become of its inhabitants." [117] This same apocalyptic spirit has been projected into the realm of Fox News Channel and of cable television by the recent rantings of the Mormon convert and true believer, Glenn Beck.

"JOSEPH SMITH OR THE SWORD" –
"ONE GORE OF BLOOD FROM THE ROCKIES TO THE ATLANTIC OCEAN"

In the summer of 1838, the Mormons were in bitter conflict with their neighbors in northwest Missouri. Groups of proslavery Missouri Border Ruffians were frequently clashing with the Mormon Danite militia. In a climate of great tension, Joseph Smith and his deputy Sidney Rigdon presided over a meeting of Mormon Saints for the purpose of discussing self-defense and military measures. Joseph Smith led off the proceedings by proposing that all lukewarm or vacillating Mormons who had failed to attend the gathering should be stripped of all their property. The crazed Rigdon, anxious to go one better, demanded that "blood of the backward be spilled in the streets" – meaning that the halfhearted Mormons should be physically liquidated.

Joseph Smith urged his followers to loot the border ruffians in retaliation for the depredations which the Mormon Saints had suffered in Missouri. Joseph Smith then continued with a violent outburst:

> "If the people will let us alone, we will preach the gospel in peace. But if
> they come on us to molest us, we will establish our religion by the sword. We

---

[117] W. Cleon Skousen, *The Cleansing of America*, online preview at books.google.com.

will trample down our enemies and make it one gore of blood from the Rocky Mountains to the Atlantic Ocean. I will be to this generation a second Mohammed, whose motto in treating for peace was 'the Alcoran or the Sword.' So shall it eventually be with us – 'Joseph Smith or the Sword!'"[118]

JOSEPH SMITH'S WHITE HORSE PROPHECY FOR MORMON COUP, MAY, 1843

According to Mormon accounts, Joseph Smith delivered an important prophecy in May of 1843 in the presence of his adepts Edwin Rushton and Theodore Turley. There are several written versions of this pronouncement, recorded in later years. The most detailed version comes from the diary of John Roberts of Paradise, Utah in an entry dated March 2, 1902. This has become known as the White Horse Prophecy. The LDS authorities have always been uneasy with the political implications of this statement, and so they have relegated it among the esoteric or "shelf doctrines" which circulate among the top leadership, but are not considered suitable for official public distribution or comment.

On May 6, 1843 Joseph Smith presided over a Grand Review of the Nauvoo Legion, his private army. On this occasion, he drank a threatening toast, inveighing against the Mobocrats and Gentiles of the surrounding counties: "I will drink a toast to the overthrow of the mobocrats…here's wishing they were in the middle of the sea in a stone canoe with iron paddles and that a shark swallowed the canoe and the Devil swallowed the shark and himself locked up in the northwest corner of Hell, the key lost and a blind man hunting it."[119]

The next day, after clashing with a critic of Mormonism over this toast, Joseph Smith took Rushton and Turley aside, and began to prophesy.

> "I want to tell you something of the future. I will speak in a parable like unto John the Revelator. You will go to the Rocky Mountains and you will be a great and mighty people established there, which I will call the White Horse of peace and safety."

The Prophet conceded that he himself (no doubt on the model of Moses) would never see this promised land. The Mormon exodus to the Rocky Mountains would be predicated on a continued pattern of persecution by the American Gentiles: "Your enemies will continue to follow you with persecutions and they will make obnoxious laws against you in Congress to destroy the White Horse, but you will have a friend or two to defend you to throw out the worst parts of the laws, so they will not hurt you so much." He instructed the Mormons to maintain their political pressure on Congress, even in the absence of immediate positive results: "you must continue to petition Congress all the

---

[118] *History of the Church*, vol. 3, p. 167..
[119] Future Prophecies Revealed at FutureRevealed.com. According to George Cobabe, "The White Horse Prophecy," online at FAIRLDS.org, original text is in John J. Roberts, *Reminiscences and Diaries 1898-1902*, microfilm manuscript, Church History Library, Salt Lake City Utah.

time, but they will treat you like strangers and aliens and they will not give you your rights, but will govern you with strangers and commissioners."

There follow the words which have become a central part of the insider folklore of the Mormon community. They contain the idea that, in a grave future crisis of the United States government, the Mormons will save the country by concentrating all political power in their own hands:

> "...you will see the Constitution of the United States almost destroyed. It will hang like a thread as fine as a silk fiber."

This trope of the Constitution hanging by a thread has become a staple of Mormon rhetoric. Is it also one of the unspoken premises of the Mitt Romney presidential campaign?

THE MORMON WHITE HORSE ALLIES WITH THE RED HORSE OF THE BRITISH EMPIRE

Putting on a long face, the Prophet continued: "I love the Constitution: it was made by the inspiration of God; and it will be preserved and saved by the efforts of the White Horse, and by the Red Horse who will combine in its defense." Here is another staple component of reactionary and proto-fascist rhetoric, which has become a favorite especially among the Austrians or self-styled libertarians. We will see it again coming from Brigham Young. It is the idea that one can hate and revile the United States government and all of its policies and officials, virtually without exception, while at the same time loudly professing a total devotion to the Constitution. Here we can see the deep ideological linkage of the Mormons with the Ron Paul libertarians. The idea of the Mormons combining with British imperialism to defend the U.S. Constitution is absurd, a hallucination.

During a Florida Republican presidential debate, Romney advanced the interpretation that the US Declaration of Independence is a universal or theological document, not limited in scope to the specifics of the American Revolution, but rather creating a "covenant between God and man."[120]

As for the Red Horse, Joseph Smith is here expressing the alliance of the Mormons to the British Empire, against the United States. To clear up any possible doubt about this, we can skip ahead to a later passage of the same White Horse Prophecy, where we read:

> "... one of the peculiar features in England is the established Red-coat; a uniform making so remarkable a target to shoot at, and yet they have conquered wherever they have gone. The reason for this will be known to them some day as red is seen in different colors threading through under all

---

[120] Sally Denton, "Romney and the White Horse Prophecy: a close look at the roots of Romney's – and the Mormon Church's – political ambitions" (Salon.com, January 29, 2012).

history. The lion and the unicorn of England come from their being so much blood of Israel in the nation."

The Red Horse is thus the power of the London oligarchy, with an included nod to the British Israelites, a school of thought which had been launched by Richard Brothers in 1794. This is the doctrine that the population of the British Isles are the direct descendents of the Ten Lost Tribes of Israel. Joseph Smith was alleged to be a descendent of the Hebrew patriarch Ephraim, and Mormons are assigned membership in one of the tribes of Israel, so that they may be gathered in during the last days. These beliefs provide a background for the Romney-Netanyahu alliance.

JOSEPH SMITH FORECASTS WORLD FINANCIAL PANIC

Continuing with his prophecy, Joseph Smith – interested as always in money-digging – predicted that the Mormons would get rich through mining in the Rocky Mountains: "...the White Horse will find the mountains full of minerals and they will become rich. You will see silver piled up in the streets, you will see the gold shoveled up like sand." At this time, the great California gold rush that started at Sutter's Mill in 1848 was still a decade and a half in the future, so this passage may represent an intelligence nugget designed by some well-informed agency to burnish Holy Joe's prophetic credentials.

But a crisis was coming in which survival, and not gold, would be the issue: "...gold will be of little value then, even in the mercantile capacity; for the people of the world will have something else to do in seeking for salvation. The time will come when the banks of every nation will fail and only two places will be safe where people can deposit their gold and treasure. This place will be the White Horse and England's vaults." Joseph Smith's rhetoric has much in common, not just with the apocalyptic preachings of our time, but also with clever sales pitches of merchants offering overpriced gold to gullible Austrian-school libertarians.

After the financial crisis, a political calamity will begin, and soon refugees will be streaming into the Rocky Mountains to take refuge with the Saints:

> "A terrible revolution will take place in the land of America, such as has never been seen before; for the land will be left without a Supreme Government, and every specie [sic] of wickedness will be practiced in the land. Father will be against son and son against father; mother against daughter and daughter against mother. The most terrible scenes of bloodshed, murder and rape that have ever been imagined or looked upon will take place. People will be taken from the earth and there will be peace and love only in the Rocky Mountains. This will cause many hundreds of thousands of the honest in heart of the world to gather there, not because they would be Saints, but for safety and because they will be so numerous that you will be in danger of famine, but not for want of seed, time and harvest, but because of so many to be fed. Many will come with bundles under their arms to escape the calamities for there will be no escape except by escaping and fleeing to Zion.

Those that come to you will try to keep the laws and be one with you for they
will see your unity and the greatness of your organization."

At this point in the prophecy, Joseph Smith began delving into geopolitics, and
specifically into the Eastern Question – the rivalry of the great powers, and especially of
Great Britain and Russia, to expand their power in the Middle East and the eastern
Mediterranean at the expense of the moribund Ottoman Empire, otherwise known as the
Sick Man of Europe: "The Turkish Empire of the Crescent will be the first power to be
disputed, for freedom must be given for the Gospel to be preached in the Holy Land."
Once again, Joseph Smith makes clear his full support for the British Empire in its rivalry
with the Russian Empire, one of the central structural geopolitical contests of the entire
19th century. He even endorses the British self-conception as the balancer in a system of
playing off other nations and groups of nations one against the other:

> "The Lord took of the best blood of the nations and planted them on the small
> islands now called England and Great Britain and gave them power in the
> nation for a thousand years and their power will continue with them that they
> may keep the balance of power; and they will keep Russia from sweeping her
> power over the world."

Joseph Smith is also aware that, after the final defeat of Napoleon in 1815, and under the
July monarchy of King Louis Philippe which was in power at the time that he was
making this prophecy, France was functioning as a junior partner of the British Empire.
He noted that "England and France are now bitter enemies but they will be allied together
and be united to keep Russia from conquering the world. The two popes, Greek and
Catholic, will eventually come together in their decline and be united." The union of the
Vatican with the Greek patriarchy of Constantinople was a project of British intelligence
which never came to fruition. The mere mention of it suggests the quality of the
intelligence which Joseph Smith was receiving from the City of London.

JOSEPH SMITH'S ADMIRATION FOR KING HENRY VIII OF ENGLAND

Joseph Smith cannot hide his admiration for the murderous psychopath King Henry VIII
of England, the monarch who had six wives – although not all at the same time – and
killed several of them while founding the Anglican or Episcopal church of England. In
doing these things, Henry VIII was profoundly influenced by advisers attuned to the
strategic goals of the Venetian Republic, the great power of diplomacy and intelligence at
the beginning of the 16th century. Joseph Smith also takes a polemical position against
the Roman Catholic Church: "The Protestant Religions do not know how much they are
indebted to Henry VIII for throwing off the Pope's bill [sic] and establishing the
Protestant faith. He was the only monarch who could do so at that time and he did it
because the nation was at his back to sustain him." The question is raised: Could a
Roman Catholic vote for Romney in good conscience?

In Joseph Smith's imagination, the Red Horse of Great Britain appears not as an agency
of empire and exploitation, but of beneficial action. This fantastic appraisal needs to be
contrasted to the prevailing and correct American view of the time, which regarded Great

Britain with much suspicion. Friedrich List stands out for his systematic critique of the destructive effects of British free trade. The Tory Prophet observes:

> "While the terrible things of which I have mentioned are going on, England will be neutral until it becomes so inhuman that she will interfere to stop the shedding of blood and history will be more properly understood. England and France would unite together to make peace, not to subdue the nations. She will find this nation [the United States] so broken up and so many claiming government, till there will be no reasonable government. Then it will appear to the other nations, or powers, as though England had taken possession of the country."

At this point, Joseph Smith introduces a new actor into his prophecy: this is the Black Horse. Mormon protestations to the contrary, there is no doubt that the Black Horse represents the Afro-American or black slaves of the United States, who in Mormon theology represent the descendents of those wretched spirits who refused to take sides in the struggle between the Mormon Jesus and the Mormon Lucifer. Joseph Smith foresees a slave rebellion in the US on the Haitian model, backed by the British:

> "The Black Horse will flee to the invaders and will join them for they have fear of becoming slaves again; knowing that England did not believe in slavery, they will flee to them that they believe will make them safe. Armed with British bayonets, the doings of the Black Horse will be terrible."

At this point, Joseph Smith paused in his prophecy, saying that he was overcome by the horror of this vision.

MORMONS SEE US AS PALE HORSE, BRINGER OF DEATH

We now find the ominous epithet "Pale Horse," the symbol of death, applied to the United States: The Pale Horse has traditionally appeared as one of the Four Horsemen of the Apocalypse in the Revelation of Saint John the Divine in the Christian Bible. The rider of the pale horse traditionally carries a bow and arrows, and is thought to represent pain and pestilence. This is a characteristic metaphor for Joseph Smith to use in describing the United States. Has this Mormon hostility to the United States abated, or is it still present consciously or subconsciously in figures like Mitt Romney? The Prophet went on:

> "During this time the Great White Horse will have gathered strength, sending out elders to gather the honest in heart from among the Pale Horse, or people of the United States, to stand by the Constitution of the United States as it was given by the inspiration of God. In these days which are yet to come God will set up a Kingdom never to be thrown down, but other Kingdoms to come into it, and those Kingdoms that will not let the Gospel be preached in their lands will be humbled until they will."

In other words, the Mormons will save the Constitution by creating an American theocracy which will conquer the world. Is this what Romney has in mind?

MORMON POWER TO ABSORB GREAT BRITAIN

The way out of the crisis will thus be opened by a massive buildup of Mormon power and influence. The gathering of the lost tribes of Israel will then take center stage:

> "England, Germany, Norway, Denmark, Switzerland, Holland and Belgium have a considerable amount of the blood of Israel among the people which must be gathered out. Those nations will submit to the nations of God [the Mormon power]. England will be the last of the nations to surrender, but when she does she will do it as a whole in comparison as she threw off the Catholic power. The nobility knows that the gospel is true, but it has not pump enough, and grandeur and influence for them to yet embrace it. They are proud and will not acknowledge the Kingdom of God or come into it until they see the power it will have."

This evidently foreshadows the merger of the Mormon power with the British Empire, but now with the Mormons as the senior partner. Apparently Joseph Smith regarded the Anglican High Church party, shortly to produce the Oxford Movement and the return to Rome of Cardinal Newman, as the key obstacle in this coming merger.

Under the world condominium of the Mormons and the British, a golden age will emerge, with its epicenter in the Rocky Mountains:

> "... peace and safety in the Rocky Mountains will be protected by the Guardians, the White and Red Horses. The coming of the Messiah among his people will be so natural that only those who see him will know that he has come, but he will come and give his laws on to Zion and minister unto his people. This will not be his coming in the clouds of heaven to take vengeance on the wicked of the world."

Is this who Romney thinks he is? Obama was certainly not lacking in messianic delusions, so there is no reason why Romney should not be asked about this.

In a prophecy which was not destined to be fulfilled, The Prophet further foretold that "temple in Jackson County, Missouri, will be built in that generation.... You will have... all the skilled mechanics you want and the Ten Tribes of Israel will help build it." This is once again perhaps an indication of help coming from Great Britain and northern Europe.

THE FINAL RECKONING WITH RUSSIA AND "THE HEATHEN CHINESE"

There were two last great enemies which Joseph Smith had to deal with: these were China and Russia, who, as always in British intelligence estimates, appear as hostile and threatening powers.

First, there was a threat of Chinese immigration to California: "There is a land beyond the Rocky Mountains that will be invaded by the heathen Chinese unless great care and protection be given. Where there is no law there is no condemnation; this will apply to them. Power will be given to the White Horse to rebuke the nations afar off and you obey it for the laws go forth from Zion."

Warding off the "heathen Chinese" was, however, only a prelude to the final apocalyptic struggle with Russia:

> "The last great struggle that Zion will ever have to contend with will be when the whole of America will be made the Zion of God. Those opposing will be called Gog and Magog. The nations of the earth will be led by the Russian Czar and his power will be great, but all opposition will be overcome and this land will be the Zion of our God. Amen.[121]

Mitt Romney has famously stated that Russia remains the "number one geopolitical foe" of the United States. Does Joseph Smith's White Horse Prophecy play a role in this strategic estimate?

In October 1918, the General Conference of the Latter-day Saints proclaimed that the White Horse Prophecy was "never spoken by the Prophet" and repudiated it. Of course, Joseph Smith and Brigham Young both denied that they were practicing polygamy at times in their lives when they knew that they were indeed doing so. The prophecy remains "on the shelf," held in abeyance until the proper moment.

ROMNEY EVASIVE ON WHITE HORSE PROPHECY

Mormon scholar George Cobabe also pronounced the White Horse Prophecy totally irrelevant. "I don't think the White Horse Prophecy is fair to bring up at all," said Cobabe. "It's been rejected by every church leader that has talked about it. It has nothing to do with anything."[122]

Strangely, Mitt Romney used exactly the same boiler plate, verbatim, in a 2008 interview with the *Salt Lake Tribune*. "I don't think the White Horse Prophecy is fair to bring up at all. It's been rejected by every church leader that has talked about it. It has nothing to do with anything," said Mitt. Was he working from Cobabe's text, or were they both quoting LDS talking points on how to deal with this potentially embarrassing subject?

As the *Mormon Coffee* blog ("It's forbidden, but it's good!") points out, there is also the embarrassing problem that Joseph Smith's religious and political heir, Brigham Young, repeatedly endorsed the White Horse Prophecy. One such moment came in 1855, when Brigham Young stated:

---

[121] Future Prophecies Revealed at FutureRevealed.com.
[122] See the Mormon Coffee blog of the Mormonism Research and Ministry at blog.mrm.com.

"And when the Constitution of the United States hangs, as it were, upon a single thread, they will have to call for the 'Mormon' Elders to save it from utter destruction; and they will step forth and do it."

In 1868, after the Civil War had ended, Brigham Young again showed his allegiance to the White Horse Prophecy:

"How long will it be before the words of the prophet Joseph will be fulfilled? He said if the Constitution of the United States were saved at all it must be done by this people. It will not be many years before these words come to pass"[123]

"IF NOT MITT, WHO?" – MITT ROMNEY, THE GREAT NEPHITE HOPE

As Sally Denton of salon.com points out, Romney grew up as the son of the celebrated George Romney, Governor of Michigan, Nixon cabinet official, presidential candidate, and the most famous Mormon politician in the United States. Romney was christened as Willard Mitt Romney in honor of the super-rich Mormon plutocrat, J. Willard Marriott. In 1970, when Romney's mother Lenore was campaigning against Philip Hart for a Michigan Senate seat, Romney was a member of the all male, lily-white, Cougar Club at Brigham Young University, named after the hardened traitor, British agent, and abuser of women we are getting to know in these pages. By this time, Romney had already served as assistant to the President of the LDS mission to France, which had over 200 missionaries in the field. As Denton recounts, the refrain of "If not Mitt, who?" was frequently heard among these rich Mormon elitists, and it meant that Mitt Romney was destined to fulfill Joseph Smith's vision of The White Horse.[124]

MITT ROMNEY: "ONE MIGHTY AND STRONG"?

According to Denton, Romney "at BYU was idolized by fellow students and referred to, only half jokingly, as the 'One Mighty and Strong.' He was the 'alpha male' in the rarefied Cougar pack, according to Michael D. Moody, a BYU classmate and fellow member of the group," in which young Mormon missionaries back from abroad were heavily represented. The expression "One Mighty and Strong" might represent a leader combining charisma and theocracy – a dangerous combination, as historical experience shows. This concept, it will come as no surprise, is rooted in visions of Joseph Smith. In a letter to his speechwriter William W. Phelps of November 27, 1832, the Prophet shared the following revelation, which he said he had received from Jesus Christ:

"It shall come to pass, that I, the Lord God, will send one mighty and strong, holding the sceptre of power in his hand, clothed with light for a covering, whose mouth shall utter words, eternal words; while his bowels shall be a

---

[123] Brigham Young, *Journal of Discourses*, 2:182 and 12:204, *Discourses of Brigham Young*, pp. 360-361, cited by blog.mrm.org.
[124] Sally Denton, "Romney and the White Horse Prophecy: a close look at the roots of Romney's – and the Mormon church's – political ambitions" (Salon.com, January 29, 2012).

fountain of truth, to set in order the house of God, and to arrange by lot the inheritances of the Saints, whose names are found, and the names of their fathers, and of their children enrolled in the book of the law of God: while that man, who was called of God and appointed, that putteth forth his hand to steady the ark of God, shall fall by the vivid shaft of lighting ... These things I say not of myself; therefore, as the Lord speaketh, He will also fulfill."[125]

Michael Moody, like Mitt Romney a BYU graduate and a prominent descendent of a family which has been part of Mormonism for seven generations, but unlike Romney now critical of Mormonism, recounts that he was indoctrinated on the need to carry out Joseph Smith's White Horse Prophecy. Moody says that the LDS Church attached great importance to having its members serve as important government officials. Moody received what amounts to a political commission as part of his Temple Endowment: "... the instructions in my [patriarchal] blessing, which I believed came directly from Jesus, motivated me to seek a career in government and politics," he relates. [126] In 1982, Moody, believing he had received a divine injunction to "expand our kingdom," ran for governor of Nevada. He was commanded to "lead the world into the millennium." "Moody was indoctrinated with the White Horse Prophecy," writes Denton. "We were taught that America is the Promised Land. The Mormons are the Chosen People. And the time is now for a Mormon leader to usher in the second coming of Christ and install the political Kingdom of God in Washington, DC," says Moody. [127]

Does such a seizure of power in Washington by the Saints under Romney's leadership constitute the long-awaited Mormon Moment, a time when legions of predatory, antinomian Mormons would seize control of the government and attempt to settle old scores, perhaps even going back to the 1844 assassination of Joseph Smith and his brother? You have been warned.

---

[125] Joseph Smith, *History of the Church*, ed. B. H. Roberts, vol. I, pp. 297-299.
[126] See Michael Moody, *Mitt, Set Our People Free!: A Seventh Generation Mormon's Plea for Truth* (Universe, 2008).
[127] Sally Denton, "Romney and the White Horse Prophecy: a close look at the roots of Romney's – and the Mormon church's – political ambitions" (Salon.com, January 29, 2012).

CHAPTER IV

SECESSION AND INSURRECTION: THE MORMON THEOCRACY OF BRIGHAM YOUNG DURING THE 1850s

"If the Mormons had behaved like other people, they would never have been driven from Illinois and Missouri; but they stole, robbed and plundered from all their neighbors, and all the time.'" – Former Mormon and Joseph Smith speechwriter William W. Phelps, (Hirshson, p. 63)

On the day that Joseph Smith and Hiram Smith were killed by the mob in Carthage, Illinois, Brigham Young was in Massachusetts campaigning for the election of the Prophet as president. A public meeting in Boston on July 1, 1844 which was addressed by Young, Lyman White, and Orson Hyde had not gone well, since "catcalls and hoots drowned out speeches...." (Hirshson, p. 48) The question immediately arose as to whether the gift of prophecy had departed from the Mormon Saints with the death of Joseph Smith, or whether the prophetic voice would continue to speak through another of the apostles. Did the LDS Church still possess the keys that would unlock or lock the kingdom of heaven? Brigham Young conferred with Mitt Romney's ancestor Orson Pratt, and soon proclaimed: "the keys of the kingdom are right here with the church.'" (Hirshson, p. 51) Naturally, Brigham Young was already preparing his own candidacy as the successor of Joseph Smith.

BRIGHAM YOUNG CHANNELS JOSEPH SMITH TO SEIZE POWER

A bitter faction fight soon followed. Brigham Young was able to dispose of the first challenge, which came from Sydney Rigdon, whose pre-Mormon career always set him apart from the tight clique of true believers. But there were still other contenders. Brigham Young was able to finally assert his primacy by using his already recognized ability as a mimic, capable of imitating the gestures and voice of other persons. Brigham Young's performance on August 8, 1844 was decisive, and became "perhaps the most famous in Mormon history." (Hirshson, p. 53) Brigham Young was able to convince the majority of those present that he was channeling the spirit of Joseph Smith, and therefore the role of successor ought to go to him. This then became an official theological dictum of the Mormon Saints: "The church insisted that at the meeting Joseph Smith occupied Young's person." (Hirshson, p. 53)

Brigham Young, like Joseph Smith, had been born in Vermont. He was an early recruit and loyal retainer. Much less interested than Joseph Smith in spirituality and doctrine, he made fewer theological pronouncements and recruited fewer converts than Mitt Romney's ancestor Parley Pratt. Like Stalin however, Brigham Young rose to the top because he was a consummate Organization Man. He had been sent by Joseph Smith to establish contact with the British, and he later made sure that his own son renewed these contacts. Brigham Young's face betrayed his brutal, carnal nature. He was given over to the passions of pride, rage, hatred, violence and vindictiveness. Charity, mercy, and pity played no role in his mentality. He loved strife. He was interested above all in power, with wealth coming in a close second. Polygamy he regarded as a means of power. Polygamy gave him power over individual women, and polygamy also allowed him to establish a cohesiveness in the Mormon community that allowed it to be impervious for many years to outside influence. In politics, he was a hardened traitor. These qualities allowed Brigham Young to successfully organize the wagon trains that carried the Mormons from Illinois to Salt Lake City. But his greed was also instrumental in creating the Mormon handcart debacle of 1857, which led to a political backlash against him.

After the Civil War, Brigham Young was trying to convince federal officials that he had always been on the side of the Union, which of course was not true. But he did this by announcing that he would have executed not just the Confederate diplomats Mason and Slidell, but every Confederate official he could get his hands on. Young "uttered this sentiment 'with such a wicked working of the lower jaw and lip, and such an almost demon-like spirit in his whole face, that quite disposed to be incredulous on those matters, I could not help thinking of the Mountain Meadows Massacre, of recusant Mormons, of Danites and Avenging Angels, and their reported achievements.'" (*Saints and the Union*, p. 265) Brigham Young was a man of blood, and the greatest terrorist in North America during the 19th century.

BRIGHAM YOUNG: MISOGYNY, RACISM, ANTI-SEMITISM

Brigham Young held women in contempt, and was an anti-black racist, as his contemptuous response to the Emancipation Proclamation will show clearly enough. The Mormon Moses also hated Jews, of whom he once said: "I would rather undertake to convert five thousand Lamanites [Indians] than to convert one of those poor miserable creatures whose fathers killed the Savior, and who say, 'Amen to the deed,' to this day. Yea, I would rather undertake to convert the devil himself, if it were possible.'" (Hirshson, p. 255) Brigham Young knew that he was hated, and that his life was often in danger from enemies within the Mormon camp. Accordingly, "when Young picnicked, he kept the place and time secret." (Hirshson, p. 249)

One of the hallmarks of Brigham Young's leadership was the systematic cultivation of a vendetta or blood feud by the Saints against the United States of America. This was expressed in the Oath of Vengeance, which Brigham Young inserted into the official Mormon temple endowment, or liturgy for divine service. This became the ideology of his theocratic regime. The leading lights of Mormons tried to outdo each other in making apocalyptic pronouncements about the utter doom and devastation which would soon overtake the ungrateful who had scorned and then murdered Joseph Smith, the Prophet of God.

MORMON ANTINOMIANISM: STEALING, RUSTLING, AND PLUNDERING

For the Mormons succumbed to the temptation of idealizing their own conduct, while demonizing that of their neighbors. Two recent scholars point out that, while the grievances of the Mormons over their expulsion from Missouri were real, the Saints "quickly forgot the farms the Danites had burned and the cattle they had rustled," but they had photographic memories and meticulous catalogs of all the wrongs done to them, and this tradition lives on in the Mormon and pro-Mormon historians of today. (*The Mormon Rebellion*, Bigler & Bagley, pp. 16-17) In the words of former Mormon William W. Phelps, "If the Mormons had behaved like other people, they would never have been driven form Illinois and Missouri; but they stole, robbed and plundered from all their neighbors, and all the time." (Hirshson, p. 63) We can detect the influence of the antinomian heresy, which suggested to the Saints that the moral law had been suspended for their benefit.

ROMNEY'S ANCESTOR PARLEY PRATT INDICTED FOR COUNTERFEITING, PREDICTS "WRECK" OF US

Brigham Young's bitterness was doubtless increased in December 1845, when an Illinois Circuit Court indicted him for counterfeiting. According to the Illinois district attorney, "from the testimony before the grand jury, it appeared that counterfeiting coin had been largely carried on at their place for some years. The defendants evade the service of process." Named in the indictment were four other Mormon leaders, including Parley Pratt, Mitt Romney's ancestor. (Hirshson, p. 68)

Mitt Romney's great-great-grandfather Parley Pratt poured out his venom against the United States in a memorable pronouncement. To punish the Gentiles, he foresaw, plagues, earthquakes, storms, tempests; and other dire calamities would strike the world and "devour the wicked." Pratt predicted "the wreck of nations; the casting down of thrones; the crash of states, and the winding up of all mere human institutions; while a new dynasty, as a universal Theocracy, shall succeed and stand forever." (Does this prophecy foreshadow the presidency of Parley's great-great-grandson, Mitt Romney?) God would then defeat the Gentiles and create his own kingdom on earth. God would "overthrow their armies, assert his own right, rule the nations with a rod of iron, root the wicked out of the earth, and take possession of his own kingdom." (Hirshson, p. 92) The Mormons would be placed in command.

In December 1847, after running the show for three years as President of the Quorum of the Twelve, Brigham Young was ordained as First President of the church. At this point, Brigham Young was the dominant personality in the Quorum of the Twelve, and also controlled the secret Council of Fifty, the broader body including non-Mormons which Joseph Smith had created for the express purpose of seizing political power in the United States and then worldwide. Because conflict between the Saints and the rest of the population had become endemic in Illinois, Brigham had moved many Mormons to winter quarters in Nebraska in 1846, and then continued on to Salt Lake Valley, where he arrived on July 24, 1847 – still celebrated as Pioneer Day in Utah, and considered much more important than the Fourth of July.

Salt Lake Valley was many hundreds of miles beyond the frontier of American settlement in the 1840s, and was still part of Mexico, but the authority of the Mexican state had grown very weak in this outlying territory. The Great Basin represented a power vacuum into which Brigham Young and the Mormons moved. Their goal was unquestionably to create an independent state, which they called Deseret (allegedly the Hebrew word for honeybee, one of Brigham Young's personal symbols, as it had been Napoleon's). Deseret was designed to include in whole or in part the modern states of Utah, Nevada, Idaho, Arizona, New Mexico, Colorado, Wyoming, and California. Now exercising dictatorial authority, Brigham Young sent out parties of Mormon settlers to build settlements and forts guarding the approaches to his new Inland Empire.

Brigham Young aimed at duplicating the kind of theocratic tyranny which Joseph Smith had established in Nauvoo during the last days, when he had concentrated all spiritual and temporal power in his own hands. In those days, Joseph Smith had been the mayor, the lieutenant general in command of the militia, the head of the city Council, and the Chief Justice of the local court. (*The Mormon Rebellion*, Bigler & Bagley, p. 19) And of course, Joseph Smith had been King of the Kingdom of God.

Emma Smith, the widow of Joseph Smith, refused to join Brigham Young in this endeavor, although he tried mightily to lure her in. Emma Smith and her sons indignantly denied that Joseph Smith had ever practiced polygamy, and on this basis created a dissident minority branch of Mormonism which exists to this day: this is the Reorganized Church of the Latter-day Saints, commonly known as the Reorganites. Another dissident branch was located in Michigan under the authority of James Strang, who set up his own theocracy on an island and ruled it for a time.

PRESIDENT ZACHARY TAYLOR WARNED
OF BREAKAWAY MORMON THEOCRACY

It was during this time that Brigham Young introduced the Mormon Oath of Vengeance against the United States of America into the Mormon Temple Endowment or ceremonial liturgy. The late Prophet Joseph Smith's son William, who was the leader of a Reorganite congregation in Covington, Kentucky, warned President Zachary Taylor and Congress about the activities of Brigham Young. William Smith compared Deseret to Sodom and Gomorrah, and told the US government that Deseret should not be admitted to the Union, because it was a theocracy. He accused Brigham Young of entertaining "treasonable designs against the liberties of American free born sons and daughters.... Their intention is to unite church and state, and whilst the political power of the Roman pontiff is passing away, this American tyrant is endeavoring to establish a new order of political popery in the recesses of the mountains of America." Raising the alarm against the Oath of Vengeance specifically, William Smith told President Taylor that "At Young's insistence fifteen hundred Saints had sworn to 'avenge the blood of Joseph Smith on this nation,' to 'carry out hostilities against the nation, and to keep the same intent a profound secret, now and forever.'" (Hirshson, pp. 101-102)

If Brigham Young wanted his Inland Empire, he would need to have the Indians on his side to defend it against the United States. In theory, Brigham Young argued that it was better to feed the Indians than to fight them, and that, as descendents of the Lamanites, their ultimate destiny was to intermarry with the Mormons and be absorbed into the community of Saints. But here, the Mormons had a very uneven record.

UTE CHIEF SOWIETTE: "AMERICAN – GOOD! MORMON – NO GOOD!"

The American or "Gentile" subagent Henry R. Day of the Bureau of Indian Affairs provided evidence of the deep suspicion the Indians held towards the Mormon Saints. Day was in touch with Chief Walker, the war chief of the Ute or Utah Indian tribe, and with Sowiette, the tribe's civil leader. Day reported that the Ute tribe was reluctant to attend peace talks with the Mormons, because "they believed it to be a trap set by the Mormons to kill them. They seem to have but little confidence in anything the Mormon people say to them and decidedly stand in fear of them…the old Chieftain, Sowiette… raising himself up to his full height said to me, American—good! Mormon—No good! American—friend. Mormon—kill—Steal.' Each year, complained Sowiette, the Saints shoved his people further away from good soil and timber. With tears in his eyes he begged the 'Great Father' in Washington to stop the aggressors before they drove the Indians into the mountains, where starvation was certain." (Hirshson, p. 114)

AFTER YEARS OF DENIALS,
BRIGHAM YOUNG PROCLAIMS POLYGAMY, 1852

There is good evidence that Joseph Smith introduced polygamy under the influence of his own carnal obsessions. The Prophet once confessed: "whenever I see a pretty woman, I have to pray for Grace."[128] Under the Joseph Smith regime, Mormon polygamy was always strictly, and vehemently, and indignantly denied in public. It also tended to be limited to the top levels of the Mormon hierarchy, and was not the rule among new converts or rank-and-file members.

A perceptive analysis of Brigham Young's use of polygamy or celestial marriage came from F. T. Ferris, the "Gentile" business manager of the Salt Lake *Daily Tribune*. Ferris said:

> "Brigham Young did not become a polygamist, nor do I believe that he enforced polygamy on his subjects simply for the indulgence of the animal passions. It was different with Joseph Smith, who was a man who could not control his passions, and who practiced polygamy even before he received the revelation making it the bounden duty of all good Mormons. In fact, the belief is common among the more intelligent Mormons that Joseph's carnal passions were the cause of the revelation. With Brigham it is different. With him, it is a matter of statesmanship. He is a shrewd man rather than a fanatic, and looks upon the building up of a power in the territory rather than to the indulgence of his passions…. He, I believe, clings to polygamy, first, because he thinks it will more rapidly build up the Mormon state, and, second, because its practice tends to isolate those who practice it from the outer world, keeps them together, and thereby renders his power more secure and stable than if the polygamic institution did not exist.'" (Hirshson, pp. 302-03)

Brigham Young's attitude was more manipulative and more calculating. He clearly viewed polygamy as a means of maintaining the unity and cohesion of the Mormon

---

[128] Brodie, p. 297.

community in the midst of a hostile American and Gentiles sea. Under Brigham's regime, polygamy was encouraged for all male Mormons who were in good standing with the church. The rule was that a man had to have at least three wives in order to be taken seriously as a Saint, since this was the minimum quota needed to become a god and rule over a planet in the afterlife. Even the poorest farmers soon had plural wives in their impoverished cabins. The result of this was to guarantee that these polygamists would remain in Brigham Young's fiefdom forever. This was because there was no place else in the United States, nor in North America, nor in the Western world and much of the non-Western world where polygamy would be tolerated. Once you were a polygamist you had to stay in Deseret, and that meant serving Brigham Young and his geopolitical-theocratic designs. Polygamy became even more of a recruiting tool.

It was in 1852 that Brigham Young reversed the Joseph Smith policy of publicly lying about polygamy, and proclaimed the Order of Jacob (meaning celestial marriage and plural wives) before world public opinion. As was now typical, Brigham Young in this pronouncement mixed theological and administrative issues according to his own demagogic needs.

MORMONS: GOD THE FATHER AND JESUS CHRIST BOTH POLYGAMISTS

The essence of his announcement was that the Mormon God, sometimes called Elohim, was a polygamist in heaven, and had descended to earth with one of his wives. The two had become incarnate in the Garden of Eden in the form of Adam and Eve. Brigham's revelation was that: "When our father Adam came into the Garden of Eden, he came into it with a celestial body, and brought Eve, one of his wives, with him. He helped to make and organize this world. He is Michael, the Archangel, the Ancient of Days about whom holy men have written and spoken—He is our Father and our God, and the only God with whom we have to do."

The Mormon apologist Edward Tullidge later touted this pronouncement, claiming that "When Brigham Young proclaimed to the nations that Adam was our Father and God, and Eve, his partner, the Mother of a world—both in a mortal and celestial sense—he made the most important revelation ever oracle to the race since the days of Adam himself." (Hirshson, p. 119)

A group of traveling notables came to Salt Lake City in that same year of 1852, and included the Speaker of the US House of Representatives Schuyler Colfax, and journalists Samuel Bowles of the Springfield *Republican*, and Albert D. Richardson of the New York *Tribune*. Before this august company, Brigham Young further embroidered his account, asserting that the Virgin Mary and Mother of God was also a wife of Adam: "That very babe that was cradled in the manger was begotten, not by Joseph, the husband of Mary, but by another Being. Do you inquire by whom? He was begotten by God our heavenly Father." The begetting was accomplished not by the miraculous action of the Holy Spirit, but materially, Brigham said, "by the process known to nature—just as men now create children." Betraying the inherent materialism and anti-Trinitarianism of Mormon doctrine, Brigham Young also pointed out that the father and the son were identical in appearance, except that God the father looked older. (Hirshson, p. 119) It was a pagan caricature of the Scriptures.

ROMNEY'S GREAT-GREAT-GREAT UNCLE ORSON PRATT:
CHRIST HAD THREE WIVES

For Brigham Young, if God the Father practiced polygamy, so did the Mormon Jesus. Mormons like Orson Pratt (the great–great-great uncle of the GOP candidate) and Jedediah M. Grant asserted that Jesus had married three wives, including Mary Magdalene, the repentant woman in Luke, and Mary and Martha, the sisters of Jesus' friend, Lazarus. (Hirshson, p. 119) The next step, obviously enough, was to claim that the Mormon Saints were the biological descendents of Christ. Brigham Young made this claim, saying "You understand who we are; we are of the House of Israel, of the royal seed, of the royal blood." (Hirshson, p. 17) In China at around the same time, the Prophet Hong Xiuquan was creating the Celestial Kingdom of the Taiping with a claim to be Christ's younger brother.

Brigham Young taught that men who died unmarried might go to heaven, but could never become gods and rule over planets in the way that polygamists could. These bachelors could only hope to become angels, meaning that they would become the servants and errand boys of those who had advanced to the level of Godhead. (Hirshson, p. 122) A society based on classes was thus projected into heaven. As for the women, their only hope of entering heaven was by being married in the temple, and their chances were increased if their husband was a Mormon bigwig, and not some obscure settler.

Brigham Young and his machine put out the word, ordering the Saints to "Make haste and get married! Let me see no boys above sixteen and girls above fourteen unmarried," as one contemporary reported. (Hirshson, p. 126)

MORMON WAR ON WOMEN

Mormonism thus established itself as an oligarchy of patriarchs ruling over extended households. These male oligarchs were the true beneficiaries of the system. The losers were the vast majority – polygamous wives, young men, and older women. The fact that powerful polygamists were monopolizing numbers of marriageable women meant that non-elite males would have trouble finding a spouse. We see the same phenomenon today in a Warren Jeffs' Fundamentalist Latter-day Saints, where hundreds of boys and young men have been driven out of the Southern Utah strongholds and forced to go elsewhere. Warren Jeffs was reported to be constantly on the lookout for minor infractions by these young males that he could use as a pretext for expelling them.

BRIGHAM YOUNG, DEAD-BEAT DAD

As for the older women, Ann Eliza Webb Young in her highly readable *Wife No. 19* tells the story of a destitute old woman who had been one of Brigham Young's wives, but whom he had expelled from his household and refused to support. This unfortunate lady would regularly confront the women still living in Brigham Young's harem, and remind them in no uncertain terms that she would have precedence over them in heaven because Brigham had married her before them. Ann Eliza Webb Young, although still young and attractive, could see the danger that she would be treated in the same way: Brigham Young, although he was a multimillionaire, came to her one day and announced that he could no longer pay her an allowance for her living expenses. At that point, she initiated divorce proceedings for abandonment and nonsupport, and was ultimately granted a divorce. She also obtained a judgment awarding her a cash settlement and alimony, but when Brigham Young refused to pay, the Mormon-controlled probate courts refused to enforce collection, and so Ann Eliza Webb Young and her children got nothing. On the basis of this, Brigham Young takes his place as one of the most famous deadbeat dads of the 19th century.

"MARRYING PA" – NOT JUST POLYGAMY, BUT INCEST AND POLYANDRY ALSO

Ann Eliza Webb Young also tells the story of two young sisters, both children when their mother married the Mormon polygamist McDonald. Here the arrangement was that the two little girls would also marry McDonald as soon as they were a little older. Eliza said she heard them talk about "Marrying Pa."[129] Polygamy in such cases also subsumed a violation of the incest taboo.

From the point of view of the women involved in some of these marriages, polygamy or polygyny for the husband sometimes implied polyandry from the point of view of the woman. This is especially the case with the wives of Joseph Smith, many of whom were married women. Once they had entered into celestial marriage with Joseph Smith, they had two husbands, and had thus crossed into polyandry.

One perceptive visitor to the Mormon Mecca was Sir Richard Burton, the author of the *Arabian Nights*. Burton had seen harems in the Middle East. He noted the economic advantages of the plural wives system for the male patriarchs: "Servants are rare and costly; it is cheaper and more comfortable to marry them. Many converts are attracted by the prospect of being wives, especially from places where, like Clifton, there are sixty-four females to thirty-six males." (Hirshson, p. 123)

Research suggests that about 20% of Mormon families practiced polygamy. According to Hirshson, of 1,748 polygamists in one sample, 66.3 per cent had two wives, 21.2 per cent had three, and only 6.7 per cent had four. Brigham Young, Jr. claimed that Utah had four women for every three men. According to another distinguished European visitor, the French naturalist Jules Rémy, there were many bachelors who could not find wives. (Hirshson, p. 124)

RICH MORMONS SCATTERED THEIR WIVES ALL OVER TOWN

Mormon architects designed houses for polygamists with separate entrances to many individual apartments, one for each wife and her children. Brigham Young's biographer Hirshson notes that "some rich men avoided domestic troubles by scattering their families all over town, but others, including Young, preferred harem life, keeping most of their wives together but apart from the husband, who had his own quarters nearby." (Hirshson, p. 124) One wonders how many rich and powerful Mormons even today stash

---

[129] Ann Eliza Webb Young, chapter XIX.

their plural wives in apartments scattered all over the United States or even all over the world, somewhat like Mitt Romney's offshore bank accounts.

The south of Utah, known as Dixie, acquired a reputation for having the most aggressive polygamists, an infamy which persists down to the present-day reign of Warren Jeffs. Southern Utah was also the home of Miles Romney the younger, great-grandfather of the candidate. "Abuses were especially common south of Salt Lake City, where the immigrants who lived in the isolated communities were subject to the bishop's absolutism. In Provo, sixty miles south of Salt Lake City, a man settled with his beautiful seventeen-year-old daughter. Many polygamists desired the girl, but the father warded them off. Early in 1857, he died. At the graveside the bishop who conducted the service ordered the girl to marry him. She had no alternative but to become his seventh wife." (Hirshson, pp. 125-26) The Romney family lived for a time in St. George, Utah, in this southern part of the state.

MORMON MARRIES WOMAN AND HER GRANDDAUGHTER

Hirshson records more cases of polygamy crossing over into incest: "A man named Winchester married his mother, and Young himself sealed a mother and daughter to their cousin, Luman A. Shurtliff. The Prophet often allowed his favorites to marry their stepdaughters, sometimes encouraged brothers and sisters to marry, and at least once sealed a half brother to his half sister. He also sealed an elderly man to a fifty-seven-year-old woman and her fourteen-year old granddaughter." (Hirshson, p. 126)

Inevitably, polygamy also created examples of what was then called the white slavery, and would today be classified as sex slavery or human trafficking: "Prominent Mormons sometimes purchased girls. Frederick Loba, the Swiss chemist the Saints converted and ordered to Utah to manufacture gunpowder, saw 'two young sisters sold by their father to General Horace Eldredge for some groceries.' In 1856, according to *The New York Times*, Kimball offered a father a yoke of oxen and a wagon for a sixteen-year-old girl." (Hirshson, p. 129)

The network for foreign recruiting which Brigham Young, Parley Pratt, and other leading Mormons had helped to found provided Deseret with a steady stream of converts who could be exploited by the church hierarchy for political, economic, military, and sexual purposes. By 1854, the LDS Church "had branches in England, Scotland, Wales, Denmark, Sweden, Norway, Iceland, France, Germany, Italy, Switzerland, Malta, Gibraltar, Australia, and the Sandwich Islands, India, Siam, Ceylon, South Africa, and British Guiana. Although the Prussian king expelled them, the Saints usually succeeded in Protestant countries, especially Scandinavia, northern Germany, and Great Britain, but convinced few people in southern Germany, Italy, Ireland, France, Spain, Portugal, and other Catholic countries. Jewish converts were almost nonexistent. Realizing the power of the written word, the Saints translated the *Book of Mormon* into French, German, Italian, Danish, Welsh, and Polynesian." (Hirshson, p. 106)

The criteria for Mormon recruiting were anything but rigorous, and one observer noted that "… Mormonism, a mixture of superstition and tradition, appealed, as Saints themselves admitted, to the fearful, the credulous, and the downtrodden." (Hirshson, p. 16)

The best results were obtained in the north of England as part of an operation which could not have been conducted without at least the tacit approval of the British government. By 1870, the travel agency which Brigham Young set up had financed the travel expenses of 38,000 Britishers, plus 13,000 people from other European countries. Another positive aspect of this for the Mormons is that these immigrants had no connection whatsoever to the United States, and had never been a part of the US. (Hirshson, p. 106)

SALT LAKE CITY "THE BIGGEST WHOREHOUSE IN THE WORLD"

One member of the Quorum of the Twelve was Heber Kimball, code-named "the Herald of Grace." In an article entitled "Among the Mormons" by Fitz Hugh Ludlow, published in the *Atlantic Monthly* of April 1864, we can see how the grotesque ran riot in the little world of Mormon polygamy. Kimball sounds like a polygamist Falstaff when he praises the various nationalities of women represented in his harem. Kimball boasted that he admired women of all nations. "I love the Danes dearly! I've got a Danish wife." he told Ludlow. Kimball then went on "the Irish are a dear people. My Irish wife is among the best I've got." Kimball kept going: "I love the Germans! Got a Dutch wife, too!" (Hirshson, p. 130)

A Mormon defector told the *New York Times* of February 15, 1852 that the reality of Salt Lake City was "licentiousness run mad." On September 21, 1857 an anonymous source identified as one of the many daughters of Brigham Young was quoted by the *New York Times* as observing "If Salt Lake City was only roofed over, it would be the biggest whorehouse in the world."[130]

ADVICE FROM THE HERALD OF GRACE:
GIRLS OF 14 AND BOYS OF 16 SHOULD "GO TO IT"

In October 1855, Heber C. Kimball advised "young men to get married at sixteen, and take two wives and a dozen if they wished." In the view of this apostle, girls "were old enough to get married at fourteen." With a strange idea of apostolic decorum, Kimball said he "wanted all the girls 14 & boys 16 to go to it and get married or rather get married and go to it." Brigham Young taught that "there were spirits of a nobler class waiting to take bodies & it was the duty of every man to be taking to himself more wives." (*The Mormon Rebellion*, Bigler & Bagley, pp. 81-82)

MORMON USURY: 12% INTEREST ON STARTUP LOANS TO CONVERTS

When the newly recruited Mormon Saints arrived in Deseret, they were not left to their own devices under some mystical regime of free enterprise, but were rather inducted into a collectivist system with overtones of debt peonage under centralized control: "In Utah the church directed the convert's activities. It inventoried his goods and if he had money told him what to do with it. An impoverished man was sent to a bishop, who gave him up to ten acres of land, seed, a wagon, and a yoke of cattle. The immigrant signed a note for

---

[130] Hirshson, p. 130.

these items plus interest as high as twelve per cent a year. Until his debt was paid, the bishop disposed of the man's harvest: a tenth went to the church as a tithe; a portion provided for the laborer's family; some went for seed; the rest paid off the debt." (Hirshson, p. 107)

The horrors of Mormon polygamy and theocracy were on display in national newspapers for all to see, but, nevertheless, on September 9, 1850, US President Millard Fillmore named Brigham Young as the governor of Utah Territory and superintendent of Indian affairs. The doughface Fillmore had become president after the very suspicious death of President Zachary Taylor, a Whig nationalist. Thanks to his appointment as governor, Brigham Young could now exercise theocratic power under the color of territorial law. (*The Mormon Rebellion*, Bigler & Bagley, p. 48) Brigham Young was always certain that Zachary Taylor and James K. Polk were going to hell, but he made an exception for Fillmore, even naming a town in Utah in his honor.

In order to make elections easier to control, the part of the Utah territorial code dealing with elections demanded that paper ballots be numbered so as to allow the name of the voter to be ascertained, in case an heretical ballot had been cast.[131]

Brigham Young regarded the building up of Utah Territory as inseparable for preparations for war against the United States. At the founding of Salt Lake City in 1847, Brigham Young was already looking ahead to an irrepressible conflict with the government in Washington. "If the people of the United States will let us alone for 10 years, we will ask no odds of them," said Young. Without doubt, the goal was always a separate country, an independent empire decidedly hostile to the United States. Charles E. Mix of the Office of Indian Affairs denounced the "policy pursued by the Mormons, which aimed at the establishment of an independent Mormon empire."[132] (*The Mormon Rebellion*, Bigler & Bagley, p. 11)

Standard Mormon practice was to insist that all federal officials operating in the Utah Territory and in surrounding regions be obedient members of the Mormon Church. If these federal officials attempted to implement policies which the Mormons did not like, they harassed them mercilessly, even putting their lives in danger. One Mormon trick was to make sure that the Utah probate courts had jurisdiction over most legal cases. Since Brigham Young controlled the juries and judges in his probate courts, any attempt to compel respect for federal law was doomed from the beginning.

At this time, Utah was a territory, and not a state. Standard practice for all territories at this time was that the territorial governor, federal judges, and other key appointments for the territories were filled by the president, acting with the advice and consent of the Senate. No territory had the right to choose its own governor or its own federal officials, although of course intensive lobbying of the Congress and the executive was carried on.

---

[131] Bigler and Bagley, page 49.
[132] *House Documents, Otherwise Published As Executive Documents:* 13th Congress, Second Session, p.125.

PRESIDENT FRANKLIN PIERCE REJECTS UTAH STATEHOOD, MORMONS APOPLECTIC

US President Franklin Pierce, who was close to the Mazzini Young America networks, refused the initial bid of Utah to become a state. The result was a situation of virtual insurrection. At the same time, we should look forward to Abraham Lincoln's policy of temporarily leaving the Mormons alone, until such time as growing federal power allowed their barbaric practice of polygamy to be dealt with effectively. The approach of President James Buchanan contrasts significantly with Lincoln's. Lincoln wanted to act from a position of strength, while Buchanan insisted on acting from a position of weakness, on the eve of the Civil War. Buchanan was notoriously a famous doughface – a free state man with slave state principles, as he showed by backing the slaveholder party in Bleeding Kansas. The Buchanan administration's malfeasance and nonfeasance opened the door wide for secessionism and civil war.

Under the disastrous Kansas-Nebraska legislation and its principle of popular sovereignty or squatter sovereignty, sporadic terrorism broke out between proslavery Border Ruffians and anti-slavery farmers, sprinkled with abolitionist provocateurs like John Brown, coming into Kansas. From the Mormon point of view, the Border Ruffians were of course the Missouri mobs who had attacked them in the 1830s.

John Brown's raid on Harpers Ferry, Virginia was intended to set off a general slave insurrection in the southern states, which might have started the Civil War years in advance. John Brown's actions were financed by a group of Boston bankers who descended from the New England secessionists of the War of 1812 era, and who were in close contact with British intelligence. Given Brigham Young's own historical pattern of keeping close to London, we may speculate that he was expecting the civil war to break out in the Midwest and the East sooner than it did, diverting federal forces away from the Utah front. If so, Brigham Young's calculation was off by several years.

As if the Kansas conflict were not sufficient, James Buchanan chose this moment to begin appointing non-Mormon officials for the Utah Territory. A more serious approach would have been to send in federal troops in advance of this announcement, so as to be able to enforce federal authority from day one. As it turned out, when the Mormons moved toward secession in 1857, the U.S. Army under the disloyal Secretary of War Floyd was unable to put a garrison into Salt Lake City until 1858, creating an unmistakable impression of weakness which may have encouraged the Confederate secessionists to move ahead with their subversive plans.

THEOCRACY VS THE CONSTITUTION

The conflict between the Mormon theocracy in the Intermountain West and the United States federal government in Washington was in many respects an irrepressible conflict, to use Seward's phrase. Rather than keep the Constitution, as they claimed, the Mormons wanted to supersede and subsume United States and all other human governments under their earthly version of the Kingdom of God, which would be a prelude to the second coming of Christ. This meant there could be no peace between Mormons and the United States government.

The theocratic-millenarian current in Mormon thought had grown in Joseph Smith throughout his prophetic career, and had been become stronger out in the wilderness of Deseret. This was inseparably linked with Mormon fantasies of world conquest and world reformation. During Joseph Smith's last days in 1844, the Prophet had intoned "I calculate to be one of the instruments of setting up the Kingdom of Daniel by the word of the Lord, and I intend to lay a foundation that will revolutionize the whole world."[133]

Brigham Young became variously the Mormon Moses, the American Moses, or the Lion of the Lord. One of Brigham Young's retainers was Jedediah M. Grant, who became second counselor in Brigham's First Presidency. Grant proclaimed: "If you maintain the fact that the Priesthood of God is upon the earth, and that God's representatives are upon the earth, the mouth-piece of Jehovah, the head of the kingdom of God upon earth, and the will of God is done upon earth as it is in heaven, it follows that the government of God is upon the earth."[134] Grant also taught that "It is a stern fact that the people of the United States have shed the blood of the Prophets, driven out the Saints of God ... consequently I look for the Lord to use His whip on the refractory son called 'Uncle Sam."

Meanwhile, on the other side of the world, another theocratic Kingdom of God had been conjured up by English-speaking missionaries. The Celestial Kingdom of the Taiping, with its capital at Nanking, was in 1857-58 near the height of its power.

As the jurisdictional conflict between the Kingdom of God on the one hand and the United States of America on the other became more acute, Brigham Young in 1857 planted his celestial banner with the rhetoric of defiance: "I am at defiance of all Earth and hell to point out the first thing that this people have ever committed where in righteousness it could be called an infringement upon our government. I am at the defiance of all hell [and] Governments, but especially ours. . . . We have observed good, wholesome rules and laws, but now they can pass over every Mobocratic spirit and institution, every violation of the Constitution, they pass over it as nothing, and raise a force to come and slay all the Latter-day Saints, men, women and children. . . . We will keep revolutionizing the world, until we bring peace to mankind, and all hell cannot help it." (*The Mormon Rebellion*, Bigler & Bagley, p. 10)

ROMNEY ANCESTOR PARLEY PRATT: UTTER OVERTHROW AND DESOLATION AWAIT THE GENTILES

Even before leaving Illinois, the ruling Quorum of Twelve had made clear its goal of establishing an independent Mormon state with the help of Native Americans. They announced their goals in a document known as the Proclamation of the Twelve Apostles.

---

[133] Joseph Smith, *History of the Church*, VI:365, online at Wikipedia article on "Theodemocracy."
[134] Elder Jedediah M. Grant, "The Power of God and the Power of Satan," *Journal of Discourses*, Vol. II, pp. 10-16.

Significantly for our purposes here, this proclamation was written by Parley P. Pratt, the great-great grandfather of Mitt Romney, the Republican presidential candidate. This bombastic tirade is addressed "to All the Kings of the World; to the President of the United States Of America; to the Governors of the Several States; and to the Rulers and Peoples of All Nations."[135] "Know Ye" – it proclaims – "that the kingdom of God has come as has been predicted by ancient prophets, and prayed for in all ages: even that kingdom which shall fill the whole earth, and shall stand before ever… the great Elohim Jehovah has been pleased once more to speak from the heavens; and also to commune with man upon the earth, by means of open visions, and by the ministrations of Holy Messengers." Parley Pratt warned the Gentile that, if they failed to repent, the Lamanites would "tear them in pieces, like a lion among the flocks of sheep." The Gentiles would be wiped out, with "an utter overthrow, and desolation of all our Cities, Forts, and Strong Holds—an entire annihilation of our race …except such as embrace the Covenant, and are numbered with Israel."

BRIGHAM YOUNG: HANG US OFFICIALS ON A GIBBET IF THEY INTERFERE

Brigham Young became even more strident once he had created the settlement at Salt Lake City. According to Isaac Bullock, in one of his key policy speeches, Young said he "hoped to live to lead forth the armies of Israel to execute the judgments & justice on the persecuting Gentiles & that no officer of the United States would ever dictate him in this valley, or he would hang them on a gibbet as a warning to others."[136] Accordingly, asserting independence became just a question of time, as the Saints gathered their forces for the inevitable collision.

On Pioneer Day, July 24, 1850, secessionist and subversive speeches included "Declaration of Independence of Deseret" and "The Constitution of Deseret." An eyewitness reported that "They said many hard things against the Government and people of the United States … They prophesied that the total overthrow of the United States was at hand, and that the whole nation would soon be at the feet of the Mormons, suing for mercy and protection."[137]

To maintain this saintly purity of the kingdom of God in Deseret, the senior Mormon Saints applied a kind of ideological cleansing to make sure that American Gentile travelers passing through on the way to California or other destinations knew that they were not welcome to stay. The Mormons embarked on a policy of confessional cleansing, in the form of systematic harassment against American pioneers. Americans were sued in the Mormon kangaroo courts, subjected to discriminatory taxes and fees, gouged with outrageous prices, spied upon, threatened, and denied justice for crimes

---

[135] "Proclamation of the Twelve Apostles of the Church of Jesus Christ of Latter-day Saints. To all the Kings of the World; to the President of the United States Of America; To the Governors of the Several States; And to the Rulers and People of All Nations." in Brigham Young, *Messages of the First Presidency,* Vol. 1, p. 257.
[136] Will Bagley, *Blood of the Prophets,* p. 28.
[137] David L. Bigler, "The Elephant Meets the Lion: Gold Rush Conflicts in the Great Basin," Trails Symposium, April 14, 1999, Salt Lake City.

committed against them. They were also subjected to a torrent of obloquy and verbal abuse. American pioneers who made the unlucky decision of spending the winter of 1851-52 in Salt Lake City were subjected to unprecedented harassment, which historians have seen as foreshadowing the ultimate break in 1857. (*The Mormon Rebellion*, Bigler & Bagley, pp. 39, 42)

MORMONS READ PRESIDENT LINCOLN'S TOP SECRET TELEGRAMS

The Mormons, like Mitt Romney today also practiced the regime of systematic secrecy, concealment, and deception. A permanent bureaucracy read and censored all correspondence going through the Utah post offices – in itself, a federal crime. Later, Mormons would also monitor the traffic on the transcontinental telegraph, including presidential messages from Abraham Lincoln going to California. The agency carrying this out was doubtless the Danite secret police. The Mormon routine was to "destroy letters containing anything against themselves."[138] (*The Mormon Rebellion*, Bigler & Bagley, p. 40)

Two Gentile travelers attending Pioneer Day in the early 1850s quoted the following choice remarks to a critic from territorial Governor Brigham Young: "[President] Zachary Taylor is dead and gone to hell, and I am glad of it!" Young explained how he knew this: "Because God told me so." Young's retainer Heber C. Kimball added: "Yes, …and you'll know it, too; for you'll see him when you get there."[139] Young raved on that any American president "who lifts his finger against this people shall die an untimely death, and go to hell."[140] (*The Mormon Rebellion*, Bigler & Bagley, p. 43)

Many travelers complained that they had been either robbed outright, or separated from their money through shady practices and the corrupt judiciary. One was so outraged that he later wrote: "Were Brigham Young to come in person and tender back the money he robbed us of, there is not a man among us but would exclaim: '*Your money perish with you! In our distress and anguish of soul, you robbed us of our all, and exposed our wives and little ones to the danger of perishing with famine, amid the wastes of the desert!* Never, *never,* NEVER!'" (*The Mormon Rebellion*, Bigler & Bagley, p. 41)

LAND TITLES FROM THE UNITED STATES, OR DIRECT FROM GOD?

One extremely important area of conflict between the Washington government and the Deseret theocracy was over the issue of land ownership and land rights. According to the Treaty of Guadalupe Hidalgo between Mexico and the United States ending hostilities on February 2, 1848, the Territory of Utah and surrounding states had been ceded by Mexico to Washington. That meant that the land titles and deeds granted by the Deseret administration during the first years of settlement were not valid. Accordingly, when federal officials arrived in Deseret for the purpose of beginning the process of surveying the land, they were subjected to extreme harassment. When the first federal surveyor

---

[138] Ibid.

[139] *New York Times*, "The Outrage at Salt Lake," December 3, 1851, online at truthandgrace.com.

[140] "The Mormons: People and Events: Brigham Young (1801-1877)," online at pbs.org.

entered Utah Territory, the Mormons saw this as an attempt by the United States government to assert authority over land which they held on perpetual lease from God. (*The Mormon Rebellion*, Bigler & Bagley, p. 49)

Agents of the Bureau of Indian Affairs found in 1851 that the top Utah officials had "no sympathy or respect for our government or its institutions," and could be "frequently heard cursing and abusing not only the government, but all who are American citizens." One official concluded that the Mormons would try to prevent the United States from "peaceably extending her laws over the territory."

At the same time, an awareness of the alliance between Mormons and the British Empire was common in the population at large. Mormons were overheard saying that "they did not fear the United States. If they needed help, they can easily get it from England." (*The Mormon Rebellion*, Bigler & Bagley, p. 56)

Not content with harassing federal officials and making their work impossible, the Brigham Young regime in the early 1850s also began promoting armed attacks on pioneer wagon trains transiting the Utah Territory, both by inciting the Indians to hostile action, as well as by having Mormons carry out the attacks themselves. Rumors soon abounded that white men, evidently Mormons, were joining in Indian attacks on pioneer wagon trains. The Mormons told the Indians "that it was all right to kill American soldiers, but not Mormons." (*The Mormon Rebellion*, Bigler & Bagley, p. 64)

In 1853, Captain John W. Gunnison of the United States Army was killed, presumably by Indians, while doing surveys for the proposed transcontinental railroad, which would most likely pass through Utah. There were many questions as to whether the Mormons had incited the Indians to carry out this murder

"THOSE DAMNED AMERICANS"

Among the Mormons, the term "American" was a sign of contempt. In one typical incident, a group of Mormons attacked a dwelling because they had heard that there were Americans inside. The Saintly assailants demanded to know from the homeowner "what he was doing with those damned Americans about his house."[141] (*The Mormon Rebellion*, Bigler & Bagley, p. 72)

Among the Indians, however, "The American" often had positive connotations. This is especially the case with Garland Hurt, an energetic Indian agent who did much for the federal cause, and who must be seen as one of the unsung heroes of the Utah Territory. Hurt worked especially with the Ute people, whom the Mormons had systematically antagonized. The result was that, just as brother Brigham was sending out his emissaries, disguised as missionaries, to recruit the Indian tribes for war, at least one federal official was preventing an important Indian nation from being goaded into conflict by the Mormon Saints. (*The Mormon Rebellion*, Bigler & Bagley, p. 72)

---

[141] Garland Hurt to Brigham Young, October 31, 1856, "Letters from Nevada India and Agents," 1856, Nevada History, *The Nevada Observer*, online at nevadaobserver.com.

THE CRISIS OF 1855: BRIGHAM MOBILIZES FOR TOTAL CIVIL WAR

In February 1855, President Franklin Pierce attempted to appoint a territorial governor to take the place of Brigham Young. In response to this, Brigham Young began the first phase of his plan for secession. During these months, he would hide behind the slogan of "sovereignty," a word which in our own time often has a similar subversive intent.

Brigham Young in 1855 therefore set out to accentuate and radicalize the existing tendencies and institutions of Mormondom, with a view to mobilizing the Utah Territory for total war against the United States. He was, in fact, executing an articulated strategy: he was willing to accept statehood and entry into the Union, but his first choice was existence as an independent, sovereign nation. Brigham Young was prepared to call attention to his landmark decision with special rhetorical fireworks. (*The Mormon Rebellion*, Bigler & Bagley, p. 73)

BRIGHAM: GATES TO HEAVEN CLOSED TO GENTILES AS OF 1855

Brigham Young proclaimed a revelation according to which salvation was no longer available to the Gentiles, meaning the Americans and all other non-Mormons. The word went out that "the day has come to turn the key of the Gospel against the Gentiles, and open it to the remnants of Israel, the people shouted, Amen, and the feeling was such that most present could realize, but few describe."[142] Young's pronouncement in effect consigned the Gentiles to damnation, through the proverbial outer darkness where there is much wailing and gnashing of teeth. From this he also derived the consequence that "the time had come to reject the colonial government Congress had imposed on God's kingdom." If Washington continued to deny Deseret the status of a sovereign state within the Union, then the obvious result would be a completely independent nation striking out on its own.[143]

MORMONS INCITE INDIAN WARS

Contemplating these events, one inevitably feels a sense of the grotesque disproportion between cause and effect. Here, for example, the mere act of a US president naming a territorial governor for Utah who happens not to be one of the anointed Mormon Saints is enough to cause cataclysmic effects in heaven, ruling out a future possibility of salvation for hundreds of millions of "Gentiles." How could this apocalyptic event be triggered by the routine actions of one Franklin Pierce, president of a nation of the middle rank at best? What kind of a religion was this? Was it a religion at all, or a thinly veiled pretext for theocratic secessionism? Brigham Young and his associates were indeed radical subjectivists who thought the drama of salvation revolved around them.

---

[142] David L. Bigler, *Forgotten Kingdom: the Mormon Theocracy in the American West, 1847-1896* (Spokane WA: Arthur H. Clark, 1998), p. 93.
[143] Bigler and Bagley, page 74

To enhance the possibilities of a military alliance with the "Lamanite" Indians, who were considered a lost tribe of Israel, Brigham ordered his missionaries out with orders to teach them farming, instruct them in the *Book of Mormon*, and teach them polygamy in practice by marrying Indian women. Eventually the red men could become "white and delightsome," like the good angels who fought on the side of the Mormon Jesus, according to the time-honored Latter-day Saint formulation. (*The Mormon Rebellion*, Bigler & Bagley, p. 74) Notice that the Mormon concept of saving the Indians includes forcing them to become white.

The Mormon hierarchy also organized in 1855 a conference of missionaries who would enter into communication with the main Indian tribes of North America, with the obvious implication of inciting them against the US federal government. In this continent-wide mobilization, one hundred and sixty Mormon missionaries went out, from the Pacific Ocean to the Mississippi, soon to be followed by more. They made contact with the principal Indian nations, including Delawares, Cheyennes, Cherokees, Kiowas, Comanches, Wacos, Witchitas, Lakotas, Choctaws, Moquis (Hopis), Mojaves, Nez Percés, Goshutes, Shoshones, Utahs, Paiutes, Omahas, Flatheads, Navahos, Shawnees, Bannocks, and Creeks. (*The Mormon Rebellion*, Bigler & Bagley, p. 74)

BRIGHAM YOUNG'S PRIMITIVE COMMUNISM

Brigham Young also mobilized what amounted to a collectivist war economy in Deseret. Modern Mormons claim to be the true apostles of the free market, but Brigham Young – alone in North America at the time – relied on a command economy using centralized planning and coercion. All important economic decisions involving the application of resources were the prerogative of the Mormon Moses. He claimed in 1867 that he had been called by God "to dictate affairs in the building up of his Zion," and that this gave him the totalitarian power to determine everything, "even to the ribbons the women wear."[144] One is reminded of the Soviet planners who wanted to control economic activity "down to the last bolt."

The Mormon statist war economy was fed by tithing. It was also fed by usury, with a rate of 12% interest per year being charged on the money the church had advanced to overseas converts making the journey to Deseret. For this reason, historians have seen many in the Mormon rank-and-file as having "the status of indentured servants." (*The Mormon Rebellion*, Bigler & Bagley, p. 80)

During the 1850s, an entire popular literature grew up around the theme of "Escape from Mormondom." Contributors included women like Ann Eliza Webb Young, who had managed to escape their marriages to Brigham Young and other Mormon bigwigs, plus European travel writers, Christian moralists, and muckraking social reformers. One well-known contributor was Sir Arthur Conan Doyle, who later began his famous Sherlock Holmes series with the story centering on the same theme. Brigham Young became the villain of Sir Arthur Conan Doyle's first entry in the Sherlock Holmes series; this was *A*

---

[144] Brigham Young, "Discourse," February 3, 1867, *Journal of Discourses*, 11:298.

Study in Scarlet, the story of two unhappy Mormons, John Ferrier and his daughter, who escape from Deseret.

1856 REPUBLICAN PLATFORM VS SLAVERY AND POLYGAMY, "TWIN RELICS OF BARBARISM"

Brigham Young was thrown into a state of complete frenzy in the summer of 1856 when he received word of the first Republican national convention, which had occurred in June in Philadelphia. Here John C. Fremont of California, the Pathfinder of the West, had been nominated for president. The Republican platform also included the following provision:

> Resolved: That the Constitution confers upon Congress sovereign powers over the territories of the United States for their government; and that in the exercise of this power, it is both the right and the imperative duty of Congress to prohibit in the territories those twin relics of barbarism – Polygamy, and Slavery.

Brigham Young was apoplectic. Although Fremont was defeated by Buchanan in the November 1856 election, in 1858 the Republicans took control of the House of Representatives with a platform that would have made it impossible for states to join the Union without prohibiting both slavery and polygamy. (*The Mormon Rebellion*, Bigler & Bagley, p. 87) This turned out to be the doom for Brigham Young's fallback option of forcing the United States government to protect polygamy in the same way that the Slave Power was making the federal government protect black chattel servitude.

The Republican stance on these issues was also tactically astute. The Mormon apostle John Taylor realized that the Republicans had now succeeded in attaching not just slavery but also polygamy to the Douglas-Democratic slogan of popular sovereignty or squatter sovereignty. Taylor saw that the Republicans had successfully "introduced opposition to Polygamy, as well as to Slavery, [as] *twin* relics of barbarism, which had thrown 'the onus of protecting & sustaining both onto the Democratic party.'" Taylor complained that this maneuver was a "mean dastardly act, in good keeping with other political moves of the present day; it is greedily swallowed by religionists of all parties … polygamy is shook at the Democrats as one of the institutions which they must defend, in conjunction with slavery.'" (*The Mormon Rebellion*, Bigler & Bagley, pp. 87-88) Brigham Young's only consolation was that the sporadic fighting in Bleeding Kansas was getting worse. Clearly, Brigham Young was hoping to see the short-term fulfillment of Joseph Smith's apocalyptic Civil War Prophecy, itself an early fruit of the cooperation of the Mormon Church hierarchy with British intelligence.

THE MORMON "REFORMATION" — BRIGHAM YOUNG'S REIGN OF TERROR

In the summer of 1856, Brigham Young proceeded to whip the population of Deseret into a paroxysm of apocalyptic and theocratic frenzy. He did this by unleashing the so-called "Mormon Reformation," which has a number of features in common with the Anabaptists of Muenster in the 16th century, with Robespierre's Reign of Terror in the

French Revolution, and with Chairman Mao's Great Proletarian Cultural Revolution. It was a chance for the Mormon hierarchy to cultivate a war psychosis or war hysteria among its subject population, and also to systematically eliminate any possible leaders of some possible future challenge to the absolute leadership of Brigham Young and The Quorum of Twelve.

Once again, Brigham Young stressed the messianic function of the kingdom of God, and in the process explicitly embraced the notion of terrorism. He announced that God's Kingdom was supposed to be "a terror to all nations." Mormondom had been divinely appointed to "revolutionize the world and bring all under subjection to the law of God, who is our law giver."[145]

BLOOD ATONEMENT – FOR CRIMES OF AMERICANS AGAINST MORMONS

Brigham Young also thought it proper at this point to introduce a theological concept, one which was once again totally alien to the tradition of Christianity. For Christians, the crucifixion of Christ on Calvary was a sacrifice which, because of the sinless and divine nature of the victim, fully atones for the scenes of mankind, no matter how monstrous they may be. The grace accorded to humankind by Christ's self-sacrifice is infinite, and any denial on this point amounts to outright blasphemy. But Brigham Young now put forth the doctrine that Christ's atonement is implicitly not enough, and that for certain heinous sins and crimes, "Blood Atonement" is required. Not surprisingly, many of the crimes he had in mind were crimes against Mormons, and the sinners he wanted to punish were very often none other than the American people.

Brigham offered the following concise summary of blood atonement in his sermon of September 21, 1856: "There are sins that can be atoned for by an offering upon an altar as in ancient days; and there are sins that the blood of a lamb, or a calf, or of turtle doves, cannot remit, but they must be atoned for by the blood of the man." [146]

Blood atonement became the centerpiece of a phase of acute hysteria about the Mormon creed. The grand inquisitor of the Mormon Reformation was Jedediah M. Grant, whom we have already encountered. The *New York Times* described Grant as "a tall, thin, repulsive looking man, of acute, vigorous intellect, a thorough-paced scoundrel, and the most essential blackguard in the pulpit." His nickname was 'Brigham's Sledgehammer.'"[147]

The inhabitants of Utah were subjected to an inquisition in which they were interrogated on 13 questions about their possible sins. They were grilled about their contributions to public sanitation. They were interrogated even about whether they managed to take a bath once a week. Brigham Young ordered that all the Mormon Saints be baptized, and demanded that girls over twelve start attending lectures on the importance of polygamy

---

[145] *Journal of Discourses*, IV, p. 41.

[146] *Journal of Discourses*, IV, p. 54.

[147] Hirshson, p. 155.

and the submission of plural wives, very much in the spirit of Chairman Mao's rectification and reeducation campaigns.

DANITE AND SHENPIP DEATH SQUADS PURGE THE RANKS OF THE SAINTS

Grant, in his role as Brigham's Torquemada, told the worst offenders that they should come forward and voluntarily arrange for their own capital execution. He told the worst offenders among the Mormons that they ought to go and confess to Brigham Young, who would then appoint a firing squad to execute them. If they paid the price of blood atonement now, they might still have some hope of getting into heaven. Utah traditionally offered death row inmates the choice between hanging and shooting, in deference to Brigham Young's idea that shedding your blood now might increase your chances to get into heaven later, assuming you were in the blood atonement category. The executioners would obviously be drawn from the ranks of the Danites,[148] and might include the Exterminating Angels, sometimes called Shenpips.

A few years later, Brigham Young Jr. confessed, not in public but in his diary entry for December 15, 1862, that the Reformation instituted by his father had been a "reign of terror." (*The Mormon Rebellion*, Bigler & Bagley, p. 95)

THE HAND-CART HECATOMB: BRIGHAM YOUNG'S GREAT LEAP FORWARD

Just as Mao used the Great Proletarian Cultural Revolution starting in 1966 to divert attention from his failures like the Great Leap Forward, so Brigham Young was able to use a smokescreen of fanaticism to cover up his own logistical blunders, most notably the great handcart tragedy of 1857. Seeking ways to promote an immediate wave of mass migration into Deseret on the cheapest possible basis to get ready for the imminent conflict, Brigham Young had ordered that newly converted Mormon adepts arriving at the Mississippi or Missouri River points of debarkation that served the overland trails west should not be provided with expensive wagons with oxen or horses, but rather with cheap wooden handcarts. These often resembled rickshaws. Each handcart was supposed to carry 400 to 500 pounds of baggage. Logistical support was limited to one wagon and three yokes of oxen for each 20 carts or 80 to 100 people. This was insufficient for food, clothing, and tents, and it was a recipe for disaster.[149]

Nevertheless, the Brigham Young personality cult generated paeans of phrase for this idea

> Oh, our faith goes with the hand-carts,
> And they have our hearts' best love;
> 'Tis a novel mode of traveling,
> Devised by the gods above.

---

[148] The Danites, a militia founded by Joseph Smith in Missouri, were the sons of Dan. "Dan shall be a serpent by the way, an adder in the path, that bites the horse's heels, so that his rider shall fall backward." (Genesis 49:17)

[149] Hirshson, p. 153.

> And Brigham's their executive,
> He told us the design;
> And the Saints are proudly marching on,
> Along the handcart line.[150]

But in 1856, a party of immigrants from England, Wales, Scotland, and the Scandinavian countries arrived late, and then had to wait for their handcarts to be manufactured. Two parties started the trek from Florence, Nebraska in August rather than in the spring. When they arrived at Laramie, Wyoming, it was found that Brigham Young had failed to honor his promise to provide the necessary food stocks for the rest of the trip. Handcarts began to break down, rations were cut by 25%, and the starving Saints began eating their supplies of axle grease to stay alive. A blizzard then arrived from the north, leaving the immigrants stranded. Out of about a thousand Mormons in the two hardest hit companies, some 210 died.

Brigham Young did everything possible to escape responsibility, despite the fact that logistics was supposed to be his strong point. The idea of using wooden hand carts had been totally his own, and they implemented it despite the warnings of other senior Mormon leaders. He had skimped on the accompanying wagons, and had failed to provide food stocks and emergency help along the way.

Brigham Young was widely blamed in Salt Lake City, and he lashed out in rage at his critics: "if any man or woman complains of me or my counselors, in regard to the lateness of some of this season's immigration, let the curse of God be on them and blast their substance with mildew and destruction, until their names are forgotten from the earth."[151] Modern-day political observers are reminded of the attitude of the Romney campaign towards its critics, which can be summed up as the same "the public be damned."

One wretched woman survived Brigham Young's handcart fiasco, only to lose her life when she had second thoughts about polygamy. She committed suicide on Christmas day by cutting her throat. The Mormon authorities were not interested in clarifying this tragic case, but the loyal American Indian agent Garland Hurt investigated. Hurt discovered that the victim had "come with the handcarts and been told that she would be denied subsistence and denounced as a prostitute if she did not become the polygamous wife of the man with whose family she was living, and the fatal razor was brought to its relief."[152]

It was in these same dark weeks of the winter of 1856-57, with the handcart tragedy and the Reformation hysteria providing the backdrop, that the Brigham Young clique carried out new steps on the path to secession.

---

[150] Hirshson, p. 153.
[151] Hirshson, pp. 153-155.
[152] *New York Semi-Weekly Tribune* Vol. VIII, No. 1332, online at *19th Century Mormon Newspaper Index.*

In December 1856, the Legislature of Utah Territory met in Fillmore, and quickly voted to move the territorial capital back to Salt Lake City, where it could be more easily defended. One observer of its proceedings found that the wind of theocratic secessionism and rebellion against the United States had reached hurricane force. The Mormons wanted independence, and they were willing to court a confrontation with the federal government to get it. (*The Mormon Rebellion*, Bigler & Bagley, p. 103)

Brigham Young railed against the few loyal United States officials in the territory, including Surveyor General Burr, Garland Hurt, and Federal District Judge William W. Drummond. These he vilified as "dogs and skunks."[153]

MORMONS ENDORSE NULLIFICATION DOCTRINE

Building a case for a declaration of independence or sovereignty, the Utah territorial legislature began voting a series of raving resolutions pledging to "resist any attempt of Government Officials to set at naught our Territorial laws, or to impose upon us those which are inapplicable and of right not in force in this Territory."[154]

They then passed a long resolution addressed to President elect James Buchanan, in which they recited all the injustices that had been afflicted on the Mormons starting from their foundation. Their major complaint was that American presidents had appointed Utah territorial officials "who seek to corrupt our community, trample upon our rights, walk underfoot our laws, rules and regulations, who neither feared God nor regard men and whenever checked in a mid-career, threaten us with death and destruction by United States troops."[155]

John M. Bernhisel was Utah's territorial delegate to the U.S. Congress in Washington, and tried to make the case for Utah's statehood to the new President Buchanan shortly after his inauguration, but Buchanan told them to submit these documents to Interior Secretary Jacob Thompson. Thompson declared that the Mormon version of nullification was nothing less than "a declaration of war." (*The Mormon Rebellion*, Bigler & Bagley, p. 106)

MORMONS IN OPEN REBELLION

At about the same time, Surveyor General Burr wrote urgently to Washington: "*The fact is, these people repudiate the authority of the United States in this country, and are in open rebellion against the general government.*"[156]

More reports came to the White House from Federal Judge Drummond about Mormon destruction of judicial records, American citizens imprisoned without due process of law, Brigham Young's suborning of juries, the Gunnison murder on orders from the Mormon Saints, and the assassination of Federal District Judge Shaver through poisoning.

---

[153] Bigler and Bagley, page 105.
[154] Edward Williams Tullidge, *Life of Brigham Young*, p. 280, online at books.google.com.
[155] Ibid.
[156] William Alexander Lynn, *The Story of the Mormons*, p. 805, online at books.google.com.

Meanwhile, the Reformation was still in full swing, and a Mormon bishop and his gang of Danite retainers castrated one man for alleged sexual misdeeds. This prompted a discussion among the sons of Brigham Young, which the patriarch concluded by prophesying "that the day would come when thousands would be made eunuchs 'in order for them to be saved in the Kingdom of God.'"[157]

BRIGHAM YOUNG SEES SEPARATION OF UTAH FROM KINGDOMS OF THIS WORLD

Brigham Young escalated his rhetoric, challenging his Salt Lake City audience to embrace the cause of secessionism and an independent Mormon theocratic empire. In his sermon of August 2, 1857, the Prophet intoned: "The time must come when there will be a separation between this kingdom and the kingdoms of this world, even in every point of view. The time must come when this kingdom must be free and independent from all other kingdoms. Are you prepared to have the thread cut now?"[158]

With many reports of a full-fledged Mormon insurrection converging on Washington, pressure mounted on the feckless and treacherous President James Buchanan to do something. The Mormons had considered Buchanan a friend, just as they had positively evaluated Millard Fillmore and Stephen Douglas, since all of them accepted the Democratic Party doctrine of squatter sovereignty, which the Mormons thought would allow polygamy to be continued perpetually. Buchanan's Secretary of War was John B. Floyd, who used his term in office to do everything possible to facilitate secessionism and rebellion. Some historians think that Floyd encouraged Buchanan to send a force into Utah because he expected the expedition to be a fiasco, and estimated that it was sure to drain the federal treasury in the process. Some have seen the motivation in the lucrative contracts that might be distributed.

Purely political factors clearly played a part. The Republicans had scored significant gains in 1856 by tying the albatross of polygamy around the neck of the Democratic Party. Now, Democrats were looking for a way to put some distance between themselves and the Mormon Saints. US Senator William Bigler wrote to Buchanan that "there is a good deal of honest indignation in the country against the conduct of the Mormons. The universal sentiment seems to demand the assertion and maintenance of the political authority of the general government over the territory, regardless of their peculiar institution. They may convince the world that a man in that country may have more wives than one; but it will be difficult to show that it gives him a right to reject the executive officer of the law."[159] At this point, Buchanan alerted 1,500 US troops to be ready to move into Utah.

---

[157] Jerald and Sandra Tanner, "Mormon Blood Atonement: Fact or Fantasy?", online at Recovery from Mormonism.

[158] *Journal of Discourses*, V:12, p. 98b.

[159] Hirshson, p. 168.

JUNE 1857: STEPHEN DOUGLAS CONDEMNS THE "TREASONABLE, DISGUSTING, AND BESTIAL PRACTICES" OF MORMONDOM

On June 12, 1857, Stephen Douglas, who was getting hammered as the defender of slavery and polygamy in the territories, also called for military action to reassert federal authority in Utah. Douglas declared that 90% of the Mormons were foreigners, aliens who rejected US citizenship. The Mormons, he said, considered Brigham Young and his regime superior to the federal government, which they hoped in the long run to subvert. The Mormons were goading the Indians into warlike acts, even as the Danites crushed internal dissent. Douglas denounced the Mormon power, declaring: "Should such a state of things actually exist as we are led to infer from the reports, and such information that comes in an official shape, the knife must be applied to this pestiferous, disgusting cancer which is gnawing into the very vitals of the body politic. It must be cut out by the roots, seared over by the red hot iron of stern and unflinching law." Douglas wanted to abolish the Utah Territory altogether by repealing the 1850 act of Congress which had created it. This was because the Mormons were "alien enemies and outlaws," unfit to be citizens of the Territory, and even more unfit to be citizens of a state. Douglas warned that "to protect them further in their treasonable, disgusting, and bestial practices would be a disgrace to the country – a disgrace to humanity – a disgrace to civilization, and a disgrace to the spirit of the age." Douglas wanted Brigham Young and his retainers to answer for any crimes they have committed in courts in Iowa, Missouri, or California.[160]

Heber Kimball replied that Douglas was trying to get elected president, which was certainly true, and that "he will go to hell," which remains to be determined.[161]

MAY 1857: ONE THIRD OF US ARMY DEPLOYED TO QUELL MORMON REBELLION

One of Brigham Young's sources in New York City reported that the US Army supreme commander, the Whig General Winfield Scott, had ordered Brevet Brigadier General William S. Harney along with his command of twenty-five hundred officers and men to occupy a line along the Oregon Trail from Fort Leavenworth to Fort Laramie. With this order, which was issued on May 28, 1857 Scott had committed about one third of the officers and men of the entire United States Army to dealing with the Mormon threat. (*The Mormon Rebellion*, Bigler & Bagley, p. 130-2)

At this time, the majority of Mormons were convinced that the apocalypse would occur during their lifetimes. Brigham Young cannily exploited this belief structure for his own political gain. "This is the kingdom of heaven—the kingdom of God which Daniel saw," Young sermonized. "This is the kingdom that was to be set up in the last days." If US troops came into Utah, Brigham Young considered that an aggression which he would meet with armed force and with the weapon of secessionism: "I shall take a hostile move

---

[160] Ibid.
[161] Ibid.

by our enemies as an evidence that it is time for the thread to be cut. I think that we will find three hundred who will lap water, and we can whip out the Midianites."[162]

BRIGHAM YOUNG PROCLAIMS SECESSION TO CHEERING MORMONS

This is also what Brigham Young was writing in his own private diary, where he recorded on August 11, 1857: "Fixed my detirmination [sic] not to let any troops enter this territory… And unless the Government assumes a more pacific attitude, to declare emigration by the overland route Stopt. And make every preparation to give the U.S. a Sound drubbing. I do not feel to be imposed upon any more." (*The Mormon Rebellion*, Bigler & Bagley, p. 139) According to an eyewitness, on August 16, 1857, Young had stated in a speech in the temple that Utah was now a separate and independent territory, owing no allegiance or obedience to any laws but their own. Mormon bigwig George Brown Bailey later wrote that "This people came out and declared their independency of the United States from this very time… The Presidency put it to the people wither [sic] they would maintain it to the last and it was carried by unanimous vote of uplifted hands and a shout of Yea which made the place echo."[163]

Young's actions depended on a kind of primitive doublethink which he constantly practiced. One aspect was to pledge support for the Constitution at the same time that he plotted insurrection. Here is how Brigham's doublethink sounded in that fateful August of 1857: "The United States had turned mob & were breaking the Constitution of the United States & we would now have to go forth & defend it & also the kingdom of God… If General Harney Came here with an armey [sic] to destroy this people we would destroy him & his armey [sic]." (*The Mormon Rebellion*, Bigler & Bagley, p. 141)

If the United States Constitution no longer applied to Utah, and the writ of the US federal government no longer ran, what exactly was going to take their place? Brigham Young fell back on Joseph Smith's slogan of "theodemocracy," which the original Prophet had cooked up for his 1844 presidential campaign. Clearly, theodemocracy was simply a way to sugarcoat theocracy, a concept which has never been popular in the United States. Theodemocracy, it turned out, meant a totalitarian regime with no opposition.

MORMON THREAT TO DESTROY US CITIES

When US Army Captain Stewart Van Vliet arrived in Salt Lake City to attempt to negotiate with the Mormon regime, Brigham Young greeted him with a tirade full of threats against the federal government:

> "'The intention of the Government is to destroy us & this we are determin[ed] they shall not do. If the government of the United States [persists] in sending Armies to destroy us in the name of the Lord we shall Conquer them…. And even should an Armey of 50,000 men get into this valley when they got here they would find nothing but a Barren waste. [Washington] must stop all

---

[162] *Journal of Discourses*, V:21, p. 99b.
[163] *Journal of George and Elizabeth Bailey*, August 22, 1857, online at stayfamily.org.

emigration across this Continent for they Cannot tread in safety. The Indians will kill all that attempt it. … If the Government Calls for volunteers in Calafornia [sic] & the people turn out to come to destroy us they will find their own buildings in flames before they get far from home & so throughout the United States."[164]

Did Brigham Young really possess a terrorist network capable of carrying out such a massive retaliatory strike against American cities? Were the Danites and Shenpips really that powerful? We do know that Nauvoo Legion officer John L. Dunyan was making similar threats in the same timeframe, telling a Mississippi traveler that, if the US Army tried to march into Mormon territory,

> *"every city, town and village in the States of California, Missouri and Iowa should be burned immediately—that they had men to do this who were not known to be Mormons!"* (*The Mormon Rebellion*, Bigler & Bagley, p. 147)

Thus, a century and a half before September 11, 2001, the Mormon chieftain was openly threatening to destroy American cities. What links might there be between the nightmare vision of Brigham Young's threats and the tragedy of 9/11? Up to now, many had imagined that no political force inside the United States could have been the author of 9/11, but this opinion clearly needs to be revised in light of threats the Mormons actually made. It should be added that the other significant force talking about burning New York City around this time was the British Admiralty.[165]

The rules of engagement given to the United States Army for the Utah deployment were to respect all inhabitants, to shoot only in self-defense, and to assist federal officials in the implementation of applicable law. This was, in other words, anything but a punitive expedition on the order of Sherman's March to the Sea. Nevertheless, Brigham Young found it politic to exaggerate the federal presence into a nightmare. On September 15, 1857, the Prophet decreed the distribution of a proclamation of martial law addressed to the "Citizens of Utah" which he had ordered printed up.

BRIGHAM YOUNG'S INSURRECTION PROCLAMATION OF SEPT. 15, 1857

According to this remarkable document, the Mormons have been "invaded by a hostile force, who are evidently assailing us to accomplish our overthrow and destruction…"[166] For the Mormon Saints, as a result,

> "Our duty to our families requires us not to tamely submit to be driven and slain without an attempt to preserve ourselves. Our duty to our country, our

---

[164] Scott G. Kenney, ed., *William Woodruff's Journal* (Midvale UT: Signature Books, 1983), vol. 5, pp. 96-97.

[165] See "Admiralty Plans to Bombard and Burn Boston and New York," in Webster G. Tarpley, "Wrap the World in Flames," tarpley.net.

[166] Brigham Young, Utah Governor, "Proclamation by the Governor: Citizens of Utah," broadside, Salt Lake City, 1857, online at law2.umkc.edu.

holy religion, our God, to freedom and liberty, requires that we should not quietly stand still and see those fetters forging around, which are calculated to enslave and bring us into subjection to an unlawful military despotism, such as can only emanate (in a country of constitutional law) from usurpation, tyranny and oppression."

Brigham Young, despite the fact that he was a private citizen and religious leader and not a government official in any way, did not hesitate to act in the name of the United States:

"Therefore, I, Brigham Young, Governor and Superintendent of Indian Affairs for the Territory of Utah, in the name of the people of the United States in the Territory of Utah,"

Brigham Young then proceeded to create a regime of martial law that included the following points:

"First - Forbid all armed forces of every description from coming into this Territory, under any pretense whatever.

Second - That all the forces in said Territory hold themselves in readiness to march at a moment's notice, to repel any and all such invasion

Third - Martial law is hereby declared to exist in this Territory, from and after the publication of this Proclamation; and no person shall be allowed to pass or repass, into or through, or from this Territory without a permit from the proper officer.

This proclamation was Utah's functional equivalent of the South Carolina ordinance of secession of December 20, 1860. Utah was acting as an independent country, hostile to the United States.

In a crescendo of provocation, Brigham Young thus announced that special safe conduct passes, like those issued by the infamous Committee of Public Safety during the Reign of Terror in the French Revolution or the internal passports of the USSR, would be required for all persons wanting to cross the borders of Utah Territory.

He followed this on September 18, 1857 with a general order to the Mormon troops recalling how "many and deep were the scars which the knife of the legalized assassin had inflicted upon us...God will avenge our many wrongs to guard the portals and bar the entrance of the polluter." Special vigilance was demanded of the armed forces to guarantee the faithful execution of Brigham Young's commands and to "to see that the requirements of the Proclamation are strictly carried out."

BRIGHAM YOUNG'S SIEGFRIED LINE TO KEEP US FORCES OUT

The main access to Salt Lake City from Colorado and points further east was Echo Canyon. Here the Mormon Saints constructed a line of fortifications. Because the

Mormons lacked competent military engineers, the trenches they built would have been highly vulnerable to assault. The Mormon breastworks "were accessible from the rear and so exposed that army sharpshooters might easily have picked off the defenders."[167] The trenches were also vulnerable to artillery attack. This is where Miles Romney the younger wanted to fight against the United States, and where his elder brother George was part of the garrison. Although these earthworks were not formidable, they nevertheless psychologically intimidated some federal officers who were already tending towards defeatism.

From a geostrategic point of view, Brigham Young's attempt to cut transcontinental communications posed a dire threat to the federal union. The transcontinental telegraph was still several years in the future, but it would go through Salt Lake City. The famous Golden Spike which completed the transcontinental railroad at Promontory Point in May, 1869 was also located in Utah. Among wagon routes, the Oregon Trail and Spanish or Mormon Trail passed through southern Idaho and Utah, both areas controlled by the Mormons. An insurrection in Utah and Southern Idaho would cut off communications between the East Coast and California, creating a grave danger that the Golden State might be subverted and detached from the Union. There was a secessionist constituency in Southern California, which came out in the open in 1860-61, so this danger was anything but academic.

In addition, if the Mormons could successfully block the overland wagon trails, then the great western migration of the American people would be stopped. In the summer of 1857, California newspapers were reporting that the number of people traveling west overland was between 25,000 and 30,000, which they estimated to be the highest level since 1853. What would be the fate of these numerous pioneers if Brigham Young were to succeed in his attempt to make Utah a zone of exclusion? Clearly, many of them would perish.

BRIGHAM YOUNG ORDERS WAGON TRAINS TO STAY OUT OF UTAH

A further complication came from the Mormon strategy of attempting to use the Indian tribes as irregular auxiliaries in shutting down westward migration through the Intermountain West. Brigham Young tried to scapegoat the Indians and use them as a pretext for his actions, lamenting that American atrocities against the Indians were stirring up Indian violence in his bailiwick. Therefore, the Americans must "stop traveling through this country," and desist from their "outrageous treatment" of the Native Americans. (*The Mormon Rebellion*, Bigler & Bagley, p. 143)

At the same time, Brigham wanted God's help in getting the Indians to fight and die for the cause of the Mormon Saints: "We pray our Father to turn the hearts of the Lamanites even the sons of Jacob unto us that they may do thy will & be as a wall of defense around us." (*The Mormon Rebellion*, Bigler & Bagley, pp. 156-57)

---

[167] Hirshson, p. 172.

THE MORMON SAINTS MASSACRE
THE BAKER-FANCHER PARTY FROM ARKANSAS

At this point, a column of US forces was moving through Wyoming, spread out over several hundred miles. It was now under the command of Colonel Albert Sidney Johnston, who would shortly join the Confederate States of America and be killed during his attack on the Union Army commanded by Ulysses S. Grant at Pittsburg Landing, Tennessee, in the battle of Shiloh in the spring of 1862. Johnston deployed his forces poorly. Cavalry was essential for fighting Mormons on horseback, as well as for warding off attacks by mounted Indians. But instead, Johnston had his infantry at the front of the column and his cavalry fought to the rear, where they could not be effective.

Brigham Young now caused the massacre of 140 peaceful Arkansas Travelers, including men, women, and children, in the infamous Mountain Meadows Massacre. This horrendous event stands still today as the third largest politically motivated terrorist attack in American history, ranking after 9/11 and the Oklahoma City bombing. It is a case of unprovoked violence against peaceful civilians by the Mormon Danite militia under the control of Brigham Young. Understandably, the Mountain Meadows Massacre has been a cause of acute embarrassment for Mormon, pro-Mormon, and anti-American historians. They have therefore attempted the classic maneuver of blaming the victims, alleging that the Arkansas Pioneers had mistreated the Indians, poisoned water wells, created friction with the Saints, or otherwise stirred up trouble. These are ludicrous and morally bankrupt subterfuges that are hardly capable of obscuring the fundamental responsibility of Brigham Young and the Mormon Church for these deaths.

The Arkansas wagon train had set out in the spring of 1857, long before Brigham Young had issued his order to close the borders of Utah. The travelers came from a group of families – the Fanchers, Bakers, Camerons, Joneses, Dunlaps, Mitchells, Huffs, Tackitts, Millers, and Woods – from Northwest Arkansas. These were prosperous settlers, and were accompanied by a considerable herd of cattle. These were truly innocent passersby, most or all of whom could have had virtually no knowledge of what was awaiting them in Utah until they had come in contact the Mormons. (*The Mormon Rebellion*, Bigler & Bagley, p. 156)

BRIGHAM YOUNG TO THE DANITE COMMANDER:
"PITCH INTO" THE ARKANSANS

Brigham Young preferred to orchestrate atrocities indirectly. Signed orders to commit war crimes were not his style. Historians have never found a piece of paper from Brigham Young that would finally establish his guilt for the Mountain Meadows Massacre. But to look for such documents is to misunderstand the leadership style of the Mormon Prophet. King Henry II of England, in the winter of 1170, is supposed to have exclaimed before his court, "Will no one rid me of this meddlesome priest?" The priest in question, St. Thomas Beckett, was soon assassinated in Canterbury Cathedral by killers who were seeking favor with the English sovereign. Brigham Young preferred to operate in precisely this fashion.

In the late summer of 1857, Brigham Young conferred with Mormon Bishop John D. Lee, his adopted son, a top leader of the Danites, and also a member of the secret Council of Fifty, the explicitly political body which Joseph Smith had created to advance Mormon power on this earth. The Mormon Prophet asked: "Brother Lee, what do you think the brethren would do if a company of emigrants should come down through here making threats? Don't you think they would pitch into them?" Visiting the site where the Mountain Meadows Massacre would shortly occur, Brigham had pointed out to Lee that the "Indians, with the advantage they had of the rocks, could use up a large company of emigrants, or make it very hot for them." [168] "Use up" was Brigham's usual euphemism for slaughter. It was practically an engraved invitation for a major atrocity.

The Mormon Prophet also telegraphed his intentions to the world at large, slyly warning the Gentile or American overland travelers that they were in immediate danger from the Indians: "'I now wish to say to all Gentiles send word to your friends that they must stop crossing the Continent to Calafornia [sic] for the Indians will kill them'" (*The Mormon Rebellion*, Bigler & Bagley, p. 161) But the killers would be Mormons, not Indians.

BRIGHAM YOUNG'S GRAIN EMBARGO AGAINST AMERICANS

The intentions of the Fancher-Baker party were entirely peaceful, but there was friction with the Mormon Saints because Brigham's followers had decided that they owned every inch of land in the Utah Territory. A conflict arose because "the nature of the terrain and Mormon communal land-use patterns made the large cattle herd and its need for forage a point of dispute over who owned the land—Uncle Sam or the Almighty?" (*The Mormon Rebellion*, Bigler & Bagley, p. 166) The Mormons were forbidden to give or sell any food to the United States Army or to the Arkansas Travelers. Young commanded them that not even a kernel of grain… "be sold to our enemies."[169]

On September 1, 1857 Young met with the leaders of the Pahvants and Paiutes. The details of this conference are still a secret, but Brigham wrote in his diary that he could "hardly restrain them from exterminating the 'Americans.'"[170] This looks like a cover story invented after the fact.

On the morning of Monday, September 7, 1857, a group of Mormon riflemen accompanied by a small screening force of Indians opened fire on the Arkansans as they prepared breakfast. The Pioneers circled their wagons, threw up earthworks, and returned fire with their Kentucky rifles. Some of the Indian screening force were killed. The Mormons realized that if they attempted a frontal assault, they could eventually overwhelm the Arkansans, but only at the cost of heavy losses to the Saints. Instead, from the Mormon point of view, a stratagem of deception was in order to convince the Arkansas people to give up their guns and deliver themselves into the hands of the Mormons, who would then slaughter them. (*The Mormon Rebellion*, Bigler & Bagley, p. 173)

---

[168] "History of the Mormon Rebellion," *The United Service*, Vol. IV, no. 5 (November 1890), p. 451.

[169] Jon Karkauer, *Under the Banner of Heaven*, p. 216, online at books.google.com.

[170] Everett Cooley, ed., *Diary of Brigham Young, 1857* (Salt Lake City, 1980), p. 71.

DANITES: "EMIGRANTS *MUST* BE DONE AWAY WITH"

The Danites conferred about what to do. One of the leaders, Colonel Dame, insisted that there must be no delay while waiting for further guidance from Salt Lake City. Said Dame: "I don't care what the council decided…My orders are that the emigrants *must be done away with.*"[171] The Mormons were able to convince the Arkansans to give up their weapons and accept a Mormon escort out of the territory. Each Arkansan male was flanked by an armed Mormon. There ensued the greatest peacetime massacre of Americans in the entire 19th century.

The Arkansas Travelers and their armed Mormon guards walked along a path which was surrounded by brush on both sides. At the signal from one of the Mormon leaders, each of the armed Saints turned and shot the disarmed Arkansas man walking next to him. Mormon men with their faces painted, accompanied by a few Indian allies, emerged from their hiding places in the bushes to kill the women and children at close range. The vast majority of the killers were Mormons, and not Paiute Indians. Older children begged for their lives, but they were killed if the Mormons estimated that they were old enough to give a credible account of what had occurred, and would thus be able to testify against the murdering Mormon Saints.[172]

The Mormons were anxious to hide their monstrous guilt from the world, so they took care to kill every adult and even the older children, leaving alive only the infants and toddlers who would not be able, they thought, to tell the story of how the Saints had committed this monumental atrocity. The last to die was a girl aged between ten and twelve, whom the Danites judged to be old enough to tell the story. A total of seventeen children survived. Later, with characteristic Mormon aplomb, the Southern Utah Saints – some of whom had taken part in the killing – who had taken these children in, presented the United States government with a bill for $7,000 for child care services rendered. In the event, they got $3,500." (*The Mormon Rebellion*, Bigler & Bagley, p. 343)

MORMON COVER STORY: ARKANSANS POISONED INDIAN WELLS

After the killing, a consensus among the perpetrators was quickly reached regarding a plausible cover story for the atrocity. The killers swore each other to secrecy, and pledged to maintain the fiction that the slayings had been the work of the Indians. To provide a plausible motive for such Indian violence, they also concocted the accusation that the Arkansas Pioneers had antagonized the tribes by deliberately poisoning some of the wells along the way. These interlocking components have furnished a cover story which has provided the matrix for Mormon apologetics about the Mountain Meadows Massacre for more than a century and a half. (*The Mormon Rebellion*, Bigler & Bagley, p. 177) Mark Twain was one of the first who accused Brigham Young of ordering the killings. Official Mormon historiography continues a massive cover-up on this point.

---

[171] Bagley, *Blood of the Prophets*, p. 132.
[172] See Bigler & Bagley, p. 175; Bagley, *Blood of the Prophets*, pp. 130-133.

The *Los Angeles Star* published an initial account of the massacre on October 10, 1857, and for the rest of October the issue was the subject of many articles in California newspapers. On November 9, 1857 the *Cleveland Daily Herald* published an account of these events. This was followed by the *Chicago Daily Tribune* on November 12, and the *New York Times* on November 17, 1857.[173]

On the 28th of September, Lee visited Brigham Young and reported on the slaughter. Young told him to keep silent, and attempted to blame everything on the Indians. The Mormon Prophet later said this to Lee about the Mountain Meadows Massacre: "…the company that was used up at the Mountain Meadowes were the Fathers, Mothe[rs], Bros., Sisters & connections of those that Muerderd the Prophets, they merittd their fate, & the only thing that ever troubled his was the lives of the Women & children, but that under the circumstance [it] could not be avoided."[174]

Many of the dead had been thrown into a ravine and covered with a thin layer of dirt. Coyotes and other predators soon swarmed over the pile of bodies. In May of the following year, Assistant Surgeon Charles Brewer of U.S. Army found masses of women's hair, children's bonnets, such as are generally used upon the plains, and pieces of lace, muslin, calicoes, and other material, part of women's and children's apparel."[175]

MORMON REVENGE FOR ROMNEY ANCESTOR
PARLEY PRATT WAS A FACTOR

The *Washington Times Insight Magazine*, reviewing Will Bagley's earlier book, *Blood of the Prophets: Brigham Young and the Massacre at Mountain Meadows*, notes that Bagley "puts blame for the massacre squarely on the shoulders of one of the most revered LDS leaders, Brigham Young" and also implicates "most of the adult males living in Southern Utah at the time."[176] In an interview with *Insight*, Bagley stressed that "just prior to the Mountain Meadows siege, a highly regarded Mormon leader, Parley Pratt, had been murdered in Arkansas – the very region where the Fancher wagon train formed up. His assailant, a jealous husband, was hailed as a hero in Van Buren, Arkansas, and never faced charges for the murder. Rage over the Pratt murder was just one log on a big fire.[177]

Bagley is convinced that the Church of Latter-day Saints has been organizing a cover-up of these events. He is especially concerned about the lack of source material, since "so little authentic material about the massacre survives that it suggests a concerted official effort to eliminate any mention of the subject in Mormon annals." Instead, the researcher finds: "a maze of duplicity built by men who lied to protect their very lives."

---

[173] See mountainmeadows.unl.edu.

[174] Cleland and Brooks, eds., *A Mormon Chronicle: the Diaries of John D. Lee, 1848 – 1876* (San Marino CA: Huntington Library, 1955), Vol. Ii, p. 314, May 30, 1861.

[175] Bagley, *Blood of the Prophets*, p. 226-7.

[176] John Elvin, "The Madness at Mountain Meadows," *Insight on the News*, 19:3, January 21, 2003.

[177] Ibid.

Bagley also believes that the Latter-day Saints have hidden the key documents in their archives: "I'm convinced they have access to a wealth of evidence that will back my interpretation, specifically minutes of key meetings of the Mormon hierarchy." Relatives have also done their part, destroying records that would embarrass or indict their ancestors or the Mormon Church. One wonders if this applies to Romney's transition director Mike Leavitt, or to US Senator Mike Lee, both of whom are lineal descendents of Mountain Meadows war criminals.

History Professor Wayne K. Hinton of Southern Utah University, by contrast, prefers to impeach the conduct of the Arkansans. The deaths were "unwarranted, but can be explained mainly by the fears and anger of the Mormons at the expectation of violence against themselves." He sees the Baker-Fancher party as a "rather unruly group … [whose] members abused Indians, killed livestock and stole and destroyed property."[178]

MORMON COVERUP OF THE MOUNTAIN MEADOWS MASSACRE

Insight writer John Elvin cites the case of Morris Shirts, a descendant of one of the Mormons, who claims that "all of the adults and older children were slain in battle." Elvin is justifiably indignant and explains: "Slain in battle? About half of those who were shot, butchered or clubbed to death (more than 50 in number) were children. The kids – alive, dying and dead – were tossed about like rags by their attackers, according to some surviving accounts, while their parents and guardians, including 30 women, were executed at point-blank range after having surrendered. Army investigators arriving later on the scene found nothing left but scattered bones and tufts of hair. They tried their best to bury properly such remains as were left by coyotes, wolves and other scavengers."[179]

To explain the massacre, Bagley goes back to Brigham Young's strategy, which had brought him to the brink of war with the United States. The Mormon Prophet was telling his followers: "We have borne enough of the oppression and hellish abuse, and we will not bear any more of it." Bagley also recalls that the "doctrine of blood atonement is denied by some Mormons, but there is substantial evidence that it was a practice from the beginnings of the movement and that Young espoused it, preaching that the killing of enemies was for their own good, "'the way to love mankind' by sending the sinner heavenward."[180]

Brigham Young wanted a test case which could illustrate his ability to stop all overland travel through Utah and environs. Everything was carefully planned well in advance. In this endeavor, he was more than willing to commit an act of terrorism to deter and dissuade parties of pioneers that were still flowing across the Great Plains and towards Utah. He wanted to show that no future transcontinental telegraph or railroad could be maintained without his permission. Most importantly, Young saw it as part of a dialectic

---

[178] Ibid.
[179] Ibid.
[180] Ibid.

of secessionism involving Confederate slaveocrat forces, California separatists, and others. His was an offensive strategy, and not just the defense of Deseret.

THE BUNGLED FEDERAL ADVANCE TOWARDS UTAH

Secessionists everywhere were undoubtedly heartened by the immense logistical problems encountered by the United States Army in attempting to reach Salt Lake City. The future Confederate Albert Sidney Johnston was appointed commander of the federal forces in September 1857. Given his mentality, he could hardly be expected to conduct a vigorous repression of secessionism. About one third of the United States Army was now spread out over the Oregon Trail from the Missouri River almost to the gates of Utah. The supply train and the infantry were in the vanguard, and the cavalry brought up the rear. This disposition was totally counterproductive. Because the advance was so slow, leading Mormons began gloating. Apostle Heber C. Kimball, part of Brigham Young's leadership clique, predicted that his own harem could deal with the federals, boasting: "I have wives enough to whip out the United States."[181]

BRIGHAM YOUNG WANTS KANSAS VIOLENCE TO ESCALATE, HOPES FOR JOHN BROWN

The conclusion reached by historians Bigler and Bagley was that Brigham Young was hoping for an additional flare-up of violence in Kansas that would force the U.S. Army to be sent in and tied down far away from Utah. If this diversion of American forces were to materialize, the Mormons would be able to hold out indefinitely in their intermountain fastness: "The border war over slavery in 'Bleeding Kansas' would lead, he believed, to the breakup of the Union, as Joseph Smith had prophesied. 'If we can avert the blow for another season,' Young added, 'it is probable our enemies will have enough to attend to at home without worrying about the Latter-day Saints."[182] But Brigham Young's hopes may have embraced a conflagration far larger than just Kansas.

Brigham Young generally operated with an excellent intelligence picture, and the hypothesis here is that he benefited from information passed to him by high-level British sources. In addition, Brigham Young's agents read all the transcontinental mail that was going to California, gleaning much from US government documents. The abolitionist firebrand John Brown, who was famously leading an armed struggle against the proslavery border ruffians in Kansas, was deployed by a group of leading Boston bankers, and it would be surprising if the British were not aware of some of Brown's intentions. Brown was already famous for having engaged the border ruffians in a small-scale pitched battle at Osawatomie in August, 1856.

DID BRIGHAM YOUNG JUMP THE GUN ON THE HARPER'S FERRY RAID?

Brown's backers were bankers known as the "Secret Six," and they included the wealthy Tappan interests. Part of John Brown's operation was Hugh Forbes, a British military

---

[181] Juanita Brooks, *The Mountain Meadows Massacre*, p. 19.
[182] *Journal of Discourses*, Vol. V, p. 229

officer. Forbes later leaked word of John Brown's intentions to certain US Congressmen, and might also have informed the government in London. In the fall of 1857, Brown was in Kansas recruiting men for his plan to attack the federal arsenal at Harpers Ferry, Virginia. If the well-informed Brigham Young had gotten wind of any of this, he might have assumed that John Brown would strike the US government during the spring of 1858. The goal of the Harpers Ferry operation was to detonate a generalized slave rebellion and insurrection across the South. Since the southern states were likely to demand the use of federal resources to protect slavery, such a crisis might have immediately precipitated secession, in which case Brigham Young's perspective would have been proven realistic. In the event, John Brown's raid did not occur until October 16-18, 1859. Perhaps Brigham Young had let his consuming rage against the United States cloud his judgment, leading him to get too far out in front of the coming wave of secessionism.

Brigham Young cynically told US Army emissary Captain Van Vliet that he wanted to keep the federal forces out in the wilderness during the fall and winter of 1857-58, and even force them to retreat to Colorado or beyond. "Either way, it would hold up the army's advance for at least eight months and allow enough time for the fighting over slavery in Kansas to spread to other states, forcing Washington to turn its attention elsewhere." (*The Mormon Rebellion*, Bigler & Bagley, p. 188)

BURN GRASS, STEAL HORSES AND LIVESTOCK, BURN WAGONS, POT SHOTS

At this time, California newspapers estimated that the Army of the Mormon Saints could mobilize some 10,000 fighters, and that the Mormons would seek to incite 50,000 Indians to fight for their cause. Brigham Young and his advisers developed a two-stage plan. During the first stage, any federal forces entering Utah Territory or other areas where the Mormons had a strong presence would be subjected to a comprehensive campaign of harassment, sabotage, and scorched earth. In this outer zone, Mormon tactics would include burning grass, stealing horses and livestock, destroying supply trains, and keeping the troops up all night with pot shots and other noise. But Young also traced an inner line of defense, which included the eastern approaches to Salt Lake City through Echo Canyon, and the northern approaches to the Mormon capital through Soda Springs, Idaho. If federal forces attempted to break this inner line of defense, the Mormons would engage them in pitched battle.

Initially, it looked like the Mormons were succeeding in inciting the Cheyenne to attack American pioneers, with one incident claiming the lives of four men from Arkansas. But, towards the end of September, the federals found that the Shoshone or Snake Indians camped along the Green River wanted an alliance with the Americans against the Mormons. (*The Mormon Rebellion*, Bigler & Bagley, p. 207)

BRIGHAM'S ECHO CANYON EARTHWORKS A FAILURE

By now the vanguard of the federal forces under Colonel Alexander was within striking distance of Echo Canyon, where the Mormons had erected some earthworks. In the following year, after the crisis was over, federal officers took the opportunity to inspect the fortification that was supposed to be so formidable. One U.S. Army Captain reported that the Mormon trench line "could have been turned easily by 500 troops."[183]

But Colonel Alexander was thoroughly intimidated by the supposed earthworks, and turned north, away from the Mormon capital. In retrospect, the federal vanguard would have had an excellent chance of forcing its way into Salt Lake City with a coup de main, thus calling Brigham Young's secessionist bluff. At the same time, the Mormon Nauvoo Legion would have attempted to prevent the federals from passing through Echo Canyon. One of Brigham Young's henchmen commented "They seem determined to force their way into the city anyhow, and we know no other way than to fight and destroy them." (*The Mormon Rebellion*, Bigler & Bagley, p. 209)

BRIGHAM YOUNG & CO INDICTED FOR TREASON – FOR THE THIRD TIME

In order to further slow the federal advance, the Mormons now carried out the greatest feat of military prowess in their history. On October 4-5, 1857 the Danite cavalry commander Lot Smith made a surprise raid to destroy 76 US wagons containing the logistics needed to keep the federal expeditionary force in the field for two months. (*The Mormon Rebellion*, Bigler & Bagley, p. 212) As the *New York Times* recently summed up this raid, "in early October, within a span of 24 hours, Smith and around 45 mounted militiamen captured and burned 76 Army supply wagons containing $1 million worth of food and clothing."[184] This feat continued to edify Mormon audiences for the next quarter century, allowing them to express their anti-American animus.

Lot Smith had a cakewalk because the US cavalry had been relegated to the tail end of the marching column, hundreds of miles in the rear. Colonel Alexander complained: "The want of cavalry is severely felt, and we are powerless on account of this deficiency to effect any chastisement of the marauding bands that are continually hovering about us."[185]

The medium-term result of the Lot Smith raid was that Brigham Young, Heber C. Kimball, Daniel H. Wells, Lot Smith, and other Mormon leaders were indicted for violence and treasonable acts. Some of them had already been indicted for treason in Missouri, and then in Nauvoo, so they were in danger of becoming three-time losers. (*The Mormon Rebellion*, Bigler & Bagley, p. 215) Additional treason indictments were also later issued against Joseph Taylor, William Stowell, and others. Taylor had blundered into a U.S. Army camp carrying orders signed by Wells. In the meantime, Young was putting out the word that any mountain man who showed signs of going over to the federals should be immediately liquidated.

---

[183] Martineau, "Seeking a Refuge in the Desert," p. 250.

[184] John G. Turner, "The Mormons Sit Out the Civil War," *New York Times*, May 1, 2012.

[185] *Report of the Secretary of War*, War Department, Washington, December 5, 1857, p. 30.

MORMON PROPHET BRIGHAM YOUNG
ORDERS THE DANITES TO KILL US TROOPS

Brigham Young now issued a direct military order to his armed retainers, instructing them to shoot to kill American soldiers. If the US troops come any closer, Brigham Young specified, "let sleep depart from their eyes and slumber from the eyelids, both day and night, until they take their final sleep. Pick off their guards and sentries & fire into their camps by night, and pick off officers and as many men as possible by day."[186]

"With us it is the kingdom of God or nothing," Brigham Young raved.[187]

In early November, Colonel Albert Sidney Johnston wrote to Washington of the Mormon Saints that "They have with premeditation, placed themselves in rebellion against the Union." The Mormon regime, he judged, was "utterly repugnant to our institutions." Since this was now an insurrection, Johnston concluded: "I have ordered that wherever they are met in arms, that they be treated as enemies."[188] Giving up any hope of entering Salt Lake City in 1857, Johnston now attempted to concentrate his forces at Fort Bridger in western Wyoming, and secure supplies to be able to survive the coming winter. One part of the US column lost 3,000 cattle, horses, and mules because they could not be fed.

The Mormons now established a red line at the western edge of Fort Bridger. If the federals tried to advance beyond that point, Brigham Young ordered the Danites to start "pitching into them." In that case, the Mormon Prophet added, the US forces "could at once be surrounded with an overwhelming force and be used up or compelled to surrender." (*The Mormon Rebellion*, Bigler & Bagley, p. 230)

During this phase, Brigham Young also considered the option of moving the entire Mormon community northwards, into Idaho, Oregon, or what is now British Columbia, which was created precisely at this time to try to keep the Mormons out. The Russian ambassador in Washington, Edward de Stoeckl, asked President Buchanan if he thought the Mormons would try to invade Russian Alaska. Buchanan replied that he did not know, but that he would be glad to get rid of the Mormons under any circumstances." (*The Mormon Rebellion*, Bigler & Bagley, p. 231)

In the meantime, the Mormons were committing a new massacre, which with six dead was on a scale smaller than Mountain Meadows, but which was still horrific. This was the Aiken party from California, whom the Mormons accused of being US espionage agents. Brigham Young's in-house Danite assassin William A. Hickman "used up" the last of this group in late November.

---

[186] Bagley, *Blood of the Prophets*, p. 182.

[187] John Taylor, "The Kingdom of God or Nothing," *Journal of Discourses*, Vol. 6. p. 18.

[188] *House Documents, Otherwise Published As Executive Documents*: 13th Congress, Second Session, p. 46.

MORMONS USE POISONS AGAINST INDIANS

Given the accusation by Mormon apologists that the Arkansas Baker-Fancher party had poisoned the Indian wells, it is worth pointing out that the Mormons had made poisoning Indians into an exact science. The Indian chief called Walker, who had been in conflict with the Mormons a few years earlier, died mysteriously one day after the visit of a Mormon missionary. On another occasion, Captain William McBride of the Nauvoo Legion wrote to an associate: "'We wish you without a moment's hesitation to send us about a pound of arsenic.... We want to give the Indians' well a flavor.... A little strickenine would be of fine service, and serve instead of salt for their too fresh meat."[189] Brigham Young may have tried to poison the U.S. Army with a shipment of salt, but Colonel Johnston refused to accept it.

Because their lucrative business of selling overpriced supplies to pioneers passing through Utah had been interrupted by Brigham Young's blockade order, tax receipts and user fees for the Mormon-owned ferries were now plummeting, creating a cash crunch for the Brigham Young regime. The Mormon Saints responded by gearing up their habitual practice of counterfeiting. Joseph Smith had been accused of counterfeiting, and accusations against the Mormon Saints that they were engaged in printing phony bills were rampant during their early decades. One of the top Mormon counterfeiters was a man named McKenzie, who engraved the plates used to produce the fake bills. The Mormons developed a plan to counterfeit up to $1 million in fake U.S. Treasury drafts to be circulated in California. Brigham Young quickly made up the shortfall by printing his own money, calling it "Deseret scrip.'" (*The Mormon Rebellion*, Bigler & Bagley, p. 274)

The Mormon rebellion, now in full swing, became one of the central topics of the State of the Union address sent to Congress by President Buchanan on December 8, 1857. Buchanan was doubtless responding to the same kind of political pressure which had moved Stephen Douglas to condemn the Mormons, but this nevertheless remains an authoritative statement suggesting that the Mormon rebellion of 1857-58 had an intrinsic importance which few American history textbooks come close to recognizing.

1857 STATE OF THE UNION: BRIGHAM YOUNG HOLDS ABSOLUTE POWER OVER CHURCH AND STATE, COLLECTIVIST ECONOMY

Buchanan started with a quick overview of the recent history of Utah Territory. The central fact here was the overweening power exercised by Brigham Young, who had now attained a position of absolute temporal and spiritual power. Buchanan referred in passing to Brigham Young's economic dictatorship as well:

> Brigham Young was appointed the first governor on the 20th September, 1850, and has held the office ever since. Whilst Governor Young has been both governor and superintendent of Indian affairs throughout this period, he has been at the same time the head of the church called the Latter-day Saints,

---

[189] Michael Eugene Harkin and David Rich Lewis, *Native Americans and the Environment*, p. 314.

and professes to govern its members and dispose of their property by direct inspiration and authority from the Almighty. His power has been, therefore, absolute over both church and state.[190]

This was far too much power for any one man. Brigham Young's increasing authority remained unchecked because of the authoritarian mentality of the Mormons in Utah, Buchanan argued.

BUCHANAN: PEOPLE OF UTAH BELIEVE IN BRIGHAM YOUNG WITH "FANATICAL SPIRIT," "COLLISION" LIKELY

Because of the Mormons, Utah had become a mono-confessional Territory. The decision for peace or war with the United States was now in the hands of the Mormon Moses, and all signs pointed to an early conflagration:

> The people of Utah almost exclusively belong to this church, and believing with a fanatical spirit that he is governor of the Territory by divine appointment, they obey his commands as if these were direct revelations from Heaven. If, therefore, he chooses that his government shall come into collision with the Government of the United States, the members of the Mormon Church will yield implicit obedience to his will. Unfortunately, existing facts leave but little doubt that such is his determination.

BUCHANAN: NO "GOVERNMENT IN UTAH BUT THE DESPOTISM OF BRIGHAM YOUNG"

The totalitarian Mormon power had either driven all federal officials out of the Territory, or else made it virtually impossible for them to carry out their duties:

> Without entering upon a minute history of occurrences, it is sufficient to say that all the officers of the United States, judicial and executive, with the single exception of two Indian agents, have found it necessary for their own personal safety to withdraw from the Territory, and there no longer remains any government in Utah but the despotism of Brigham Young.

BUCHANAN: RESTORE CONSTITUTION AND LAWS IN UTAH BY MILITARY FORCE

Finally recognizing the seriousness of the situation, Buchanan had dispatched new appointees, accompanied by military units:

> This being the condition of affairs in the Territory, I could not mistake the path of duty. As Chief Executive Magistrate I was bound to restore the supremacy of the Constitution and laws within its limits. In order to effect this

---

[190] James Buchanan, *First Annual Message to Congress on the State of the Union*, December 8, 1857, online at The American Presidency Project.

purpose, I appointed a new governor and other Federal officers for Utah and sent with them a military force for their protection and to aid as a *posse comitatus* in case of need in the execution of the laws.

BUCHANAN: OPINIONS, NOT ACTIONS, PROTECTED BY FREEDOM OF RELIGION

Buchanan was careful to point out that he did not intend to interfere with the religious beliefs of the Mormons, but that overt acts were subject to applicable laws, and did not acquire immunity simply because of the claim that they were religiously inspired:

> With the religious opinions of the Mormons, as long as they remained mere opinions, however deplorable in themselves and revolting to the moral and religious sentiments of all Christendom, I had no right to interfere. Actions alone, when in violation of the Constitution and laws of the United States, become the legitimate subjects for the jurisdiction of the civil magistrate.

BUCHANAN: "ACTS OF HOSTILITY" LEADING TOWARD "OPEN REBELLION" BY SAINTS

Buchanan had delayed sending troops for as long as political expediency allowed, so he had a kind of sincerity in asserting that sending the Army had been his least preferred alternative. But now rebellion loomed:

> ...a hope was indulged that no necessity might exist for employing the military in restoring and maintaining the authority of the law, but this hope has now vanished. Governor Young has by proclamation declared his determination to maintain his power by force, and has already committed acts of hostility against the United States. Unless he should retrace his steps the Territory of Utah will be in a state of open rebellion.

BUCHANAN: BRIGHAM YOUNG'S WAR PREPARATIONS

In retrospect, Buchanan pointed out, Brigham Young could be shown to have been preparing for war with the United States over a prolonged period. He was capable of protracted guerrilla warfare in the mountains. As evidence, Buchanan cited the reports of Major Van Vliet:

> There is reason to believe that Governor Young has long contemplated this result. He knows that the continuance of his despotic power depends upon the exclusion of all settlers from the Territory except those who will acknowledge his divine mission and implicitly obey his will, and that an enlightened public opinion there would soon prostrate institutions at war with the laws both of God and man. "He has therefore for several years, in order to maintain his independence, been industriously employed in collecting and fabricating arms and munitions of war and in disciplining the Mormons for military service." As superintendent of Indian affairs he has had an opportunity of tampering

with the Indian tribes and exciting their hostile feelings against the United States. This, according to our information, he has accomplished in regard to some of these tribes, while others have remained true to their allegiance and have communicated his intrigues to our Indian agents. He has laid in a store of provisions for three years, which in case of necessity, as he informed Major Van Vliet, he will conceal, "and then take to the mountains and bid defiance to all the powers of the Government."

BUCHANAN: "FRENZIED FANATICISM" OF MORMONS HAS CREATED "FIRST REBELLION" IN US TERRITORIES

The sad bottom line, Buchanan observed, was that – courtesy of the Mormon Saints – the United States was now forced to deal with the first rebellion to take place in any of its territories. Immediate and decisive action was required – although the Buchanan administration was proving incapable of precisely this. Buchanan warned that

> ... no wise government will lightly estimate the efforts which may be inspired by such frenzied fanaticism as exists among the Mormons in Utah. This is the first rebellion which has existed in our Territories, and humanity itself requires that we should put it down in such a manner that it shall be the last. To trifle with it would be to encourage it and to render it formidable. We ought to go there with such an imposing force as to convince these deluded people that resistance would be vain, and thus spare the effusion of blood. We can in this manner best convince them that we are their friends, not their enemies.

BUCHANAN: FOUR REGIMENTS NEEDED TO SUPPRESS MORMON "INSURRECTION"

Although the Panic of 1857 was continuing to disrupt federal finances, Buchanan asked for four new regiments to be used to suppress the insurrection in Utah:

> In order to accomplish this object it will be necessary, according to the estimate of the War Department, to raise four additional regiments; and this I earnestly recommend to Congress. At the present moment of depression in the revenues of the country I am sorry to be obliged to recommend such a measure; but I feel confident of the support of Congress, cost what it may, in suppressing the insurrection and in restoring and maintaining the sovereignty of the Constitution and laws over the Territory of Utah.

The head of the Democratic Party, and a supporter of the Jeffersonian theory of enumerated powers under the constitution, had thus been compelled to take action. The Democratic party doctrine of popular sovereignty or squatter sovereignty in the territories was revealed as bankrupt, for it had allowed a growth an alien theocratic power on national territory.

Brigham Young replied by claiming that Congress had no more power to govern territories than it could govern states. But, in Article Four of the Constitution, the Congress is given the final say in the governance of all US territories: "The Congress shall have power to dispose of and make all needful Rules and Regulations respecting the Territory or other Property belonging to the United States...." This is the Territorial or Property Clause. Needless to say, Article Four of the U.S. Constitution was anathema to Brigham Young, since it also contains the requirement that "the United States shall guarantee to every State in this Union a Republican Form of Government," which obviously rules out the Mormon theocracy.

Brigham Young tried to create a right of rebellion for territories that were being trampled on by the Congress. When Washington acted "clearly without the pale of those authorities and limitations, unconstitutionally to oppress the people, it commits a treason against itself, which demands the resistance of all good men, or freedom will depart our Nation."[191] (*The Mormon Rebellion*, Bigler & Bagley, p. 264) Brigham Young's crank reading of the Constitution foreshadows equally fantastic readings of that document put forward by reactionary antigovernment libertarians in our own time.

BRIGHAM YOUNG WANTS TO INCINERATE THE US ARMY

But by January, 1858, even the inefficient Buchanan administration was marshaling its forces to curb the Mormons. General Winfield Scott got the war Department to approve his plan of sending 3,000 regular troops into Utah in the springtime. Like other dictators facing long odds, Brigham Young began to look around for secret weapons (*Wunderwaffen*) he could use to redress the balance in his favor. One of these was apparently a kind of napalm or liquid fire being developed back in Nauvoo, Illinois by Uriah Brown, one of just three non-Mormons who were members of the secret Council of Fifty, the explicitly political board which Joseph Smith had established as part of his plan for world conquest. Uriah Brown wanted to create a system of napalm mines in Echo Canyon to burn up the advancing federals. But the promised secret weapon failed to materialize. (*The Mormon Rebellion*, Bigler & Bagley, p. 267)

The Utah territorial legislature approved a lengthy list of Mormon grievances for Buchanan and the Congress. It culminated with the demand to "withdraw your troops, give us our CONSTITUTIONAL RIGHTS, and we are at home."[192] But theocracy was explicitly forbidden by the Constitution, and no right of polygamy has ever been found there.

Facing the prospect of a new federal effort against him in the spring of 1858, Brigham Young fell back on the option he had been preparing to move the Mormons north and west. American mountaineers, however, were out looking for food supplies for the US garrison cooped up in Fort Bridger, and their attention was attracted by the 300 cattle and 40 horses concentrated at a Mormon outpost called Fort Limhi (today Lemhi) on the border between Idaho and Montana. Because of accumulated grievances against the Mormon Saints, some 250 of the Bannock and Shoshone Indians of the area joined in the

---

[191] *The Latter-day Saints' Millennial Star*, vol. 20, p. 237, online at books.google.com.

[192] Ibid. vol. 20, p. 254, online at books.google.com.

attack on Fort Limhi, with John Wesley Powell of later Grand Canyon fame playing a prominent role. This incident, which occurred on February 25, 1858, acquired a strategic significance, since it meant that the Indians of Idaho had turned against the Mormons, rendering Brigham Young's escape plan via the northern route no longer practical. With these events, Brigham Young's option of retreating into the northern Rockies was no longer feasible. (*The Mormon Rebellion*, Bigler & Bagley, p. 280)

THE MORMON STANDING ARMY OF 1858:
A MIDDLE EAST RELIGIOUS MILITIA

Brigham Young first considered dealing with the federal spring offensive by creating parties of guerrilla fighters and assigning them to attack travelers along the Overland wagon trains. When this idea failed to gain traction, Brigham Young responded by creating a permanent military establishment in the Utah Territory under Mormon theocratic control. This was not a mere territorial militia, but a permanent standing army, for which he intended to procure better weapons in the future. The Kingdom of God, the materialist Brigham Young evidently believed, needed professional soldiers. The result was the self-styled Standing Army of Israel, a military "more closely resembling a Middle Eastern religious militia" than an American force. (*The Mormon Rebellion*, Bigler & Bagley, p. 271) Even if large-scale secessionism was not to emerge during 1858, the crisis was nevertheless imminent, as Brigham Young knew very well. He obviously wanted to be better prepared to act against the United States during the next phase of the crisis, which would soon arrive.

Brigham Young now launched a bewildering array of simultaneous and contradictory initiatives. He turned to public relations gestures. He pretended to be concerned that the troops in Fort Bridger might be getting hungry, so he sent them some beef cattle and flour. Simultaneously, the Mormons launched a campaign of character assassination against Buchanan, designed to paint the Saints as the victims. He also developed an operation code-named "Sebastopol" which called for the burning of the existing Mormon settlements. In this context, Brigham Young also issued an order for many of the poorest and least influential Mormons – up to perhaps a third of the total population – to be forced out of the Salt Lake City area and into southern Utah. It is among the descendents of these wretched persons that the practice of polygamy remains the most widespread. The destinations of the Mormons deported by Brigham Young are today the strong points of the polygamist Fundamentalist Latter-day Saints, of whom Warren Jeffs is an infamous leader.

BRIGHAM YOUNG THREATENS ANNIHILATION OF US TROOPS

There were reports in the eastern press of bloodcurdling threats made by the Mormon Moses against Colonel Johnston. The *St. Joseph's Gazette* reported that Brigham Young had issued an ultimatum to the U.S. Army to leave Utah Territory by no later than March 10. Otherwise, the troops would be annihilated by the Mormons.[193]

---

[193] "Important from Utah: Brigham Young Threatens to Annihilate the US Troops," *New York Times*, April 10, 1858.

By the spring of 1858, numerous refugees, called "apostates" by the Mormon leaders, were fleeing east at the risk of their lives. In other cases, those desiring to leave were required to pay a year's taxes in advance. The refugees told a reporter that "fully one-half the entire Mormon community would embrace the opportunity to flee from the moral and physical slavery in which they are held."[194] Surely John Stuart Mill was aware of these reports that Utah was a giant prison house, yet he ignored them in writing his famous defense of Mormondom in *On Liberty*.

Brigham Young was keeping his options open. According to one report, he was keeping 50 to 60 high-quality mules ready at all times so that he and his wives could flee The Kingdom of God. The Mormon Prophet continued to inveigh against the United States government: on April 4, 1858 he accused the United States Government of "Cursed meanness," "wickedness corruption and abomination," and a "Disposition to Destroy us from the face of the Earth."[195]

BUCHANAN: "A STRANGE SYSTEM OF TERRORISM"
BY MORMONS IN UTAH

Then news arrived of the proclamation issued in Washington on April 6, 1858 by President Buchanan.[196] Here, for the first time in American history, an American president spoke in his official capacity of terrorism – meaning the Mormons. The theocratic regime, Buchanan noted, tolerated no dissent: "Indeed, such is believed to be the condition to which a strange system of terrorism has brought the inhabitants of that region that no one among them could express an opinion favorable to this Government, or even propose to obey its laws, without exposing his life and property to peril."

Buchanan deplored the anti-American sentiment in Utah, which was now impelling the Mormons towards an armed clash with federal forces: "the hatred of that misguided people for the just and legal authority of the Government had become so intense that they resolved to measure their military strength with that of the Union."

BUCHANAN: REBELLION AND TREASON IN UTAH

Buchanan warned of rebellion and treason, with the dire consequences that must necessarily follow from the Mormon "determination to oppose the authority of the Government by military force has not only been expressed in words, but manifested in overt acts of the most unequivocal character. Fellow-citizens of Utah, this is rebellion against the Government to which you owe allegiance; it is levying war against the United States, and involves you in the guilt of treason." Buchanan offered the people of Utah amnesty for the treason committed so far. But, if they proved obdurate, then treason trials would follow: "I offer now a free and full pardon to all who will submit themselves

---

[194] Ibid.

[195] *Journal of Discourses*, vol. 6, p. 39.

[196] For full text, see Appendix.

to the just authority of the Federal Government. If you refuse to accept it, let the consequences fall upon your own heads."

Buchanan's offer of amnesty found one very influential taker right off the bat: this was none other than the Mormon Prophet Brigham Young, who, after all of his bluster, bombast, and bloodcurdling threats, cravenly accepted the offer coming from the notoriously weak Buchanan. After much negotiation, US forces marched through Salt Lake City on June 26, 1858. The streets were utterly deserted, except for small groups of Danite militiamen armed with clubs and pistols, who had been given orders to burn the city under certain circumstances. The federals did not permanently occupy Salt Lake City, which turned out to be a serious mistake. Instead, they crossed the Jordan River and proceeded southwards some 40 miles, and stopped at Camp Floyd. Since the mission of these troops was to assist federal officials in executing the laws of the United States, especially in regard to Utah territorial government in Salt Lake City, the location of Camp Floyd was already an act of appeasement and capitulation.

US ARMY WANTED "EVERY DAMNED MORMON HUNG BY THE NECK"

The US Army showed commendable discipline in avoiding clashes with the Mormon plug-uglies. Colonel C. F. Smith commented that "as far as the army was concerned, it 'would like to see every damned Mormon hung by the neck.'"[197] (*The Mormon Rebellion*, Bigler & Bagley, p. 324)

Three US officials were now playing prominent roles. One is Alfred Cumming of Georgia, soon to be a secessionist, who was appointed governor of Utah Territory by Buchanan. Cumming shows the path of cowardice and appeasement in his dealings with Brigham Young. The Mormon Prophet did not hesitate to threaten this federal official with insurrection. On one occasion, Brigham Young growled to Governor Cumming, "Toe the line, and mark by the law, and do right or I shall crook my little finger, and you know what will come then."[198] Cumming was trying to convince Colonel Johnston that there was no need for the U.S. Army to march through Salt Lake City.

Having been encouraged by Democratic Party politicians to mediate the dispute, the Philadelphia political fixer Thomas L. Kane also arrived in Salt Lake City. Kane was notable for an uncanny ability to ignore the polygamy and other illegal activities carried out by the Mormons. According to Bigler and Bagley, Kane did everything possible to muddy the waters concerning Brigham Young's direct personal responsibility for the Mountain Meadows Massacre. Kane had studied in Great Britain and in France, and was a correspondent of Thomas Carlyle's protégé Ralph Waldo Emerson, as well as of Horace Greeley. So it is not so surprising that he lacked a moral compass. In any case, his overall impact on the situation in Utah was deplorable.

JUDGE CRADLEBAUGH SCORES MORMONS
AS TOOLS AND DUPES OF TYRANNICAL DESPOTISM

---

[197] "Camp Floyd," *Deseret News*, October 28, 2005.
[198] Van Wagoner, *Complete Discourses at Brigham Young*, 5:1882, July 7, 1861.

One loyal, effective, and energetic federal official was John Cradlebaugh, who became the federal judge of the second District of Utah Territory. Cradlebaugh set out to punish the perpetrators of the Mountain Meadows Massacre, along with the killings of former Mormons seeking to leave the territory, as well as travelers crossing through Utah. His work was sabotaged at every turn by Mormon juries acting to sabotage the law under orders from their tyrant ruler. In response to one such incident on April 12, 1859, Cradlebaugh confronted the Mormons with their moral depravity:

> "'You are the tools, the dupes, the instruments of a tyrannical Church despotism. The heads of your Church order and direct you. You are taught to obey their orders and commit these horrid murders. Deprived of your liberty, you have lost your manhood, and become the willing instruments of bad men. I say to you it will be my earnest effort while with you, to knock off your ecclesiastical shackles and set you free.'"[199]

Judge Cradlebaugh was reprimanded by Washington doughfaces for his efforts to bring justice to Utah. Cradlebaugh was an American hero who went on to Congress and later fought with distinction during the Civil War. But, as long as the Mormons controlled the probate courts, and the probate courts had original jurisdiction in most cases, justice was doomed to miscarry.

BRIGHAM YOUNG AUTHORIZES MURDER:
SAVE THE SISTER'S SOUL BY CUTTING HER THROAT

Governor Cumming, responding to persistent newspaper reports that many women were being held in the Mormon territories against their will, offered to assist any of them who needed help to exit the territory. Very few came forward. John Stuart Mill and others concluded from this that the Mormon women were reasonably content. But one documented case may suggest what was actually happening. Mormon bigwig Milo Andrus had eleven wives, but one of them began objecting to polygamy, and was observed planning to escape. Andrus asked Brigham Young how she should be dealt with. Young reportedly replied that "the only way to save the sister's soul was to cut her throat." While the woman was on her knees begging for her life, Andrus cut her throat from ear to ear and held her in an iron grip until she ceased to struggle.[200]

By the summer of 1858, the Buchanan administration in Washington was thoroughly dominated by doughface, subversive, and outright secessionist forces. Buchanan was not interested in investigating the Mountain Meadows Massacre, or other Mormon atrocities. He now ordered that the U.S. Army should not assist the federal courts in enforcing US federal laws. He sent a message to Colonel Johnston warning him that he could not use troops in support of the federal judiciary without permission from Governor Cumming.

---

[199] Edward Wheelock Tullidge, *History of Salt Lake City*, p. 227, online at books.google.com.
[200] Jesse Augustus Gove, *The Utah Expedition, 1857-1858: Letters of Captain Jesse A. Goff to Mrs. Dove and Special Correspondence of the* New York Herald (New Hampshire Historical Society, 1928), pp. 283-284, online at books.google.com.

And since the soon-to-be secessionist Cumming was determined to appease Brigham Young, this meant that Utah was doomed to relapse into theocratic anarchy. The Danites had not been broken up, women were still being kidnapped and terrorized, and murder went unpunished. Most important, Brigham Young was free to continue his preparations for secession.

BRIGHAM YOUNG'S CONTEMPT FOR MEDICINE AND SCIENCE

The eastern press pointed out that, under the theocratic dictatorship, Utah had no public schools whatsoever, and only a few church schools which could not serve the existing population. Much of this was due to the Mormon Moses himself, who "disliked education and feared educated men." Brigham's views about medical doctors remind us of the comic characters who appear in Molière's plays, which were written almost two centuries earlier. Young "believed diseases were demonic possessions curable only by exorcism, said he had not allowed a doctor into his house for forty years, and insisted Salt Lake City had no illness until doctors, too lazy to work like others, arrived and made people ill so they might make a living treating them." (Hirshson, pp. 245-46)

Public awareness of the Mountain Meadows Massacre grew slowly. The New York newspaper editor Horace Greeley visited Utah in the summer of 1859. During his trip, Greeley got the first interview Brigham Young ever conceded. Brigham told Greely he believed in the devil, but not in the existence of the Danites. Setting a Mormon pattern which persists until our own day, a Mormon Prophet, who was also a multimillionaire, gave a lowball estimate of his own personal fortune at a mere $250,000, and accompanied this by underestimating the size of his personal harem at a mere 15 wives, when the reality at this time was more than three times that figure.[201]

HORACE GREELEY: MORMONS ROBBED, MAIMED, KILLED

Greeley also investigated the stories of Mormon atrocities. In an important article, he wrote: "Do I, then discredit the tales of Mormon outrage and crime—of the murder of the Parishes, the Mountain Meadows massacre, &c., &c., —where with the general ear has recently been shocked? No, I do not. Some of these may have been fabricated by Gentile malice—others are doubtless exaggerated—but there is some basis of truth for the current Gentile conviction that *Mormons have robbed, maimed, and even killed persons in this Territory, under circumstances which should subject the perpetrators to condign punishment, but that Mormon witnesses, grand jurors, petit jurors and magistrates determinedly screen the guilty. I deeply regret the necessity of believing this; but the facts are incontestable.*"[202]

---

[201] Horace Greeley, "Two Hours With Brigham Young," in *An Overland Journey from New York to San Francisco in the Summer of 1859* (New York: C. M. Saxton, Barker and Co., 1860), pp. 209-16.

[202] Horace Greeley, "The Mountain Meadow Massacre – Popular Sovereignty," *New York Tribune*, August 4, 1859, online at mountainmeadows.unl.edu.

Mormon atrocities also attracted increasing attention. When a man who was suing Brigham Young for $25,000 was shot to death by three Danites on the eve of his day in court, the *New York Times* condemned the Mormon power, writing that the outrages in Utah went far beyond "anything to be found within the jurisdiction of any civilized government on the globe. In saying this, we have Algeria, the Punjab and the Caucasus directly before our mind's eye. We take into account the turbulence of the Kabyles, the restless activity of the Nena Sahib, the ferocity of the Sikhs, and the cut-throat propensities of the Circassian mountaineers. And yet we assert that the United States possesses inhabited territory, occupied by a competent force of its troops, within a month's march of a frontier inclosing thirty millions of law-abiding citizens, which, for disorder, insecurity, bloodshed, contempt for the law and its officers, beats anything of the kind which either France, England or Russia can produce."[203]

FAILURE OF THE BUCHANAN ADMINISTRATION TO QUELL THE MORMONS

The entire purpose of sending a garrison to Utah was thrown out the window by the cowardice and stupidity of Buchanan, Floyd, Johnston, and other federal officials. This meant, that when secession boiled over once again a few years later, the insurrectionary theocracy of the Mormons would be intact and combat-ready, still capable of threatening the future existence of the United States during the ordeal of the Union.

---

[203] *New York Times*, September 29, 1859.

CHAPTER V

BRIGHAM YOUNG AGAINST THE UNION: THE MORMON SAINTS DURING THE CIVIL WAR

"The number of their wives their lusts decree;
The Turkish law's their Christian heresy."[204]

The wave of secessionism threatening to break up the American federal union which Brigham Young had hoped for in 1858 finally arrived in late 1860 and early 1861. Since the Mormon theocracy and Brigham Young's personal dictatorship had foolishly been left intact by the feckless Buchanan administration, Brigham Young now had a second chance to establish his Inland Empire of Deseret as the United States broke apart.

Brigham Young attempted to use Confederate secessionism for his own purposes. And during the Civil War, the Mormons were in a thinly disguised united front with the slaveocrats in Richmond, Virginia. Both were serving a geopolitical design developed by such British strategists as Lord John Russell, Lord Palmerston, and William Gladstone.[205] Partly to facilitate this coordination, Brigham Young kept his son and political heir apparent, Brigham Young, Jr., in London during 1862 and 1863, the decisive years of the secession crisis.

British grand strategy against the United States included a four-pronged envelopment carried out by the Confederacy, by British troops in Canada, by the French army in Mexico, and by the Mormon Danite and Nauvoo Legion forces, perhaps supplemented by Indians, in the Intermountain West.

E. B. Long correctly notes that "The American Civil War, 1861 to 1865, can be and often is studied without reference to the vast western frontier, thus giving an incomplete account of that struggle. And central to the American West during the Civil War is Utah Territory. The story of this region …received scant attention in Civil War histories and only a little more in volumes on the American West."[206] Many who know the story of the Gettysburg and Vicksburg campaigns in great detail know little or nothing about the Civil War in the Intermountain West. But events west of the 100th meridian exercised an important influence over the course of the hostilities, and even a cursory glance reveals that in this theater of operations the Mormons represented a threat to the United States that was no less than that posed by the Confederates.

---

[204] From a royalist propaganda sheet of 1643, targeting pro-polygamy writings of the poet John Milton and other backers of Oliver Cromwell. (Christopher Hill, *Milton and the English Revolution*, p. 130)

[205] For the geopolitics of the American Civil War, see Webster G. Tarpley, "' Back the World in Flames' – The US-Russian Alliance That Saved the Union," April 11, 2011, Tarpley.net.

[206] E .B. Long, *The Saints and The Union* (Urbana IL: University of Illinois Press, 1981), p. xi.

DESERET AS A BRITISH GEOPOLITICAL GAMBIT AGAINST THE USA

Within the framework of the policy universe thus defined by the British Foreign Office, Brigham Young planned to use the Confederates, and they cordially reciprocated this intention. The Confederate strategy was to strike out west from Texas and attempt to secure control of the New Mexico Territory, meaning the present-day states of New Mexico and Arizona. "Confederate leaders were ambitious to acquire even greater areas. The Territory of New Mexico extended west from Texas to California. This prize, if secured, would place the Confederacy almost on the Pacific Ocean ... it was of major importance for the Confederacy to acquire New Mexico."[207]

The goal of this strategic thrust was to plant the Confederate flag on the shores of the Pacific Ocean in California. "With the Pacific slope in their possession through conquest or by alliance with a Western Confederacy, the world would be open to the Confederates, making an effective Union blockade impossible. It would provide an opportunity for Confederate cruisers and privateers to prey upon Union commerce, and it would afford an excellent chance to develop Asiatic trade."[208]

If the Mormon Saints were located astride the essential American lines of communication between the Missouri River and California, they were also sitting on the right flank of the planned Confederate March to the Pacific.

BUCHANAN AND FLOYD PULL OUT US FORCES, RE-OPEN DOOR TO UTAH SECESSION

As a result of the Mormon Rebellion of 1857-1858, a small United States garrison had remained in Utah Territory, and was located about 30 miles south of Salt Lake City, on the west side of the Jordan River, in an Army post named Camp Floyd. During the last phase of the Buchanan administration, Secretary of War Floyd (after whom this camp was named) carried out an orgy of treason, doing everything possible to weaken the United States and transfer military assets to the Confederacy.

In May 1860, Secretary of War Floyd ordered the partial closure of Camp Floyd and removed more than half of its troops. As one historian points out, this garrison had failed to enforce federal law in Utah, but it did provide a powerful stimulus for the economy, which even ungrateful Mormons could not fail to notice. According to the *New York Tribune*, "Many persons who, two years ago, did not possess the first half of an animal now boast of ox teams and mule teams; while the numerous Mormon belles and dames literally revel in calicoes and crinolines—all these furnished, too, through the overflowing generosity of the good old uncle." (Hirshson, p. 254)

Here we can see a clear harbinger of the ideological hypocrisy of many so-called red states, which benefit out of all proportion from the US federal budget through corporate

---

[207] Ray C. Colton, *The Civil War in the Western Territories: Arizona, Colorado, New Mexico, and Utah* (Norman OK: University of Oklahoma Press, 1959), p. 3.
[208] Colton, p. 4.

welfare and defense spending, even as they issue ideological manifestoes against the evils of big government.

MORMONS GET OVERTURES FROM CONFEDERATES AND PACIFIC SLOPE SECESSIONISTS

Whitney's *History of Utah* (1893) "claimed that Brigham Young rejected overtures from the Southern Confederacy and from a group which proposed a Pacific Slope Federation...."[209] But having been burned once before, in 1857-58, the Mormon Prophet had learned that it was unwise to take an exposed position in the expectation that help would be arriving from elsewhere.

Nevertheless, the Confederate leaders thought they could count on at least the benevolent neutrality of Utah, since the Mormons would never do anything to help sustain the Union. Instead, "it was assumed by the Confederate leaders that the Mormons in Utah would readily accept allegiance to almost any other government than back in Washington."[210]

As we will see, Union General Patrick E. Connor thought that Brigham Young was waiting for either the military collapse of the Union forces, and/or military intervention by Britain and France. Until that time, the Mormon Prophet would take a low profile and let the Confederates weaken the Union and do his fighting for him.

MORMONS CONTROLLED OVERLAND TRAILS, TELEGRAPH LINES, RAIL ROUTES

The danger posed by the defection of Utah from the Federal Union was a very serious one: "Had Utah, in its key position on the overland route, seceded at the outbreak of the Civil War, a danger risking east-west cleavage could have compelled the federal government to expend considerable money and manpower to reroute the telegraph, mail, and stage lines."[211]

The Salt Lake City area was widely considered to be the hub of the Intermountain West, and with good reason. "Utah was located, by an accident of geography, astride the principal communication lines between the eastern and western states. Across its land went the great and vulnerable emigrant roads, the Overland Trail to California, the Pony Express, stage lines, the telegraph—all becoming even more vital when Civil War came and the southern routes were disrupted. Utah, it was generally held, would likely be crossed by the first transcontinental railroad. Salt Lake City was the only major city between far western Missouri and California." (Long, p. 3)

Whether it was really an accident that Brigham Young had decided to utter his famous proclamation, "This is the place!" only when he reached Salt Lake City remains to be

---

[209] Colton, p. 180, n. 12.
[210] Colton, p. 9.
[211] Colton, p. 180.

determined. If the entire Mormon project in the Intermountain West had been inspired to some degree by British intelligence, it would have made sense to locate the Mormon Zion where geography would allow it to have the greatest effect.

Brigham Young had originally planned to carve out even larger swaths of territory for his Mormon Inland Empire. But, as soon as the Confederates had left the Congress in Washington, the Republican majority in March 1861 carved the Nevada Territory out of Utah in an attempt to cut the Mormon New Jerusalem down to size.

CONFEDERATE INVASION OF NEW MEXICO, 1862: VALVERDE

At first, the Texas-based forces of the Confederacy invading New Mexico seemed to be gaining the upper hand. The Confederates won a victory at the Battle of Valverde near the Rio Grande in New Mexico on February 21, 1862. In the wake of this Union reverse, Texas troops swarmed over much of New Mexico and Arizona: "The Confederate campaign had reached its zenith. The major portions of New Mexico and Arizona were now under Southern control. The capital, Santa Fe, and most of the towns of the Territory were dominated by the conquerors…. The military fortunes of the Union forces in the Intermountain West, on the other hand, were at their lowest ebb…. Finally the federal government and the commanding generals in the middle West were becoming conscious of the seriousness of the Confederate invasion of New Mexico…."[212]

The next step for the Confederates would have been to push northwards into Colorado, thus cutting the Union lines of communication between Kansas and California without any assistance from the Mormons. The Confederates, however, proved incapable of penetrating into Colorado.

GLORIETA: COLORADO DEFEATS TEXAS FOR CONTROL OF NEW MEXICO

The Confederates soon became overextended, and their triumphal march through New Mexico lasted little more than a month. A decisive change in the New Mexico situation was brought about by the influx of capable units of Colorado volunteers on the Union side. In a rapid reversal of fortunes, the Confederate forces suffered a crushing defeat in the Battle of Glorieta, southeast of Santa Fe, on March 26-28, 1862. This encounter is variously remembered as the Gettysburg of the West, or the Waterloo of the Confederates in New Mexico. In this battle, Colorado defeated Texas. The decisive moment at Glorieta came when Union forces, in a daring flanking maneuver, destroyed upwards of 80 Confederate wagons with all their contents, while spiking one artillery piece. Utterly bereft of food, ammunition, clothing, and blankets, the Confederates began a long retreat towards El Paso.

There is some evidence to suggest that the public statements by Brigham Young had become more bellicose after the Confederate success at Valverde, but then became somewhat attenuated when news of the Union victory of Glorieta arrived in Salt Lake City. Brigham Young's potential for strategic blackmail was further diminished by the

---

[212] Colton, p. 40.

Battle of Bear River in January 1863, in which Union forces under Patrick Connor defeated a large party of Indians. The Mormons had been counting on the Indians to tie down and harass federal forces, but after this engagement, the Indian violence subsided and the Mormons were left high and dry.

MORMONS IGNORE LINCOLN'S CALL FOR VOLUNTEERS

After the fighting began at Fort Sumter, President Lincoln issued a call for 75,000 troops from state militias to be placed under his command to deal with the rebellion. Brigham Young never dreamed of responding to this call, and it seemed a foregone conclusion all around that the Mormons would do nothing for the United States. (This was also the case when conscription began in July 1863 – the Mormons contributed nothing, and Mitt Romney and his sons – even though they profess themselves leading warmongers today – are all chickenhawks with no military service.) However, the authorities in Washington did send a personal request to Brigham Young, even though he was no longer the territorial governor of Utah, to contribute Lot Smith and his cavalry to an effort to secure overland travel and communication through Utah against possible interference by marauding Indians. Brigham Young was obviously glad to do this, since it was a way for him to seize control of the overland trails and Pony Express routes. A few months later, Brigham Young ended this cooperation. This brief episode was the only participation of Utah Territory in the American Civil War. The Mormon Saints looked at the great national struggle as outside spectators – they acted as what they were, a separate nation.

BRIGHAM: "I WILL SEE THEM IN HELL BEFORE I WILL RAISE AN ARMY FOR THEM"

Young was grudgingly willing "to furnish a home guard for the protection of the telegraph and mail lines and overland travel within our boundaries," but he refused to furnish either money or manpower to defend the Union. "I will see them in Hell before I will raise an army for them," he blustered in late 1861. "With the exception of Lot Smith's company, Utah raised no volunteers for the Union Army, and the Territory's Mormon population eschewed displays of wartime patriotism."[213]

According to a recent article in the *New York Times*, "Young decided that the Mormons would sit out the Civil War. He saw the conflict as God's punishment of the United States for its past mistreatment of his church, especially its failure to protect Joseph Smith, the Mormons' founder who was murdered by an Illinois mob in 1844. In Young's view, the war was a prelude to the 'winding-up scene,' the end times in which American society would collapse under the weight of divine judgment and Mormons would save the Constitution, welcome the return of Jesus Christ and participate in his millennial reign."[214]

---

[213] John G. Turner, "The Mormons Sit Out the Civil War," *New York Times*, May 1, 2012.
[214] Ibid.

The *New York Times* author concludes that "Young was careful to tread the line between dissent and treason...."[215] Quite the contrary: by his conduct during the Civil War, the Mormon Prophet Brigham Young entered deeply into treason for the second time. This can be shown in some detail.

On February 10th, 1861, less than a week after the creation of the Confederate States of America with seven states participating, Brigham Young addressed the Saints in the Tabernacle, posing the question: "Is the form of the Government ruined? Has its form become evil? No! but the administrators of the Government are evil. As we have said many times, it is the best form of human government ever lived under; but it has as corrupt a set to administer it as God ever permitted to disgrace his footstool. There is the evil. Can they better the condition of our country? No! they will make it worse every time they attempt to do so." (*Saints and the Union*, p. 19) This was the usual Mormon doublethink: the Constitution was divine, but the officials staffing the federal government were radically evil, and the only answer was a militant Mormon theocracy.

BRIGHAM YOUNG: "THERE IS NO MORE A UNITED STATES"

Brigham Young and his associates had been nourished for almost three decades by Joseph Smith's 1832 Civil War Prophecy. Now that they saw the Union breaking up, the Mormon leaders were manic with gloating and *Schadenfreude*. Abraham Lincoln they regarded with open hatred, not least because of his mentor, Henry Clay, whom the Mormons accused of being part of the assassination of Joseph Smith. Brigham Young made clear that he considered the United States a doomed nation: "There is no more United States. Can they amalgamate and form a government? No. Will they have ability to form a government and continue? No, they will not ... and if a state has a right to secede, so has a Territory, and so has a county from a State or Territory, and a town from a county, and a family from neighborhood, and you will have perfect anarchy.... What will King Abraham do? I do not know, neither do I care. It is no difference what he does, of what any of them do. Why? God will accomplish his own purposes, and they may do or not do, they may take the road that leads to the right, or they may take the road that leads to the left, and which ever road they do take they wish they had taken the other.... 'Mormonism' will live and God will promote it." (*Saints and the Union*, p. 19)

Brigham Young viewed the breakup of the US Federal Union as irreversible and irrevocable; it was an act of the Almighty. According to this analysis, "God has come out of his hiding-place, and has commenced to vex the nation that has rejected us.... It will not be patched up—it never can come together again—... in a short time it will be like water spilled on the ground, and like chaff upon the summer threshing floor, until those wicked stewards are cut off. If our present happy form of government is sustained, which I believe it will be, it will be done by the people I am now looking upon in connection with their brethren and their offspring."[216]

---

[215] Ibid.
[216] *Journal of Discourses*, 8:81.

RICHARD BURTON ON THE DANITE ESPIONAGE SYSTEM

The political situation of the Mormon home front was the subject of a profile drawn up in the middle of 1860 by the British intelligencer Richard Burton. Burton was impressed by the State Law and order maintained in Salt Lake City, and above all the pervasive surveillance maintained by the Danite political police. Burton recorded that "Gentiles often declare that the Prophet is acquainted with their every word half an hour after it is spoke…. There is no secret from the head of the Church and State; every thing from the highest to the lowest detail of private and public life, must be brought to the ear and submitted to the judgment of the father confessor-in-chief (Young)."[217] The Danites were as oppressive as the Venetian Council of Ten.

Brigham Young's machinations against the United States were doubtless facilitated by the large part of his subject population which had never wanted anything to do with this country. According to one estimate, "by 1860 about a third of the population was from Great Britain, with a sizeable contingent of Danes, Swedes, and Norwegians, plus those born in America, primarily from New England, the mid-Atlantic states, and the Midwest." (*Saints and the Union*, p. 23)

BRIGHAM INFORMED OF FT. SUMTER
IN ADVANCE – BY GOD OR BY LONDON?

On January 23, 1861, with secession claiming one slave state after another, Brigham Young was described as being in high spirits, specifically because of the tragedy now impacting the United States: "The President is unusually cheerful, the present distracted state of the affairs of the U.S. following so soon after their wicked attempts to root up the Kingdom of God, and afflict his saints inspires the President with strong hopes for the prosperity of the cause of God…." (*Saints and the Union*, p. 24)

As usual, Brigham Young was operating from a remarkable intelligence picture. He seems to know certain events were coming before they occurred. On January 28, Young shared a revelation that "the news from the States would be extremely interesting about the middle of next April." (*Saints and the Union*, p. 24) When the Confederates opened fire on Fort Sumter in Charleston, South Carolina harbor in the night of April 12-13, 1861, some of those who remember this prophecy might have been astounded by the Mormon Prophet's charismatic gifts. More likely is that he had been familiarized with the approximate timetable of Southern secession by emissaries of the British imperial "Red Horse," which had excellent sources inside Scottish Rite Freemasonic circles in and near the Confederates' seats of power.

According to Brigham Young's Office Journal, the Mormon Prophet "knew the reason why this Government was in trouble, they had killed Joseph Smith and they would have to pay for it as the Jews did in killing Jesus…. The President further remarked there is no union in the North or in the South—the nation must crumble to nothing. They charged us

---

[217] Richard F. Burton, *City of the Saints* (New York: Harper, 1862), p. 224, online at books.google.com.

with being rebels and rebels they will have in their Government. South Carolina has committed treason, and if Prest. Buchanan had been a smart man he would have hung up the first men who rebelled in South Carolina." (*Saints and the Union*, p. 25)

The historical record shows that the Mormons were not in the least distraught about the terrible conflict which was now beginning. On the contrary, they felt a deep sense of satisfaction that the prophetic powers of Joseph Smith were being vindicated, and they looked forward eagerly to the suffering which they were about to witness visited on their tormentors, both Unionists and Confederates. Historians agree that Joseph Smith's Civil War Prophecy of 1832 provided the conceptual framework for the thinking of Brigham Young and other Mormons during the war of 1861-1865.

MORMON GLEE OVER AMERICA'S DOOM

The *Deseret News*, the only newspaper published in Utah Territory, and the party organ of the Mormon Saints, stressed on March 6 and again on April 24 that the federal union was doomed. (*Saints and the Union*, p. 26) Brigham Young recommended a policy like that of Mao Tse-tung during the 1950s – go to the top of the mountain and watch the Tigers fight. At the Church Conference in Salt Lake City in April 1861, Brother Brigham gloated about the good fortune of the Mormons under his administration; 'We are not now mingling in the turmoil of strife, warring, and contention, that we would have been obliged to have mingled in had not the Lord suffered us to have been driven to these mountains—one of the greatest blessings that could have been visited upon us....'[218]

Mormons generally cultivated a millenarian or chiliastic (latter-day) outlook which held the end of the world as perpetually imminent. Towards the end of the same April 1861 oration, Brigham prophesied apocalyptic events which would redound to the advantage of the Mormon Saints: "Shame, shame on the rulers of the nation! I feel myself disgraced to hail such men as my countrymen.... The whole government is gone; it is as weak as water.... Mobs will not decrease, but will increase until the whole Government becomes a mob, and eventually it will be State against State, city against city, neighbourhood against neighbourhood, Methodists against Methodists, and so on.... It will be the same with other denominations of professing Christians, and will be Christian against Christian, and man against man; and those who will not take up the sword against their neighbours must flee to Zion. Where is Zion? Let us be prepared to receive the honourable men of the earth—those who are good."[219] Brigham Young was illiterate, but note the British spelling used by his secretaries, most of whom were foreigners.

The Mormons still professed their theory that it was the exclusive prerogative of the Saints to name the territorial officials of Utah. The Constitution said different, and the Mormons professed to revere the Constitution as divinely inspired, so this was another example of their usual subversive doublethink.

---

[218] *Journal of Discourses*, vol. 9. p. 2.
[219] *Journal of Discourses*, vol. 9. p. 5.

As always, Brigham Young placed the Mormon peculiar institution of polygamy in the center of attention as the hallmark of his faith: "The time is coming when the Lord is going to raise up a holy nation. He will bring up a royal Priesthood [the Pratt-Romney family?] upon the earth, and he has introduced a plurality of wives for that express purpose, and not to gratify lustful passion in the least.... I never entered into the order of plurality of wives to gratify passion."[220] It would be more accurate to say that Brigham Young regarded polygamy as an instrument of power – be it his power over individual women, or his power to bind the Mormon community to gather in contradiction to the outside world.

ANTI-AMERICAN TIRADES FROM SAINTS
JOHN TAYLOR AND HEBER KIMBALL

The opinions of the Mormon Prophet Brigham Young represented the compulsory doctrine of the State of Deseret, but Brother Brigham was not alone in professing these subversive and anti-American sentiments. John Taylor, born in Britain, married to at least seven women, and destined to take the helm one day as third First President in Brigham's stead, lashed out at the United States on April 28, 1861, just two weeks after Fort Sumter: "The people of this nation [the United States] are evidently bent upon their own destruction, and they are full of enmity, and hatred, a war and bloodshed. To all human appearance, it would seem that they will not stop short of the entire destruction of this great nation." As usual, Taylor put the grievances of the Mormons at the center of the moral universe, alleging of the United States that "they have neglected righteousness, justice and truth for years that are past and gone; they have allowed the honest, the virtuous, the just, and the true hearted [i.e., the Mormons] to be abused and afflicted and they have winked and mocked at their sufferings; and not only so, but they have unblushingly used their force and strength to bring about the destruction of God's people...." (*Saints and the Union*, p. 30)

And then there was Heber Kimball, Brigham Young's top adviser, who had forty-three wives, and who could always be counted on for a ranting anti-American tirade. Speaking in the tabernacle on April 14, 1861, Kimball pontificated that "in this country the north and south will exert themselves against each other, and ere long the whole face of the United States will be commotion, fighting one against another, and they will destroy their nationality. They have never done anything for this people, and I don't believe they ever will. I have never prayed for the destruction of this government, I know that dissolution, sorrow, weeping, and distress are in store for the inhabitants of the United States, because of their conduct towards the people of God [the Mormons]."[221] As for the prophecy that the United States would never do anything for Utah, Kimball struck out completely: the transcontinental telegraph would arrive soon, and the transcontinental railroad would soon follow. The Mormon rhetorical tradition, like the libertarianism that is based on it today, simply ignores reality.

---

[220] *Journal of Discourses*, vol. 9. p. 36.
[221] *Journal of Discourses*, 9:11.

Kimball's bad temper may have been made worse by the fact that he had built his large personal harem based on quantity rather than quality. In 1869, after Kimball had died, "the *New York World's* Utah correspondent noticed Kimball's widows at the theater and commented: 'I do not think that I ever saw a homelier collection of women anywhere.'" (Hirshson, p. 188)

Thanks to the Pony Express, and soon to the transcontinental telegraph, the reading public of Chicago, Cleveland, New York, Boston, and Philadelphia heard every word of this slanderous abuse. As E. B. Long notes, "This flow of highly colored rhetoric together with long-standing suspicions undoubtedly caused much of the Gentile wariness and hostility that bordered on perceiving the Mormons as treasonous." (*Saints and the Union*, p. 31)

MORMON *SCHADENFREUDE* AS AMERICA BLEEDS

With four more states having seceded from the Union in response to Lincoln's call for volunteers after the firing on Fort Sumter, and with a bloody civil war looming, Brigham Young celebrated every day. According to his Office Journal of May 1, 1861, the Prophet was "pleased with the news which showed more and more secession, and each party was preparing for war, thus giving the Kingdom of God an opportunity of being established upon the Earth." (*Saints and the Union*, p. 31) Note the connection between American disaster and the coming of the Kingdom of God. The Mormon Saints plan was to play the role of the *tertius gaudens* – the laughing bystander – while the Union and the Confederates bled to death, all in conformity with Joseph Smith's Civil War Prophecy of 1832. This mood of gloating pervaded the entire Mormon establishment. As *The Deseret News*, the Mormon *Pravda*, complacently wrote on May 22, 1861, "... while peace reigns in Utah, civil war, with all its horrors prevails among those who earnestly desired to see the soil of these valleys crimsoned with the blood of the Saints."[222]

BRIGHAM YOUNG SEES LINCOLN AS "SUBJECT TO THE INFLUENCE OF A WICKED SPIRIT"

Using his habitual jargon of aggression and slaughter, the Mormon Prophet's Office Journal recorded his view that "Old 'Abe,' the President of the US has it in his mind to pitch in to us when he had got through with the South... Pres. Young was of the opinion the sympathy of the people for the South was in case they should be whipped, and the northern party remain in power he thought they wanted the war to go [on so] both parties might be used up." (*Saints and the Union*, p. 36)

Young reserved special venom for Abraham Lincoln, the US president who most successfully frustrated the Mormon strategic designs. In August 1861 Brother Brigham told his office staff that "Abraham was a pretty good man, but he acted as he would rather the Kingdom of God [Deseret] was out of the way; he was not the man to raise his voice in favor of Joseph Smith when his enemies were persecuting him, he with many others had assented to the deaths of innocent men, and through that he is subject to the

---

[222] *Saints' Herald*, vol. II, p. 116, online at books.google.com.

influence of a wicked spirit."[223] Lincoln served in the Illinois legislature between 1834 and 1842, but he was a lawyer practicing in Springfield, Illinois during the final 1844 events around Joseph Smith in Nauvoo.

According to Brigham Young's Office Journal of September 16, 1861, the Mormon Prophet, still elated over the Confederate victory at Bull Run in June, was making it known that "he would be glad to hear that Genl. Beauregard had taken the President & Cabinet and confined them in the South." (*Saints and the Union*, p. 41)

Whether through divine revelation or intelligence reports from his correspondents, the Prophet was by the end of the year focused on the impending conflict between Deseret and the United States. Brother Brigham, "warm" about his frictions with Washington, was more than six months ahead of the news when he repeated that "he had no disposition to respond to the calls of a government, that had to lately shown their bitter hostilities against us, not alone by sending an army, but by burning the remnant of their arms rather than we should possess them, he felt like contending for our rights, and we were as well prepared to meet a million of the United States soldiers as 10,000, he believed now that an army was on the way to us." (*Saints and the Union*, p. 41)

Brigham wrote to Mormon President George Cannon in Liverpool, England on November 15, 1861, pointing out that the new transatlantic telegraph had been cut near the Utah border in the neighborhood of Fort Bridger, Wyoming. But he stressed that, thanks to Mormon administration, "While strife and bloodshed are wasting the States, we continue to enjoy the rich blessings of peace, in whose various occupations, according to localities and season, the people are most industriously occupied."[224]

From April 1860 to the fall of 1861, the news arrived in Salt Lake City primarily via the Pony Express. But on October 17, 1861 the transcontinental telegraph line from the East reached Salt Lake City. Within a short time, this line would be extended on to San Francisco,

BRIGHAM USES THE NEW TRANSCONTINENTAL
TELEGRAPH FOR PROPAGANDA

Brigham Young immediately began exploiting the transcontinental telegraph for propaganda purposes. On October 18, 1861 – only the second day that the telegraph was functioning – he informed the president of the telegraph company in Cleveland that "Utah has not seceded, but is firm for the Constitution and the laws of our once happy country, and is warmly interested in such useful enterprises as the one so far

---

[223] Brigham Young Office Journal, August 13-21, 1861, cited by Michael T. Griffith, *Abraham Lincoln, the Mormons, and the Civil War: An LDS Perspective on "Honest Abe"*, online at mtgriffith.com.

[224] Arrington, *American Moses*, p. 272, online at books.google.com; also available on DailyPaul.com, April 17, 2012, with comments revealing an ample convergence of Mormons and Paulbearers/Paultards in their hatred of Lincoln.

completed."[225] In reality, Utah had done none of these things. This telegram from Brigham Young was pure deception, designed to create the fictitious picture of a loyal Utah in the minds of the people in the Midwest and East. And it worked: many observers, perhaps unfamiliar with the Mormon theory that the Constitution meant whatever they want it to mean, were momentarily duped by Brigham Young's meaningless gesture.

For years the Mormons had been seeking to get Deseret admitted to the Union. If they had succeeded in doing this without addressing the issues of polygamy and of the Mormon theocratic regime which was focused on preserving plural marriage, they could hope to practice polygamy indefinitely – although, as it turned out, the 14th amendment was soon to prevent the states from sanctioning such monstrous abuses. In the fall of 1861, President Lincoln had named a new slate of territorial officials for Utah, none of whom were Mormons or natives of Utah. Lincoln chose John W. Dawson of Indiana as territorial governor, replacing the secessionist Cumming who had fled to join the Confederacy.

Dawson had no illusions about the difficulty of the task he was taking up. While still in Washington, he wrote to Secretary of the Interior Caleb Blood Smith on October 26th, 1861 that the Mormons, "…though they are professedly loyal to the constitution and obedient to the laws of the United States, they nevertheless, from the nature of their domestic institutions & from past causes of embittered feeling between them & the gentiles … are inclined to independence which may approximate rebellion should federal authority & arms prove in any considerable degree ineffectual during the existing war in maintaining our national colors beyond disputed boundaries.'" (*Saints and the Union*, p. 54)

In early December 1861, Governor Dawson was ambushed and badly beaten while traveling east, forcing him to flee. Dawson said that they were Mormon Danites, and there is every reason to credit his account. Writing to Lincoln from Ft. Bridger, Wyoming on January 13, 1862, Dawson pronounced the Mormons disloyal, and explained the reason they were demanding statehood: "The whole purpose of these people is to gain admission into the Union on an equal basis & then the ulcer polygamy will have a sovereign protection…. The horrid crimes that have been committed in this territory & which have gone unpunished, have no parallel among civilized nations."[226]

BRIGHAM YOUNG SLIMES LINCOLN AS "CURSED SCOUNDREL"

On December 10, 1861, Brigham Young was still propounding the Mormon doublethink theory of the U.S. Constitution: "I do now, and always have, supported the Constitution, but I am not in league with cursed scoundrels as Abe Lincoln and his minions who have sought our destruction from the beginning. Lincoln has ordered an Army from California, for the order has passed over the wires. A senator from California said in Washington the short time since that the 'Mormons' were in the way and must be

---

[225] D. S. Spencer, "Utah and Telegraphy," Genealogy Trails.com.
[226] John W. Dawson to Abraham Lincoln, January 13, 1862, online at truthandgrace.com.

removed. Lincoln feels that he will try to destroy us, as Buchanan was unable to do." (*Saints and the Union*, p. 50) Note that the Prophet was tapping President Lincoln's telegraph messages.

While claiming that he supported the U.S. Constitution, the Mormon Prophet refused, as always, to defend the constitutional order against secessionism. In instructing Utah's territorial delegate about the course to pursue in Washington, Young told him: "I also wish you, if the question arises whether we will furnish troops beyond our borders for the war, to tell them no, but that, if necessary, we are ready to furnish a home guard for the protection of the telegraph and mail lines and overland travel within our boundaries, upon such terms as other volunteer companies employed by the Government." (*Saints and the Union*, p. 51) When, in 1862, the US Army asked Young (a private citizen) to allow Lot Smith's cavalry to be used as needed, including outside the territory, "Young tersely refused, and Utah's only military contribution to the Civil War came to an abrupt end."[227]

At the beginning of 1862, the Mormons organized a Utah State convention for the purpose of once again demanding admission to the Union on their own terms – with polygamy, with theocracy, and with the Danites all still intact and functioning. *The Deseret News*, Brigham Young's house organ, pointed out that if the request for statehood were to be denied once again, then the obvious recourse for Utah would be to declare itself an independent nation. The paper wrote: "in the event of the request for admission into the family of States should be refused, they feared not the consequences of throwing off the Federal yoke and assuming the right of self-government, of which they have so long been deprived...." (*Saints and the Union*, p. 63)

In spite of all of this verbiage, the Mormons were hoping that the Confederacy would cripple the power of the federal union, which posed the more immediate threat to Zion. Young Informed W. C. Haines in London on February 25, 1862 that "The South at this time is being worsted. The sympathies of our brethren are divided some for the Union and some for the South, but the South gets the greatest share."[228] In the following month, Young conferred with his principal advisor Heber C. Kimball and inveighed once again against "the wicked course the American Nation has taken with this people," since the federal government was "running into despotism.... The President observed that Abraham Lincoln was a sagacious man, but believed he was wicked."[229]

MORRILL ACT OUTLAWS POLYGAMY IN US, 1862

One of the leading nation builders in Washington was Congressman Justin S. Morrill of Vermont, a leading exponent of the American System of political economy who successfully advocated the Morrill Tariff, a protective system which finally placed the United States on the necessary road to becoming the premier industrial power of the world. He was also a great promoter of the transcontinental railroad, at that time the greatest civil engineering project in human history. The Morrill Act or Homestead Act

---

[227] John G. Turner, "The Mormons Sit Out the Civil War," *New York Times*, May 1, 2012.

[228] "Today in Mormon History," Feb. 25, 1862, today-in-mormon-history.blogspot.com.

[229] *More Musings of a Miniature Man*, swinson1979.blogspot.com .

was one of the great land reforms of the modern world. Morrill was also responsible for the provision which specified that some of the proceeds from the sale of public lands would go to finance the state land-grant colleges, which were tasked with instruction in agriculture and mechanical arts. Morrill also played a role in the creation of the National Academy of Sciences. It is not surprising that this champion of human progress also judged it essential to mobilize the power of the federal government against the barbaric relic of polygamy.

On April 8, 1862, Morrill introduced a House bill "to punish and prevent the practice of polygamy in the Territories of the United States, and for other purposes, and to disapprove certain acts of the Legislative Assembly of the Territory of Utah." (*Saints and the Union*, p. 71) Mormon polygamy would endure officially for almost 3 more decades, and unofficially continues to this day, but, with the Morrill Act of 1862, the handwriting was already on the wall for the demise of the Mormons' hallmark practice.

BRIGHAM YOUNG STANDS FIRM FOR POLYGAMY

On July 6, 1862 Brigham Young responded to Morrill with a speech delivered in a place called the Bowery, which was a shelter with a roof made of tree branches, but no walls. The Mormon Prophet tried to argue that polygamy had to be respected because it was divinely ordained. He asserted that "monogamy, or restriction by law to one wife, is no part of the economy of heaven among men." He mocked the hubris of the U.S. Congress, which was blasphemously attempting to "dictate the Almighty in his revelations to his people.... Why do we believe in and practice polygamy? Because the Lord introduced it to his servants in a revelation given to Joseph Smith, and Lord's servants have always practiced it."[230]   Later in the day, he returned to the same theme, preaching that "the world is at war against the truth and against those who propagate it." (*Saints and the Union*, p. 78)

Naturally, many religions make sweeping absolute claims and demand that their revelations be respected. But the experience of Western civilization, starting with the wars of religion in the 16th century in particular, was that the needs of public order and the avoidance of civil war require that the demands of all faiths, without exception, be judged according to enlightened reason of state.

Despite the sweeping power explicitly given to the Congress in the Constitution to manage the affairs of the territories, Brother Brigham could not give up his mantra that the territories were supposed to be immune from congressional interference. He wrote to one Mormon elder in San Francisco on July 17, 1862 that the "Congress has no Constitutional right to pass such an act as the one against polygamy, except for the District of Columbia, but the Constitution is an instrument of writing that of late seems to be very readily disregarded when interfering with partisan purposes.'" (*Saints and the Union*, p. 78)

---

[230] Sandra Tanner, "LDS Leaders Still Believe There Will Be Polygamy in Heaven," online at utim.org.

In another appearance in the Bowery on August 31, 1862, Brigham Young once again reminded his audience of Joseph Smith's Civil War Prophecy of 30 years before. Abraham Lincoln, he noted, had told Horace Greeley that his main object was to save the Union, but Brother Brigham was very skeptical. In Brigham's view, Lincoln's actions all converged on the realization of Joseph Smith's prophecy. In the meantime, the Mormons had to push on with the creation of the "Kingdom of God." He urged his followers to proceed "onward and upward." Mormon salvation would be accompanied by American disaster, he opined: "Our course is onward to build up Zion, and the nation that has slain the Prophet of God and cast out his people will have to pay the debt. They will be broken in pieces like a potter's vessel; yes, worse, they will be ground to powder."[231]

MORRISITES REJECT POLYGAMY, REBEL AGAINST BRIGHAM YOUNG

Like all modern gnostic sects based on alleged direct revelation, Mormonism contained inherent structural elements of instability and was constantly plagued by factions, defections, split-offs, and schisms. The mechanism for producing these disturbances was built into the Joseph Smith narrative. If Joseph Smith had enjoyed extra-scriptural revelations coming directly from God, and if oracles had indeed not ceased, then what was to prevent a dissident Mormon from declaring himself a prophet and starting a faction fight? This is exactly what happened in Salt Lake City in the summer of 1862. Among the Mormons was a certain Welshman named Joseph Morris, who claimed to be receiving revelations and communications direct from God. In fact, Joseph Morris claimed that his line to God was better than Brigham Young's. Already in the late 1850s, these divine messages convinced Morris that polygamy was not part of God's plan. (*Saints and the Union*, p. 90) Salt Lake City was full of impoverished and disgruntled victims of Brigham Young's regime of exploitation and oppression, so this new prophet was able to assemble a following known as the Morrisites. In mid-June, 1862, armed Morrisites seized control of Brigham Young's favorite public stage in the Bowery and engaged in firefights with the Danites. Morris was murdered by the Danites, but his movement went on. Before long, the Church of Jesus Christ of Saints Most High, generally known as the Morrisites, had seized Kington Fort on the Weber River, 35 miles north of Salt Lake City. Soon there were gun battles between Morrisite and mainline LDS gunmen, and Brother Brigham had to unleash his judicial apparatus through the probate courts to put some of the heretics in jail.

PATRICK CONNOR, LIBERATOR OF UTAH AND FATHER OF UTAH MINING

But now, shortly after the passage of the Morrill Act, a worthy American antagonist of the Mormon secessionist Brigham Young finally appeared on the scene. This was Colonel Patrick Connor, born Patrick O'Connor on St. Patrick's Day in 1820 in Killarney, County Kerry, Ireland, and then transplanted to New York City. Connor, an officer of the regular army who had fought in the Mexican War, was selected to lead a regiment of California volunteers into Utah for the purpose of securing the transcontinental telegraph and the Overland trails. "California Volunteers for Salt Lake," headlined the *Deseret News* of June 25, 1862, naming Colonel Connor as the commander

---

[231] *Journal of Discourses*, vol. 9, p. 368.

of the Third California volunteers, which had already arrived in Stockton, California on May 31. Connor was destined to become the "Liberator of Utah" and the "Father of Utah Mining."[232] The Roman Catholic Irishman Connor represented a Union Army which, as destroyer of slavery and polygamy, and as bringer of the land reform contained in Justin Morrill's Homestead Act, was a revolutionary force on this planet.

Connor was a far more formidable figure than the secessionists like General Albert Sidney Johnston and Governor Cumming or the doughfaces and appeasers of Mormondom like the Kanes of Philadelphia, with whom the American Moses had generally been dealing up to this point. Connor was a Stephen Douglas Democrat evolving into a Lincoln Republican, and above all he had Brigham Young's number. Thanks to Connor, the Mormon Prophet's scheming and subversive intrigue were now destined to be contained.

Connor benefited first of all from his essentially realistic appraisal of the Mormon power which was then current among US Army officers stationed in California. One of these was Major James H. Carleton, who wrote to Pacific Headquarters in San Francisco from a camp near Los Angeles on July 31, 1861, giving a profile of the Salt Lake City Saints. Carleton had studied the Mormons in the area of San Bernardino, California, which Brigham Young had destined to be part of the Inland Empire. Accordingly, he knew what he was talking about. Major Carleton informed the Army:

> "Nearly all Mormons are foreigners. Among these are Welsh, English, Norwegians, Swedes, some Germans, and a few French. They are evidently of the lowest and most ignorant grade of the people in the several countries from whence they have come. Mixed in with these are a few low, unprincipled Americans. The most intelligent and crafty of these, commencing with Brigham Young, are the directors and rulers of the whole mess ... their government is solely a hierarchy, and notwithstanding, in theory, they are assumed to be a population obedient to the laws of our common country, practically they scorn and deride, and set at defiance all laws that interfere with their safety or interest, save those promulgated by the great council of the church."[233]

Connor was able to verify and confirm this profile as his forces marched through Nevada to Fort Church. Here, on August 3, 1862 he reported to San Francisco: "I find since entering this Territory that there are many sympathizers with the Southern rebels along our entire route; but while they are loud-mouthed brawlers before our arrival, are very careful in the expressions of such sentiments during our stay at any point. Still, they are

---

[232] Brigham D. Madsen, *Glory Hunter: a Biography of Patrick Edward Connor* (Salt Lake City UT: University of Utah press, 1990), pp. 273-276.

[233] *Official Records of the War of the Rebellion*, Series I, vol. 50, Part I, Chapter LXII– Correspondence, p. 1055.

known and can be identified as open and avowed secessionists."[234] Unlike so many of his predecessors, Connor understood what he was dealing with. At this point Connor's Utah column had 850 infantryman, with six artillery pieces, plus 50 teams and wagons, with each wagon weighing 23,000 pounds.

COLONEL CONNOR TO THE MORMON SAINTS:
"ENOUGH OF YOUR TREASON"

Connor had a simple and effective plan of action: he would take up a fortified position above Salt Lake City and "say to the Saints of Utah, enough of your treason."[235] He also had a long-term strategy for undermining the Mormon theocracy: "Connor was quick to see that bringing in Gentile [i.e., American] miners would afford an opportunity to secure an economic footing in the great basin and break the Mormon monopoly." The Union force in Utah, made up to a significant degree of "miners in uniform," was well suited to be the vanguard of this effort.[236]

The obvious path to economic development in the Intermountain West was mining, to exploit the vast mineral wealth of this huge land area. But Brigham Young, ever the sectarian thinker, was opposed to mining because it would inevitably mean the ingress into the land of the Saints of many American Gentile working people. In the choice between economic development and sectarian-gnostic purity, the Mormon Moses chose the latter. Patrick Connor therefore represented the economic future of the West, in contrast to Brigham Young, who had a Malthusian anti-development policy lurking behind the slogans of the Mormon faith.

CONNOR: SALT LAKE CITY FULL OF
"TRAITORS, MURDERERS, FANATICS, AND WHORES"

With his army now well advanced on the road to Salt Lake City by September 1, Connor traveled ahead in civilian clothes to reconnoiter the situation in Salt Lake City. The Mormons knew who he was, but they did not interfere with him. Based on what he was able to learn, Connor once again reported to Army headquarters in San Francisco on September 14, 1862. He wrote:

> "It will be impossible for me to describe what I saw and heard in Salt Lake, also as to make you realize the enormity of Mormonism; suffice it, that I found them a community of traitors, murderers, fanatics and whores....The people publicly rejoice at reverses to our arms, and thank God that the American Government is gone, as they term it, while their prophet and bishops preach treason from the pulpit. The Federal officers are entirely powerless, and talk in whispers for fear of being overheard by Brigham's

---

[234] "US Army Operations in Nevada and Utah Territories, 1862 (July-December)", *Official Records of the War of the Rebellion*, Series I, vol. 50, Part 2, p. 48, online at Nevada Observer.com.
[235] Colton, p. 186.
[236] Colton, p. 186.

spies. Brigham Young rules with despotic sway, and death by assassination is the penalty of disobedience to his commands. I have a difficult and dangerous task before me, and will endeavor to act with prudence and firmness."[237]

Albert Sidney Johnston had been content to march his forces through the streets of Salt Lake City one time, and then to disappear from view at Camp Floyd, on the west side of the Jordan River 40 miles south of the Mormon metropolis. This was one of the things that rendered the Floyd-Johnston mission so impotent, and Connor had no intention of repeating such a feckless maneuver.

During his reconnaissance trip, Connor had identified a much better place to post his men. This was a small plateau or bench land three miles northeast of Salt Lake City, surrounded by timber and sawmills, where hay, grain, and other produce could easily be purchased. Here Connor intended to create Fort Douglas. Connor received requests from the few federal officials hanging on in Salt Lake City to post his men as close as possible to the Mormon Mecca. General Wright in San Francisco approved Connor's plan, saying that this position was "most eligible for the accomplishment of the objects in view" since it sought "a commanding position, looking down on the city, and hence has been dreaded by the Mormon chief." (*Saints and the Union*, p. 102) Pressing resolutely ahead, Connor with his small force reached the old Camp Floyd on October 17, and crossed the Jordan River on the following day.

CONNOR WARNS DANITES HE WILL ENTER SALT LAKE CITY "IF HELL YAWNED BELOW HIM"

According to the *San Francisco Bulletin*, Connor now sent word to Bill Hickman, the infamous assassin and the head of the Danites, that the US Army intended to "cross the river Jordan if hell yawned below him." (*Saints and the Union*, p. 109) This message had its desired effect. Although Hickman had reportedly been taking bets that no federals would ever pass the Jordan River, the Brigham Young regime, despite all of its bluster, now ignominiously backed down, just as when Albert Sidney Johnston's force was finally approaching in 1858. Brigham Young, it would seem, had the psychology of a bully, eager to attack the weak, but equally anxious to avoid a clash with those who would not capitulate. Connor had bested the Mormon Prophet with a decisive show of strength that proved him to be an aggressive and determined commander. Compared to Connor, Brother Brigham was blowing smoke.

As Connor and the Californians paraded through the streets, there were only large crowds of gawkers looking on in sullen silence. "There were none of those manifestations of loyalty that any other city in a loyal Territory would have made."[238]

In a recent evocation of these events published in connection with the Romney campaign, the *New York Times* recalled that Connor warned that persons nourishing "'treasonable

---

[237] *Official Records of the War of the Rebellion*, Series I, vol. 50, Part I, Chapter LXII–Correspondence, p. 119.
[238] Tullidge, *History of Salt Lake City*, p. 281.

sentiments in this district ... must seek a more genial soil, or receive the punishment they so richly merit.' He bivouacked his men on a plateau overlooking Salt Lake City from the east, only three miles from Young's principal residence."[239] The Mormons began quarreling with everything Connor did, including his decision to name the new army post after Stephen Douglas, whom the Saints still resented because he had called their signature practice of polygamy a disgrace to humanity and to civilization.

OCTOBER 22, 1862: US TROOPS ENTER SALT LAKE CITY AS BRIGHAM BACKS DOWN

On the same day that federal troops arrived in Salt Lake City, *The Deseret News* proclaimed the contempt of the Mormons for President Lincoln's Emancipation Proclamation, which had just been issued in preliminary form. As could be predicted, the party organ of Mormonism based its rejection of emancipation on a frivolous argument that the move was unconstitutional. *The Deseret News* wrote: "We demand to be informed whence the President derives his power to issue any such proclamation as he has now published. Not from the Constitution surely, for it is in plain violation of some of its leading provisions... He is fully adrift on the current of radical fanaticism. We regret for his sake, we lament for the sake of the country, that he has been coerced by the insanity of radicals, by the denunciation of their presses, by the threats of their governors and senators." (*Saints and the Union*, p. 106) In reality, Lincoln was forced to limit the Emancipation Proclamation to areas that were in insurrection against the United States, where it could be justified as a war measure. That fact had certainly not escaped the more judicious of the Mormon Saints. But these observers could also see that the abolition of polygamy might someday be proclaimed in a similar form, especially should the Saints start a secessionist insurrection of their own. On the last day of 1862, the *Deseret News* branded the Emancipation Proclamation, which would become operative on January 1, 1863, as "this ultra measure," and predicted it would help only the Confederates. (*Saints and the Union*, pp. 117-118)

The *San Francisco Bulletin* had sincerely expected the Mormons to resist with armed force the entry of the United States Army into their metropolis, and this paper was still justifiably indignant. Now the paper stressed that Mormons and Confederates were both operating on the same immoral plane, declaring that "if our troops are to march on the United States territory wherever Government sends them, then those who resist their march, because of polygamy, are as really traitors as those who resist because of slavery, and are to be dealt with as such."[240]

THREAT OF "GULF STREAM OF BAYONETS" TO END MORMON ABUSES

The *San Francisco Bulletin* also commented that the small American garrison was vastly outnumbered by Brigham Young's 8,000 Mormon main force troops and reserves of perhaps 50,000 more. Brother Brigham could indeed wipe out the federal garrison, wrote the *Bulletin*, "but Young could expect within two or three years that the federal

---

[239] John G. Turner, "The Mormons Sit Out the Civil War," *New York Times*, May 1, 2012.

[240] Tullidge, *History of Salt Lake City*, p. 278.

government 'could flood his valley with regiments, and sweep it with a gulf stream of bayonets.'" (*Saints and the Union*, p. 110)

Brigham Young, having failed to keep the federal troops out, was now concerned to limit any fraternization between them and his subject populations, since this might lead to an erosion of his ideological control. He therefore augmented his system of surveillance and spying. According to one Mormon summary, the Prophet "considered it important that some regulations should be made in each ward of this city by which the people might be kept from association with the troops that have come into our city. To this end he recommended that the Teachers of the several Wards should be constituted policemen to look after the interest of the people…that if these Teachers become suspicious of any person in their Wards they should watch them day and night until they learned what they were doing and who frequented their houses. If they found any of the sisters going to Camp, no matter under what pretence, they should cast them forth from the Church forthwith." (*Saints and the Union*, p. 112) The contemporary Austro-Hungarian Empire had the Bach system, with its standing army of troops, its sitting army of bureaucrats, its kneeling army of priests, and its creeping army of spies, but Bach had nothing on Brigham Young. Brigham did find time to establish guidelines for Mormon price gouging in selling supplies to the American garrison.

CONNOR: BRIGHAM BETTING ON US DEFEAT, FOREIGN INTERVENTION

Late 1862 and the spring of 1863 was the time of the greatest and most sustained danger of British and French intervention on the side of the Confederacy, and Connor accurately estimated what Mormon intentions were. He wrote at this time to army headquarters in San Francisco:

> "I am reliably informed that the so-called President Young is making active preparations indicating a determination on his part to oppose the Government of the United States in the spring, provided Utah is not admitted into the Union as a State, or in case of a foreign war or serious reverse to our arms."[241]

Britain and France were proposing to intervene in the second half of 1862, and then once again in the summer of 1863. They were deterred by the firm stance of the Russian Empire on the side of the Union, and then by the twin Union victories at Gettysburg and Vicksburg. But if things had gone otherwise, Brigham Young would have activated his plan for secession and rebellion.

Connor could also see that the Mormon strategy was now to deliberately cut the transcontinental telegraph in hopes that the federal garrison would have to be scattered across hundreds of miles in order to protect the wires. The Mormons were also facilitating Indian attacks on pioneers. He so informed the Army in San Francisco: "I am creditably informed and believe that the Mormons have instigated the late attack by Indians on the telegraph station at Pacific Springs in order to draw my forces to that

---

[241] *Official Records of the War of the Rebellion,* Series I, vol. 50, Part I, Chapter LXII– Correspondence, p. 257.

point. Mormons also, in the northern part of this valley, encourage depredations by the Humboldt Indians by purchasing of them property of which massacred immigrants have been despoiled by giving them in exchange therefor powder, lead and produce."[242]

Governor Harding was a new Lincoln appointee, but he had showed some doughface tendencies in publicly regretting that the presence of the Army in Salt Lake City had been deemed necessary. But now even Harding was learning in Brother Brigham's hard school. Harding wrote to Secretary of State William Seward in Washington in late August of 1862 that
he now understood that the Mormons were disloyal to the government of the United States: "Brigham Young and other leaders are constantly inculcating in the minds of their ... audience who sit beneath their teachings every Sabbath that the Government of the United States is of no consequence, that it lies in ruins, that the prophecy of Joseph Smith [The Civil War Prophecy] is being fulfilled to the letter." Once both the Union and the Confederacy are decimated and exhausted, "then the Saints are to step in and quietly enjoy the possession of the lands and all that is left of the ruined cities and desolated fields and that 'Zion is to be built up' not only in the valley or the mountains but the great centers of their power and glory, is to be in Missouri, where the Saints under the lead of their prophet, were expelled many years hence."[243]

On September 3, 1862, Governor Harding went to hear Brother Brigham's speech in the Bowery, and reported back to Secretary of State Seward that the theme of his sermon had been: "Nothing I can say can save the Government of the United States. It could have been saved if the people had accepted Joseph Smith for their President." (*Saints and the Union*, p. 120)

Around this time, the Mormon chief put out a contract on the life of Colonel Connor. Connor revealed in 1886 that "Bill Hickman told me a half hour after it occurred that Brigham had promised him a thousand dollars if he would send a ball through my brain and lay the murder to the Indians. I don't believe that those men [the Danites] were butchers by nature, they were fanatics in their belief that they could not be saved if they would not obey any order of the prophet, right or wrong." (Hirshson, p. 262)

LINCOLN'S MAN HARDING CONFRONTS
THE UTAH RUBBER-STAMP LEGISLATURE, DEC. 10, 1862

Governor Harding addressed the territorial legislature on December 10, 1862. This Utah territorial assembly was a rubber stamp parliament of an extreme type. It generally met only one day a year, and mechanically voted up every measure which Brigham Young and his lieutenants demanded. Harding started off by reproaching the Saints for their lack of patriotism: "I am sorry to say that since my sojourn amongst you I have heard no sentiments, either publicly or privately expressed, that would lead me to believe that

---

[242] Charles Griffin Coutant, *History of Wyoming*, chapter XXX, online at rootsweb.ancestry.com.
[243] Eugene E. Campbell, *Establishing Zion: The Mormon Church in the American West*, 1847-1869 (1988), p. 292, online at mormonthink.com.

much sympathy is felt by any considerable number of your people in favor of the government of the United States, now struggling for its very existence…"[244]

As was inevitable, Harding then addressed the question of polygamy, wherein the Mormons were totally exceptional and isolated, and which he characterized as an "anomaly throughout Christendom…. I lay it down as a sound proposition, that no community can happily exist with an institution so important as that of marriage, wanting in all those qualities that make it homogenial with institutions and laws of neighboring civilized communities having the same object."[245] Harding was especially concerned about the way in which Mormon polygamy also induced incest and polyandry: "That plurality of *wives* is tolerated and believed to be right may not appear so strange; but that a mother and her daughters are allowed to fulfill the duties of wives to the same husband, or that a man could be found in all Christendom who could be induced to take upon himself such a relationship, is, perhaps, no less a marvel in morals than in matter of tastes…. No community can long exist without absolute social anarchy unless so important an institution as that of marriage is regulated by law."[246] This is the sound proposition which Ron Paul called into question during the 2011-12 Republican presidential debates with his proposal to deregulate marriage.

HARDING: RELIGIOUS FREEDOM COVERS BELIEFS, NOT OVERT CRIMINAL ACTS

Harding agreed that liberty of conscience, the freedom to worship, and freedom of religion had to be maintained. He pointed out that "when religious opinions assume new manifestations, and pass from the condition of *mere sentiment* into *overt acts*, no matter whether they be *acts of faith* or not, they must not outrage the opinions of the civilized world, but, on the other hand, must conform to those usages established by law, and which are believed to underlie our very civilization." Harding called for elections by secret ballot, abolishing the practice of making each voter sign his paper ballot. (*Saints and the Union*, p. 122-3) The legislature railroaded 20 measures, but Harding vetoed 14 of them. The Mormons refused to print the governor's message, as had been customary in the past.

MORMONS SEE ATTACK ON POLYGAMY AND INCEST AS "TOCSIN OF WAR"

The Mormon leaders were apoplectic. One wrote that Harding's speech "was a toxin of war, and was considered a very offensive document, it was interpreted as an open and gratuitous insult on the part of the Executive."[247]

---

[244] Cannon and Knapp, *Brigham Young and His Mormon Empire* (New York: Fleming H. Revell, 1913), p. 331.
[245] Catherine van Valkenburg Waite, *The Mormon Prophet and His Harem; or, An Authentic History of Brigham Young, His Numerous Wives and Children* (New York: Hurd and Houghton, 1866), p. 89, online at books.google.com.
[246] Waite, *The Mormon Prophet and His Harem;* p. 90.
[247] Waite, *The Mormon Prophet and His Harem*, p. 84, online at Internet Archive.org

Back in Washington, Senator Benjamin Wade of Ohio got the U.S. Senate to print a thousand copies of Harding's speech. The Committee on Territories on February 13, 1863 concluded that "the customs which have prevailed in all our other Territories in the government of the public affairs have had but little toleration in the Territory of Utah; but in their stead there appears to be, overriding all other influences, a sort of Jewish theocracy, graduated to the condition of that Territory. This theocracy, having a supreme head who governs and guides every affair of importance in the church, and practically in the Territory, is the only real power acknowledged here, and to the extension of whose interests every person in the Territory must directly or indirectly conduce.'" (*Saints and the Union*, pp. 123-124)

This report went on to outline how the Mormon theocracy functioned, with special attention to the Mormon doublethink theory of the Constitution which is still circulating in our own time. The report stated:

> "Contrary to the usages of the whole country, the affairs of this Territory are managed through church instrumentalities, and no measure is permitted to succeed in the Territory which will, for one moment, conflict with the interests of the church; in other words, we have here the first exhibition within the limits of the United States of a church ruling the State.... Another opinion—the subject of both public and private teaching—is that the government of the United States will not and ought not to stand. They make a difference between the Constitution and the government of the United States; to the Constitution they claim to very loyal, but to the government they owe no particular allegiance.'" (*Saints and the Union*, p. 124)

The report also established that "Polygamy of the most unlimited character, sanctioning the cohabitation of a man with the mother and her daughters indiscriminately, is not the only un-American thing among them."[248]

US WINS BATTLE OF BEAR RIVER, JANUARY 29, 1863, CLOSING MORMON NORTHERN OPTION

In late January 1863, Connor and some 300 of the Californians went on an expedition northwards from Salt Lake City. On January 29, Connor won a decisive victory attacking a fortified Indian village which had been the source of attacks on the Overland Mail and on local settlers. This was an event of considerable strategic importance, since it deprived Brigham Young of the "Lamanite" allies he was constantly seeking to incite against the US forces and against American pioneers. In the evaluation of historian Ray C. Colton, this "victory completely broke the power of the Indians in northern Utah and Southern Idaho and conveyed a threat to them which was never necessary to repeat."[249] General Halleck in Washington promoted Connor to the rank of brigadier general. Governor Harding saw the hand of "secret agents of the church... employed to form a

---

[248] Waite, *The Mormon Prophet and His Harem*, p. 94.
[249] Colton, p. 166.

league for a common safety and a common purpose." He told Washington that the Mormons had kept in close contact with the fortified camp dispersed by Connor.[250]

With the latest Mormon request for statehood under consideration in Washington, Connor used his reports to call attention to the abuses by the Mormon regime. On February 19, 1863, he wrote to San Francisco: "I can only allude briefly to the frequent and flagrant violations of the law and the audacious interference with its operations. The law for the prohibition of polygamy is daily violated under the very eyes of the Federal courts by citizens and members of the Mormon Church, who are composed chiefly of the very lowest class of foreigners and aliens." (*Saints and the Union*, p. 148) In Connor's view, the mentality and outlook of the Mormons had not changed. He observed that "The people, from Brigham down to the very lowest, are disloyal almost to a man, and treason, if not openly preached, is covertly encouraged and willful and infamous misrepresentations as to the intention of the Government toward this people constantly made under the guise of heavenly revelations."[251]

BRIGHAM STILL HOPING FOR THE CHANCE TO SECEDE

Connor warned his superiors once again that Brigham Young was still betting on either a catastrophic defeat of the Union, or foreign intervention, most likely by the British and French. He repeated that Brother Brigham "only awaits a serious reverse to our arms, or a foreign war, to break out into open rebellion, and if I understand the significance of his preparations; they mean rebellion and nothing else.'" Connor was certain that the only thing saving Brigham Young from the righteous anger of the American people was the fact that their attention was fixed on military operations in the East and Midwest. Otherwise, the calls for massive action against Utah would have become overwhelming: "…if the crimes and designs of this people were known and understood by the people of the United States as I understand and know them, it would cause such a burst of indignation as would result in the utter annihilation of this whole people."[252]

It was now very likely that 1863 would prove to be the decisive year for the Confederacy. But this battle was being fought on a broader scale. In January 1863, the British Mazzini networks were able to foment a rebellion in the Polish and Lithuanian regions of the Russian Empire. There was immediately talk of French and British intervention. If this had occurred, war between the Russian Empire and the Anglo-French was a likely result. Given the political dynamics existing in the world at that time, it was then quite possible that a Russo-American alliance might have found itself in conflict with London, Paris, and Richmond. Once again, Brigham Young's grasp of the larger world dynamics was impressive, and highly suggestive of high-level intelligence sources in the British Isles, where his son was a missionary at this time, and had a number of well-informed correspondents.

---

[250] *Official Records of the War of the Rebellion*, Series I, vol. 50, Part I, Chapter LXII–Correspondence, p. 315.
[251] Ibid., p. 319.
[252] Ibid.

On March 3, 1863 Brigham Young and his retainers organized a mass meeting in the tabernacle in Salt Lake City to protest the speech recently delivered by Governor Harding to the Utah Territorial Legislature. Brigham Young's rhetorical stance was now that he supported the transcontinental telegraph and the transcontinental railroad, and wanted to defend them from unprincipled saboteurs in the Washington administration. Since Brigham Young was eager for the lucrative contracts associated with these infrastructure projects, there was some truth in this pose. Brigham Young was met with a thunderous ovation, and he quickly warned Governor Harding that if he thought his bread was buttered, "there was poison underneath" – a typical Mormon theme. The Mormon Moses alleged that "there seems to be a secret influence existing, among a class that I do not know what others call but that I call Black-hearted Republicans, against the Pacific railroad and the overland mail route and telegraph line…. If a military government can be established in this Territory, it is universally believed that the people of Utah would not bear it. [Cries of 'No'] There [in Utah] it is expected that the telegraph wires would be severed, the mail be stopped, and the free travel across the continent put an end to.'" (*Saints and the Union*, p. 152) In other words, moves to enforce federal law against the church hierarchy would lead to acts of domestic terrorism, for which the federal themselves would have to be held responsible. Brigham harped on the theme that federal officials were "trying to break up civil government in Utah and set up a military despotism, and woe be to that man who undertakes to introduce despotism in Utah; in such an attempt they will then learn who is Governor (great applause) ….'" (*Saints and the Union*, p. 153) For the moment, the Mormon theocracy was still intact.

By now, Brigham Young was attempting to censor the accounts and transcripts of his public tirades which were telegraphed to American newspapers on the East and West coasts. He wanted to be able to use his demagogy to whip his followers into a frenzy, but at the same time he realized that the backlash against this rhetoric might become dangerous to him. He began harassing newspaper reporters, some of whom in those days knew shorthand and often recorded his speeches verbatim. As part of the new public-relations strategy, he often ordered the *Deseret News* to tone down his remarks.

BRIGHAM YOUNG: LINCOLN'S MAN IN UTAH
A "N****R WORSHIPER"

But Connor was able to report passages from Brigham Young's March 3 speech which did not show up in the published versions. Connor informed the Army in San Francisco that Brother Brigham had launched a bitter personal attack on Governor Harding, against whom he railed in these terms: "This man, who is sent here to govern the Territory— man, did I say? Thing, I mean; a n****r worshipper. A black-hearted abolitionist is what he is and what he represents—and these two things I do utterly despise."[253] The March 3 mass meeting passed resolutions demanding the ouster or resignation of Governor Harding.

---

[253] Waite, *The Mormon Prophet and his Harem*, p. 101.

GOV. HARDING: IF DANITES KILL FEDERAL OFFICIALS, UTAH WILL BE RAZED

When a committee of Mormon leaders went to Governor Harding's office and delivered the resolutions calling on him to resign, he replied in kind. Harding told the delegation that if they killed him, Union forces would massively retaliate and destroy the Mormon metropolis: "I, too, will prophesy if one drop of my blood is shed by your ministers of vengeance while I am in the discharge of my duty, it will be avenged, and not one stone or adobe in your city will remain upon another. Your allegations in this paper are false, without the shadow of truth."[254] Governor Harding was evidently learning to reciprocate the language of threats which he had heard so often from Brigham Young.

A few days later, Brigham Young launched the next step in his spring 1863 propaganda offensive. On March 8, he delivered an oration entitled "The Persecutions of the Saints.—Their Loyalty to the Constitution." Here he was at pains to refute the growing and widespread awareness that he was preparing anti-American moves in the military sphere if the campaigning season of 1863 were to result in serious defeats for the Union. The Mormon Moses complained that the Saints were "objectionable to our neighbors. We have a warfare.... We are accused of disloyalty, alienation, and apostasy from the Constitution of our Country. We are accused of being secessionists. I am, so help me God, and ever expect to be a secessionist from their wickedness, unrighteousness, dishonesty and unhallowed principles in a religious point of view; but am I or this people secessionists with regard to the glorious Constitution of our country? No."[255]

MARCH 1863: BRIGHAM YOUNG RAGES AGAINST EMANCIPATION; DEATH PENALTY FOR INTERRACIAL MARRIAGE

Since the Emancipation Proclamation was now in full force, the war aims of the Union now included the extirpation of slavery, and this Brother Brigham found to be simply intolerable. He attempted to paint Abraham Lincoln as an abolitionist: "The rank, rabid abolitionists, who I call black-hearted abolitionists, have set the whole national fabric on fire. Do you know this, Democrats? They have kindled the fire that is raging now from the north to the south, and from the south to the north. I am no abolitionist, neither am I a pro-slavery man; I hate some of their principles and especially some of their conduct, as I do the gates of hell. The Southerners hate the negroes, and the Northerners worship them; this is all the difference between slave-holders and abolitionists. I would like the President of the United States and all the world to hear this. Shall I tell you the law of God in regard to the African race? If the white man who belongs to the chosen seed mixes his blood with the seed of Cain, the penalty, under the law of God, is death on the spot."[256] The deeply rooted racism of Mormon theology was clearly reflected in this philippic. Despite what Romney claims, these policies have only been changed at the

---

[254] *Official Records of the War of the Rebellion*, Series I, vol. 50, Part I, Chapter LXII–Correspondence, p. 373.

[255] *Journal of Discourses*, 10:25.

[256] Ibid.

level of regulations, but never at the level of the Mormon sacred texts from which they derive.

Since the arrival of Connor and the Californians, Brigham Young's home had been organized as a fortress. The house was surrounded by high walls, and scaffolding was erected on the inside to provide firing platforms for the garrison. A Mormon observer with a telescope stationed on the roof of Brigham's house (maintained by Miles Romney) permanently monitored what was happening at Camp Douglas. Ammunition was being manufactured. Brigham's home was heavily guarded, especially at night, and might have had as many as 300 sentries during times of tension. The raising of the flag over the domicile of the Mormon Moses was the signal for thousands of Danite militia to come running.

DANITE MOBILIZATION OF MARCH 9, 1863:
A MORMON WAR PROVOCATION?

On March 9, 1863, Brigham Young ran his emergency warning flag up the flagpole over his house, and a phalanx of 2,000 armed Mormons soon surrounded the premises. The Mormons alleged that they had picked up signs that Connor was going to try to arrest Brigham Young and round up some of his lieutenants. Connor denied that he had any such plan. Instead, Connor wrote to San Francisco that the Mormon emergency mobilization had been designed as a provocation to get the U.S. Army to initiate hostilities. Connor's intelligence estimate was that "the late armed display was a mere ruse to frighten the proscribed Federal officers from the Territory; or else they desire to have a conflict with the Government, and are endeavoring to provoke me into inaugurating it. The latter I believe to be the real motive, however Brigham Young may try to disguise the fact."[257] The Mormons duplicated this stunt on March 12.

Connor told the commanders in San Francisco that the federal anti-polygamy legislation was universally ignored. In addition, non-Mormon residents were subjected to systematic discrimination and denied the equal protection of the laws. And, despite the illusions of John Stuart Mill and Thomas Carlyle, it was extremely difficult for residents to get out of Deseret. Connor reported: "The law against polygamy is a dead letter on the statute books. Brigham Young has lately violated it, and boasts that he will have as many wives as he desires, and advises his people to pursue the same course. American citizens (who are not Mormons) can not hold real estate in the Territory, and those who undertake to do so are abused and threatened, their property stolen or confiscated by the Mormon courts upon a charge manufactured for the occasion. I have applications daily from people of the Mormon faith who desire to leave the Territory, and who say they cannot do so without protection from me, as they fear they would be arrested, their property taken from them on some trumped up charge, and probably their lives taken."[258]

---

[257] *Official Records of the War of the Rebellion*, Series I, vol. 50, Part I, Chapter LXII–Correspondence, p. 371.
[258] *Executive Documents for the Senate of the United States, Congressional Serial Set*, Issue 2679. p. 158.

The Danite mobilizations of March 9 and March 12 had been duly reported by journalists present on the scene, and these reports created a furor, especially in California. In Washington, the mood in Congress was that if the Mormons wanted Utah to be admitted to the Union, they should hold a constitutional convention to prohibit polygamy in the future state constitution. One bill in the House of Representatives offered Utah immediate admission if slavery and polygamy were both banned, but the Utah territorial delegate objected. Other bills put forward during 1863 would have mandated the popular election of judges in the probate courts – which Brigham used to prevent Mormons – including himself – from being punished. There was also a failed bid to fight polygamy by giving women the right to vote. (*Saints and the Union*, p. 167)

The Mormon defensive posture now depended on further attempts to incite the Indians against Connor and the Californians. (*Saints and the Union*, p. 174) Connor still lacked enough cavalry for his needs. After clashes with the Indians, Brigham Young attempted to exercise his purely personal authority over them, writing to the recalcitrant tribes: "I have always been your friend and have endeavored to do you good, and *you must* abide *my command.*"[259] This was the voice of the theocratic dictator, not of the territorial governor.

Connor tried to create humanitarian corridors so that refugees from Brigham Young's regime could exit the Territory without risking the loss of their lives and property. With the help of some residual Morrisites, he created a safe zone north of Salt Lake City in Idaho Territory. On November 20, 1863, the US Army at Camp Douglas began publishing the first daily newspaper in the territory, *The Union Vedette*. This paper featured extensive coverage on mining and natural resource issues, and engaged in lively polemics with the *Deseret News*. Brigham Young's mind control was correspondingly diminished.

DESPOTISM AND FANATICISM OF THE MORMON REGIME

On June 24, 1863, on the eve of Gettysburg and Vicksburg, Connor once again sent to San Francisco a comprehensive profile of conditions in Utah Territory. His fundamental objection was, once again, to the Mormon theocracy:

> "The world has never seen a despotism so complete, so limitless, so transcendent, controlling not alone the outward and internal civil polity of the Territory, but entering into all the details of everyday life and the minutia of the domestic economy of each individual, as exhibited in the construction of the Mormon Church.... Of that church Brigham Young is the acknowledged head and recognized despot. Upon his will alone depend as well the acts of public officials as the course, temper, and feeling of the humblest member of his flock. Fanaticism can go no further than it has in this case."[260]

---

[259] Mormon Wiki, June 15, 1863.
[260] *Official Records of the War of the Rebellion*, Series I, vol. 50, Part 2, p. 491 ff.

Contempt against the American government by the Mormon hierarchy was openly proclaimed, Connor pointed out, with "striking and undutiable evidences of hatred to the Government, disloyalty to the Union and affiliation and sympathy with treason in the East and savage massacre and plunder all around and about us." He called attention to the Sunday "harangues" by the Mormon prelates, always full of "flippant expressions of disloyalty and vulgar threats against the Union," interspersed with "mock tears and sneering lamentations" whenever there was a federal defeat.[261]

Connor reiterated his accusations that Indian attacks on the Overland Mail were systematically fomented by Mormon agents. They also complained that he never received warnings from the Mormon authorities about the military operations of the Indians; this he attributed to the "insidious and damnable" Brigham Young.[262]

LINCOLN: FROM "ONE WAR AT A TIME" TO
"I PROPOSE TO LET THEM ALONE"

During the *Trent* affair several years earlier, Lincoln was confronted by Secretary of State Seward and other members of his cabinet who thought that a war with Great Britain would help reunify the country. Knowing that Britain's Lord Palmerston was eager to intervene in the side of the Confederacy, Lincoln had ruled out this possibility. He summed up his policy with the famous "one war at a time" dictum of November 8, 1861. This meant that the captured Confederate diplomats Mason and Slidell would be turned over to the British, and the crisis defused.

In the spring of 1863, President Lincoln told Brigham Young's hand-picked territorial delegates that matters between Washington and Salt Lake City "had come to a pause, a stand still, that there was no immediate danger of an outbreak, and therefore he thought it was best to let things alone." (*Saints and the Union*, p. 168)

Now, in the hour of maximum danger to the Union, with Grant besieging Vicksburg, and Lee's army on the march in Maryland and Pennsylvania, Lincoln sent a back channel message to Brigham Young through T. B. H. Stenhouse, the editor of the semi-official *Deseret News*. Asked by Stenhouse what he was going to do in regard to the Mormons, Lincoln replied simply "I propose to let them alone." The president went on: "Stenhouse, when I was a boy on the farm in Illinois there was a great deal of timber on the farms which we had to clear away. Occasionally we would come to a log which had fallen down, it was too hard to split, too wet to burn and too heavy to move so we plowed around it. That's what I intend to do with the Mormons. You go back and tell Brigham Young that if you will let me alone I will let him alone."[263] In the framework of Lincoln's policy what now followed was a prolonged stalemate between Connor and Brigham Young.

---

[261] Ibid.

[262] Ibid.

[263] "Abraham Lincoln," Mormonthink.com.

The well-known writer Fitz Hugh Ludlow was passing through on July 4, 1863, and noted that the Mormons kept replacing "Union" with "Utah" in the patriotic speeches of the day. He also composed a quick profile of Brigham Young, whom he compared to "Louis Napoleon, *plus* a heart." Agreeing to some extent with Carlyle, Ludlow found that "Brigham Young is the farthest removed on Earth from a hypocrite; he is that grand, yet awful sight in human nature, a man who has brought the loftiest Christian self devotion to the altar of the Devil."[264]

Connor used the new *Union Vedette* newspaper to highlight mining activity in the Territory, stressing the potential for gold, silver, copper, lead, and other minerals. He was sure that an influx of "Gentile" miners would be the key in the long run to building a pro-American counterweight against the theocracy. Brigham Young was vulnerable on this point. In 1849, the Mormon Moses had warned: "if anybody comes here discovering gold and distracting my people, sure as the Lord that is, I'll cut that man's throat." (*Saints and the Union*, p. 213)

MORMONS PLOT GREENBACK PANIC
TO INTRODUCE BRITISH GOLD STANDARD

Checkmated for the moment in their plans for armed rebellion, the Mormons fell back on economic sabotage against the Union war effort. One of their ploys reveals an ideology obsessed with gold and silver, just like Andrew Jackson and the Locofoco Democrats before them and the Ron Paul Austrian libertarians in our own time. On July 9, 1864 Connor warned the Army in San Francisco about a "persistent effort on the part of a few merchants and traders doing business in Great Salt Lake City to institute a forced change in the currency of the territory, viz, from national Treasury notes [greenbacks] to gold coin." Connor wanted to arrest those fomenting "so unpatriotic and suicidal a policy." Connor was concerned that the planned money panic might "disseminate among us suspicious people the opinion that the government was fast going to pieces, and its pledge securities little better than blank paper. The efforts of bad men among them to sneer at the importance of the government and depreciate it in any manner would be furthered, and our great nation become a byword and reproach among a deluded community, already deeply inoculated with enmity and disloyalty towards it." Connor saw the danger of a monetary coup in which "a very few disloyal and greedy merchants, owing and neither feeling any allegiance to nor regard for the nation, may consummate a most disastrous stroke in the forcible change of the currency."[265] The *Deseret News* was hyping a greenback depreciation of hyperinflationary proportions in order to bring on this coup. (*Saints and the Union*, p. 237) During the 19th century, the world gold market was controlled by London, and proposals for a return to the gold standard were thus automatically proposals to submit to the political dominion of the British Empire.

Here we can see clearly that the belief structure and rhetoric of the modern gold-obsessed Austrian school libertarians of the Ron Paul ilk, closely allied to the Romney campaign, owe a great deal to the example of Brigham Young, "a man hardly second in disloyalty

---

[264] "Fitz Hugh Ludlow, Wikipedia.
[265] *Official Records of the War of the Rebellion*, Series I, vol. 50, Part II, p. 889.

and evil intent to Jefferson Davis himself." Connor responded by establishing a provost guard in downtown Salt Lake City.

The news from the East was now about the great battles of the Wilderness, Spotsylvania Courthouse, Cold Harbor, and Petersburg, accompanied by reports of heavy casualties on both sides. This was the last chance for the Confederacy, whose hopes depended entirely on the crisis of defeatism gripping the northern states on the eve of the November 1864 presidential election. Brigham Young, as usual, coordinated his actions according to a sophisticated intelligence picture that included all of these factors.

Connor tried to alarm his superiors on July 13, 1864 with a warning that "encouraged by the unfavorable news from the east, the Mormons are assuming a very hostile attitude. They have about 1,000 men under arms and are still assembling, and threaten to drive my provost guard from the city; alleged excuse for armed demonstration, the presence of the provost guard in the city."[266] By some strange coincidence, Brigham Young had decided to mount this demonstration at exactly the same time that the Draft Riots had broken out in New York City. (*Saints and the Union*, p. 238)

But Sherman took Atlanta, Sheridan defeated Early in the Shenandoah Valley, and Lincoln's election victory was soon followed by the destruction of Hood's Confederates before Nashville at the hands of George Thomas, the Rock of Chickamauga and now the Sledgehammer of Nashville. By the beginning of 1865, the military situation of the Confederacy was most dire. As a result of these developments, Brigham Young and the Mormons adopted a lower and lower profile as the day of reckoning at Appomattox approached. But the Mormon Moses was still defiant, growling in January 1865 that "If General Connor crosses my path, I will kill him."[267]

The capitulation of the Confederacy in April 1865 was a devastating defeat for Brigham Young. Reflecting the new political realities, the Mormons put on a show of mourning the death of Lincoln; the choice comments Brigham Young might have made behind the scenes are not reported. The Mormon Moses had already consigned Zachary Taylor and James K. Polk to the Inferno.

The Danites kept killing and maiming. Salt Lake City was constantly plagued by violent crimes arising from conflicts involving polygamy. In April 1866, a man dared to marry the polygamist wife of a Mormon who was serving as a missionary in Europe. He was soon assassinated. The incident came to the attention of General William T. Sherman, now serving as the army commander in the West. Sherman pledged to protect all persons "regardless of religious faith.... Those murderers must be punished, and if your people resort to measures of intimidation those must cease," Sherman pointedly warned Brigham Young. (Hirshson, p. 270)

---

[266] *Official Records of the War of the Rebellion*, Series I, vol. 50, Part I, Chapter LXII– Correspondence, p. 901.
[267] John G. Turner, "The Mormons Sit Out the Civil War," *New York Times*, May 1, 2012.

BRIGHAM YOUNG? "HIS DAY IS OVER"

With the completion of the transcontinental railroad in 1869, the U.S. Army acquired the ability to reinforce its presence among the Saints in short order. A senior US officer commented at the time to the *New York Herald*, "We used to have some anxiety about Utah. That is over. In forty-eight hours we can pour in all the troops wanted. There need be no more uneasiness about the rebellion of Brigham Young. His day is over." (Hirshson, p. 280) Brigham Young had claimed he was welcoming the railroad, and indeed he tried to make money off the construction contracts.

The notoriously ignorant and provincial Brigham Young could have learned something from the great Italian statesman Count Cavour, who had written an essay about the critical role of railroad building in national unification and in bringing modern culture and civilization to backward areas. As it turned out, the railroad became a potent weapon against the barbarism of Utah. Stanley P. Hirshson pointed out that "in Salt Lake City the railroad killed plural marriage. There a Mormon woman heard from outsiders how the world despised her. Peeking into store windows, she saw eastern finery a husband might be able to give one wife but not two, three, or four. Handsomely dressed Gentile women constantly reminded her of her plight." Hirshson, p. 324) At the same time, polygamy was placed under increased national and international scrutiny, since, thanks to the new transcontinental railroad, writers and reporters from all over the world, plus Gentile Americans, including the top leaders of the federal government, visited Salt Lake City and its environs." The railroad also interfered with Brigham Young's long-standing policy of preventing the denizens of Zion from fleeing: "If the railroad came in, it also went out. Dodge described how one of Young's daughters tried in October 1868 to reach the Union Pacific's track and the East." (Hirshson, pp. 280-81)

BRIGHAM'S SON JAILED IN ENGLAND; HIS GRANDSON CONVICTED OF MURDER IN NEW YORK

Brigham Young had always expected that his son Brigham Jr. would be his successor. But scandals enveloped the career of the Mormon Dauphin. According to John D. Lee of the Danite intelligence, Brigham Jr. had been put in jail in England, and $26,000 was misdirected from the perpetual emigration fund to secure a cover up of his activities. Then, in February 1876, one of the crown prince's daughters fled with a Gentile. Brigham Jr. had to go to court to get her returned to him. (Hirshson, p. 321)

Brigham Young's grandson was William Hooper Young. In 1902, this grandson was sentenced to life in prison in Sing Sing by a New York City court. He was convicted of stabbing a woman to death, and then dumping her body in the Jersey Meadows. The Mormon theory that polygamy produced superior individuals seemed to be in trouble. (Hirshson, p. 325)

NEW YORK TRIBUNE, NEW YORK TIMES:
RURAL POLYGAMY REDUCES WOMEN TO SLAVERY

The outside world had always been horrified by polygamy. Already in 1859, the *New York Tribune's* correspondent was reporting that "No where else on the Continent of North America are white women to be seen working like slaves, barefooted, in the field. It is notorious to all here that large numbers of Mormon women are in a state of great want and destitution, and that their husbands do not pretend to provide them even with the necessaries of life.'" (Hirshson, p. 132) The *New York Times* pointed out in 1877 that a poor farmer with half a dozen able-bodied wives automatically possessed a loyal low-wage workforce, allowing him to act as overseer or superintendent. The women were disciplined with a whip. "Farmers with four, five, six or more wives are numerous, and it is among these people that polygamy has its greatest strength. Polygamy in Utah, especially among the rural population, is nothing more nor less than slavery, and its popularity arises almost wholly from its profitableness. It is the system of the South twenty years ago, with more lines of parallel than many of us might suspect." (Hirshson, pp. 323-324) The twin relics of barbarism turned out to be closely linked in practice.

ENGLISH AND WELSH GODBEITES REBEL AGAINST BRIGHAM'S
CALVINIST-SCOTTISH-SCANDINAVIAN REGIME

A significant challenge to Brigham Young's power emerged in 1869, when Brigham Young's anti-American propaganda campaign finally boomeranged. Deseret had always depended heavily on converts coming from abroad. The self-identity of Mormons was the LDS Church, and they did not in the least consider themselves Americans. This distinction was kept alive by Brigham's constant tirades against the United States. But this meant that there was no national identity the immigrants could assimilate to. Therefore, the new Mormons kept whatever nationality they brought with them. In a climate of growing American nationalism during and after the Civil War, Brigham Young's American recruits were becoming fewer and fewer. But the Mormon Moses estimated that three out of every four American converts had defected. Other Mormon estimates put this figure as high as five out of six. This meant that Brigham Young's inner circle of Calvinists from New England, New York, and Ohio had to reach out to other groups to stay in power. Brigham Young leaned especially on Scots, and on Scandinavians from Denmark, Sweden, and Norway. This policy offended the Welsh and especially the English, who complained that despite the fact that they were the biggest single national group in Deseret, they were represented in the supreme councils of the Church by only one important figure, John Taylor. This situation led to a factional revolt for which a prominent spokesman was William S. Godbe, an Englishman. The Godbeites were excommunicated, but a number of very prominent Mormons, including the editor Thomas B. H. Stenhouse and his wife Fanny, joined the schism, going on to write influential books about Mormonism. (Hirshson, p. 292 ff.)

BRIGHAM YOUNG: PRESIDENT GRANT A GAMBLER AND A DRUNKARD

In April 1869, Brigham Young allowed himself a rage-filled outburst against the government in Washington: "Who goes to the White House in these days? A gambler and a drunkard. And the vice president is the same. And no man can get either office unless he is a gambler and a drunkard or a thief. And who goes to Congress? You may hunt clear through the Senate and House, and if you can find any men that are not liars, thieves, whoremongers, gamblers, and drunkards, I tell you they are mighty few, for no other kind of men can get in there." (Hirshson, p. 279) With this intemperate rhetoric, Brigham had made an enemy out of President Grant.

Grant never forgot Young's insults. In November 1869 Brigham Young, Jr., opened up the wounds by commenting to the *Philadelphia Morning Post*: "Undoubtedly Grant has great abilities as a commander in the field, but his political abilities, we think, consist simply in knowing how to hold his tongue." As for Congress, Brigham Jr. opined that it contained the most "dissipated set of men anywhere." (Hirshson, pp. 303-04)

BRIGHAM YOUNG BUSTED FOR LEWD AND LASCIVIOUS COHABITATION

Grant was a Methodist, and the Methodists were the denomination that suffered most from Mormon recruiting, including in England. Some Methodist clergyman who were influential with the President wanted to go after Brigham Young, either for lewd and lascivious cohabitation, or for bigamy. They also wanted investigations of the Mountain Meadows Massacre and various assassinations carried out by Brigham's personal hitman, Bill Hickman. Grant appointed a group of tough federal officials for the territory. In 1871 a group of leading Mormon saints were indicted for lewd and lascivious cohabitation. Others were incriminated for killings committed during the Mormon war of 1857. Then, on October 2, 1871, Brigham Young himself was indicted for lewd and lascivious cohabitation with 16 of his wives. Brigham discussed with his top lieutenants whether he should resist with an armed uprising, or with a scorched earth policy to destroy irrigation ditches, burn buildings, and then flee en masse to Mexico. Brigham Young decided to surrender to the authorities, secure in the knowledge that Utah juries were always controlled by the Mormon Saints. Armed gangs of Mormons tried to intimidate the court, but two companies and federal soldiers caused them to disappear.

When P. T. Barnum passed through, the Mormon Moses asked him: "Barnum, what will you give to exhibit me in New York and the eastern cities?" Barnum's answer was: "Well, Mr. President, I'll give you half the receipts, which I will guarantee shall be $200,000 per year, for I consider you the best show in America." (Hirshson, p. 279)

NO STATEHOOD FOR UTAH IF POLYGAMY IS KEPT

The Mormons continued to press for statehood, while insisting that polygamy remain intact. The *New York Tribune* spoke out in 1872 against admitting the polygamist theocracy to the Union. This paper warned that "To throw the political and judicial machinery of Utah (or Deseret) into the hands of the Mormon leaders would be to give a hierarchy of morbid fanatics powers which would drive from the country every 'Gentile' person, and build up in the basin of Great Salt Lake an impregnable State, intolerant of all non-Mormon influences, governed by a hierarchy hostile to ordinary immigration, and infested with a secret system of priestly espionage which is at variance with the spirit of our institutions.'" (Hirshson, p. 309)

On the other side were the Mormon hardliners, who spoke through the *Deseret News*, which editorialized that: 'It is not consistent that the people of God should submit to man-made governments. There is but one true and perfect government—the one organized by God; a government by prophets, apostles, priests, teachers, and evangelists; the order of the original Church, of *all* Churches acknowledged by God.'" (Hirshson, p. 309)

Statehood for Deseret, commented an observer familiar with Utah, meant Young as governor, George Smith as lieutenant governor, and Wells as head of the Supreme Court. This Gentile asked: "What chance would a man like me have for justice with Mormon Danites as constables to arrest, and Mormon Elders as Magistrates to bind over; a Mormon Bishop as Circuit Judge to try, and a Mormon Supreme Court High Council to appeal to—presided over by High Chief Justice, President, Lieut. Gen. Daniel H. Wells—a cruel and remorseless bigot who knows as much of law outside of Mormonism as Red Cloud does of *Blackstone's Commentaries*?'" (Hirshson, pp. 309-310)

Congress had already struck down the Utah law which had incorporated the Church of Jesus Christ of Latter-day Saints and giving the Mormons the power to perform and regulate marriages in the territory. (*The Mormon Rebellion*, Bigler & Bagley, p. 353) In 1874, Congress passed the Poland Act, which stripped the Mormon-dominated probate courts of their original jurisdiction in most cases, and thus deprived them of the civil and criminal powers bestowed by Utah lawmakers. At about the same time, the U.S. Supreme Court voided the territorial law that had granted such jurisdiction. (*The Mormon Rebellion*, Bigler & Bagley, p. 358)

Then, on January 6, 1879 the Supreme Court affirmed the constitutionality of the Morrill Act of 1862, allowing the ban on polygamy in the territories to stand. Many polygamous marriages were automatically dissolved, and their offspring declared illegitimate. Henceforth numerous Mormon patriarchs would be convicted, joining the ranks of what the Saints like to call "polygamous martyrs."' (*The Mormon Rebellion*, Bigler & Bagley, p. 361)

Brigham Young and his favorite wife Zina Huntington kept predicting disaster for the hated United States. They foresaw a second civil war to bring about the collapse of the federal government. So far, the second civil war has not occurred. These were variations on a theme by Joseph Smith, who had prophesied that in 1866 – the year of two sixes – United States would be swimming in blood. He foresaw another disaster for 1890. (Hirshson, p. 326)

IGNORANCE AND BACKWARDNESS OF MORMONDOM

Brigham Young had tried to build his New Jerusalem on the foundation of ignorance and backwardness. Perhaps this is unavoidable for tyrants. The *New York Times* pointed out in 1869 that "there is not a free school in Mormondom… The result is a general lack of intelligence, except among the leaders, and the intelligence they possess is by no means of the highest order. The newspapers, of which there are several, are very guarded, and give the most meager accounts of everything." Brigham Young wanted totalitarian control, and not the inquiring mind, and as a result he "made Utah the thinking man's graveyard." (Hirshson, p. 322) The Latter-day Saints like to compare themselves to the people of Israel, but a comparison of Mormonism and Judaism shows that while the Mormons placed a much greater emphasis on proselytizing and recruiting, they neglected education and had contempt for learned individuals. This intellectual backwardness and contempt for science still hangs like a heavy pall over the American Intermountain West.

Finally, in order to obtain statehood, the Mormon hierarchy announced a new revelation, which was made public on September 24, 1890. Mormon president Woodruff claimed he was putting an end to polygamous marriages among the official LDS Church. At the same time, the theological justification for polygamy was reaffirmed, and loyal saints were reminded that when they took their places as gods ruling over planets, polygamy would be the order of the day. The Fundamentalist Saints, with their center of gravity in the backward regions of southern Utah and northern Arizona, have never stopped practicing polygamy; their most recent leader of note has been Warren Jeffs, currently serving a life sentence in a federal penitentiary.

Utah finally became a state on January 4, 1896.

The post-Civil War reforms had been more effective in driving Mormon abuses underground than in ending them. Important elective offices in the state of Utah are still preponderantly controlled by representatives of the Mormon hierarchy, and even by the descendents of participants in the Mountain Meadows Massacre of 1857. In many ways, the Mormon Insurrection of 1857 and the subversive campaign of Brigham Young during the Civil War have never ended. On the contrary, after a long march through the institutions, a representative of these values is now within striking distance of seizing the White House.

MORMON THEOCRACY STILL INTACT IN UTAH

As of 2002, Mormons "constituted 63% of Utah's population.... Virtually all statewide elective offices, from the governor down, are held by Saints ... the state legislature is overwhelmingly made up of white Mormon Republican males. Three fourths of the state judiciary is Mormon. The entire United States Congressional delegation from Utah is Mormon. School boards, city councils, municipal agencies, and mayors offices are dominated by Mormons." The editor of the *Salt Lake Tribune* summed it up thus: "The fact is, we live in a quasi-theocracy. 80% of officeholders are of a single party, 90% of a single religion, 99% of a single race, and 85% of one gender."[268] The constitutionally mandated separation of church and state is much neglected in Utah. The majority of public junior high schools and high schools have an in-house Mormon seminary which serves for religious studies. This is the Mormon tradition, and it is therefore difficult to imagine that a Romney cabinet would look like America. It might well look more like Utah, where Salt Lake City may well be the most lily-white city on the planet.

---

[268] Lawrence Wright, "Lives of the Saints: at a Time When Mormonism Is Booming, the Church Is Struggling with a Troubled Legacy," *New Yorker*, January 21, 2002.

In 1875, John D. Lee was charged with the Mountain Meadows Massacre, but this trial ended in a hung jury. In the following year, he was put on trial once again, and this time the Mormon Church chose to hang him out to dry. He was sentenced to death, and he chose the firing squad. In an autobiography and numerous interviews and statements given to the world press in the last months of his life, Lee accused Brigham Young of ordering the killing, and portrayed himself as a scapegoat. Just before his execution, he called on his family and friends to leave vengeance to God. Nevertheless, until the end of his life, Brigham Young had to maintain a large security detail and was constantly accompanied by bodyguards. (Hirshson, p. 316 ff.)

By the mid-1870s, Brigham Young's health was in decline. This was when he called on the Romneys to help build his winter palace in St. George, Utah. Common parlance was that the Mormon Moses was "just well enough to sit up in bed and get married now and then." (Hirshson, p. 315) Brigham Young died on August 23, 1877. He was succeeded as Mormon Prophet by the Englishman John Taylor.

MORMON LONG MARCH THROUGH US FEDERAL INSTITUTIONS

Before his death, Brigham Young had succeeded in getting one of his sons, Willard, appointed to the US military Academy at West Point. President Grant later swore that if he had known about it, he would have blocked Willard Young from entering the Academy. Perhaps Brigham Young was already thinking about a long march through the institutions which would allow the Mormons to bore into the US federal government from within. If so, they have succeeded admirably.

Brigham Young established another important precedent. Young admitted in 1863 that he had in 1837 bought a "fine tavern establishment" in Auburn, New York, which was still his property. In Nauvoo, the Saints consumed large quantities of rum, whiskey, brandy, wine, and beer. In December 1843, Joseph Smith was given a liquor license by the Mormon-controlled city Council of Nauvoo so he could serve drinks in his hotel. In Utah, the head of the LDS Church, Brigham Young, always dominated the liquor trade. Rival distillers were systematically driven out of business. Brigham Young was the founder of Las Vegas, and we can see here the foreshadowing of the heavy Mormon involvement in gambling and prostitution, especially in Nevada. (Hirshson, p. 284-6) Today, Utah produces Five Wives Vodka and Polygamy Porter for polygamist Saints who want to tipple.

CHAPTER VI

POLYGAMY, ANTI-AMERICANISM, AND OTHER ROMNEY FAMILY VALUES

"The system of the subjection of women here [Utah] finds its limit, and she touches the lowest depths of degradation." – Susan B. Anthony, letter from Utah, 1871.

"Among my great-grandparents, we had at least two who were polygamous."
– Mitt Romney to Lawrence Wright of the *New Yorker*, 2002

"Christianity...is a perfect pack of nonsense...the Devil could not invent a better engine to spread his work than the Christianity of the nineteenth century."
– LDS President John Taylor.[269]

"I believe in my Mormon faith, and I endeavor to live by it. My faith is the Faith of my fathers. I will be true to them and to my beliefs. Some believe that such a confession of faith will sink my candidacy. If they are right, so be it," said Mitt Romney during his 2008 campaign.[270]

The first Romney to belong to the Mormon Church was a carpenter from Lower Penwortham, near Liverpool, England. This was Miles Archibald Romney, who, along with his wife Elizabeth, had been converted by Mormon missionaries preaching in their town square in 1837. Miles and Elizabeth Romney, the great-great-grandparents of the Mitt, became some of the very first converts to Mormonism in the British Isles. Naturally, at this point, nothing was being said about polygamy. By 1841, the Romneys took advantage of the immigration system set up by Brigham Young to make the journey to Nauvoo, Illinois. Miles A. Romney was a skilled worker, a carpenter and builder. He was quickly named master mechanic and put in charge of building the Nauvoo Temple. Joseph Smith's collectivist administration granted the Romneys a small stone house, where Elizabeth would soon give birth to a boy named Miles Park Romney, who arrived on August 18, 1843. Within less than a year, Joseph Smith had been assassinated, but the Romney family stayed behind for a time to finish work on the temple. The Romneys were too destitute to proceed directly to Salt Lake City as part of the wagon trains organized by Brigham Young. Instead, they had to join a group of impoverished Mormons living in places like Burlington, Iowa and St. Louis, Missouri while Miles the elder attempted to accumulate the resources necessary for the journey west. After four years of this nomadic existence, the family was able to begin a 1300 mile trek to Salt Lake City. Here Miles Romney was immediately put to work on the Salt Lake City Temple.

---

269 *Journal of Discourses*, vol. 6, p.167.
270 Kranish and Helman, p. 31.

During the Utah War of 1857-58, George Romney, the eldest son of Miles A. Romney and Elizabeth, joined a Brigade of Mormon Danite militia preparing to hold a line of trenches blocking passage through Echo Canyon, the principal route for forces arriving from Colorado and further east. George Romney was thus ready to take up arms and wage civil war against the United States Army units under General A. S. Johnston sent by President Buchanan to put down Brigham Young's attempt at theocratic secession. George's younger brother Miles Park Romney wanted to join the Danites in the Echo Canyon trenches, but Mormon authorities ordered him to remain in Salt Lake City.[271]

Mitt Romney usually avoids discussing any of these topics, particularly polygamy and treason. But Mitt had said, concerning these events, "they were trying to build a generation out there in the desert, and so he [Miles P. Romney] took additional wives as he was told to do. And I must admit I can't imagine anything more awful than polygamy."[272] This is the same fictitious argument peddled by Glenn Beck, who describes polygamy as a practical response by the Mormons to a demographic crisis caused by having so many men killed by persecuting mobs. In reality, Mormon polygamy was started by Joseph Smith and his inner circle in the early 1830s, probably before any Mormons were killed.

So this is doubletalk. Romney has told us that he loves his Mormon faith, which is the faith of his fathers. A central aspect of the Mormon creed, especially after the 1850s, is the open practice of polygamy by the entire Mormon community, including the rank-and-file. The GOP candidate, we fear, is talking out of both sides of his mouth. After the 1890s, the practice of polygamy was supposed to be limited to the afterlife, but it was continued surreptitiously.

HANNAH HOOD HILL ROMNEY:
A VICTIM OF POLYGAMY AND ABANDONMENT

Miles P. Romney was a Mormon true believer and fanatic of the Latter-day Saints. He was also a hard-line polygamist. When Miles P. Romney turned 18, Brigham Young ordered him to get married as soon as possible. Miles P. Romney chose Hannah Hood Hill, a recently arrived 19-year-old woman from Toronto, Canada. Shortly after Miles had married Hannah, he was ordered by Brigham Young to become a Mormon missionary in Britain. Hannah Romney had to support herself as a washerwoman, drudging "all day from sun up to sundown for a dollar."[273] She could have sued Miles Romney for child support, but the Mormon-controlled probate courts would of course have thrown out her case.

The unfortunate Hannah Hood Hill Romney (1842-1929), who was thus forced to accept polygamy and menial labor, wrote a memoir in which she described the difficulty of sharing her husband with another woman. Mitt discussed the case of Hannah with Lawrence Wright of the *New Yorker* in 2002: "She talks about how she and her husband

[271] Ibid., p. 37.
[272] Ibid., p. 36.
[273] Ibid., p. 37.

wept together when he was asked by Brigham Young to marry another woman," Romney said at that time, and added: "My great-grandmother prepared a room for this new wife and knitted her a rag rug. Brigham Young ultimately asked him to take five additional wives. It was the great trial of the early Mormon pioneers." Romney told Wright that when his father ran for President his friends kidded him that there wouldn't be enough room in the White House for a family gathering. "My dad had something like two hundred and thirty-two first cousins," Romney said.[274] The moral of this tragic story in Romneyland: too bad for poor old Hannah. If the status of women is one of the best barometers for the progress of civilization, the Mormons surely qualify as barbarians.

MILES P. ROMNEY SLANDERS UNITED STATES FOR BRITISH SAINTS

When Miles P. Romney got to Britain, he penned a savage attack on the United States government under the headline "Persecution" for *The Millennial Star* of October 1864. Miles P. Romney attempted to portray the Mormons exclusively as victims of evil forces in America: "Many, now, wonder why it is that we are so despised," Miles wrote. "Many likewise, will argue... that if we had the Truth we would not be so despised by the great majority of mankind." But Miles argued that "from the earliest ages of the history of man, Truth and those who strictly adhere to its principles have been unpopular."[275] Miles P. Romney thus comes across as self-righteous and focused on the sufferings of Mormons, not of slaves, while ignoring the greater suffering caused by the Civil War as a product of the same principles of secessionism this young Romney embraced.

In another article, Miles P. Romney wrote: "The Lord has said that his people should no longer be driven from their homes; they are now in the 'secret chambers of the Lord,' and they are living in peace and safety, while their persecutors are suffering death and destruction. The judgments of the Almighty have overtaken the wicked; the American Republic has met with punishment for the rejection of the testimony of the servants of God, and the same awaits every other people who persecute the Saints of God and repent not of their sins, for thus the Lord has spoken through his servants. Then why not take warning by the history of the past?"[276]

"The Saints have a form of godliness, and enjoy the power thereof this causes the ministers to feel quite uncomfortable, because they know their old crazy, shattered craft is in great danger of being wrecked, and, likewise, that finally the Saints will take the lead in the fashion... [Utah's] brave sons are taught from their infancy to respect and protect female virtue as they would with their lives. Hence, the wicked and corrupt, because their deeds are evil, do not like the Society of the people of God.... Here again

[274] Lawrence Wright, "Lives of the Saints," *New Yorker*, January 21, 2002.
[275] Kranish and Helman, pp. 37-38.
[276] Miles P. Romney, "Persecution," *Millennial Star*, October 1, 1864, p. 629, in Thomas Cottam Romney, *Life Story of Miles P. Romney* (Independence MO: Zion Publishing, 1948), pp. 34-40.

that we are out of fashion, which causes the wicked and corrupt to despise us as they did Jesus and his humble followers."[277]

October 1864 was a time when American patriots were fighting under Grant before Petersburg, under Sherman in Georgia, under Phil Sheridan in the Shenandoah Valley, and under George Thomas in Tennessee. It was just a few weeks before the decisive election of November 1864, in which a defeat for Abraham Lincoln would have meant the destruction of the Union. It was at this time that Romney's ancestor, Miles P. Romney, whose portrait hangs in the foyer of Mitt Romney's palatial home in Belmont, Massachusetts, chose to attack the United States from abroad. How much of the treasonous spirit of Miles P. Romney lives on in his great-grandson Mitt?

Miles P. Romney returned to Utah in October 1865, and Hannah Romney was granted a brief interlude of happiness. This ended in 1867, when Brigham Young ordered Miles to join the ranks of the polygamists by taking a second wife. "Brother Miles, I want you to take another wife," the Prophet said. Like any normal woman, Hannah Romney fell into despair: "I felt that was more than I could endure, to have him divide his time and affections. I used to walk the floor and shed tears of sorrow…. If anything will make a woman's heart ache it is for her husband to take another wife, but I put my trust in my heavenly father and prayed and prayed with him to give me strength to bear this trial….I was able to live in the principle of polygamy and give my husband many wives." The wretched Hannah was forced to prepare a room for her husband's new concubine.[278]

MILES P. ROMNEY A HOUSE SERVANT FOR BRIGHAM YOUNG

The tyrant Brigham Young then ordered his slavishly loyal retainer Miles P. Romney to sell his home in Salt Lake City at the drop of a hat, and move his family to the town of St. George in desolate Southwest Utah. The reason was that Brigham Young wanted to create a kind of winter palace for himself in the St. George region. Miles A. Romney, despite his advanced age, accompanied his son and took part in the building projects: "the Romneys were also hired by Young to help build this winter home in St. George. Father and son took on the task with zeal, constructing one of the era's most lavish residences in Utah, an adobe and sandstone dwelling with high ceilinged rooms and an elaborate porch painted red and green."[279] The Romneys can thus be seen as family retainers for the hardened traitor and secessionist, the anti-American Brigham Young.

In the meantime, the inevitable tragedy of polygamy was playing out in the Miles P. Romney household. Hannah wrote that his second wife "was very jealous of me. She wanted all my husband's attention. When she couldn't get it there was always a fuss in

---

[277] Miles P. Romney, "'You Had Better Be Out of the World Than Out of the Fashion,'" *Millennial Star*, Vol. 26, p. 694, in Thomas Cottam Romney, *Life Story of Miles P. Romney* (Independence MO: Zion Publishing, 1948), pp. 34-40.
[278] Kranish and Helman, pp. 38-39
[279] Ibid., p. 39..

the house. [Miles] being a just man, didn't give way to her tantrums."[280] This second marriage soon ended in divorce.

Politicians in Washington were now attempting to enforce the federal laws outlawing polygamy, and one such measure passed the House of Representatives. Miles P. Romney and four other Mormon leaders produced a statement in 1870 declaring that "the anti-polygamy bill... is an act of ostracism, never before heard of in the Republican government and its parallel hardly to be found in the most absolute despotism, disenfranchising and incriminating as it does, 200,000 free and loyal citizens, because of a particular tenet in their religious faith." This same reasoning could have been used to defend widow-burning or human sacrifice, both mandated by existing religions. Friends and puppets of the Saints made sure this bill never passed the Senate.[281]

Hannah gave birth to Gaskell Romney, the grandfather of the current Republican candidate. Two years after that, Miles became acquainted with Catherine Cottam, considered the prettiest girl in St. George, and decided to add her to his harem. The two were married in Salt Lake City on September 15, 1873. Poor Hannah recalled that she had to "do my duty" even "if my heart did ache... many nights I would cry myself to sleep."[282]

In 1877, the elderly Miles A. Romney was seriously injured at the age of 70 while doing construction work at the Mormon Tabernacle of St. George, Utah. His son, who had now acquired a reputation as a wino, responded by adding a third wife.

MILES P. ROMNEY SENT TO ARIZONA TO PRACTICE POLYGAMY

At this point, the theocratic dictatorship of the Mormon Church had a new brainstorm. A new attempt would be made to create Mormon communities throughout the Great Basin, replacing those which had been liquidated by Brigham Young in 1857 when he called back all the isolated outposts to prepare for war against the United States. At this point, the Romneys were ordered to leave everything they had built a second time and trek some 400 miles southeast across the Colorado River to St. John's, Arizona.

Polygamy as a political issue now became the dominant question in the lives of Romney and his family in Arizona. The federal government was attempting once again to suppress polygamy, now under a new statute, the Edmonds Anti-Polygamy Act of 1882, which was backed up by federal marshals. Local newspapers called for action, including violent action, to expel the polygamists in their midst. Romney worked with Mormon Bishop David Udall, of another well-known Mormon political family, to defend the relic of barbarism. Romney edited a newspaper called the *Orion Era*, which battled the anti-Mormon organ, *The Apache Chief*. The latter paper attacked Miles P. Romney as "a mass of putrid pus and rotten goose pimples; a skunk, with the face of a baboon, the

---

[280] Ibid., pp. 39-40.

[281] Ibid., p. 40.

[282] Ibid., p. 41.

character of a louse, the breath of a buzzard and the record of a perjurer and common drunkard."[283]

MITT ROMNEY'S GREAT-GREAT UNCLE GEORGE JAILED FOR POLYGAMY

Around this time, Miles' elder brother George, who had become a top Mormon official in Salt Lake City, was arrested under the federal anti-polygamy law and spent six months in prison. It was a special federal prison in Detroit, Michigan for polygamy offenders. Miles Romney sent two of his three wives into hiding in the mountains of New Mexico. He was also accused of lacking proper title to the land they occupied. Miles P. Romney had to flee to avoid arrest, and Mormon leaders ordered him to proceed to Mexico to create a new Mormon colony where the practice of polygamy could continue. In April, 1885, Miles P. Romney expatriated from the United States and fled into Mexico. He had no idea that he would never return. In Romney family values, polygamy trumped patriotism.

When given a choice between loyalty to the United States and loyalty to the principle of polygamy, Miles P. Romney immediately chose polygamy. Miles P. Romney stopped running when he reached the banks of the Piedras Verdes River, where he founded Colonia Juárez, where he and one wife lived in a hut. By 1890, the polygamist settlement was prospering.

MORMON LEADERS CLAIM TO END POLYGAMY ONLY UNDER THREAT OF EXPROPRIATION

But then, on September 24, 1890, first President William Woodruff of the LDS, realizing that Utah could never join the Union as long as polygamy was practiced on a vast scale, officially and formally repudiated the practice. The Mormon First President had undergone a miraculous revelation, perhaps having something to do with the fact that the United States government was now proposing to confiscate all the assets of the Latter-day Saints, considered as a society devoted to polygamy. It was something similar to the present day Racketeer Influenced and Corrupt Organizations Act (RICO), but it had been specifically designed to wipe out "plural marriage." "I now publicly declare that my advice to Latter-day Saints is to refrain from contracting any marriages forbidden by the law of the land," read this proclamation.[284] Romney took refuge in a quibble about whether the reference here was to the laws of the United States or to Mexico, where the suppression of polygamy was much less energetic. In 1897, disregarding the directive of the first presidency, Miles P. Romney, by now aged 53, married yet another wife, a wealthy widow named Emily Henrietta Eyring Snow. At this point he had four wives and 30 children.

---

[283] Ibid., p. 43.
[284] Ibid., p. 46.

ROMNEYS LEAD MORMON POLYGAMIST COLONY IN MEXICO

Miles P. Romney was by 1897 the leader of an autonomous fundamentalist/polygamist community in defiance of the directives of the official Mormon Church – a situation not unlike that of polygamist theocrat Warren Jeffs, who was recently sentenced to life in federal prison.

At the same time, the 1890 Mormon church decree directed against polygamy was more of a public relations gesture than an actual prohibition. So many Mormons stayed in polygamous marriages and contracted new ones that the church hierarchy realized that a backlash from the federal government might soon ensue. Therefore, a decade and a half after the first ban on polygamy, a second one was solemnly promulgated. But the second ban did not stop the First President of the Latter-day Saints, by now the Prophet Joseph Smith's nephew Joseph Fielding Smith, from continuing to live in polygamy and from continuing to induct more wives into the harems of other Mormon Saints.

Lawrence Wright recalls that "When Congress demanded that furtive polygamists be rooted out, Joseph F. Smith, who was a nephew of the founder and had become president of the Church, issued a Second Manifesto, in 1906, in which he declared that anyone who participated in the practice would be excommunicated. Nonetheless, Smith himself continued to perform secret plural marriages." Another antinomian First President caught lying! In any case, starting in 1933 Church President Heber J. Grant began yet another campaign to convince the American public that the Mormons had turned away from polygamy.[285] After the death of Heber J. Grant in 1945, Mormon First Presidents have no longer practiced polygamy in public.

MITT ROMNEY 2004: POLYGAMY A LEGITIMATE "RELIGIOUS BELIEF"

Mitt Romney presents a sketch of these events in his 2004 book, *Turnaround*, obviously written to assist his gubernatorial and later presidential ambitions. The remarkable thing about this account is that the word "polygamy" never once appears, despite the fact that the peregrinations of the Romney family were dictated by the need to flee United States law enforcement in order to maintain this relic of barbarism. Instead, as a good Mormon boy, Romney tries to portray his ancestors as victims: "theirs was a life of toil and sacrifice, of complete devotion to a cause. They were persecuted for their religious beliefs but they went forward undaunted."[286] We are not told that the issue was not simply a belief, but the institution of polygamy, which has been alien to Western civilization for two millennia. The implicit idea is that the claim of a mountebank like Joseph Smith trumps the public laws of the United States.

MITT ROMNEY 2010: US BAN ON POLYGAMY IS "RELIGIOUS PERSECUTION"

In Romney's more recent 2010 campaign biography, written with his eyes exclusively on the White House, this same conception prevails. Here he dispenses with Miles Senior

---

[285] Lawrence Wright, "Lives of the Saints," *New Yorker*, January 21, 2002.
[286] *Turnaround*, p. 9.

and Miles Jr., and goes directly to his father George. "My father," writes Romney, "knew what it meant to pursue the difficult. He was born in Mexico, where his Mormon grandparents had moved to escape religious persecution."[287] How interesting that Mitt Romney in the year 2010 still regards federal efforts to suppress polygamy as a form of religious persecution. Will he demand that reparations be paid to the long-suffering Mormon Saints for the federal tampering with their peculiar institution?

At the same time, Romney is uncomfortably aware that his family choice of polygamy over loyalty to the United States may create a problem. In *Turnaround*, he tries to get around this issue by stressing that the mere fact of fleeing to Mexico carried no hint of anti-Americanism: "despite emigrating, my great-grandfather never lost his love of country. He had an abiding loyalty to America and a deep interest in politics."[288] Why, Romney tells us, Miles Jr. was even a Democrat, and a supporter of Grover Cleveland, the president who turned over control of the US public debt to J.P. Morgan acting for the City of London! Surely it would be evidence of anti-Mormon bigotry if we were to read disloyalty into Miles Junior's repudiation of the United States, including during the Civil War, when national existence itself was at stake. Here again we see the typical 19th-century Mormon pattern of loud protestations of constitutional loyalty, combined with betrayal of the nation in practical actions.

Gaskell Romney, the grandfather of the current candidate, had gone to Salt Lake City for the usual course of Mormon indoctrination. In 1895, he married Anna Amelia Pratt, the granddaughter of Parley P. Pratt, one of the stars of the first generation of Mormon leaders. Pratt had married 12 wives, and had been selected by Joseph Smith as an apostle to the British. Parley P. Pratt was also the Paris of the Mountain Meadows Massacre, since it was his carrying off of an Arkansas woman (the Helen of Troy of this tragedy) which had provided Brigham Young with the pretext for the Mountain Meadows Massacre of 1857. It is thanks to this connection that the Romneys joined the ranks of Mormon royalty.[289]

NEW YORK WORLD (1870): THE PRATTS (ROMNEY'S FAMILY) ORIGINATED MORMONISM

Edward Tullidge, in an article published in the *New York World* on September 25, 1870, paid tribute to the central importance of Parley Pratt in shaping the entire Mormon project. "Parley and Orson Pratt stand out incomparably beyond their compeers. They were not so much society builders as Brigham Young, but they were far more apostolic. Indeed, Brigham has grown out of such men as the Pratts. It is questionable if Brigham has made 20 converts in all his life…. Orson and Parley Pratt have directly or indirectly converted 20,000 to Mormonism. Ask the people what brought them into the church, and you would hear from every direction Parley Pratt's 'Voice of Warning,' or 'Orson Pratt's

---

[287] Mitt Romney, *No Apology: The Case for American Greatness* (New York: St. Martin's Press, 2010), p. 5.

[288] *Turnaround*, p. 9.

[289] Mitt Romney and Timothy Robinson, *Turnaround: Crisis, Leadership, and the Olympic Games* (Washington, DC: Regnery Publishing, 2004), p. 2.

Tracts,' until it would almost seem to you that the Pratts had created the church. Indeed, the best part of Mormon theology has been derived from them, and so it may be said that they also, to a great extent, originated Mormonism."[290]

Romney's pride in having Parley P. Pratt as an ancestor is prominent down to the present day. In Romney's ghostwritten campaign biography *Turnaround: Crisis, Leadership, and the Olympic Games*, Romney introduces this key figure thus: "my ancestors were Mormon pioneers who made the arduous journey across what was then Indian Country to the Salt Lake Valley. The precipitous mountain pass that led the pioneers down into the Salt Lake Valley and still is the route of access from the east on Interstate 80, was first explored by my great-great grandfather, Parley P. Pratt. He had worked a road up along 'Big Canyon Creek" as an act of speculation when his crop failed in the summer of 1849. He charged tolls to prospectors making their way to California at the height of the Gold Rush and even had a Pony Express station commissioned along his pass." Already here, the pattern of speculation and privatizing public resources is clear to be seen. But these are the least of Parley P. Pratt's abuses.

According to the official Romney family historiography, Gaskell chose not to follow his father down the traditional Mormon path to polygamy. We are told that, despite the fact that the entire purpose of the Mormon colony in Mexico was to cultivate polygamy, Gaskell was content with a single wife. This question must remain open for the time being. In 1907, Gaskell and his wife Anna became the parents of George Wilcken Romney, the future president of American Motors, Governor of Michigan, and father of the current Republican presidential contender. The Romneys by now were wealthy ranchers.

ROMNEY CLAN WANTED TO STAY IN MEXICO, BUT PANCHO VILLA DROVE THEM OUT

The Romney clan had made their final choice to abandon the United States forever because polygamy was more important to them. The Romneys might never have returned, had they not been driven out by the revolutionary army of Pancho Villa. In 1910, the Mexican Revolution broke out when the armies of Francisco Madero, Pancho Villa, and Emiliano Zapata rebelled against the dictatorship of Porfirio Diaz. Pancho Villa's northern army soon took over the state of Chihuahua, and began to carry out a land reform in a country in which 95% of the land had been owned by 5% of the population. The revolutionaries were understandably not impressed by the assurances of neutrality offered by the Mormons, who counted as very rich farmers and had gotten along very nicely with the tyrant Porfirio Diaz. Revolutionary forces demanded that the Romney family contribute their guns and their horses. Gaskell's half brother Junius refused to cooperate, saying that he "would die before ordering our people to give up their arms."[291] Within a few days, 2,300 of the 4,000 Mormons who had resided in the polygamist colony were fleeing north towards Texas.

---

[290] Hirshson, p. 323.
[291] Kranish and Helman, p. 48.

The remark by Junius Romney just cited illustrates once again the fanatical Mormon reliance on deadly force which has gotten them into so much trouble, again and again and again. The constant harping on killing and vengeance which we observe in so many Mormons from Joseph Smith on down is of course totally alien to Christian doctrine. The Mormon insistence on armed militia and private armies carrying out the policies of the theocracy has repeatedly generated a military backlash from those around them. Who lives by the sword will die by the sword, but the Mormons have never been able to learn this lesson. Armed struggle against the United States was implanted in the early Mormon DNA, and has never been removed, as we can see in southern Utah and northern Arizona even today.

GEORGE ROMNEY ACCUSES PANCHO VILLA OF THE POLITICS OF ENVY

George Romney later wrote of these events in his campaign autobiography, *The Concerns of a Citizen*. Here we can see that George Romney was infected by the same obsessive materialism that we find in his son Mitt – a materialism which is of course rooted in the doctrine of the Mormon Church, where God and Jesus are supposed to be material beings just like human beings, rather than existing as spirits. This is, after all, the church where Joseph Smith promised Heber Kimball, one of his acolytes, an estate bordering his own in heaven.

Looking back at the Mexican Revolution from Michigan in 1968, George Romney whined that his family had to be considered among "the first displaced persons of the 20th century." This reflects astounding ignorance and concern with one's own problems while ignoring much more serious difficulties faced by others. The first displaced persons of the 20th century may well have been the Afrikaners or Boers of South Africa, who were put into concentration camps by the British colonialists. There was also the war between Italy and the Ottoman Empire starting in 1911 – a war which took place largely in what is today's Libya. George Romney ignored all of this, in order to nurse his own grievance – a typical Mormon stance. Elsewhere in this book, George Romney presents himself as a member of the most persecuted religious minority in the history of the United States.

According to George Romney, the Mexican Revolution was based on envy. He wrote: "I was kicked out of Mexico when I was five years old because the Mexicans were envious of the fact that my people… became prosperous." George Romney also alleged that "the Mexicans thought if they could just take it away from the Mormon settlers, it would be paradise. It just didn't work that way, of course."[292]

The notion that any principled objection to the outrageously inequitable distribution of income in the United States represents sheer envy has of course become a staple of the Romney for President campaign. The unprecedented income disparities in this country have destroyed any illusions of upward social mobility, leaving the United States with a

---

[292] Tom Mahoney, *The Story of George Romney: Builder, Salesman, Crusader* (New York: Harper, 1960), pp. 53-54. George Romney, *The Concerns of a Citizen* (New York: G .P. Putnam and Sons, 1968), pp. 263-267.

more rigid class system than any country in Western Europe with the sole exception of the oligarchical paradise, Great Britain. But for Mitt Romney, this topic is taboo – except in "quiet rooms."

George Romney also reflects a racist spite against the Mexicans who wanted a land reform. He implies that the Mexicans were too backward to administer the farms created by the Mormons after their confiscation and land reform had been carried out. This must be considered the politics of greed.

MITT'S COUSIN PARK ROMNEY:
MORMON CHURCH IS "AN AMERICAN CULT"

One prominent dissident in the Romney clan is Mitt Romney's second cousin, Park Romney, who warns that the Mormon Church is "an American cult." Park Romney warns against putting cousin Mitt in the White House. His reason is that "obedience to the leadership of the Mormon Church is part of the covenant of the temple ordinances to which Mitt Romney is absolutely a party."[293] Park Romney also says that the LDS authorities carry on "brainwashing."

After scorning and reviling the United States government for decades, and swearing to exact revenge from the American people, the Romneys now demanded that the US government make good some of their losses. Thanks to this lobbying, the Congress established a $100,000 relief fund for Mormon refugees. Even under these conditions, the Mormons hesitated to commit themselves to a future in the United States. The *El Paso Herald* of October 25, 1912, reported that Gaskell Romney and his family, including son George, had fled to Los Angeles "until it is safe for his family to return to the colonies." But the Mexican Revolution would go on, and there would be no return. Gaskell moved to Salt Lake City, and – doubtless with a little help from his fellow Mormon Saints – rebuilt his fortunes. Then came the Great Depression, and the Romneys were not immune.

Gaskell proved as tenacious in attempting to extract payment for damages from the Mexican government as his grandson Mitt has shown himself tenacious in seeking the presidency. In 1938, Gaskell, a reactionary Republican, prevailed in the lawsuit *Gaskell Romney v. United States of Mexico*, and was able to collect $9,163.[294]

GEORGE ROMNEY JOINS ALCOA, PART OF NAZI CARTEL SYSTEM

George Romney attended George Washington University in Washington, DC, and went to work for US Senator David Walsh, a Democrat of Massachusetts. George Romney then traded on this Senate connection to get a job with the Aluminum Company of America. George Romney was soon a lobbyist for Alcoa.

---

[293] Dana Milbank, "Meet Mitt Romney's Cousin," *Washington Post*, February 2, 2012.
[294] Kranish and Helman, p. 49.

The Aluminum Corporation of America was controlled by the Mellon, Davis, and Duke families. Alcoa was part of the Nazi-dominated world aluminum cartel, and it attempted to keep its cartel arrangements in force as long as possible. According to George Seldes, "by its cartel agreement with I. G. Farben, controlled by Hitler, Alcoa sabotaged the aluminum program of the United States Air Force. The Truman Committee heard testimony that Alcoa's representative, A. H. Bunker, $1-a-year head of the aluminum section of the Office of Production Management, prevented work on our $600,000,000 aluminum expansion program. Congressman Pierce of Oregon said in May, 1941: 'To date, 137 days or 37 ½ percent of a year's production has been wasted in the effort to protect Alcoa's monopolistic position.... This delay, translated into planes, means 10,000 fighters or 1,665 bombers."[295] George Romney was a flack for these pro-fascist policies. Alcoa was a part of a massive sitdown strike by US corporate executives between May and October 1940, aimed at sabotaging Roosevelt's defense preparedness program, and logistical support for the survival of Great Britain.

In the words of US Secretary of the Interior Harold Ickes on June 26, 1941: "If America loses the war it can thank the Aluminum Corporation of America."

GEORGE ROMNEY AS FLACK FOR PRO-FASCIST SABOTEURS AT GM AND FORD

George Romney then became the chief of the Detroit office of the Automobile Manufacturers Association, a post which he held during all the years of World War II. He thus represented the big car companies. Who was George Romney working for in his new job?

One leading figure was Henry Ford, the notorious anti-Semite and fascist sympathizer whose portrait for many years hung behind Hitler's desk in the Brown House, the Nazi party headquarters in Munich. Hitler had gotten money from Henry Ford even before his abortive 1923 beerhall putsch. Ford was the owner of his own German automobile company, the *Ford-Werke* of Cologne, which rapidly converted to serve the Nazi war economy. In the United States, Ford was supposed to create a bomber plant at Willow Run, Michigan, but his approach was so incompetent that bomber production did not begin until the middle of 1943.

Henry Ford later hired a notorious Nazi sympathizer Charles Lindbergh, who had been the main spokesman of the America First Committee of Roosevelt haters and fascist supporters.

George Romney was also working for General Motors, which at this time was controlled by the Dupont family. Dupont had important cartel arrangements with I. G. Farben. Irénée Dupont was a notorious admirer of Hitler and the Nazis. Top GM official Alfred P. Sloan was a notorious reactionary who funded anti-union and pro-fascist groups like the Crusaders, the American Liberty League, and the Southern Committee to Uphold the Constitution. General Motors was tied to Nazi Germany because of its ownership of the

---

[295] Seldes, *Facts and Fascism*, p. 262.

Adam Opel AG car company, which had reconverted to making tanks and trucks for the Nazis

ROMNEY'S BOSS KNUDSEN OF GM SAW HITLER'S GERMANY AS "MIRACLE OF THE TWENTIETH CENTURY"

General Motors President William S. Knudsen told the *New York Times* on October 6, 1933 that Hitler's Germany was "the miracle of the 20th century." General Motors was responsible for the Los Angeles tank arsenal, a factory which failed to produce any complete armored vehicles until May of 1943. General Motors was also the main contractor for the M-7 tank, a project which was simply abandoned because of failures and delays.

Seldes notes: "The Big Three of the auto industry, General Motors, Chrysler and Ford, refused to convert to war production, refused to expand plants, refused to give up civilian production, insisted on government cash and business as usual, thus delaying war production of tanks, guns and planes while labor offered excellent war plans."[296] Despite World War II, George Romney thus found a way to remain loyal to the anti-American tradition of his Mormon forebears. How he managed to avoid military service is another interesting question.

George Romney was then hired by Nash Kelvinator Corporation, which later merged with Hudson Motor Car Co. to become American Motors Corp. American Motors later absorbed Studebaker Packard.

GEORGE ROMNEY BACKED PRO-FASCIST BUCHMANITE IDEOLOGY OF "MORAL RE-ARMAMENT"

George Romney was also deeply interested in the international movement known as Moral Rearmament, also known as Buchmanism, after its American founder, Dr. Frank Buchman.

Seldes describes Buchman as "a notorious fascist, who had endorsed Hitler many years ago, and who made an excellent living getting money from big business men to preach a 'philosophy' of appeasement to labor. Everyone was to cooperate, there were to be no strikes, the lion and lamb were to lie down together." Among strong backers of Buchman, Seldes lists the notoriously stingy Henry Ford, plus SS boss Heinrich Himmler, Rudolf Hess (number three in the Nazi hierarchy), the reactionary publisher Harry Chandler of the *Los Angeles Times*, William Randolph Hearst, Harvey Firestone, George Eastman, and other super-rich businessmen.

---

[296] Seldes, *Facts and Fascism*, p. 262.

JEWISH WAR VETS CONDEMN MORAL RE-ARMAMENT
AS FASCIST, ANTI-SEMITIC

The Jewish War Veterans of the United States, at their national convention, unanimously approved a resolution stating:

> "*Whereas,*   Dr. Frank N. D. Buchman, founder of Moral Rearmament, also known as the Oxford Group Movement and Buchmanism, is also the author of the expression, 'Thank God for Hitler....';
>
> *Whereas,* Buchman has been exposed in the British Parliament;
>
> *Whereas,* Dr. Guy Emery Shipler, leading Protestant editor, has exposed the Buchmanites as largely anti-Semitic;
>
> *Whereas,* Dr. Buchman has cooperated with leading Buchmanites in all enemy nations, notably Himmler, the arch murderer in Nazi Germany, and the leading Japanese war makers;
>
> *Whereas,* when the call to fight Nazi-ism came in both Britain and America the Buchmanites claimed exemption from the draft saying they were really a religious movement;
>
> *Whereas,* both in Britain and America public officials have denounced Buchmanites as draft dodgers, and force them to register;
>
> *Whereas,* in general, the Moral Rearmament movement may be described as fascist, subsidized by native Fascists, and with a long record of collaboration with Fascists the world over;
>
> *Therefore*, be it resolved by the Jewish War Veterans of the United States, that they join in denouncing Buchmanism, the Oxford Movement and Moral Rearmament as Fascist in viewpoint, as un-American, and as a menace to the world's war against the common enemy of mankind."[297]

One wonders whether George Romney used his support for Moral Re-Armament and Buchmanism as a means of escaping the draft.

Buchman told a gathering in East Ham Town Hall, London, on May 29, 1938: "The Crisis is fundamentally a moral one. The nations must re-arm morally. Moral recovery is essentially the forerunner of economic recovery. Moral recovery creates not crisis but confidence and unity in every phase of life." These ideas were later the basis of the 1965-2000 musical spin-off operation called Up with People, which featured relentlessly banal singing productions by clean-living, straight-arrow young people. Up with People was prominent during the last years of the Cold War, after which it lost its corporate funding, and was designed to counter communism and socialism on the one hand, and the hippie subculture on the other. The internal life of the group was built around reactionary politics, with a definite cultist overtone involving arranged marriages. The affinity with Mormondom is quite evident.

---

[297] Seldes, *1000 Americans, the Real Rulers of the USA,* pp. 217-218.

Seldes sums up: "… Moral Rearmament was pretty well discredited when its founder, Reverend Dr. Frank N. P. Buchman, was publicly quoted as thanking God for Hitler."[298]

GEORGE ROMNEY'S 1968 WHITE HOUSE BID
BASED ON MORAL RE-ARMAMENT

George Romney's personal papers from the 1920s to 1973 are available for scholars in the Michigan Historical Collections in the Bentley Historical Library of the University of Michigan. According to the overview available online, about 15 boxes of George Romney's correspondence deal with either Moral Rearmament directly, or with Governor Romney's Governor's Ethical and Moral Panel which he set up in order to promote these ideas.

In his role as liberal Republican governor of Michigan, George Romney came under attack from labor unions, which tried to expose him with a pamphlet entitled "Who is the Real George Romney?" One of the themes was that Governor Romney deliberately misled voters, showing that he had talked on the stump of Michigan's need for 100,000 new jobs, but later prevaricated that he never promised to create these jobs.[299]

When George Romney ran for president in 1967-68, he assumed the profile of a stern Buchmanite moralist calling his fellow citizens to account for their multiple failings. He announced that the problems of the United States were due to rampant godlessness, and to public immorality. He lamented the decline of religious belief, and of virginity. He warned against a disintegration of the family which was robbing the American people of their wholesome traditional values. George Romney was at the same time very vague about the issues. He suggested that the solution to these problems was to be found in personal responsibility, and in traditional American principles. The remedy would have to start in the home. His campaign, he said, was designed to be an appeal to conscience that could begin a crusade. But he did say that the U.S. Constitution was divinely inspired – the traditional Mormon line. Like father, like son.

Some concluded that George Romney felt that his actions were ordered by God, and that his opponents were necessarily the Devil's disciples. The *New York Times* noted in 1965 that Romney's critics saw him as a "sanctimonious, intractable, egotistical tyrant."[300]

"At a Romney campaign stop in San Francisco, a black teenager turned to her boyfriend and said 'That Romney, he's a pretty cool governor.' The answer was, 'He belongs to a church where you ain't got no soul.'" A black woman in Atlanta asked Romney how he could feel comfortable in the racist Mormon Church, but he was unable to reply.

The *New York Times Magazine* commented that "the impromptu speech in which Romney is most completely at ease is the inspirational appeal, with its stress on the

---

[298] Ibid., p. 216.
[299] Kranish and Helman, p. 24.
[300] Dennis L. Lythgoe, "The 1968 Presidential Decline of George Romney: Mormonism or Politics?", BYU Studies, pp. 219-241., online at scribd.

divinely inspired nature of American government and the sure ability of every individual to achieve happiness and success through faith and good works." Like father, like son.

GEORGE ROMNEY PREACHES STOICAL ACCEPTANCE OF DEATH TO VIETNAM G.I.S

Time magazine described Romney's trip to Vietnam, noting his tendencies to "lecture the troops" and "even to preach." Incredibly, Romney recommended "stoical acceptance of death on the battlefield." In the holiday spirit at a Christmas dinner at Cu Chi, Romney told the G.I.s "we have to lose ourselves for others. Some have to lose lives young and some when we are older." A black Marine asked Romney, "Is the governor letting Negroes into his church yet?" Perhaps this incident can help us understand why Mitt Romney's speech to the Republican national convention was so utterly devoid of compassion for wounded veterans and their suffering families.

Many accounts attribute George Romney's failure to take the Republican presidential nomination in 1968 to his complaint that he had been "brainwashed" by the U.S. Army during his Vietnam trip, but in reality Romney was hurt more by his vagueness and lack of specific programs on current issues, even racist practices of his Mormon Church, and his sanctimonious piety, which some saw as hypocrisy because of the interests it served.

MITT ROMNEY COVERS UP LDS OLYMPIC CORRUPTION

The sharp contrast between self-righteous moralism and corruption can also be observed in Mitt Romney's career. One key example is Romney in the 2002 Salt Lake City Winter Olympics. Our thesis here is that Romney was called in to carry out a cover-up benefiting Governor Mike Leavitt and top officials of the Mormon Church.

In his earlier campaign biography, *Turnaround*, Mitt Romney admits that he was personally acquainted with Tom Welch, the dominant figure of the Salt Lake Organizing Committee for the 2002 Winter Olympic Games. Tom Welch and Dave Johnson, both leading Mormon Saints, were indicted in US federal court for a systematic campaign of bribery of Olympic and foreign officials in order to secure the 2002 Winter Olympics for Salt Lake City. The Salt Lake City boosters had been edged out for the previous 1998 Winter Games by Nagano, Japan, and they attributed this to the bribes and expensive gifts, including laptop computers, which were distributed by the Nagano backers to officials of the International Olympic Committee and others. So, the Salt Lake City committee decided to fight back with systematic bribery.

Their chosen vehicle was an entity calling itself the National Olympic Committee Assistance Program, which was to "provide tuition, travel, and lodging expenses to athletes and coaches from third world nations" – in itself a legitimate practice allowed as humanitarian aid under Olympic rules. But when the payments were made to relatives of Olympic officials who were not athletes or coaches, the line into bribery had been crossed. Investigation revealed "nearly $400,000 in payment for education and 'athletic training' made to 13 people, six of whom appeared to be relatives of voting IOC members." The countries involved were primarily in Africa and in Europe, and included

Mali, Cameroon, Swaziland, South Korea, Finland, and the Republic of Congo. Three African voting members of the International Olympic Committee had received direct bribes.[301]

Romney was obviously called in to make sure that Welch and Johnson were made the scapegoats for behavior which in all probability involved high officials of the State of Utah like Governor Mike Leavitt, the City of Salt Lake, and the Mormon hierarchy itself. (This pattern recalls Brigham Young's 1877 use of John D. Lee as his own scapegoat for the Mountain Meadows Massacre.) In fact, Welch and Johnson always contended that they were acting with the complete approval of higher-ups. As Romney writes, "It has always been Jim's and Dave's assertion that other members of the board knew of the suspect payments being made from the fund, including the governor."[302] This means Mike Leavitt, public apologist for polygamy, active in covering up the actions of his ancestor Thomas Leavitt in the Mountain Meadows Massacre of 1857, and today the boss of Mitt Romney's transition team. A local television station noted that "Welch and Johnson feel powerful leaders, like Governor Mike Leavitt and Salt Lake Olympic President Mitt Romney, have orchestrated a campaign to make Welch and Johnson scapegoats for the scandal."[303]

CORRUPTION CHARGES IN LDS OLYMPIAD THROWN OUT BY MORMON JUDGE DAVID SAM

According to Lawrence Wright of the *New Yorker*, "the United States Attorney's office indicted two of the Salt Lake committee's leaders, David Johnson and Thomas Welch, both prominent members of the Mormon Church, on bribery and other charges. It was expected that their trial might implicate other leading members of the Mormon establishment, including Michael O. Leavitt, the governor of Utah. [In August 2001] the federal judge in the case, David Sam, who was also a Mormon, threw out the key charges, calling them an 'uninvited federal intrusion' into the state's affairs." The Mormon judge Sam dismissed the entire case in November 2001.[304]

Welch and Johnson escaped conviction. What happened to them reminds us of how Brigham Young shifted exclusive responsibility for the Mountain Meadows Massacre to John D. Lee, the only person to be executed for that crime. In the 2002 Winter Olympics scandal, Mitt Romney made sure that none of the bigger Mormon fish were caught in the net. The close alliance between Mitt Romney and Mike Leavitt which we see on display today was actually forged in the midst of a cover-up of Olympic proportions which saved not only Leavitt, but unknown bigwigs of the antinomian Mormon Saints.

Romney has always harped on the openness and transparency of his efforts in regard to the 2002 Salt Lake City Winter Olympics. However, the main document archive left

---

[301] *Turnaround*, pp. 23-26.

[302] *Turnabout*, p. 28.

[303] KSL-5 TV, February 8, 2001.

[304] Lawrence Wright, "Lives of the Saints: at a Time When Mormonism Is Booming, the Church Is Struggling with a Troubled Legacy," *New Yorker*, January 21, 2002.

over from that event has always been strictly closed to reporters and researchers. As of this writing, Romney is promising that these documents will be released before November 2012. However, insiders have admitted that this archive is already "pretty well scrubbed," with "all legally privileged or confidential information" already long since destroyed.[305] In particular, all internal documents were destroyed in 2002.[306]

MORMON FRATERNIZATION WITH THE NAZIS

George Romney, as we have seen, was incapable of taking a strong anti-fascist stance, and was profoundly influenced by the pro-Nazi appeasement rhetoric of the Moral Rearmament Movement. In these tendencies, George Romney was not acting alone, but mirrored the general orientation of the Mormon Church, which saw its cooperation with the Nazis based on appeasement.

Around 1930, Germany had a larger number of Mormon Saints than any other country except the United States. It was estimated that there were 12,000 Mormons in Germany. Total LDS Church membership was estimated at 670,000 in the year 1930.[307]

The ideological affinities between Mormonism and National Socialism are easy to see. Both belief systems had a strong racist component, with the white race classified as axiomatically superior, while black people were viewed as structurally inferior. The Mormon perspective of making the Lamanite Indians become "white and delightsome" had a certain appeal to the devotees of National Socialist blood and soil thinking. The Mormon notion of eternal progression with the final goal of becoming a God was not so different from the concept of the Nietzschean Superman or *Übermensch*.

From the very beginning of the Nazi regime in 1933, the Mormon Church was singled out for privileged treatment. After the Nazi seizure of power, most religious organizations except the Roman Catholics, the Lutherans, and the Reformed (or Calvinist) churches were dissolved. The Nazis terminated 34 religious denominations and sects, with special attention for religions that were considered American cults, including Jehovah's Witnesses, Anabaptists, and Seventh-day Adventists; the Baha'i movement was also prohibited. The Jehovah's Witnesses were persecuted with special ferocity, because they refused to swear an oath of allegiance to Hitler and refused to serve in the armed forces.

1933: *DESERET NEWS* LAUDS HITLER, GOEBBELS FOR "WORD OF WISDOM"

During the first year that the Nazis were in power, the Mormon Saints signaled from Salt Lake City that their goal was to cooperate with the Nazis. A favorable portrayal of the new Nazi regime is contained in the article "'Mormonism' in the New Germany" by Dale

---

[305] *Washington Post*, July 23, 2012.
[306] Yahoo, August 5, 2012.
[307] For the following, see Douglas F. Tobler, "The Jews, the Mormons, and the Holocaust," online at WebRing.com

Clark, published in the December 9, 1933 *LDS Church News*, published in the official *The Deseret News.*[308]

Clark starts off by reassuring his readers that the Nazis have not interfered with Mormon missionary work, and by stressing the affinities between the LDS and the NSDAP: "The rise of the Hitler movement in Germany caused a great many to fear that religious activity in missionary work would meet with disastrous opposition. Since the National Socialist party had come to power a few sects have been prohibited or restricted, but activities in the 'Mormon' Church have been carried on about the same as before. As a matter of fact, a number of interesting parallels can be seen between the Church and some of the ideas and policies of the National Socialists."

The Mormons were not interested in these "few sects (which) have been prohibited or restricted," be they Jews, radical Protestants, Jehovah's Witnesses, or others. None of them is mentioned in the article. The Mormons, as always, were relentlessly focused on their own persecution narrative, to the total exclusion of suffering by other groups.

Clark reports that the Nazis consider their introduction of fast days to finance their *Winterhilfe* cold weather charity campaign as an example of Hitler's organizing genius, but also comments that this is merely what the Mormons have been doing all along: "it was just another application of the effective method that has been in use in the "Mormon' church for decades. The author particularly admires the Nazi *Winterhilfe* because it "has the important purpose of developing that spirit of sacrifice that is so being stressed in the new Germany, and also of creating more of a feeling of unity and brotherhood through voluntary mutual help."

DESERET NEWS: HITLER LOVES CLEAN LIVING, NO ALCOHOL OR SMOKING

The Nazis also seemed to be respecting some of Joseph Smith's prohibitions, the author points out: "there is another noticeable trend in the 'Mormon' direction. It is a very well-known fact that Hitler observes a form of living which 'Mormons' term the 'Word of Wisdom.' He will not take alcohol, does not smoke, and is very strict about his diet, insisting on plain and wholesome foods, largely vegetarian."

This article promotes the cult of personality around Hitler which was being fostered by the National Socialists. Concerning the Nazi leader, we read that:

> "As a specimen of physical endurance Hitler can easily take his place along side the athletes who are usually taken as classic examples. His 14 year struggle which brought him to power in Germany put him to a terrific physical strain. Besides the great responsibility there has been trials and conflicts, and campaigning so strenuous that it has required his attention night and day, many times making it necessary for him to travel great distances by auto or plane, catching up on his sleep underway to fit him for the multitudes who would gather to hear him wherever he had time to stop."

---

[308] Online at exmormon.org.

Since church organizations in Nazi Germany had to deal with propaganda and Culture Minister Joseph Goebbels, Clark was careful to ingratiate himself with this Nazi bigwig as well. Goebbels was touted as being another follower of Joseph Smith's prohibition of alcoholic beverages: "a lady who has had several dinners that Dr. Joseph Goebbels, the conqueror of Berlin, attended told me that the rich assortment of liquors on hand were never there for his benefit. It was always necessary to serve him nonalcoholic drinks."

Our Mormon author was deeply impressed by the rise of clean living in Nazi Germany, as shown in the examples of Hitler and Goebbels: "These two colorful leaders of the new Germany, in the gigantic struggle for political supremacy, have needed capable bodies and clear brains and have trained like athletes. Their very popularity is making intemperance more unpopular. The fact that they are worshipped may be one big reason for a growing dislike for smoking and drinking in Germany today." The author does not mention that Ernst Röhm, who at the end of 1933 was still leading the SA Brownshirts, was a notorious morphine addict – a foible he shared with other top Nazis.

The campaign against smoking has been supplemented by a decline in the use of cosmetics, the article points out: "posters from youth organizations fighting the use of tobacco have actually appeared on the street. The same movement has even extended itself to the use of cosmetics and its effectiveness may be seen by the fact that a woman recently told me that the slump in the cosmetic business was the cause of her losing her job."

This 1933 article expresses special satisfaction about the shared interest of Mormons and Nazis in the question of genealogy, which had increased in Germany because of the Nazi demand that individuals prove their status as members of the "Aryan" race. And because of this new interest, the Mormons were:

> "... finding that at least one branch of their church work has received its greatest boon since Germany's adoption of Hitlerism. It was always difficult for genealogical workers to get into the archives of the recognized church to trace back family records. When the pastor learned of the intention, access to the records was often denied. Now, due to the importance given to the racial question, and the almost necessity of proving that one's grandmother was not a Jewess, the old record books have been dusted off and stand ready and waiting for use. No questions are asked. In fact some of the Saints instead of being refused by the pastors now have received letters of encouragement complimenting them for their patriotism. All genealogical workers who are interested in tracing back family history in Germany should take advantage of the present unusual opportunity."[309]

---

[309] Two Mormon scholars comment: "Hitler enjoyed at least as much popularity among German Saints as he did among the population in general. His apparent dynamism and self-confidence seemed to show a way out of the chaos and weakness of the Weimar years. Moreover, as 'good Germans,' the Mormons were acutely aware that Hitler had risen to power through legal channels... Some Church members even saw Hitler as God's instrument, preparing the world for

The German magazine of the Mormon Church, *Der Stern*, advocated a line of resignation and cooperation with the Nazi regime. In 1935, *Der Stern* stressed that Utah Senator Reed Smoot, a leading Mormon, had always been part of the fifth column friendly to Nazi Germany. LDS Church President Heber Grant visited Germany in 1937, and told the 12,000 Mormons living there to stay where they were, to keep the commandments, and to work for the greatest possible cooperation with the regime so the church would remain intact and missionary activity continued.

VÖLKISCHER BEOBACHTER, APRIL 1939:
MORMONS, NAZIS HAVE MUCH IN COMMON

To symbolize the cordial relations between the Mormon Saints and the Nazi regime, Alfred C. Rees, the president of the West German Mormon mission, was allowed to contribute an article to the *Völkischer Beobachter*, the official national daily newspaper of the Nazi party, on April 14, 1939. The article, entitled "Im Lande der Mormonen" – "In the Land of the Mormons," stresses the deep affinities and history of friendly relations between Nazi Germany and the Mormon Saints. Notice that the title of this article does not refer to the United States, but only to the land of the Mormons.

April 1939 is very late in the day. Hitler had re-armed, had re-militarized the Rhineland, had absorbed Austria through the *Anschluss*, had seized control of Czechoslovakia in two separate phases, had carried out the *Krystallnacht* pogrom of November 1938, and was loudly signaling his intention of attacking Poland. The main British pro-appeasement group, the Cliveden set, had become disillusioned with Hitler in March 1939.

Keele and Tobler summarize the Rees article as follows:

> In their eagerness to coexist with the [Nazi] government, American officials of the German Church resorted to public relation efforts . . . Probably the clearest example of this tendency is an article by West German Mission President Alfred C. Rees entitled "In the Land of the Mormons." The article appeared in a special issue of the Nazi Party organ *Der Volkische Beobachter* dated April 14, 1939. In the Editor's Preface to the article, President Rees is called 'the representative of the Church in Germany,' who 'paints for our readers a portrait of Mormonism today, a church which views the New Germany with sympathy and friendship.' Whether President Rees originally wrote the article in German or not, the language of the piece abounds in such loaded terms as *Volk* and *Rasse* (race), and a picture of Brigham Young bears

---

the millennium. Superficial parallels were drawn between the Church and the Nazi party with its emphasis on active involvement by every member... The vital importance of 'Aryan' ancestry gave new significance to genealogical research. And the Fuhrer himself, the non-smoking, non-drinking vegetarian who yielded to no one in his desire for absolute law and order, seemed to embody many of the most basic LDS virtues." Alan F. Keele and Douglas F. Tobler, "The Führer's New Clothes: Helmuth Huebner and the Mormons in the Third Reich," *Sunstone*, v. 5, no. 6, pp. 20-29

the caption, 'Fuhrer der historischen Mormonenpioniere.' [Leader of the Historic Mormon Pioneers] But the significance of these linguistic gaffes is magnified by hindsight. More disturbing is the way President Rees blatantly parallels Mormonism with Nazism. As Rees warms to his topic, Mormonism begins to sound like a fulfillment of Nazi teachings, providing "the practical realization of the German ideal: 'the common good takes precedence over the individual good.'" Rees concluded by assuring his readers that "Mormons are people who put this healthy doctrine into action." Reading articles such as this, it would have been easy for a German Saint to mistakenly conclude that the seal of official Church approval had been placed on the Nazi regime."[310]

According to Keele and Tobler, some of the Mormon Saints in Germany were convinced that Hitler was an instrument of Divine Providence, since he was hastening the arrival of the millennium.

DESERET NEWS APPEASES HITLER, 1939

The Mormon appeasement line in regard to Hitler in the official publications of the Church was deeply disturbing to Fawn Brodie. She criticized the editorial position of the *Deseret News*, the official Mormon Church newspaper in Salt Lake City. "If the *Deseret News* is careful not to offend [Nazi] Germany, and I gather … that it is falling backwards on the attempt, it is my guess that first of all the Church is afraid of complete banishment."[311] By the time Fawn Brodie wrote this in June 1939, even Sir Neville Chamberlain had been forced to condemn Hitler in public, but the Mormons held fast to their appeasement policy. Angry that the *Deseret News* was intent on appeasing the Nazis, and failed to condemn Nazi persecution of Jews, Fawn Brodie wrote her uncle, "I can just hear the good brethren... at home saying – 'of course the persecution of the Jews is terrible but God moves in mysterious ways, his wonders to perform.'"[312]

One German Mormon who did distribute leaflets calling for the overthrow of Hitler and the Nazi Regime was Helmuth Hübener, who died a martyr at the age of 17 in 1942, tortured and beheaded. Hübener's story is included in the 1969 novel by Günther Grass entitled *Local Anesthetic* (*Örtlich betäubt*). Hübener was excommunicated by local Mormon authorities before his death. Hubener's branch president was a fanatical Nazi who played Hitler's speeches on the radio for all the local Saints to hear.

The first major condemnation of Nazism by a religious leader was that of Pope Pius XI in 1937 with his encyclical, *Mit brennender Sorge* (With burning consternation).

[310] Alan F. Keele and Douglas F. Tobler, "The Fuhrer's New Clothes: Helmuth Huebner and the Mormons in the Third Reich," *Sunstone*, v. 5, no. 6, pp. 20-29
[311] Fawn M. Brodie to Dean Brimhall, June 14, 1939, Brimhall Papers, Special Collections, Marriott Library; quoted at exmormon.com
[312] Fawn M. Brodie to Dean Brimhall, 14 June 1939; Newell G. Bringhurst, *Fawn McKay Brodie: A Biographer's Life* (Norman OK: University of Oklahoma Press, 1999), online at WebRing.com.

According to reports on the Internet, Mormon recruiting in Germany after World War II was relatively successful, since former Nazi supporters could be converted by stressing that Mormonism was a "white" religion which aimed at the racial transformation of dark skinned peoples. According to one of these accounts, "former Nazis saw in Mormonism a spiritual version of Hitler's policies."

EZRA TAFT BENSON: RACIST MORMON PROPHET (1985-1994) AND THE VIETNAM WAR

Ezra Taft Benson has been noted for his reactionary politics and his support of the right-wing extremist John Birch Society. Benson served as US Secretary of Agriculture under Eisenhower from 1953 to 1961. During this time, he made a significant contribution to the onset of the Vietnam War.

During the 1950s, the leading US expert on land reform was the agricultural economist and researcher Wolf Ladejinsky, who had worked with General MacArthur in Tokyo between 1945 and 1954 on the highly successful Japanese land reform which, for the first time in history, had broken the power of absentee landlords and established prosperous family farmers. He had also been active in mainland China under the KMT Nationalist regime of Chiang Kai-shek, and later helped design the landmark land reform carried out under Chiang's auspices in the Republic of China on Taiwan, which was one of the indispensable components of the Taiwan economic miracle. He also worked in India.

Ladejinsky was land reform adviser to President Ngo Dinh Diem of South Vietnam between 1955 and 1961. He was a Jew born in the Ukraine in 1899, who had studied with Rexford Tugwell at Columbia University and who became an anti-Communist New Deal Democrat. He was described as "no typical bureaucrat, but an impassioned reformer,"[313] and was according to author James Michener "Communism's most implacable foe."

Ladejinsky's career was sabotaged by the reactionary Mormon Ezra Taft Benson, who revoked his security clearance, and had him fired from the post of agricultural attaché in Tokyo. Benson grotesquely slandered Ladejinsky as a "security risk" and alleged without any proof that he had been a member of two Communist front organizations. Ladejinsky was quickly hired in 1955 by Harold Stassen of the US Foreign Operations Administration to work on land reform in South Vietnam. President Eisenhower was questioned about this matter, but did not offer a forceful defense of Ladejinsky. Since it was clear to all that Ladejinsky did not enjoy the full support of Eisenhower and the entire US government, he was unable to implement this program in South Vietnam. If this land reform had succeeded, the root causes of the later Vietnam War could very well have been eradicated. So perhaps we can thank the reactionary racist Mormon Prophet Ezra Taft Benson for some of the suffering of the Vietnam War.

---

[313] Wikipedia article on Wolf Ladejinsky.

BENSON: "CIVIL RIGHTS A TOOL OF COMMUNIST DECEPTION"

Benson's racism has been documented by his grandson, Steve Benson, who writes: "In the mid-1960s, I was in junior high school. It was a time when the nation was being rocked by the tumultuous struggle for civil rights.... During those uncertain days, I remember my grandfather telling me that Dr. King was a tool of the Communist conspiracy and urging me to read John Birch Society literature on King's supposed true nature and Communist-inspired agenda."[314] Ezra Taft Benson's daughter was a "card-carrying Bircher."

By the 1960s, Ezra Taft Benson was already planning for race war: "He reassured white patriots, however, that even 'if Communism comes to America . . . the Negro represents only 10 percent of the population. In any all-out race war which might be triggered, there isn't a chance in the world that Communist-led Negro guerilla units could permanently hold on to the power centers of government, even if they could capture them in the first place.'"[315]

Ezra Taft Benson wrote of Martin Luther King: "The man who is generally recognized as the leader of the so-called civil rights movement today in America is a man who has lectured at a Communist training school, who has solicited funds through Communist sources, who hired a Communist as a top-level aide, who has affiliated with Communist fronts, who is often praised in the Communist press and who unquestionably parallels the Communist line. This same man advocates the breaking of the law and has been described by J. Edgar Hoover as 'the most notorious liar in the country.'"

In a letter to Mormon hotelier J. Willard Marriott, Ezra Taft Benson argued that "Martin Luther King had been affiliated with at least the following officially recognized Communist fronts," three of which he then went on to list. In the same letter, he coldly warned Marriott that "the Communists will use Mr. King's death for as much yardage as possible." Steve Benson also recalls: "A year later, in another letter to Marriott, my grandfather continued his attack on the dead black minister, writing that 'the kindest thing that could be said about Martin Luther King is that he was an effective Communist tool. Personally, I think he was more than that.'... My grandfather's hate-filled utterances directed at Rev. King brought like-minded rank-and-file LDS bigots out of the woodwork, rallying to his anti-Communist/anti-civil rights cause." Ezra Taft Benson published a pamphlet entitled: "Civil Rights: Tool of Communist Deception."

Steve Benson notes that Ezra Taft Benson's extremism was an embarrassment, but it was a viewpoint shared by many other top Saints: When Mormon Apostle Mark E. Petersen spoke on "Race Problems—As They Affect the Church" at the BYU campus in 1954, he stated the following: "...if the Negro accepts the gospel with real, sincere faith, and is really converted, to give him the blessings of baptism and the gift of the Holy Ghost, he

---

[314] Steve Benson, "Ezra Taft Benson: Mormonism's Prophet, Seer, and Race Baiter," July 20, 2005, exmormon.com.
[315] Steve Benson, "Signs of the Un-True Church," mormoncurtain.com, January 23, 2008.

can and will enter the celestial kingdom. He will go there as a servant, but he will get celestial glory."

Mormon racism was pervasive: "Some time before the 'revelation' [allowing blacks to enter the Mormon priesthood] came to chief 'Prophet' Spencer Kimball in June 1978, General Authority Bruce R McConkie had said: "The Blacks are denied the Priesthood; under no circumstances can they hold this delegation of authority from the Almighty. The Negroes are not equal with other races where the receipt of certain blessings are concerned, particularly the priesthood and the temple blessings that flow there from, but this inequality is not of man's origin, it is the Lord's doings."[316]

The Mormon explanation for the decision to abandon open racism is this: "We are told that on June 8, 1978, it was 'revealed' to the then president, Spencer Kimball, that people of color could now gain entry into the priesthood. According to the church, Kimball spent many long hours petitioning God, begging him to give worthy black people the priesthood. God finally relented."[317]

In addition to their other racist and reactionary policies, the Mormon Church is also anti-labor, anti-worker, and anti-union. They are determined to keep Utah as a "right to work" or more accurately a union-busting or scab state where organizing for collective bargaining is practically impossible. The LDS Church has meddled blatantly in politics in order to secure these results: "As recently as 1965, church president David O. McKay wrote letters to the 11 Mormons in Congress urging them to vote against the move to repeal section 14 (b) of the Taft-Hartley Act, which authorizes state right to work laws."[318]

POLYGAMY: A NEW FRONT IN THE REPUBLICAN WAR ON WOMEN

> "And if he had ten virgins given them to him by this law, he cannot commit adultery, for they belong to him, and they are given it to him; therefore he is justified." Joseph Smith's 1831 revelation on polygamy, *Doctrine and Covenants*, section 132, verse 62.

The official leadership of the Mormon Church of Latter-day Saints held fast to the Joseph Smith – Brigham Young tradition of polygamy until 1890. At this point, polygamy was repudiated under the First Presidency of Wilford Woodruff. Woodruff had waited until the last possible moment, awaiting the outcome of an appeal before the US Supreme Court of a law which disenfranchised the Mormon LDS Church and threatened to destroy the religion altogether. Starting in the 1880s when the handwriting was on the wall, hard-line polygamists gravitated to southern Utah and northern Arizona, giving rise to the de facto theocratic communes of Hillsdale, Utah, Short Creek, Arizona, and Colorado City, Arizona. The latter two communities are located in Mohave County, where prosecutions against polygamists were attempted from the 1930s to the 1950s. According

---

[316] *Mormon Doctrine*, pp. 526-527. See Steve Benson, "After 'The Speech': 10 Top Extreme Beliefs of Mitt the Mormon, Kooky Candidate from Kolob," Mormon Curtain, December 10, 2007.

[317] Freerepublic.com; see also Mormon Coffee.

[318] Hewitt, p. 223.

to the *Los Angeles Times*, there were some 30,000 polygamists in the United States west of the Mississippi at the beginning of the 21st century.

The most famous polygamist of the modern age may be Warren Jeffs of Hillsdale, Utah, leading light of the polygamist Fundamentalist Church of Jesus Christ of Latter-day Saints. Warren Jeffs is now serving a life plus twenty years sentence in Texas after being convicted on child sex abuse charges. Jeffs has clearly been sacrificed to protect more important polygamists. At the same time, depraved libertarians are taking up the polygamy issue as a question of human rights – on the side of the polygamists.

In the summer of 2012, Kody Brown and his four wives (Meri, Janelle, Christine, and Robyn), all of them members of the Apostolic United Brethren and all of them stars of the TLC cable channel series *Sister Wives*, were in court before US District Judge Clark Waddoups to argue their case that the Utah anti-bigamy law, which might subject them to criminal prosecution, should be overturned. In Utah, bigamy is a third-degree felony carrying a penalty of up to five years in prison. The policy of the Utah Attorney General's Office is that the state will not prosecute consenting adult polygamists unless other crimes are being committed.

The *Sister Wives* series represents a major propaganda initiative by pro-polygamy forces, designed as an effort to humanize the horrors of plural marriage, in much the same way that *The Sopranos* served to humanize the Mafia.

However, Utah does not openly accept that polygamy amounts to the exercise of religious freedom. "It is not protected under religious freedom because states have the right to regulate marriage," according to Paul Murphy, the spokesman for Utah Attorney General Mark Shurtleff.[319] Brown and his four *Sister Wives* are represented by Jonathan Turley, known to cable TV viewers as a constitutional law professor from George Washington University in Washington, DC who supported the impeachment of Bill Clinton a dozen years ago and then made a left turn under Bush. Turley's argument is based on a US Supreme Court ruling striking down a Texas sodomy law, based on which he argues that private intimate relationships between or among consulting adults are protected by the Constitution.

The notion that polygamy could be restored in the United States in the 21st century may appear to be an absurd contention, but a combination of right wing libertarian anarchists and left wing permissive social liberals is acting today to resurrect this relic of barbarism. Polygamy is attempting to make a comeback by attempting to establish false analogies with gay marriage or the abolition of sodomy laws. According to Jane Schacter, constitutional law professor at Stanford University: "in many ways, the movement for the rights of polygamists is just not advanced enough to the point where the claim is going to seem legitimate to the courts." She added that there is "much more acceptance of gay couples, of homosexuality in general," while polygamy "opens up a whole can of

---

[319] Brian Skoloff, "'Sister Wives' Family Back in Court to Challenge Utah Bigamy Law," AP-*Salt Lake City Tribune*, July 25, 2012.

legal worms that is not really opened with the same-sex marriage issue," especially because polygamous households so often involve underaged girls.[320]

In Canada, British Columbia has been practicing a policy of not prosecuting polygamists for the past 20 years. The toleration of polygamy under the cover of religious freedom began under the left-of-center New Democratic Party. A spokeswoman for the Utah-based group Tapestry against Polygamy (TAP) criticized this Canadian neglect, pointing out that women trapped in polygamous marriages suffer appalling abuse. "Polygamists are every bit as bad as the Taliban in the way they treat women. They use them as property, they barter and trade them and they force them into marriages at very young ages." "Some polygamists demand that the women have a child per year."[321] TAP attempted to intervene at the Salt Lake City Winter Olympics in 2002 to call attention to the "dirty little secrets" of polygamy in places like Utah and British Columbia.

According to journalist Frank Stirk, Canada has its own polygamist Mormon theocracy in British Columbia: "in the rural area near Creston, B.C., is the 1,000 member Bountiful commune, an affiliate of a fundamentalist Mormon sect which split from the LDS Church after it renounced polygamy in 1890. Bountiful's leader is Winston Blackmore, reputed to have 30 wives and 80 children. In 1992, the Royal Canadian Mounted Police recommended charges under section 239 be laid against Blackmore and Elder Dalmin Oler. But Attorney General Colin Gabelmann decided not to prosecute, after being advised that the law banning polygamy is invalid. Gabelmann also said polygamy is a 'social problem'...."[322]

Another Canadian commentator, Susan Martinuk, predicted that "it won't be long before polygamy is viewed as a legitimate marital state in our tolerant nation." Canada may thus emerge as a world magnet for polygamists, setting the social condition of women and children back by decades or centuries.

REACTIONARY SHERIFF JOE ARPAIO WINKS AT POLYGAMY

Arizona, another part of Brigham Young's Inland Empire, also has a large polygamist population. Here, as in Utah, polygamy is outlawed by the state constitution. In 1953, law enforcement officials launched a midnight raid on the polygamist community at Short Creek, with hundreds of children being separated from their polygamous households and dozens of men indicted for bigamy and statutory rape.[323] About 20 girls between 11 and 15 years of age had been forced into polygamous unions with older men. Some 26 men later pleaded guilty on charges of unlawful cohabitation, and were given sentences of one year's probation at Mohave County Superior Court. The 40 women and 160 children were taken into protective custody by the family court in Phoenix. Two judges agreed that the welfare of the children was in danger, so the mothers and children

---

[320] Fox News, July 25, 2012.

[321] Frank Stirk, *Christian Week Canada*, March 5, 2002.

[322] Ibid.

[323] Tim Molly, "It's a Felony, but Polygamy Isn't Prosecuted in Arizona," Associated Press, August 12, 1998.

were sent to live with Mormon families in various parts of Arizona. But this ruling was struck down by the Arizona appeals court in 1955, and this finding was upheld by the Arizona Supreme Court. How many Mormons sat on these courts? In any case, the polygamist community of Short Creek was soon restored to its status quo. After that, the elected officials of Arizona basically stopped all enforcement of the anti-polygamy laws.[324]

Joe Arpaio, the sheriff of Maricopa County, Arizona, has become nationally famous as the new Bull Connor for his policies of racial profiling. Arpaio is a Romney supporter and has been endorsed by Romney. But the widespread practice of polygamy in Arizona, including Arpaio's immediate jurisdiction, is a topic scorned by Arpaio. Despite the obvious multigenerational association of the Romney family with polygamy, many journalists are also ignoring this topic, leaving it to Internet readers like this one to make the obvious connection concerning Sheriff Joe: "Why isn't he cracking down on all the polygamist Mormon communities that live in Arizona at or near the Utah border? In case Arpaio doesn't know it, polygamy is illegal in the United States, and so is child abuse."[325]

POLYGAMOUS MORMON THEOCRACIES IN UTAH AND ARIZONA TODAY

In reading about the monstrous abuses of Brigham Young's Mormon theocracy in Utah Territory – justly labeled as a "strange system of terrorism" by President James Buchanan, many readers no doubt find it unbelievable that such an outrageous system had ever existed on the territory of the United States. But there is considerable evidence that just such a reign of terror persists in parts of the old Mormon Inland Empire down to the present day.

The localities in question are Hildale, Utah, and Colorado City, Arizona (formerly called Short Creek), both controlled by the polygamist Fundamentalist Church of Jesus Christ of Latter-day Saints (FLDS), whose most famous member is none other than the felon Warren Jeffs. These towns, where some 10,000 polygamists are reported to have settled, have notoriously denied American citizens the equal protection of the laws, making it difficult or impossible for them to own or rent housing, receive protection from the police force, or enjoy their fair share of public services. As a recent blog entry reports,

> In what is certainly a novel approach, the Department of Justice has sued two polygamist towns for religious discrimination against non-members and expelled members of the Fundamentalist Church of Jesus Christ of Latter-day Saints (FLDS). This includes "denying non-FLDS individuals housing, police protection, and access to public space and services". The joint lawsuit is against neighboring Hildale, Utah and Colorado City, Arizona, which are controlled entirely by FLDS members.

---

[324] Jim Dougherty, "Eyes Wide Shut: from Governor Janet Napolitano down, Arizona Authorities Have Protected Polygamous Sexual Predators With Their Indifference," *Phoenix New Times*, August 7, 2003.
[325] Robin Ferruggia, *Huffington Post* comment, July 18, 2012.

According to Bob Morris, a former two-year resident in nearby Cedar City, Utah, law and order means nothing to these Mormon theocratic polygamists:

> I once mentioned to someone raised in Utah that I thought hiking near polyg ("polyg" is Utah slang for polygamist) areas could be dangerous. He smiled and said, "They'd never find the body." A garbage truck driver told me he drove to remote polygamist encampments once a week. The men drag the trash bins out to the public road and stand with rifles to ensure he doesn't enter their land.[326]

According to John Doherty of *Phoenix New Times*, "Colorado City polygamists have thrived in the remote enclave beneath Canaan Mountain about 240 miles by highway from Mohave County's administrative center in Kingman. Prominent polygamists live in huge homes… that house plural 'wives' and children." Colorado City is located in the so-called Arizona Strip, cut off from the rest of the state by the Grand Canyon.

The Colorado City Police Department is by all accounts controlled by polygamists. Most of the cops are reported to be polygamists, including Chief of Police Roundy. One of the main perpetrators whose case has come to light is Dan Barlow Jr., the son of Dan Barlow Sr., who was for many years Mayor and Fire Chief of Colorado City. After molesting five of his own daughters for 10 years, the younger Barlow was given a sweetheart plea bargain of one felony count of sexual abuse and was sentenced to 120 days in the county jail. The district attorney cited the wishes of the community – where many are polygamists themselves – for the lenient treatment. But the Mohave County Superior Court reduced the sentence to time served plus seven years probation. All in all, Barlow served 13 days in jail. Colorado City, Arizona, is a company town, and Mormon fundamentalism is the name of the company.

ORRIN HATCH, SENATOR FROM KOLOB:
"POLYGAMISTS … ARE VERY FINE PEOPLE"

In 2003, US Senator Orrin Hatch, while attending a town meeting in the town of St. George in southern Utah (once the home of the Romney family), was confronted by anti-polygamy activists who demanded that he condemn this practice. The activists came from the group called Help the Child Brides. Responding to demands that he do something about polygamy and child abuse in the twin polygamous towns of Hildale, Utah and Colorado City, Arizona, Hatch lamely responded: "I'm not here to justify polygamy. All I can say is, I know people in Hildale who are polygamists who are very fine people. You come and show me evidence of children being abused there and I'll get involved – bring the evidence to me." Hatch declined to "sit here and judge anybody just

---

[326] Bob Morris, "Justice Department Sues Polygamist Towns in Utah and Arizona." Politics in the Zeros, June 26, 2012 at http://polizeros.com/2012/06/26/ustice-department-sues-polygamist-towns-utah-arizona/

because they live differently than me. There will be laws on the books, but these are very complicated issues."[327]

POLYGAMY DATING WEBSITES

Internet links include one labeled "Polygamy Dating – find women to join your family!" One website asks, "Are You Seeking a Polygamist Relationship? Join Polygamy Dating Today and Explore the Polygamist Lifestyle. Search for Others, in Your Area, We Share the Same Ideals and Beliefs and Connect Instantly Right Now!" The site goes on to laud "Polygamy Dating, a Hidden Lifestyle with Ancient Roots." Here we read: "If the idea of polygamy strikes a chord in you, if you like to share your man with other women, or you are a man that can handle many women, then join our polygamy singles club and start meeting others that share the same lifestyle. We won't get into why polygamy is attractive to many people, but it is. Whether it satisfies an ancient need to be part of a group, or some other inexplicable need, you be the judge. There are, of course, polygamists from various traditions, Christian, Muslim, and some of them that are none of the above. We welcome polygamists of all faiths and backgrounds, recognizing that polygamy has long traditions in various parts of the world and is still widely practiced in many countries."

JANET NAPOLITANO SOFT ON POLYGAMY

The willingness to tolerate polygamy among Utah and Arizona elected officials especially is thoroughly bipartisan. As Attorney General and later as Governor of Arizona, Obama's Homeland Security Secretary Janet Napolitano distinguished herself for her craven failure to come to grips with polygamy. One press account of almost 10 years ago stated: "Arizona leaders – from Governor Janet Napolitano down – have also given the polygamists a virtual free pass by refusing to enforce the laws to protect children when local officials failed to do so. Instead, Arizona's political leaders have mostly ignored the abuses in the remote town [Colorado City] while emphasizing instead the clean-cut image promoted by Colorado City's leaders."[328] And further: "Among the charges made against Napolitano is the allegation that she was Attorney General, Napolitano opened a criminal investigation into allegations of sexual misconduct, welfare abuse, school fraud and weapons violations. But the timid probe has been conducted primarily from Phoenix, with very little on the ground work in Colorado City, and has resulted in no arrests.... In an interview with *New Times* recently, Napolitano expressed frustration with the Colorado City situation, but continued to offer no solution. So far, she has ruled out another state raid to stop the wholesale sexual abuse of young girls – which, sources say, she fears might result in a violent confrontation. She told *New Times* she fears for the safety of any state workers sent to investigate the Mormon fundamentalists' apparent misuse of public money for schools and welfare."

---

[327] *Casper Star Tribune*, April 18, 2003.

[328] Jim Dougherty, "Eyes Wide Shut: from Governor Janet Napolitano down, Arizona Authorities Have Protected Polygamous Sexual Predators With Their Indifference," *Phoenix New Times*, August 7, 2003.

GOVERNORS BABBIT AND SYMINGTON REASSURE THE POLYGAMISTS

Napolitano's "record on this issue has been abysmal," wrote *New Times*. Her main excuse was that she was unable to find witnesses willing to testify. And Napolitano is not alone. During recent decades, two Arizona governors, the Democrat Bruce Babbitt [later Clinton's Secretary of the Interior] and Republican J. Fife Symington III publicly declared a policy of hands off polygamy. They "publicly assured fundamentalist Mormon leaders that the state would not interfere with their unique religious lifestyle." Colorado City has traditionally practiced the bloc voting under strict orders from polygamist bosses which was pioneered by Joseph Smith in Missouri and Illinois, and later perfected by Brigham Young in the Utah Territory.

One firm prediction which can be made concerning the policies of a Romney administration is that polygamy would experience an unprecedented resurgence in the United States and beyond. We have already seen that Mitt Romney thinks that the suppression of polygamy amounts to religious persecution, while probable White House Chief of Staff Mike Leavitt thinks that polygamy is covered by religious freedom. Mike Lee and Orrin Hatch, the two senators from Kolob, are on the same line, as is the Utah state government. The Ron Paul libertarians are also determined to deregulate marriage and replace it with the law of the jungle. With so many top officials determined to tolerate polygamy, it is bound to experience exponential expansion. With this, the Republican Party will have come full circle, from opposition to polygamy as a relic of barbarism in 1856 to a vehicle for the covert promotion of this monstrous practice.

In the words of anti-polygamy activist Penny Peterson, in Arizona, "to get away with the rape of young girls, all you have to say is you're a polyg."

CHAPTER VII

BISHOP ROMNEY'S ATTEMPT TO SEIZE THE WHITE HOUSE

"A member of the white boys' club" – Joseph Kennedy, 1994

Mitt Romney served as governor of Massachusetts from 2003 to 2007. During these years, he was also preparing his bid for the Republican presidential nomination, and then for the White House. During the 2008 Republican primaries, Romney was given a bitter lesson about what a weak candidate he was. Over the entire primary season in that year, Romney was able to get only a little bit more than 22% of the Republican votes – slightly less than half the votes garnered by his victorious rival, Senator John McCain. Despite Romney's ability to obtain generous campaign contributions from his plutocratic Wall Street friends and Bain Capital partners, he was only able to do slightly better than the populist preacher Mike Huckabee, who was notoriously under-funded. Huckabee claimed to be the candidate of the Sam's Club Republicans, and not of the country club set. Romney obviously represented the latter. But Romney also had the backing of Limbaugh, Hannity, the Mormon Glenn Beck, and a number of other reactionary radio voices.

In 2007, Romney kicked off his effort by raising $23 million, in the first quarter, more than any Republican, and almost as much as Hillary Clinton and Barack Obama. The co-chair for finance of the Romney campaign was plutocrat Meg Whitman, the boss of eBay, who had worked together with Romney at Bain Capital. During early 2007, Romney got more money from Wall Street than any other candidate in either party. By the end of 2007, Romney had raised almost $63 million for his campaign.

In the first Republican poll of 2008, Romney seemed to be in the lead, but he was surpassed by Huckabee in the Iowa caucuses, where Romney had organized using the vapid slogan "Ask Mitt Anything," and had won the Ames straw poll. Such strength as Romney was able to demonstrate mainly depended on the notorious block voting behavior of the Mormons. Romney was able to win a Wyoming caucus thanks to his LDS backing, but this was widely ignored. After losing in New Hampshire, Romney secured an absolute majority of 51% in the caucuses in Nevada, another LDS stronghold. In addition to his strength in the Mormon-dominated Great Basin, Romney would also call Michigan and Massachusetts his home states – the first because his father had been governor there, and the second because of his own governorship. Romney won the 2008 Michigan primary by 9%. But, the Bishop posted a weak fourth-place finish in the South Carolina primary, and was beaten by McCain in Florida 36% to 31%.

On February 2, 2008, Romney prevailed in the Maine caucus with 52% of the vote. And Super Tuesday, February 5, Romney was the winner in Alaska, Colorado, Massachusetts, Minnesota, Montana, North Dakota, and Utah. But McCain won Arizona, California, Connecticut, Delaware, Illinois, Missouri, New Jersey, New York, and Oklahoma – all in all a more important group of states. Romney failed to gain traction and was forced to drop out of contention on February 7, 2008, having outlasted Fred Thompson, Duncan

Hunter, and Rudy Giuliani. In quitting, Romney made a strange and sanctimonious speech saying that he wanted to "stand aside, for our party and our country… in this time of war, I simply cannot let my campaign be a part of aiding a surrender to terror." Exactly why Romney chose or was forced to drop out at this point remains something of a puzzle.

2008 GOP PRIMARY HOPEFULS ALL HATED ROMNEY

Political observers noted how Mitt Romney was personally hated by his Republican rivals. Huckabee accused Romney of practicing underhanded techniques of voter suppression, and called Romney "presumptuous and arrogant." During one debate, Huckabee conceded that Mormonism might be a religion rather than a cult, but then asked: "Don't Mormons believe that Jesus and the devil are brothers?" (The answer is that they do.) But already in January 2008, Ron Paul came to Romney's defense, saying: "One thing I'm a little bit afraid of is that they might be doing that for religious reasons, and I don't like that."

But for McCain, Giuliani, Fred Thompson, and their staffs, Romney was an object of scorn. "Within the small circle of contenders, Mr. Romney has become the most disliked… the almost visceral scorn directed at Mr. Romney by his rivals has been overshadowed….," wrote the *New York Times*, quoting Huckabee's campaign manager Ed Rollins' remark: "What I have to do is make sure that my anger with a guy like Romney, whose teeth I want to knock out, doesn't get in the way of my thought process." Front runner John McCain and his handlers were described as "irked by what they perceive as misleading attacks and Mr. Romney's willingness to say anything to be elected. 'He doesn't play by the same rules the rest of us do,' said Charlie Black, a senior McCain strategist."[329] Having made a hard reactionary turn to pander to the GOP's crazed petty bourgeois base, Romney had become a sanctimonious hypocrite.

According to one GOP operative, "The degree to which the other campaigns' personal dislike for Mitt Romney has played a part in this campaign cannot be underestimated." Ann Marie Cox found that "while sharp words have been exchanged between practically every Republican candidate at one point or another on the campaign trail, the aversion to Romney seems to go beyond mere policy disagreements. It's also a suspicion of what they see as his hypocrisy and essential phoniness – what one former staffer for Fred Thompson called Romney's 'wholesale reinvention.'" According to one Huckabee adviser, "what Romney has done is attack people for positions they once held. That annoys people. And he uses his own money to do it, which rubs it in." Romney criticized McCain for views on campaign finance reform which he once endorsed himself, attacked Huckabee for tax increases which were indistinguishable from Romney's fee hikes, and faulted all his fellow Republicans for the very same softness on illegal immigration which he once shared. And, he paid the price by being targeted for many acrimonious tirades in the GOP debates.[330]

[329] Michael Luo, "Romney Leads in Ill Will Among GOP Candidates," *New York Times*, January 24, 2008.
[330] Anne-Marie Cox, "The 'I Hate Romney' Club," *Time*, February 3, 2008.

Romney's 2008 experience, in short, showed that he had grave problems as a candidate – problems that no amount of money might ever be able to heal. Nevertheless, Romney and his LDS backers wanted the presidency. What was to be done?

George H. W. Bush had once solved similar problems by arranging scandals to eliminate his most formidable opponents early on: Gary Hart had fallen victim to such machinations. But Romney chose another route. During the 2012 primaries, it was also evident that the militant reactionaries and proto-fascists of the "Tea Party" had shifted the GOP terrain in ways that might make Romney's victory even more difficult. This meant that an elaborate apparatus had to be constructed to shape the 2012 GOP outcome in ways favorable to Romney.

ROMNEY'S 40% CEILING IN THE 2012 GOP PRIMARIES AND CAUCUSES

In retrospect, we can see that the 2012 version of GOP presidential candidate Mitt Romney had a ceiling of about 40% across-the-board in the Republican caucuses and primaries. In Southern states where evangelical Protestant voters, especially Baptists, were dominant, Romney's ceiling went down to 30% or even less. Here was the essence of Romney's problem. If the best he could do was about 40%, that left 60% of the vote which might conceivably coalesce around a single rival – as it turned out, the clerical authoritarian Santorum. The post-Tea Party Republican Party had a country club wing of almost 40%, plus a Sam's Club and Born Again Christian faction which added up to almost 60%.

ROMNEY'S SOLUTION: WINGMAN OR STALKING HORSE CANDIDATES

The only way to prevent this was to make sure that the anti-Romney vote remained fragmented. It was not enough to hope for this; Romney had to guarantee that his opposition would remain divided.

Romney needed wingmen – stalking horses to protect each of his flanks. These stalking horse candidates had to be weak enough so that they would be structurally incapable of outgrowing their assigned roles and taking the nomination away from Mitt. At the same time, they had to be strong enough to lock up 10% or 15% of the vote, as needed, to make sure that this support would never go to a serious candidate actually capable of eliminating Mitt from the race. The Mormon combine also had to make sure that the wingmen had money and resources to do their assigned job.

ROMNEY'S LEFT WINGMAN: COUSIN JON HUNTSMAN, MORMON BILLIONAIRE

The Bishop needed one wingman on his moderate flank – the quarter from which he had been defeated by McCain in 2008. This was less likely in 2012, but Romney's inherent weakness dictated an excess of caution to ward off a McCain, a Donald Trump, a Giuliani, or a Bloomberg. If any candidate with this profile got into the race, they would have to compete for votes with Romney's left wingman. This turned out to be Romney's billionaire Mormon cousin Jon Huntsman, who played the part of the classic liberal Republican. Huntsman served as a foil for Romney, supporting cap and trade, endorsing anthropogenic global warming, and embracing a series of other issues which made Romney look more reactionary, and therefore more electable for Republicans, by comparison.

Nobody should have been fooled by this, since Huntsman was none other than Romney's cousin, and, in addition, a leading Mormon. Both Mitt Romney and Jon Huntsman are descendents of Parley P. Pratt, a Mormon polygamist whose celestial attentions for an Arkansas woman he wanted as his twelfth wife led to his own death and set up a quarrel which contributed to the infamous 1857 Mountain Meadows Massacre, in which 140 peaceful Arkansas travelers going to California were massacred by Brigham Young and his secessionist Danite militia.

During the campaign, Huntsman told George Stephanopoulos of ABC News: "I believe in God. I'm a good Christian. I'm very proud of my Mormon heritage. I am a Mormon." Jon Huntsman is the son of Jon Huntsman Sr., a billionaire businessman and the boss of Huntsman Corporation, a global chemical company with 12,000 employees and revenues in excess of $9 billion. He served as Deputy US trade Representative in the George W. Bush administration, and then as governor of Utah between 2004 and 2009. After that, he was made US ambassador to China by Obama.

As it turned out, Huntsman played a relatively minor role during the primaries. He came in third in the New Hampshire primary with 17% of the vote, trailing Mitt's 39% and Ron Paul's 23%. But some of Huntsman's New Hampshire votes might have gone to Newt Gingrich, who in the event got only 9%. And it may well be that Huntsman's presence deterred other moderate candidates from entering the field and thus posing a potential threat to Romney. Huntsman inherited the liberal Republican media constituency which had previously belonged to McCain, and the fact that this support was no longer up for grabs may have scared off a candidate coming from the Trump-Giuliani-Bloomberg area of the GOP.

ROMNEY'S RIGHT WINGMAN: RON PAUL, NEO-CONFEDERATE FREEMASON

Mitt Romney, as we have seen in detail, represents the reactionary and racist Mormon political establishment, a social formation which has always been subversive against the United States. Ron Paul, by contrast, must be considered a creature of the Southern Jurisdiction of the Scottish Right of Freemasonry. Paul's father was a Freemason. Paul's wife is a member of the Eastern Star, the ladies' auxiliary of the Freemasons. Paul's daughters were members of the Rainbow Girls, the girls' Masonic organization. Ron Paul's son Rand was a member of the freemasonic NoZe Brotherhood at Baylor University, where he harassed a young woman in the notorious "Aqua Buddha" incident.

We recall that, in 1861, President Abraham Lincoln was confronted by several secessionist forces. One was the slaveocrat Confederate States of America, dominated by the Southern Jurisdiction of the Scottish Rite Freemasons. These later variously morphed into the Ku Klux Klan, the Redeemers, and the Dixiecrats. This is the racist and reactionary tradition of Nathan Bedford Forrest, Albert Pike, Strom Thurmond, Jesse Helms, and Trent Lott. Ron Paul has privately denied that he is a Freemason, but he is associated with a fraternity which is traditionally considered an inner elite above and behind the Freemasons. In this context, Ron Paul appears as a modern doughface in the tradition of Caleb Cushing and James Buchanan, northern men with slaveocrat principles.

The other secessionist threat was Brigham Young and his Mormon Saints. If the Confederate *soldatesca* had succeeded in their 1862 or 1863 invasions of Maryland and Pennsylvania, and especially if the British and French had intervened on the side of the Confederacy, Brigham Young would have joined the Confederates in secession, opening up a second front which would have caused potentially fatal difficulties for the Union. The United States might have been broken up into a multitude of petty, squabbling, impotent, racist, oppressive entities.

RON PAUL'S DEREGULATION OF MARRIAGE MADE TO ORDER FOR MORMON POLYGAMISTS

The convergence of Mormon Saints and Dixiecrats has deep roots. Mormon theology holds black people in contempt, and this view is shared in practice by the neo-Confederate Freemasons of the Ron Paul type, as seen in many articles of his racist newsletters. Worthy of note are also Ron Paul's sallies in favor of the total deregulation of marriage. Paul wants each state to decide what constitutes a marriage, and he recommends that the states ought to accept whatever any church or religious organization chooses to call a marriage. This solution he calls "liberty across the board."[331] Such an approach would clearly take us back to Brigham Young's Deseret, thus opening the doors of Hell. It would allow the legalization of polygamy, polyandry, and instant divorce, rolling back centuries of legal progress in affording protections to women and children.

And who, pray tell, might be interested in Ron Paul's bid for allowing states to define marriage according to their own criteria? Perhaps the polygamists of Utah, Arizona, Nevada, Idaho, Colorado, and other areas might be interested in taking up Paul's offer. As we can see, the alliance of Romney and Paul was directed against the elementary prerequisites of human civilization as we have known it.

The deal between Mitt Romney and Ron Paul was denounced by the present writer on Twitter and on World Crisis Radio during the first week of January 2012. It was finally reported in a minimalist version by the *New York Times* on February 16, 2012, in an article by Richard A. Oppel Jr. entitled "Amid Rivalry, Friendship Blossoms on the Campaign Trail." Here we read that "in a Republican presidential contest known for its angry rivalries, the Romney-Paul relationship stands out for its behind the scenes stability. It is a friendship that, by Mr. Paul's telling, Mr. Romney has worked to cultivate. The question is whether it is also one that could pay dividends for Mr. Romney as he faces yet more setbacks in his struggle to capture the 1,144 delegates needed to win the nomination."

---

[331] Ironically, Ron Paul's approach might also be the only way sharia law could come to the United States – the outcome GOP activists say they fear most.

Fraternization between the Mitt Romney and Ron Paul campaigns goes back to the 2007-2008 cycle, and kept going into the 2012 contest. As the same *New York Times* piece reported, "When Mr. Paul's campaign jet broke down last year in Wolfeboro, New Hampshire, Mr. Romney's wife offered to let Mr. Paul, and one of his granddaughters stay the night at their summer home on Lake Winnipesaukee. When Mr. Romney arrived later, he offered his jet to take them home to Texas. Mr. Paul, not wanting to impose, was grateful but declined both offers." Santorum complained that Ron Paul and Romney were colluding against him, noting that "their commercials look a lot alike, and so do their attacks."

The deal between Romney and Ron Paul was also backed up by some very significant financial power. During this year's meeting of the Bilderberg group in Chantilly, Virginia at the end of May, it became evident that the Bilderberg financier elite of the NATO countries preferred a Romney presidency. Because of Romney's weaknesses as a candidate, helping Romney to win necessarily involved support for Ron Paul. Because Ron Paul's fascist austerity was just what the Bilderberg group wanted to propagate in any case, they found it relatively easy to support Romney's right wing man.

ANARCHO-CAPITALIST PETER THIEL OF BILDERBERG STEERING COMMITTEE, RON PAUL'S FINANCIAL ANGEL

A leading member of the Bilderberg group's steering committee is now Peter Thiel, a right wing anarchist or anarcho-capitalist. Thiel made money initially on PayPal, and then became one of the early investors in Google. He may therefore be implicated in the debacle of the Google initial public offering, but that is another story. Thiel's great project in life is to build offshore floating colonies outside the territorial waters of any country, where, in a juridical vacuum, all kinds of practices can be promoted which are illegal in the United States and other countries. On these offshore anarchist islands, there would be no laws against narcotics, no minimum wage, no child labor laws, and none of the norms of modern civilization. Thiel wants to build such a colony off the coast of California, so he can compete with Silicon Valley, but outside the reach of the California and US labor laws. Needless to say, there would be no Medicare, no Medicaid, no Social Security, no unemployment insurance, and so forth. In promoting this project, Thiel has worked together with the former Google engineer Patri Friedman, the grandson of crackpot Chicago school economist Milton Friedman, who specialized in dumbing down the Hayek-Mises Austrian economics for US business school consumption. Thiel's name has also been linked romantically to that of Patri Friedman, but the two have lately had a falling out.

Thiel, according to Federal Election Commission reports, has contributed $2.6 million to Endorse Liberty, the principal Super PAC supporting Ron Paul's presidential candidacy. It is clear that Thiel fully supports Ron Paul's role in spewing the ideological poison of Austrian libertarianism and in making genocidal austerity presentable in polite society. He is also backing Ron Paul because this is the way to procure the nomination for Romney. Some protesters at this year's Bilderberg meeting seemed to think that the elitists and plutocrats assembled there held some kind of grudge against Ron Paul. Quite the contrary: the Bilderberg elite has provided millions of dollars to support the Ron Paul wingman presidential campaign, and Thiel is a leading example. The Bilderbergers generally support Romney, who made a semi-secret visit to their gathering.

Peter Thiel represents the kind of predatory young wolves who are now emerging as the dominant force inside the Bilderberg group. Leading Bilderberg figures like David Rockefeller, Zbigniew Brzezinski, and Henry Kissinger belong to a generation which is gradually leaving the historical stage. Thiel and his ilk are bidding to replace them, and Ron Paul is a part of their strategy for duping the younger generation.

PRO-RON PAUL SUPER PAC LOCATED IN THE MORMON MECCA

Endorse Liberty was created in December, 2011. Some details about Endorse Liberty indicate the way in which the Romney-Ron Paul alliance actually works. Endorse Liberty happens to be headquartered in the Mormon Mecca of Salt Lake City, and not in Lake Jackson, Texas or some other location closer to Ron Paul's political-administrative center of gravity. Endorse Liberty is run by political operatives Jeffrey Hartman, Stephen Oskoui, and Abe Niederhauser. Hartman, of Provo, Utah, supported Romney in 2008 but then switched to Paul. The fourth key figure at Endorse Liberty is Ladd Christensen, a longtime business associate of Jon Huntsman, Sr. Christensen helped the elder Huntsman, a top Mormon, to create the Huntsman chemical concern back in the 1970s. The elder Huntsman thus emerges as the Mormon link between Romney's right wing man, Ron Paul, and his left wing man, Jon Huntsman, Jr.[332]

Five relatives of Mitt Romney, or at least five persons whose name is Romney, endorsed Ron Paul in early 2012. These included attorney Ty Romney of Great Falls, Montana; Travis Romney of Spokane, Washington; Chad Romney of Boise, Idaho; Jarrod Romney of Salt Lake City; and Troy Romney, also of Salt Lake City.[333]

RON PAUL RUNS INTERFERENCE FOR ROMNEY IN GOP DEBATES

No fewer than twenty debates among the Republican presidential candidates stretched across most of the year 2011. The one constant of all of these debates was that Ron Paul consistently ran interference for Romney. The basis of Ron Paul's technique was to start from an evaluation of who the most dangerous adversary for Romney was in a given situation. A study by Think Progress showed that Ron Paul had attacked Bachman once, Cain four times, Rick Perry four times, Gingrich eight times, and Santorum 22 times. But Ron Paul had never but never assailed Romney. Not reflected in the study was the critical timing of Paul's attacks, which generally came at moments when Romney was already under fire, and his bitter rivals were trying to gang up on the Bishop to administer

---

[332] Matt Canham, "Utah-based Super PAC supports Paul-not Romney," *Salt Lake Tribune,* February 21, 2012.
[333] "Five Members of Romney Family Endorsed Ron Paul for President; Free to Speak at Idaho Caucus Sites," RonPaul.com, March 5, 2012.

a knock-out blow. Because of the animus against Romney, there was often a grave risk that the entire Republican pack would join in tearing down the assumed front-runner.[334]

For example, in the October 18, 2011 GOP presidential debate, Rick Perry began criticizing Romney for his Massachusetts individual mandate health plan, which he referred to as "Romneycare." Ron Paul immediately went into action, counterattacking the Texas governor: "First off, you know, the governor of Texas criticized the governor of Massachusetts for 'Romney care,' but he wrote a really fancy letter supporting 'Hillary care.' So we probably ought to ask him about that."

When the actual voting began, Romney's more urgent need was for a wingman on his right flank. Here, Romney had to make sure that reactionary candidates like Gingrich, Santorum, Bachmann, and Cain could never get more than 40% of the votes and become competitive with Romney. The ideal choice was still Ron Paul. The hope was that Ron Paul could attract between 10% and 15% of Republican voters, thus making sure that these votes would be taken off the table and put into a deep freeze where they could never benefit a candidate with a serious chance of winning. Ron Paul would lock up this 10% to 15% and essentially take it off the table.

Ron Paul proved able to fulfill this function. In the primaries and caucuses of the early states, Romney racked up slightly less than 41% of the votes. Ron Paul provided decisive help by attracting a little over 11% of Republicans. This configuration allowed Romney to win all but four of the contests between the Iowa caucus on January 3 and Washington State on March 3. Romney was significantly helped in the Iowa caucuses by hundreds of thousands of dollars of ads attacking Gingrich that were paid for by Ron Paul.

RON PAUL DEFENDS ROMNEY FROM NEWT AND PERRY ON BAIN LOOTING

In the South Carolina primary campaign, a firestorm of criticism engulfed Romney because of the predatory activities of Bain Capital in looting manufacturing companies and then shutting them down, destroying jobs, lives, and communities in the process. Newt Gingrich touted a movie about the Bishop called *When Mitt Romney Came to Town*, featuring the testimony of working people victimized by Romney and his asset-stripping cohorts from Bain. Rick Perry denounced Romney as a "vulture capitalist."

Gingrich pointedly asked on Fox News: "Is it fair to have a system, is it right, is it the kind of country you want to live in, to have a system where somebody comes in to take over your company, take out all the cash and leave behind a wreck, and they go off to a country club having a great time and you go off to the unemployment line?"

Ron Paul immediately sprang to Mitt's defense, using his odious Austrian school ideology to justify Romney's unscrupulous methods. "I think it's a big distraction," said Paul. "And they are picking up on this and those who are condemning him for it, I think,

---

[334] Judd Legum, "Study: Ron Paul Never Attacked Romney Once during 20 Debates, but Attacked Romney's Rivals 39 Times," *ThinkProgress*, February 27, 2012.

are arguing like Democrats… the principle of restructuring is a good thing in the marketplace," he continued. Notice Paul's structural inability to come to grips with the reality of looting and layoffs, which are destroying the US economy.

Focusing on Gingrich, who had sold influence to Freddie Mac for $1.6 million under the guise of historical consulting, Paul ranted: "For conservatives to come forward and say restructuring is bad, I think there is a big difference if you are restructuring in the free market and you are doing a positive thing versus somebody who may have taken money from Freddie Mac."[335]

RON PAUL SAVES ROMNEY FROM MICHIGAN AND OHIO DEFEATS

Another important contest was the February 28 Michigan primary. It was widely felt that Michigan was one of Romney's home states, and that he therefore had to win there. In the event, Romney outdistanced Santorum by 41% to 38%, a relatively narrow victory. The decisive margin for Romney was evidently provided by Ron Paul, who got 12% of the Michigan vote. If Ron Paul had not been in the picture, Santorum might well have received enough of those ultra-reactionary votes to win. Ron Paul had declined to campaign personally in Michigan, but did commit significant resources to running anti-Santorum television ads. This behavior documents how he was functioning as Romney's wingman, rather than as a serious candidate in his own right. Amazingly, Ron Paul's fanatical supporters were generally unable to understand this swindle.

Newt Gingrich had won South Carolina by 12 points over Romney, largely on the strength of his aggressive performance in the debates. Romney was anxious that this not be repeated in nearby southern states where Gingrich's name recognition was still quite high. Newt's home state of Georgia was scheduled to have a Republican candidates' debate during the run up to Super Tuesday, and the Romney campaign did everything possible to get this debate canceled. But the Romney camp also feared the perception that they were afraid to stand up to Gingrich in a debate. In so doing, they were assisted by Ron Paul, who took the same line and provided them with precious cover. The Georgia debate was canceled.

Ron Paul had an opportunity to mobilize his reactionary base through a triumphal appearance at the Conservative Political Action Conference of the American Conservative Union (CPAC), held in Washington on February 11, 2012. Ron Paul had won the CPAC presidential straw poll in 2010 and 2011. But in the midst of the 2012 primaries, he declined the invitation to appear, saying that he was too busy campaigning. This was a subterfuge so obvious that even the densest among his stupefied libertarian stoners became uneasy. As for the CPAC 2012 Straw poll, even with Ron Paul sabotaging his own support down to 12%, Romney came in with an anemic 38%, Compared to 31% for Santorum. If Paul had appeared, Romney might have come in third.

---

[335] Jonathan Easley, "Ron Paul Defends Romney, Bain Capital from GOP Attacks," *The Hill*, January 10, 2012.

On Super Tuesday, Romney scored about two points below his expected 40% ceiling, but thanks in large part to an 11% showing by Ron Paul, Romney was able to win six states while losing four. Here the big event was Ohio, where Romney narrowly defeated Santorum by 38% to 37%. Once again, Ron Paul's vote total of 9% was one key reason why Santorum was unable to win, since many of his votes came from ultra-reactionaries who would have gone to Santorum over Romney.

RON PAUL WRECKS HIS OWN VIRGINIA CAMPAIGN TO HELP ROMNEY

The Virginia primary was an interesting case to illustrate Ron Paul's role as Romney's wingman. Here Gingrich and Santorum had been thrown off the ballot for technical infractions, and this decision had been upheld in the courts. Virginia was therefore a rare case of Romney against Paul one-on-one, with no other important candidates on the ballot. Because of the danger that Paul might inflict a humiliating defeat on Romney, with serious consequences for the Republican nomination, the Paul campaign proceeded to sabotage their own support in every conceivable way. It was political hari-kari, for the benefit of Romney, and ultimately for the benefit of little Rand Paul.

Veterans for Ron Paul had organized a rally and march on the White House in the District of Columbia on February 20, but this event was pointedly snubbed by the Ron Paul campaign, which refused to send any speakers or representatives, or to offer encouragement or support in any form. The disaffection of Adam Kokesh and other veterans who had been supporting Paul escalated in the wake of this betrayal.

The local commentator "DC Dave" Martin notes that "Virginia represented a perfect storm for Paul. And what did he do? He did as close to nothing as he could possibly do and still call himself a candidate. In fact, what little campaign he mounted seemed to be directed entirely towards testing the loyalty of his band of long-suffering followers. These followers – and these followers alone – were given what can only be described as a meager, pitiful show of a campaign while the general public, all those people out there thirsting for someone they can believe in and waiting to be wooed, weren't even given that."

According to DC Dave, there was no visible Ron Paul campaign in Virginia for weeks on end, and there was no television or radio advertising. Paul did make one campaign appearance about a week before the primary, but this was not publicized in the press. Ron Paul's single event in Virginia was held in a ballroom near the infamous Springfield Mixing Bowl, site of the worst rush-hour traffic in the entire region. Despite this, people were told to arrive between 6 and 6:30 p.m., the height of the rush hour. The seating capacity was too small, and parking was impossible to find.

As DC Dave argues, "a real campaign with a genuine candidate for president, would have rented a larger facility such as the easily reached 10,000 seat Patriot Center at George Mason University in Fairfax, and the rally would have been announced far and wide. In fact, had Paul been serious about winning Virginia, with any sort of publicity at all he could have easily filled basketball arenas in all of Virginia's population centers in a series of rallies. We may contrast that with Mitt Romney, who might be able to fill a good-sized restaurant, but only if he buys all the drinks."[336]

Romney became slightly weaker in the mid-March primaries and caucuses, with an average of 35% support during this phase. Despite lack of funds, Santorum was able to match Romney's results with a 35% showing of his own. One reason was that Ron Paul's support had shrunk to only 3%. But Romney still took seven out of 10 contests, largely because his opponents Gingrich and Santorum were low on cash.

In the April primaries, Santorum collapsed to 25% and Gingrich to 9%, while Mitt Romney pulled away with 53%, winning all the contests. But again, Ron Paul's 12% helped make this possible in Wisconsin, where Romney defeated Santorum by 43% to 38%. Gingrich dropped out on March 27, and Santorum quit on April 10. Even so, Santorum remained competitive in some states, such as Nebraska. In Oregon, a candidates' debate on Pacific Northwest regional issues had been scheduled in advance of the primary there on May 15, but Romney wanted that canceled, as usual. Once again, Paul obliged in working to sabotage this debate, which was called off.

RON PAUL'S GOAL: WIN ENOUGH DELEGATES TO BUY LITTLE RAND PAUL A PLACE ON THE GOP TICKET

Ron Paul was thus perfectly suited to become Romney's wing man or stalking horse to guard his constantly threatened right flank. By 2012, Ron Paul was a perennial presidential candidate looking for a last hurrah, and especially concerned about the nepotistic political patronage needs of his own extended family. Paul was especially concerned to provide for the future of his mediocre, racist son, Senator Rand Paul of Kentucky. Paul's fondest wish was to win enough convention delegates to make his support for Romney indispensable in getting the Bishop the 1,144 votes needed to go over the top at the Tampa convention in August. In that scenario, the vice presidential slot for Little Rand would be the *quid pro quo* exacted to get the Paulbearer delegates to vote for Mitt.

Ron Paul was frequently called an incorruptible candidate, but this applied as little to him as it did to Maximilian Robespierre, the author of the Reign of Terror in the French Revolution. Ron Paul was in reality one of the most corrupt and duplicitous of all the candidates.

According to Citizens for Responsibility and Ethics in Washington, Ron Paul was among the champion nepotists in Washington. During the 2008 and 2010 election cycles, Congressman Ron Paul dished out salaries and/or fees to six of his own relatives, the most of any member of Congress in either party. These relatives received a total of $304,599. Family members also received reimbursements of $47,421. The relatives involved included Paul's daughter Lori Pyeatt, his grandson, his daughter's mother-in-law Nora Leblanc, his granddaughter Laura Paul, his granddaughter Valori Benton, his

---

[336] Dave Martin, "Ron Paul's CPAC and Virginia Cop- outs: The Last Straw, March 14, 2012, DC Dave.com.

grandson-in-law Jesse Benton, and one other relative. In addition, his campaign committee reimbursed the congressman, his wife Carol Paul, his son Rand, his son Robert, and several other relatives, and furthermore sent money to his brother's accounting firm. Ron Paul's leadership PAC, called Liberty PAC, dispersed money to the congressman and his brother's accounting firm, and also paid Paul's daughter a salary. The brother in question is Wayne A. Paul, the owner of Paul, Phipps and Company accounting firm.[337]

But that was back in 2008-2010. By early 2012, it was widely reported that Ron Paul had a grand total of 61 relatives on his congressional office, PAC, presidential campaign, and other payrolls. And this count was limited to nepotism centering on Congressman Ron Paul. In 2011, Little Rand Paul, taking advantage of his father's national fundraising base, had entered the Senate representing Kentucky, and was doubtless building up a nepotistic empire of his own, even as his father strove to get him on the national ticket.

One egregious case was that of campaign manager Jessie Benton, resented by the libertarian True Believers as an incompetent mediocrity. Jessie Benton was married to Ron Paul's granddaughter, and by May 2012 had received over $322,000 from Liberty PAC, plus $264,000 from the Ron Paul presidential campaign, for a grand total of $586,616.[338]

RON PAUL: ANARCHO-CAPITALIST CRACKPOT

Ron Paul's personal ideology was a jumble of von Hayek, von Mises, and the Austrian or psychological school of economics, which had been created in its modern form mainly by the London School of Economics and by David Rockefeller to oppose the American School (Hamilton-Carey) and the German School (Friedrich List) of economics. Ron Paul was also an admirer of the Russian neofascist novelist Ayn Rand (after whom Little Rand was named), and of the anarcho-capitalist crank Murray Rothbard.

When Senator Rand Paul endorsed Mitt Romney for president at the beginning of June 2012, just after Romney had made a secret visit to the Bilderberg group meeting in Chantilly, Virginia, many Paulbearers were deeply disappointed. But the lesson of this was not just that Ron Paul and Rand Paul were scoundrels, nepotists, and deceivers. Austrianism and libertarianism represent a synthetic ideology, based on the economics of David Ricardo with a strong infusion of the radical subjectivism of Ernst Mach, fostered over the years by Lionel Robbins and his colleagues at the London School of Economics, financed by David Rockefeller, and systematically promoted by the Mount Pelerin Society, one of the most sinister ideological organizations of the past hundred years. For most people, to choose libertarianism is indeed to choose self-destruction.

---

[337] Citizens for Responsibility and Ethics in Washington (CREW), *Family Affair* (Washington, 2012).

[338] *Economic Policy Journal*, May 2012; OpenSecrets.org.

Some candidates run for president because they want to win and have a real chance to win. Other candidates run because they delude themselves they can win, even though this is exceedingly unlikely. Then there are candidates who are aware that they probably cannot win, but who are focused on spreading ideological poisons throughout the body politic. Independent candidate John Anderson represented this third class of ideological spewers in 1980. This is the other role Ron Paul plays today.

"RESTORE AMERICA": RON PAUL'S PLAN FOR GENOCIDAL AUSTERITY

In October 2011, Ron Paul's campaign website published Restore America, his program to cut $1 trillion from the US federal budget in one year, on the way – Paul claimed – to balancing the budget within a single presidential term. Paul's trillion dollars in cuts were ten times more concentrated than what was being attempted by the Super Committee or Twelve Tyrants enacted as part of the Satan Sandwich enacted to settle the debt ceiling confrontation of August, 2011. This would represent about 27% of the US federal budget. According to my estimates, this meant that Ron Paul's austerity plan was at least twice as severe as the devastating cuts implemented by the German "Hunger Chancellor" Heinrich Brüning between 1930 in 1932, which had destroyed the German political and economic institutions, opening the door wide to Hitler. Ron Paul would thus represent the most radical austerity that any modern industrial or postindustrial society had ever experienced.

Ron Paul had often told his supporters that he wanted to cut military spending on foreign wars and foreign bases in order to "take care of our people here at home." The Restore America Plan allowed citizens to see exactly how he intended to take care of them. Although the entire federal budget was to be cut 27% in the first year, the Pentagon budget would be cut by only 15%. Ironically, this was the cut that was already baked in the cake, without any input from Ron Paul. Obama was embracing a Pentagon cut of about 8%. And, because of the failure of the Super Committee or Twelve Tyrants to agree on a plan of their own, another cut of seven or 8% was already in the works. That meant that Ron Paul was not adding any military spending cuts of his own on top of what was already in the works.

Instead, the duplicitous libertarian Leprechaun took dead aim at the old, the sick, children, women, the disadvantaged and defenseless, seeking to largely wipe out the frayed US social safety net. On the chopping block would be the Women Infants Children Program (WIC), designed to provide high protein meals to pregnant women, nursing mothers, and infants. This program has been highly effective in reducing cognitive impairment because of insufficient protein consumption during gestation and the first months of life. Ron Paul demanded that WIC be cut by 33%, more than twice what he wanted to cut out of the Pentagon.

The State Children's Health Insurance Program (S-CHIP) represents the largest expansion of health coverage for children since the enactment of Medicaid in the mid-1960s. Ron Paul wanted to cut S-CHIP by 44%. Ron Paul also demanded 35% cuts in Medicaid, which provides medical care for poor people but also protects the middle class by paying for nursing home care.

Most brutal of all was Ron Paul's plan for Food Stamps or SNAP – the Supplemental Nutrition Assistance Program of the US Department of Agriculture, a New Deal program started around 1940 under Franklin D. Roosevelt. Food Stamps now serve almost 50 million Americans. These 50 million people are the most at risk in our society. According to recent studies, many of them are in dire poverty. They cannot get welfare payments, because what previously existed as welfare – Aid to Mothers with Dependent Children under the Social Security Act of 1935 – had already been destroyed by Bill Clinton as part of his 1996 reelection campaign. As many noted at the time, that was the worst thing that Clinton ever did. Real unemployment in the United States today amounts to about 30 million, and if we add in dependents, we get back to that same 50 million ball park. They have no jobs, and most of them have exhausted the 99 weeks or usually far less of unemployment benefits granted them under existing law. This is also the part of the US population that has no medical care.

PELLAGRA PAUL SPARES PENTAGON, ATTACKS 50 MILLION US DESTITUTE

So what does Ron Paul want to do about these 50 million Americans, people who are in every way on the brink of the abyss? He wants to stab them in the back by cutting Food Stamps by 63%. According to chef Mario Battali, who lived on food stamps for a few weeks recently, this program gives the average recipient in the New York City area about $150 per month to buy food. This comes down to about $1.50 per person per meal. It is already next to impossible to achieve good nutrition for so little money, as Battali has pointed out. Ron Paul would bring us down to between 50¢ and 60¢ per person per meal. That kind of a diet is a one-way ticket to rickets, pellagra, and scurvy. The congressman has already been jeered as Pellagra Paul on the Internet.

Most importantly, the proposal to cut 63% out of the food stamp allowance of 50 million at risk Americans will kill people. How many hundreds of thousands, how many millions of Americans must lose their lives for the greater glory of the crackpot Austrian school? Here we see the real function of the Ron Paul campaign. In the 1940s or 1950s, proposals like the one advanced by Paul might have gotten their bearer a one-way ticket to a mental hospital. But, if they were taken seriously, the response could well have been, "Nazi go home!" But now, thanks to Paul and others, proposals for genocide against the American people were presentable, respectable and acceptable – at least in the Republican Party – as the basis for polite discussion. Ron Paul had earned his pay. He had consolidated a massive moral and intellectual degradation of the American people, to the point where a Republican audience would seriously entertain demands for mass death of fellow Americans.

Nor was this all. Ron Paul wanted to wipe out the Davis-Bacon Act, which guarantees union wages on federal construction projects. Both Ron Paul and Rand Paul, who claimed to be partisans of states rights, wanted to force all states to become right-to-work states. They were eager to trample on states' rights if they could bust unions in the process. Under Ron Paul, the Bush tax cuts would remain. There would be no capital gains tax and no estate tax on plutocrats. The corporate income tax would be cut to 15%.

There would be no tax on foreign profits. All of these measures would benefit plutocrats, but there was no specific tax relief whatsoever for the average American wage earner.

Ron Paul wanted to eliminate the Department of Energy. Critical scientific research would cease to exist. There would be no more Department of Housing and Urban Development. There would be not even the pretense of low-cost public housing. The Department of Commerce, the Weather Service, and efforts to promote exports would go to zero, as would the Department of the Interior – the national parks. The Department of Education would cease to exist, and with it would disappear the Pell grants and Stafford loans, the only way most poor kids can hope to go to college. Total federal employment would be cut by 10%, meaning half a million new jobless. Maryland, Virginia, and the District of Columbia would become depressed areas, and many others would join them.

RON PAUL WOULD END US EMERGENCY FOOD AID, LEAVING MILLIONS ABROAD TO STARVE

In addition to inflicting genocide against the American people, Ron Paul also wants to impose genocide abroad. He would do this by wiping out all US foreign aid, to the tune of between $50 and $60 billion. Much US foreign aid is used for meddling in other countries, but this is not the whole story. The United States still provides about 57% of all the emergency food aid in the world. Every year, the United States Food for Peace program distributes 2.5 million metric tons of food aid worth about $2.6 billion to about 44 countries. In places like Somalia, South Sudan, Kenya, Bangladesh, in Haiti and Pakistan after recent natural disasters, this food aid unquestionably saved lives. Under Ron Paul, it would end, and all these people would die.

Ron Paul's austerity program has been presented here in some detail, precisely because this document is of more than retrospective interest – quite the contrary. The Ron Paul austerity plan gives us an idea of the crushing cuts which are to be imposed during the early months of the next presidency – regardless of whether the president is Obama or Romney. This effort is already under way, with the hysterical propaganda about the fiscal cliff and the need for a grand bargain during the lame-duck session in December 2012, or immediately thereafter. Ron Paul is serving the ruling financier elite by circulating this plan in the guise of his demagogic "Liberty Agenda" to convince his myrmidons and dupes to fight for it, or at least to neutralize any resistance they might otherwise offer.

Ron Paul supporters often have the mentality of scabs, of strikebreakers. Among them there are many disgruntled war veterans looking for scapegoats, and operating with a right-wing anarchist world outlook. These characteristics take us back to Italy and Germany between the world wars to the emergence of fascist movements.

SENATOR RUBIO: MORMON APOSTATE, OR CRYPTO-MORMON?

The flaw in this elaborate intrigue, at least from the point of view of Ron Paul and Rand Paul, became clear when Romney was able to clear the hurdle of 1,144 convention votes on his own power. Ron Paul had been eager to sell his pathetic duped delegates to

Romney in exchange for getting little Rand on the national ticket, but now Romney no longer needed them. Rand had begun endorsing Romney in the last week of May, and became totally explicit during the first week of June. But Romney appeared to be looking elsewhere – to the austerity ghoul Paul Ryan, to the Bonapartist General David Petraeus, to Governor Christie (the Garden State Göring), or to Senator Marco Rubio.

The obvious difficulty with Rubio was that he had also been a Mormon. Rubio's campaign autobiography, *An American Son*, reveals that the Florida senator and his cousins were all baptized into the Mormon Church. "We were in the Mormon church I guess by the time I turned eight," Rubio told David Muir of ABC News on June 18, 2012. Rubio attributes his joining of the Mormon Church to his mother, who was supposedly looking for a family-friendly environment and found it in the LDS Church. At this time, Rubio was living with his family in Las Vegas, Nevada, and became a fan of the musical group, the Osmonds. Rubio claims that he returned to the Roman Catholic Church by the time he was 12 or 13. "… in our lives and our family in Las Vegas, we have a large extended family of cousins, second cousins and others who are still part of the LDS Church," Rubio added. The question remains: should Rubio be considered a Mormon apostate, or rather regarded as a crypto-Mormon?

AYN RAND DEVOTEE AND BIRCHER PAUL RYAN, ROMNEY'S VEEP PICK

By early August of 2012, Romney's incorrigible ineptitude, his obsessive secrecy, and the incompetence of his tight Boston clique of advisors had put his presidential campaign on the path to decline. The *Wall Street Journal* and other citadels of hard-line reactionary politics continued to criticize him for excessive moderation and insufficient fighting spirit. The rightist harpy Laura Ingraham shrieked on her radio program that "Romney's losing!"

This widespread disaffection with Romney created the danger that the militant right-wing extremists so important to the Republican base would come to regard Romney's efforts with indifference or lukewarm commitment, giving Obama the margin of victory.

Romney had considered a number of vice presidential candidates. One was Senator Rubio, but Rubio's 10 years of affiliation with Mormonism might focus excessive attention on an issue which Romney was anxious to avoid. General David Petraeus of the Pentagon and the CIA would add background in foreign policy, but this option did not pan out, perhaps because Petraeus did not want to be subjected to the degrading ordeal of a presidential campaign – or perhaps he wanted to be appointed to national office at some future time. Rand Paul was eager for the vice presidency, but he already had acquired a deserved reputation as a right-wing extremist of the DeMint-Lee-Toomey school in the Senate, and this would surely attract criticism. Ron Paul had wagered everything on the hope that Romney would need extra delegates to reach the GOP magic number of 1,144 convention votes, but Romney had sufficient delegates in hand. Therefore, the main reason to choose Rand Paul had disappeared. Senator Portman from Ohio might have helped to win a critical Electoral College mega-state, but Portman was just another white bureaucrat like Romney for most voters. Governor Pawlenty, although a solid reactionary, was similarly bland. Condoleezza Rice would have attracted attention as a black woman, but she was not extremist enough on abortion and other social issues to please the Limbaughs and Hannitys.

Romney therefore chose Congressman Paul Ryan of Wisconsin, the chief ideologue of Schachtian austerity of the House Republican caucus. Ryan was the main author of the House Republican "Path to Prosperity" program, which would abolish the existing Medicare program, replacing it with a voucher which would fall far short of the real cost of health insurance for elderly recipients. In effect, Ryan wanted to shift the risk for future increases in medical costs off the federal budget and onto the backs of low income seniors. It amounted to the utter destruction of Medicare as it had existed since 1965.

Medicare has been one of the most successful programs in world history in reducing the rates of morbidity and mortality among people over 65. Ryan wanted to destroy these benefits, because they were hated by right-wing ideologues, and because his wealthy backers did not want to be taxed to keep somebody else alive. Ryan had learned the art of the deceptive euphemism, and called his demolition of Medicare "premium support," a dodge designed to befuddle gullible old people.

Along with the end of Medicare went massive tax cuts for the rich, even as taxes on working people and the middle class went up. Ryan also wanted to privatize Social Security, turning it into a system of private accounts. Here again, the risk is shifted from the government to the hapless elderly. Colossal commissions would go to the Wall Street brokers executing orders for the system.

Reactionary commentators like Bill Bennett and Peggy Noonan tried to tout Ryan as a serious intellectual, a man of ideas, a deep policy thinker sincerely concerned with the future fate of the United States. In reality, Ryan represented the reactionary petty bourgeoisie of the American Midwest. In a word, he was George Babbitt out of the pages of Sinclair Lewis's famous novel – but without any of the openness to the issues of working people which Babbitt showed during at least one phase of his life. Ryan's approach is that of a small-town or suburban Chamber of Commerce booster, relying on cracker barrel clichés and Friedmanite or Rothbardesque slogans to defend unjustifiable privileges and status claims for the wealthy. Ryan was a classic philistine.

PAUL RYAN'S WIFE FROM A PRO-WALLACE RACIST CLAN

Four years ago, I argued that, while Obama was attempting to hide many things about himself and his wife, much could nevertheless be learned about this candidate by looking at the woman he had chosen to marry. That was true then, and it is true now in regard to Romney and Paul Ryan. Ryan's wife is Janna Little Ryan, who comes from a well-to-do family holding energy interests in Oklahoma. Janna's grandfather was Reuel Little, an active supporter of the racist Governor George Wallace of Alabama in his 1968 bid for the presidency, and a co-founder and stalwart of Wallace's racist American Party. Reuel Little, a lawyer and rancher of Madhill, Oklahoma, was the American Party's candidate for governor of Oklahoma in 1970.[339] If Little family values live on in Jana, then we

---

[339] *The Oklahoman*, December 4, 1993, online at newsOK.com, August 11, 2012.

have learned something important about Ryan's view of race relations. Governor Wallace came close to making an explicit alliance with Mormondom: Quorum of Twelve member Ezra Taft Benson, also a committed racist, seriously entertained the idea of running for vice president on Wallace's ticket.[340]

When Michael Leahy of the *Washington Post* attempted to reconstruct some of the contacts that had led up to Romney's decision to tap Ryan as vice president, he found that the congressmen most able to talk about the Ryan-Romney relationship were Mormons serving in Congress. One of Ryan's biggest supporters for the veep nod was Republican Congressman Jason Chaffetz of Utah, a leading Mormon. Chaffetz was so eager to get Ryan on the national ticket that he "sent an endorsement note to Mike Leavitt, the former Utah governor and a Romney campaign official thought to be a possible White House Chief of Staff in a Romney administration." Readers of this book know about Leavitt. Another advocate of a Romney-Ryan ticket was Republican Congressman Jeff Flake of Arizona, who in late 2010 urged Ryan to attempt a coup d'état against John Boehner to become Speaker of the House. Flake, now a candidate for Senate in Arizona, clearly regarded Ryan as the most reactionary figure who would still be able to defeat Boehner. Ryan emerges from this article as a special friend of the Mormon caucus in the House.[341]

RYAN'S ROOTS IN THE JOHN BIRCH SOCIETY, A MORMON-KOCH BROTHERS FRONT

The matrix for Ryan's ideology is not hard to find. While Ryan represents Democrat Les Aspin's district in the Chicago suburbs, if we look a few hundred miles to the north, in the town of Appleton, Wisconsin, we find the headquarters of the John Birch Society. The John Birch Society is of course the archetypal reactionary organization of post-World War II America. It was founded in 1958, the year after the death of the scoundrel Senator Joe McCarthy – another Wisconsin institution – to keep right-wing extremist ideas at the center of national attention. It was funded by Fred Koch, the father of the two reactionary Koch brothers whose political meddling has attracted so much interest in recent years. It uses the classic trick which we have observed in Joseph Smith and in Brigham Young of idolizing the U.S. Constitution, while vilifying and condemning every aspect of the United States government and its personnel. It claims to support the Constitution, but in reality the Constitution it is talking about turns out more often than not to be the Confederate Constitution of 1861. It is racist, xenophobic, anti-labor, and anti-women.

For several decades after its founding, the John Birch Society was a laughingstock, as seen in the movie *Dr. Strangelove*, in Walt Kelly's *Pogo* comic strip, and in the songs of Bob Dylan and the Chad Mitchell Trio.

---

[340] Jon Meacham, "The Mormon in Mitt," *Time*, October 8, 2012.
[341] Michael Leahy, "The Willing Lightning Rod: Paul Ryan's Stance in Daring to Touch Entitlement Reform Most Accounts for His Rise to a Bigger Stage," *Washington Post*, August 20, 2012.

But the John Birch Society has never been a laughing matter. Among its members were Kennedy assassination figurehead Guy Bannister, and the *golpista* General Edwin Walker. There was also hatemongering columnist Westbrook Pegler, widely regarded as a fascist sympathizer in the 1930s and 40s. The JBS ideological influence has been highly destructive, and quite considerable. What was considered a bad joke or a curiosity in the Kennedy era is contending for power 50 years later. Nothing could show more clearly the ideological decadence and degeneration of the United States over that time. Whatever the specific details of Paul Ryan's relation to the John Birch Society may be discovered to be, it is clear that Ryan comes from the JBS tradition.

The Mormon Saints represent a very important faction of the John Birch Society. In the early years of the Birchers, one of their main boosters was none other than Ezra Taft Benson, who had been Eisenhower's Secretary of Agriculture for eight years, and who then went on become the First President and Prophet of the LDS Church. Ezra Taft Benson supported the John Birch Society, even though the Birchers were spreading the idea that President Eisenhower, who had appointed Benson to his cabinet post, was either objectively or subjectively a communist agent. The Mormons were careful to cover their embrace of the Birchers with a pro forma 1963 statement putting a little distance between the LDS and the fanatics of Appleton, Wisconsin.

MORMON PROPHET EZRA TAFT BENSON A FANATICAL BIRCHER

According to an account by Benson's grandson, "in 1966, an organization spearheaded primarily by John Birchers and known as the 1976 Committee, nominated my grandfather as its choice for President of the United States, with avowed racist and South Carolina senator Strom Thurmond as his running mate." This project did not succeed, and the leadership of the white supremacist cause was taken over by Alabama Governor George Wallace, who "made serious attempts to generate Ezra Taft Benson's interest in joining his third-party presidential ticket as Wallace's running mate." Eventually, the veep nod went to former Air Force General Curtis LeMay, who wanted to "bomb Vietnam back into the stone age."

Benson was an outspoken racist, who considered Martin Luther King a communist agent. On December 14, 1963, Elder Benson addressed a meeting in Logan, Utah, sponsored by the John Birch Society: The official Mormon newspaper reported the event in these terms:

> "LOGAN, UTAH – Former Agriculture Secretary Ezra Taft Benson charged Friday night that the civil-rights movement in the South had been 'formatted almost entirely by the Communists.' Elder Benson, a member of the Council of the Twelve of the Church of Jesus Christ of Latter-day Saints, said in a public meeting here that the whole civil-rights movement was 'phony'." (*Deseret News*, Dec. 14, 1963)

Elder Benson's son, Reed Benson, went to work for the John Birch Society, serving as public relations director.[342] Ezra Taft Benson had been made a member of the Quorum of the Twelve Apostles in 1943 by First President Heber J. Grant, who had signaled his support for European fascism by visiting Germany in 1937. Mormon writers attempt to argue that Benson was punished for his John Birch Society activities by being sent to lead the missions in Europe for several years. But Benson never paid a serious price for promoting the Birchers, and he was promoted to President of Quorum of the Twelve Apostles in 1973, and then made Prophet and First President of the LDS church, a post he held from 1985 to 1994. Benson was part of a continuity of government operation during the Eisenhower administration. He was named administrator designate of the Emergency Food Agency, which was in turn part of a secret apparatus known as the Eisenhower Ten, created in 1958 in preparation for a possible national Emergency. Mormons have traditionally attempted to infiltrate continuity of government operations, possibly because they have Joseph Smith's White Horse Prophecy in mind. On September 11, 2001 Mormon Brent Scowcroft was aloft in one of the doomsday aircraft, and might have become the highest authority in the US government under certain circumstances.

Between 2004 and 2005, the boss of the John Birch Society was G. Vance Smith, the leading Mormon activist. Published accounts have accused Smith of packing a hierarchy of the JBS with Mormon loyalists, making the Birchers more than ever a satellite of Salt Lake City.

CLEON SKOUSEN OF THE FBI MORMON MAFIA, TOP BIRCHER IDEOLOGUE

The most important ideologue of the John Birch Society has been the late Cleon Skousen. Skousen, the author of *The Naked Capitalist*, is widely regarded as the originator of the slogan "The New World Order," which he coined to designate and mischaracterize the future plans of Anglo-American imperialism. This slogan has always been profoundly misleading, since it leads away from recognizing the centrality of Anglo-American finance capital. There is little to no place at the table for Russia and China as nation states. The slogan of the New World Order obscures this reality, and opens the door wide to chauvinistic scapegoating of other nations, while providing a smokescreen for Wall Street and the City of London.

Cleon Skousen has also been the most important political ideologue of the Mormon Church. The overlap here is doubly significant. Skousen had a career with the FBI and later as chief of police in Salt Lake City. Cleon Skousen's biography touches that of Romney in some respects: Willard Cleon Skousen (1913-2006) was born in Raymond, Alberta, Canada, where many Mormons had gone because it was easier to practice polygamy there than in the United States. Willard Cleon Skousen was the grandson of a half brother of Eliza Skousen Brown, who was one of the five wives of the Mormon polygamist Orson Pratt Brown.

---

[342] Steve Benson, "Ezra Taft Benson: Mormonism's Prophet, Seer, and Race Baiter," July 20, 2005, exmormon.com.

Skousen's father was Royal Pratt Skousen, quite possibly a relative of the same Pratt family to which Mitt Romney's grandmother belonged, or the son of Pratt admirers. At the age of 10, Skousen moved to Colonia Juarez in Mexico, the same town from which Gaskell and George Romney had fled 14 years before. Skousen then served as a Mormon missionary in Great Britain, the country so often visited by members of the Mormon elite. Skousen's rather tenuous connections to the United States did not prevent him from later assuming the profile of a chauvinist super-patriot – just like Romney.

Skousen then got a law degree at George Washington University, where FBI Director J. Edgar Hoover had also studied. The Mormons, as noted, have always maintained a large faction inside the FBI, as well as in the CIA and other government agencies. Skousen then became the chief of police of Salt Lake City, serving in this post for four years. Skousen was for many years professor in the religion department at Brigham Young University, where he retired in 1978.

SKOUSEN METHOD: SLIME CRITICS AS COMMUNISTS

Although like Ezra Taft Benson he may never have been a card-carrying member of the John Birch Society, Skousen was one of the favorite authors of the JBS rank-and-file, and was also one of the most effective defenders of Bircherdom against attacks. His method was simple: anybody attacking the John Birch Society was *ipso facto* a communist. An example of this was his pamphlet, "The Communist Attack on the John Birch Society." Later, during the 1970s, when the Mormon Church was increasingly criticized for its policies of excluding blacks by refusing to ordain them into the priesthood, Skousen wrote another screed, this time entitled "The Communist Attack on the Mormons." Here he argued that those demanding the abolition of this racist exclusion were "distorting the religious tenets of the Church regarding the Negro, and blowing it up to ridiculous proportions" – thus playing into the hands of the world Communist conspiracy. When the Mormon leadership caved to the pressure to desegregate in 1978, that was followed by a directive telling Mormon organizations to stop pushing Skousen's writings.

When Georgetown Professor Carroll Quigley, in his book *Tragedy and Hope* (1966), made an important contribution to the understanding of how the ruling Anglo-American financier oligarchy actually functions, he was targeted for harassment by the FBI and various networks, including the Mormon Mafia. Skousen contributed to the distortion of Quigley's ideas so as to make it easier for establishment pundits to dismiss them. Skousen also accused Quigley of being a part of the conspiracy he was describing, and thus, by implication, a communist.

Skousen was at pains to defend the Mormon Church against any and all criticism. Edwin Brown Firmage, Law Professor at the University of Utah, commented that Cleon Skousen taught "right wing fundamentalism with a constitutional veneer.... How anyone can prove that civil rights and welfare are unconstitutional is beyond me. For [Skousen's] people, 'constitutional' is just a right wing buzzword."[343]

---

[343] For Cleon Skousen, see his biography on Wikipedia.

Skousen demanded the full reactionary program of total deregulation, no minimum wage, no unions, no laws against discrimination, no public lands, no national parks, no direct election of Senators, no federal income tax, no estate tax, and no division of church and state. He also wanted to end the Federal Reserve System, but by abolishing it completely he would have increased the power of the Wall Street banks. He was hostile to Social Security, and wanted to replace it with a system of individual retirement accounts – exactly the plan embraced by Paul Ryan. Another example of his views in a current Mormon political figure is the demand by Utah Senator Mike Lee that the child labor laws be abolished, allegedly because they are unconstitutional.

Cleon Skousen's nephew is Joel Skousen, who carries on the same traditions today. Joel Skousen is an entrepreneur of survivalism, which he calls "strategic relocation," dispensing advice for those obsessed with future apocalyptic events. Skousen claims that the best place to be a survivalist is in the Intermountain West of the United States. He praises Utah and Idaho as the two most reactionary and refractory states, where federal encroachment meets with the most vigorous resistance. By coincidence, these are also two Mormon fiefdoms.

Joel Skousen handles his fellow Mormons with kid gloves. In an Infowars interview of January-February, 2011, he gravely discussed the positive potential of the raving crackpot Mormon Glenn Beck, seeking strategies to save poor Glenn from the clutches of the insidious globalists. In the same interview, Skousen adamantly protested that Mitt Romney, unlike Newt Gingrich and Rick Perry, is NOT part of "The System," and is therefore opposed by globalists who fear that he might resist their policies if he were to become president. This fantastic view may have collapsed of its own dead weight when candidate Romney made a covert visit to the Bilderberg meeting in Chantilly, Virginia in early June 2012.

After the present writer exposed and denounced the Romney-Ron Paul alliance at the time of the Bilderberg meeting in Virginia, on June 8, 2012, Joel Skousen joined Stan Montieth in devoting an entire radio program to attempt to discredit the present writer. In good JBS-Mormon tradition, they focused on the accusation of "socialism."[344]

Romney's choice of Paul Ryan for Vice President therefore reflects and expresses the role of the John Birch Society in spreading the ideology of right-wing Mormonism far beyond the confines of the Mormon confession. In the Romney-Ryan ticket, we see a combination of Mormonism's reactionary mainstream, supplemented by its most robust ideological tentacle. This may explain why commentators repeatedly cited the excellent personal chemistry between Mitt and the young congressman. They find each other congenial because they both derive from the same ideological template.

BISHOP ROMNEY'S 2012 CAMPAIGN

Romney's 2012 campaign contains a series of echoes that hearken back to the Mountain Meadows Massacre of 1857, in which 140 peaceful Arkansas travelers of the Baker-

---

[344] I am in fact an exponent of the Hamilton-List-Clay-Lincoln-FDR American System of Political Economy, and a critic of Karl Marx as a British asset – see Chapter III of this book.

Fancher party were slaughtered by Brigham Young's Danite militia. (*The Mormon Rebellion*, Bigler & Bagley, p. 156)

PARLEY PARKER PRATT'S ANCESTOR
ANNE HUTCHINSON BANNED IN BOSTON

The first echo involves the top of the ticket – Romney himself. Romney's status as belonging to one of the first families of Mormondom derives from his great-great-grandfather, Parley Parker Pratt. Parley Pratt came from a family whose ideology had been tinged by antinomianism for two centuries: Pratt was a descendent of Anne Hutchinson, the founder of the antinomian group in Boston during the 1630s. The argument of this group was that the imperatives of obeying the moral law and the need to do good works of charity were suspended for the elect. Although much admired by modern feminists, there was little theological merit in Anne Hutchinson's tenets. Rather, her antinomian clique posed a real practical and political danger to the future of Massachusetts Bay colony. Anne and her followers were expelled from Boston, and soon joined Roger Williams and his eclectic group of seekers in Rhode Island. She later moved on to Eastchester in the Bronx, where she was killed by Indians. Joseph Smith's mother was also an antinomian, and the social practice of Mormonism as a whole was decidedly on the wild side of antinomianism.

Pratt was a part of Joseph Smith's original quorum of supporters, and became a member of the Quorum of the Twelve apostles in 1835. He then took part in Brigham Young's mission to Great Britain between 1839 and 1841. He later spent time in San Francisco, hoping to recruit enough Mormons to detach California from the Union. Pratt was one of the most prestigious and popular early Mormon oligarchs, variously called "the Apostle Paul of Mormonism" or "the Archer of Paradise." His brother, Orson Pratt, was another LDS bigwig. Parley Pratt practiced polygamy with great gusto, taking no fewer than a dozen wives who gave him thirty children. Pratt married his second wife so quickly after the death of the first that even Joseph Smith had to criticize his unseemly haste. Not only Mitt Romney, but also Jon Huntsman, are descendents of Parley Pratt.

If Parley Pratt was supposed to be the Archer of Paradise, it was Cupid's bow which proved to be his undoing. While on church business in San Francisco, Parley Pratt had met and seduced Eleanor McLean, who was still legally married to Hector McLean. Eleanor became a Mormon, and brought along her elder sons with her. Hector did not want his sons and daughter to be forced to live under the leadership of Brigham Young, so he sent them to New Orleans to live with their grandparents. Eleanor McLean came to New Orleans and took the children off to Salt Lake City. There she formalized her union with Parley Pratt, being sealed to him in celestial marriage. Hector McLean was able to get Pratt arrested in Oklahoma Territory in 1857 on charges of kidnapping and stealing the children's wardrobe. Pratt was acquitted on these charges. But on May 13, 1857, Hector McLean caught up with Pratt near Van Buren, Arkansas and inflicted fatal wounds by shooting and stabbing. Pratt died protesting that he was merely trying to save Mrs. McLean from oppression. In life, he was variously described as dour, humorless, and antisocial – traits which live on in his distinguished great-great-grandson.

Brigham Young in public speeches put the death of Parley Pratt into the same category of glorious martyrdom as Joseph Smith and Hyrum Smith. At the time of the Mountain Meadows Massacre a few months later, the entire Mormon community was animated by insatiable thirst for revenge and blood atonement against peaceful travelers simply because they happened to be from Arkansas, the same state where Parley Pratt was finally overtaken by the backlash from his polygamist escapades. Mitt Romney is thus the scion of the polygamist line that provided the pretext for the Mountain Meadows Massacre.

MIKE LEAVITT, MITT'S RIGHT-HAND MAN

A second echo of Mountain Meadows in the Romney camp today is the role of former Governor Mike Leavitt of Utah, who is the boss of Romney's transition team. Leavitt as a doctrinaire Mormon required his staff to read the *Book of Mormon* every morning.[345] In 1998 he publicly defended polygamy as being covered by religious freedom. Mike Leavitt is a lineal descendent of (Thomas) Dudley Leavitt, who was one of the Mormon butchers at the Mountain Meadows Massacre.

Several years ago, the site of the Mountain Meadows Massacre was being prepared for a ceremony marking the 150th anniversary. Forensic research carried out by the state of Utah was beginning to reveal additional and hitherto unknown details about the brutality of the massacre, including female and child victims shot at point-blank range, and other grisly details.

The Mormon cover story has generally been that the Arkansas pioneers were responsible for what happened to them because they were mistreating the Indians and picking fights with the local population. According to this cover story, the Arkansas people were killed by Paiute Indians – not Mormons. The weakness of this deception is that the Indians had very few firearms, and relied instead on bows and arrows, clubs, and other primitive weapons. It was the Mormon Danite militia that was armed to the teeth.

According to John Elvin, writing in the old *Washington Times Insight* magazine, the evidence unearthed while the site was being prepared for the anniversary "supports the execution version of the story. In preparing the site, now owned by the Mormon Church, for a new monument a few years ago, piles of bones were turned up in mass graves. On advice from Ron Loving, president of the Mountain Meadows Association (MMA), a group of descendants of victims, the church decided to keep the find secret. Though the remains of murder victims had to be turned over to a medical examiner under state law, the state also agreed to keep the find quiet. But the secret quickly became public knowledge, sparking protests by a rival group, the Mountain Meadows Monument Foundation, that groups of descendants had been unaware of the discovery of their ancestors' bones."

TRANSITION BOSS MIKE LEAVITT COVERS UP FOR HIS TERRORIST ANCESTOR AT MOUNTAIN MEADOWS MASSACRE

Mike Leavitt's crude and illegal attempt to cover up the evidence for Mormon butchery at Mountain Meadows caused a bitter division between the descendants of the Arkansas

---

[345] Ibid.

victims and those of the Mormon killers. "There's a sense among some of our members that it's like having Lee Harvey Oswald in charge of JFK's tomb," commented Scott Fancher, a descendent of the victims. A spokesman for the pro-Mormon side claimed that "the reason for the quick and surreptitious reburial was to protect the sensibilities of the families" and to guarantee that "no unnecessary tests were conducted on the remains." The pro-Mormon view was that "Utah state forensics experts were conducting precisely such 'unnecessary tests' to determine who was responsible for the massacre."

But before Mike Leavitt was able to stop the investigation with an illegal executive order and bury the evidence, "the University of Utah's Shannon Novak, leader of the team of scientific examiners, discovered that many of the dead men and women were shot as they faced their assailants, and none died, as had been claimed, from arrows shot by Indians." Governor Leavitt had a double conflict of interest, first because he was a leading Mormon, and secondly because his ancestor [Thomas] Dudley Leavitt was "a massacre veteran" – or, more accurately, one of the assassins.

Hiding behind spokespersons, Leavitt repeatedly told the public that he was unaware that his interference with the investigation constituted a violation of state law. Leavitt stuck to his story that he was concerned about the mental anguish of the descendents of the victims. John Elvin commented: "Despite the rush to rebury the bones, the finding that the men, women and children had been shot just about demolished the popular tale that Indians killed the travelers."[346]

MOUNTAIN MEADOWS RINGLEADER JOHN D. LEE AND UTAH SENATOR MIKE LEE

A third echo is that one of Romney's Utah backers is fellow Mormon Senator Mike Lee, who is a direct lineal descendant of John D. Lee, the leader of the Mormon killers at the Mountain Meadows Massacre. According to some accounts, Lee raped some of the female victims before murdering them, and his polygamist wives were later seen wearing the clothing and jewelry of the dead Arkansas women. John D. Lee in 1877 became the only one of the perpetrators to be executed (by firing squad) for the Mountain Meadows Massacre. Lee went to his death saying that he had been scapegoated by Brigham Young, and indeed there is reason to believe that John D. Lee, while certainly guilty of multiple murders, was taking the rap to protect other Mormon bigwigs. The extremely reactionary (or protofascist) Senator Mike Lee, a Tea Party fanatic, has declared that child labor laws are unconstitutional, a position previously embraced by the Mormon John Birch Society ideologue Cleon Skousen.

In another echo of the Mountain Meadows Massacre, Jared Lee Loughner, the suspect in the shooting of Congresswoman Gabby Giffords in which several other people died, is also a descendant of John D. Lee. Other prominent descendents of John D. Lee include New Mexico Democratic Senator Tom Udall and Colorado Democratic Senator Mark

---

[346] John Elvin, "The Madness at Mountain Meadows: a New Book and Forensic Evidence Suggest That the Mormon Church Has Long Covered up Complicity in the 1857 Massacre of US Civilians in Southern Utah," *Insight on the News*, January 21, 2003.

Udall. In the previous generation, Stewart Lee Udall and Morris Udall represented this wing of the Mormon Lee clan.

GOP SUPPRESSION OF MINORITY VOTERS MESHES WITH RACIST MORMON TRADITION

The Republican strategy for winning back the White House in 2012 depended to a significant degree on voter suppression, targeting especially black and Hispanic voters in states like Florida, Pennsylvania, Iowa, and Michigan. Republican measures to make voting harder were energetically advocated by ALEC, The American Legislative Exchange Council, an entity notoriously funded by the reactionary Koch brothers. The strategy was always the same: allege widespread voter fraud, and then proceed to create obstacles between minority voters and the ballot box. This outrageous Republican ploy was of course perfectly coherent with the racism which pervades Bishop Romney's Mormon tradition. Harold Meyerson of the *Washington Post* raised the issue of the legitimacy of a possible future Romney presidency, if it were to be discovered that Romney's margin of victory was significantly smaller than the number of minority voters who were kept away from their polling places by the Republicans. Meyerson asked, "And what should Democrats do if Romney comes to power on the strength of racially suppressed votes? Such an outcome and such a presidency, I'd hope that they contend, would be illegitimate – a betrayal of our laws and traditions, of our very essence as a democratic republic. Mass demonstrations would be in order. So would a congressional refusal to confirm any of Romney's appointments. A presidency premised on the racist restriction of the franchise creates a political and constitutional crisis, and responding to it with resigned acceptance or inaction would negate America's hard-won commitment to democracy and equality."[347]

ROMNEY CLIQUE'S BUNGLING AND INEPTITUDE

The Republican presidential primary contest effectively ended on April 10, when the clerical-authoritarian candidate Santorum announced that he was dropping out. It was a case of Santorum's right-wing Jesuit networks being bested by a combination of Mormon and Scottish Rite Southern Jurisdiction freemasons in the form of the Romney and Ron Paul campaigns. The futurologist Newt Gingrich had run only a token campaign after March 27, when he lost the Louisiana primary, but he too dropped out on May 2 after losing in Delaware.

The Romney forces therefore could have used May and June, the last two months of the Republican primary season, to begin projecting a positive image of their candidate, necessarily including some specific ideas about what a Romney presidency might do for the United States. But Romney's handlers refused to use this opportunity. They were dominated by the obsessively held idea, repeated ad infinitum by media commentaries over many months, that the 2012 presidential election will be exclusively a referendum

---

[347] Harold Meyerson, "The illegitimate aims of voter suppression," *Washington Post*, July 25, 2012.

on Obama, with the popularity and policies of the Republican nominee playing no role whatsoever.

Because of this amateurish misconception, the Romney campaign stagnated in May, June, and July of 2012, when Romney backers had hoped to build up an insuperable lead over the feckless Obama. During this time, the Axelrod-Plouffe-Valerie Jarret Chicago clique who run Obama's campaign began to assail the Mormon plutocrat using the obvious issues pioneered against Romney by Senator Kennedy in 1994: Romney had asset stripped and destroyed viable businesses for short-term super-profits when he was running Bain Capital. An important feature of the Bain looting process was that US plants were shut down, and the jobs outsourced and shipped overseas. Romney refused to release more than one or two years of his federal income tax returns, feeding reports that he had avoided paying income tax altogether in one or more years. Romney was discovered to have hidden tens of millions of dollars of proceeds from his asset stripping activities in more or less secret accounts in the Cayman Islands (where he invested in a dozen funds); in his very own, wholly owned Sankaty High Yield Asset Investors Fund in the Bermudas; and in others in Ireland, Switzerland, Luxembourg, Bermuda, Germany, and Australia.

GOP NOMINALISTS NOT HAPPY WITH ROMNEY'S "BOSTON COTERIE"

When, at the end of June 2012, the Supreme Court validated the Affordable Care Act commonly known as Obamacare, the immediate Pavlovian reaction of the reactionary Republican congressional leadership was to seize on the part of the majority opinion which declared that the individual mandate feature of Obamacare was constitutional because it constituted a tax. The mantra that Obamacare was bad because it was a tax fit smoothly into the nominalistic-hysterical Republican world outlook, and thus represented the neatest and easiest way to package this issue to reassure the credulous Republican base. The Obama administration, by contrast, insisted that the money paid to the government by those who refused to buy health insurance in defiance of the individual mandate had to be considered a penalty or a fee, not a tax.

Top Romney adviser Eric Fehrnstrom appeared on television to agree with Obama: an additional payment assessed on those who do not buy insurance has to be considered a penalty or a fee. This line robbed the reactionary Republicans of their slogan that Obamacare had raised taxes on the middle class, in direct betrayal of Obama's election-year promises of 2008. Fehrnstrom was evidently concerned that if the Obamacare individual mandate represented a tax, then so did the money collected in Massachusetts under Romneycare from those who similarly refused to buy a health insurance policy.

Faced with a hue and cry from reactionaries, Romney, in a July 4 interview went back to calling Obamacare "a tax." By early July, the militant reactionaries who run the *Wall Street Journal* editorial page were thoroughly alarmed, and declared a state of emergency.

> If Mitt Romney loses his run for the White House, a turning point will have
> been his decision Monday to absolve President Obama of raising taxes on the

middle class. He is managing to turn the only possible silver lining in Chief Justice John Roberts' Obamacare salvage operation – that the mandate to buy insurance or pay a penalty is really a tax – into a second political defeat.[348]

The *Wall Street Journal* assailed Fehrnstrom and Romney campaign spokeswoman Andrea Saul, whom it described as being part of a "Boston coterie" motivated by fear that Romney would be "labeled a flip-flopper." If so, they got the worst of all possible worlds when Romney reverted to calling Obamacare a tax.

According to the reactionary flagship, the "Boston coterie" represents the Romney "campaign's insular staff and strategy that are slowly squandering an historic opportunity… the Romney campaign thinks it can play it safe and coast to the White House by saying the economy stinks and it's Mr. Obama's fault. We're on its e-mail list and the main daily message from the campaign is that 'Obama isn't working.' Thanks, guys, but Americans already know that. What they want to hear from the challenger is some understanding of why the president's policies aren't working and how Mr. Romney's policies will do better."

Rupert Murdoch's minions were also upset by the photo opportunities arranged by the campaign during the nominee's vacation a few days earlier, which featured the candidate on jet skis and riding in an expensive speedboat. The jet ski cameo resembled John Kerry's windsurfing debacle of 2004, and the speedboat hearkened back to George H. W. Bush cavorting in his Don Aronow cigarette boat in the waters off Kennebunkport, Maine. "The Obama campaign," wrote the Murdoch team, "is assailing Mr. Romney as an out of touch rich man, and the rich man obliged by vacationing this week at his lakeside home with a jet ski cameo… team Obama is now opening up a new assault on Mr. Romney as a job outsourcer with foreign bank accounts, and if the Boston boys let that one go unanswered, they ought to be fired for malpractice."

ERIC FEHRNSTROM'S ETCH-A-SKETCH STRATEGY

Eric Fehrnstrom has been described by the *New York Times* as Mitt Romney's David Axelrod – "the keeper of the candidates narrative, the guy who has been with Mr. Romney since before he was governor of Massachusetts and has stuck like glue through two grueling presidential campaigns—he has been the defiant defender of Mr. Romney when he has been accused of being a flip flopper or having no core principles."

Fehrnstrom had been responsible for the notorious "Etch-a-Sketch" episode of mid-March 2012. Asked about when Romney might begin to jettison some of his most extreme reactionary posturing to appeal to persons less fanatic than the typical Republican primary voter, Fehrnstrom remarked: "everything changes. It's almost like Etch-a-Sketch. You can kind of shake it up and restart all over again."[349] It was one of the best summations heard in recent years of the cynical hypocrisy which pervades

---

[348] "Romney's Tax Confusion," *Wall Street Journal*, July 5, 2012.

[349] Michael D. Shear, "For Romney's Trusted Advisor, 'Etch-a-Sketch' Comment Is a Rare Misstep," *New York Times*, March 21, 2012.

American politics during the late empire. Gingrich and Santorum began carrying Etch-a-Sketch toys to their campaign rallies, as the Democrats would surely do in October.

Fehrnstrom was working as an advertising copywriter when Romney recruited him. That day, he recalls, he was "working on a press release for a new, spicy menu at Popeye's Fried Chicken. I said to myself, 'there have to be more interesting things in life than spicy fried chicken.' I hung up the phone, walked down the hall and quit."

A month after the editorial blast at Romney's inner circle of handlers, the *Wall Street Journal* was still deeply concerned about the cliquishness and drift of the Romney campaign: "Nearly every presidential candidate relies on a handful of trusted advisors who have been longtime loyalists. Mr. Romney's inner circle includes a large number of people from fields other than politics. Many say they have little taste for campaigning, have no plans to move on to another job in the political world and are in the campaign only to help a friend become president. Outside the campaign, some conservatives have questioned whether Mr. Romney is too reliant on longtime aides and friends – whether the team is too tight-knit to sufficiently consider the advice of others who also want Mr. Romney to succeed. Polling suggests that Mr. Romney's team has not successfully conveyed Mr. Romney's strongest qualities to voters or parried the Obama campaign's efforts to cast his business career as a pursuit of profits at the expense of workers."[350]

During July, Romney hired a number of experienced Republican hacks with backgrounds in national political campaigns. These included Ed Gillespie, a former chairman of the Republican National Committee who had also served in the White House under George W. Bush. There was also Michelle Davis, who had been a top Treasury official under Bush the younger.

But the inner circle of Romney's handlers continued to be dominated by long-term cronies. One of these was Bob White, who had been Romney's partner in asset stripping at Bain Capital, and who was described in the press as a "longtime friend and senior advisor to Romney." Another was Spencer Zwick, often called Romney's sixth son, who was a student at Brigham Young University when he was recruited by Romney for the purpose of covering up the bribery and corruption perpetrated by the Mormon Saints in the preparation of the Salt Lake City Winter Olympics. Zwick then went on to serve Romney when he was governor of Massachusetts and in the 2008 and 2012 campaigns. He is a partner in an investment company he co-owns with Romney's eldest son.

Yet another long-term Romney aide is Beth Myers, who was given the assignment of evaluating possible choices for the vice presidential slot on Romney's ticket. She served in Romney's gubernatorial campaign in Massachusetts, and then as his chief of staff in the State House in Boston.

---

[350] Colleen McCain Nelson, "Following Romney Again and Again: Some of the Candidates Close Circle Work for Him Multiple Times, but Not for Love of Politics, *Wall Street Journal*, August 4-5, 2012.

Most important of all is former Utah Governor Mike Leavitt, who brought Romney in to cover up the crimes of the Mormon Saints who had violated the Foreign Corrupt Practices Act by bribing foreign officials to bring the Winter Games to the heart of the Mormon Inland Empire.

Leavitt was appointed as director of Romney's presidential Transition Team in early June 2012, quite possibly the earliest date at which this post has been filled and announced by any candidate in recent decades. Leavitt, a Mormon true believer, will thus control appointments to every political patronage post in the federal Plum Book. Based on the pattern displayed by Romney so far, we can expect that the Mormon Saints will be heavily over-represented in the new regime. US propaganda rails against the Syrian Baath party regime of President Bashar Assad as bad because it is overstocked with members of the Alawite minority, but this may be nothing compared to the narrow, Mormons-only, personnel policies of a Romney regime. A predatory Mormon yoke may be about to descend on the United States.

Michael Okerlund "Mike" Leavitt was governor of Utah from 1993 to 2003. He then became Administrator for the Environmental Protection Agency in the Bush the younger Administration from 2003 to 2005. He was then Secretary of Health and Human Services from 2005 to 2009.

Romney's appointment of Leavitt generated significant criticism from reactionary circles. According to one account, "Mitt Romney is under fire from conservatives for selecting a man to run his White House transition team who has championed a key element of 'Obamacare' and benefited financially from the law – and the Romney campaign is already working to ease the right's concerns." This criticism alleged that Leavitt was not reactionary enough for the extremists at FreedomWorks and similar outfits. Leavitt was accused of being "a high profile Obamacare profiteer" through his company Leavitt Partners. But behind these attacks may have also lurked the dawning realization that, in a Romney administration, the lion's share of the corporate welfare would go to the Mormon Saints.

ROMNEY TRANSITION BOSS MIKE LEAVITT: POLYGAMY PROTECTED BY FIRST AMENDMENT AS RELIGIOUS FREEDOM

In 1998, Governor Leavitt was asked why polygamy is not frequently prosecuted. His answer was that "it may fall under religious freedoms."[351] He later retreated to the safer position that polygamy is and should be illegal.

Leavitt later commented: "I was asked sitting in this [governor's] chair whether I thought it [polygamy] was constitutional, and I said I didn't know."[352]

---

[351] *Salt Lake City Tribune*, August 9, August 29, 1998.
[352] Dennis Romboy, "'Polygamy Is against the Law,' Leavitt Stresses," *Deseret News*, May 25, 2001.

In May, 2001, Mike Leavitt was forced to cancel a scheduled appearance at the National Press Club in Washington, DC, where he had been planning to make a pitch for investment in Utah based on a new report from the Center of the New West. But this report was forced to include a section on "The Polygamy Issue." This section would have doubtless piqued the curiosity of the Washington press corps, especially since Tom Green, a noted Utah polygamist who had proclaimed his practices on television, had just been convicted on four counts of bigamy and one count of criminal nonsupport. This case had been the first polygamy prosecution in many decades.

Interestingly, the Juab County Prosecutor who brought this case against Tom Green was David Leavitt, the brother of Governor Mike Leavitt. Both Leavitts are descended from Mormon polygamists. The policy of modern Utah prosecutors seems to focus on low level polygamists who have little or no standing in the hierarchy of the Latter-day Saints Church – polygamists of the Warren Jeffs variety, for example – as a way of reassuring the public that polygamy is under control. But this leaves open the question of the polygamy reportedly practiced by top-level Mormon bosses.

MIKE LEAVITT COVERS FOR AMERICAN TALIBAN

The prosecution of Tom Green was also regarded as a piece of Mormon window dressing to reassure reporters and possible visitors to Mitt Romney's 2002 Olympic Winter games that the issue of polygamy was under control in Utah. The Utah Legislature voted for the appointment of a full-time polygamy investigator (or polygamy czar) in the year 2000. They acted under pressure from anti-polygamy groups, often composed of women fleeing from polygamous households, such as Tapestry against Polygamy (TAP). TAP's favorite slogan is that polygamists represent "the American Taliban." Utah polygamy investigator Ron Barton produced only one important prosecution in 2000-2002, and this was the "flamboyant polygamist" Tom Green. When Green went to jail, it was the first conviction for polygamy in Utah in 50 years. Anti-polygamy activists described the case as a "show trial."

One TAP organizer pointed to the obvious problem of tackling polygamy in Utah: "They've been slow to respond to the issues. I don't think Utah can really tackle this problem without outside help. They can't do it themselves because everyone is too connected to polygamy." This is especially true in a state like Utah where 70% of the population are Mormons, and 90% of elected officials are members of the official LDS.[353]

TRANSITION BOSS LEAVITT SCORNS FEDERAL BAN ON POLYGAMY

At Leavitt's monthly news conference for the Utah media, he repeated a mantra as: "polygamy is against the law. It has been for 100 plus years in the state, and it ought to be." But this remark shows that Leavitt is still defying the Morrill Act of 1862, which

---

[353] Julie Cart, "Groups Airing 'Utah's Dirty Little Secret': As Activists Gather, They Say States in Action on the Issue Allows Sexual Assaults, Child Abuse, Welfare Fraud to Go Unchecked," *Los Angeles Times*, August 18, 2002.

outlawed bigamy under federal law. If he had wanted to respect the Morrill Act, Leavitt could have said that polygamy had been outlawed for almost one and a half centuries. After all, when federal law banned bigamy, then polygamy became illegal in Utah Territory as well. Leavitt's hundred year time frame, by contrast, shows that he thinks polygamy only became illegal in Utah when the state code was altered to say that it was, as a part of Utah's successful effort to finally join the Union on January 4, 1896.

Today, Utah, Arizona, and other states of Brigham Young's former Inland Empire notoriously refuse to bring cases against known polygamists. Would Leavitt call that a policy of salutary neglect of US law? The governor's 2001 answer was evasive: "Those are decisions that local prosecutors need to make. It's against the law, it ought to be, and I believe that the outcome of this [Tom Green] trial was an appropriate one." Not surprising, since the prosecutor was Leavitt's brother.

ROMNEY WIN WOULD BRING A "MORMON MOMENT" FOR PATRONAGE JOBS

At the beginning of 2012, Washington journalist Wayne Madsen warned about a massive increase in the numbers and power of the Mormon Mafia in the eventuality of a Romney victory: "The word from federal departments and agencies that have experienced a steady influx of Mormon senior officials over the past few years is that one thing that can be expected from a Mitt Romney presidency is the type of rampant nepotism and cronyism already witnessed at the Department of Health and Human Services (HHS), Environmental Protection Agency (EPA), and CIA, but on a much wider scale."[354]

Madsen cited Mike Leavitt as one of the Mormon officials of the Bush administration most determined to pack the federal bureaucracy with his coreligionists. He noted that Leavitt, at both EPA and HHS, "ensured that his Mormon friends and members of their families were appointed to high-level positions in both agencies. Leavitt's conflicts of interest at EPA and HHS were even more stark when considering that he inherited the Leavitt Group regional insurance company founded by his father and served on the board of Utah Power & Light."

One notorious example of Leavitt's Mormon cronyism had been his hiring of his old pal Charles Johnson: "Johnson was Leavitt's chief financial officer for EPA and his Assistant Secretary for Budget, Technology, and Finance at HHS. Johnson, in turn, hired his niece as the director of the grants program at HHS. President Obama kept Johnson on at HHS, and Johnson's niece managed to burrow down from a political appointment to a career civil service position before the Bush to Obama transition. As a further example of Mormon nepotism, Johnson served as President of Huntsman Cancer Foundation and as Vice President of Huntsman LLC in Utah. Jon Huntsman, Jr., a former Utah governor

---

[354] Wayne Madsen, "A Romney presidency? Get ready for massive Mormon nepotism," Wayne Madsen Report, February 1-2, 2012.

who ran unsuccessfully for the Republican nomination for president, served as Obama's ambassador to China. Huntsman and Romney are cousins."[355]

Corrupt bureaucrats sometimes attempted to justify all this cronyism with the argument that Mormon clean living made the new hires more stable and less subject to blackmail: "… CIA and FBI … have instituted hiring preferences for Mormons in the belief that they are squeaky-clean when it comes to alcohol and drug use. In addition, many Mormon recruits have proficiency in at least one foreign language, a result of their foreign Mormon missionary work. But for those who believe that all Mormons are squeaky-clean and besides the fact that Romney has destroyed entire towns through the actions of his vulture capital company, Bain Capital, consider the close ties between the Mormon Church and organized crime in the Western states."[356]

In reality, the Mormons were up to their necks in gambling, prostitution, and related activities in Las Vegas and Reno. Madsen recalled the case of Don Bolles, an investigative journalist for the *Arizona Republic*, who was killed by a car bomb on June 2, 1976, while probing the links between the Mormon Mafia gambling operations and the Intermountain West.[357] During his last years, the mentally disturbed billionaire recluse Howard Hughes had been surrounded by Mormons. Though Hughes died in April 1976, a last will and testament allegedly sworn by Hughes was discovered in the office of a Latter-day Saints official in Salt Lake City. Among the beneficiaries, Madsen writes, was the Mormon Mafia stalwart Bill Gay, who was president of Hughes's Summa Corporation, the owner of The Sands, Silver Slipper, Frontier, Landmark, Castaways, and Desert Inn hotel-casinos in Las Vegas. This "Mormon Will" attributed to Howard Hughes was thrown out as a forgery by a Nevada court. Madsen also notes that U.S. Senate Majority Leader Harry Reid is traditionally regarded as the interface between the Mormon Saints and organized crime.[358]

MORMON ROOTS OF ROMNEY'S PROWESS AS A LIAR

Romney's extraordinary achievements as a liar and a flip flopper, this book has argued, are rooted in the Mormon belief in the suspension of the moral law for the Saints as the end of the world approaches. Romney, in other words, is a typical Mormon antinomian. Romney's antinomianism was displayed in grand style during his first debate with Obama on October 3, 2012. Here, Romney's strategy was to evade all responsibility for the extreme reactionary policy positions he had taken during two years of presidential campaigning, and to reinvent himself on the spot as a moderate. In a breathtaking series of lies during the first 10 minutes or so of the debate, Romney repudiated his own platform concerning a $5 trillion tax cut for the very rich, concerning his desire to wreck Medicare, and concerning his intent to loot Social Security. As Paul Krugman and John Stewart noted, this was simply a strategy of blatant lying and prevarication. The only

---

[355] Wayne Madsen, "A Romney presidency? Get ready for massive Mormon nepotism," Wayne Madsen Report, February 1-2, 2012.
[356] Ibid.
[357] Ibid.
[358] Ibid.

possible effective answer by Obama would have been to condemn Romney on the spot as a pathological and compulsive liar. But since Obama is a notorious weakling and coward, since Obama fears the image of the angry black man, since Obama feels he must preserve his likeability as his principal remaining asset, and since Obama believes that the so-called independents do not like acrimony, the craven president let this cascade of lies pass almost without comment.

Romney had long been known as a flip flopper, but in this debate he outdid even himself in mendacity. What is notable about Romney is his ability to lie effortlessly, without skipping a beat. Other candidates lie, but they often display symptoms of bad conscience, fear, or anguish. None of that is seen in Romney's case: as this text has shown, Romney's striking ability to lie without any apparent internal friction is the heritage of 182 years of Mormon deception and prevarication, especially about polygamy and related practices. As an antinomian, Romney is way ahead of Richard Nixon and virtually all other recent US political figures, and in this, he is standing on the shoulders of Joseph Smith and his successors.

"A WILD AND CRAZY MAN… JUST WAITING TO COME OUT"

The 2012 election campaign has revealed many disturbing facts about Bishop Romney. It has been revealed that Romney launched Bain Capital with money from wealthy and reactionary Central American families, who were implicated in illegal drug trafficking and in the operations of right-wing death squads operating in a civil war in El Salvador.[359]

We have read the story in the *Washington Post* of the young Mitt Romney's leading role in a campaign of hazing, harassment, and bullying against John Wilder, a gay student at the expensive Cranbrook School in Bloomfield Hills, Michigan, in 1965. Romney led a gang assaulting Wilder, and personally cut off much of Wilder's hair, supposedly to make him conform to his own idea of what a Cranbrook student should look like. Wilder was severely traumatized by this event. Ann Romney has observed: "there is a wild and crazy man inside of there just waiting to come out." What if the proverbial 3 a.m. phone call announcing an international crisis should be answered by this "wild and crazy man"? The consequences for the American people might well be tragic.[360]

We have also learned from national media reports of young Romney's strange hobby, practiced when he was an undergraduate at Stanford University in California, of dressing up in a Michigan State Trooper's uniform (the gift of his father, the Governor of Michigan). Romney would reportedly attach a flashing red light to the roof of his white Rambler automobile, and harass motorists by pulling them over to the side of the road.

---

[359] Ryan Grim and Cole Stangler, "Mitt Romney Started Bain Capital with Money from Families Tied to Death Squads," *Huffington Post*, August 9, 2012; Joseph Tanfani, Melanie Mason, Matea Gold, "Bain Capital Started with Help of Offshore Investors," *Los Angeles Times*, July 19, 2012.
[360] Jason Horowitz, "Romney's Pranks Could Go to Far: Classmates at the Elite Cranbrook Boys' Prep School Recall Much Joking by Their Friend, but Also Troubling Incidents," *Washington Post*, May 11, 2012.

According to one account, Romney had also equipped this car with a siren. The targets of Romney's harassment included his own friends and acquaintances, but apparently also chance passers-by. Fraudulently impersonating a police officer is a serious crime in both California and Michigan. Incidents like these, combined with Romney's cruel indifference to working people at companies assets stripped by Bain Capital, unavoidably raises the question of whether the bishop is actually a sadist.

BISHOP ROMNEY AT STANFORD: "PRETTY WEIRD … CREEPY"

A woman who was attending Stanford in those years and who knew about Romney's strange hobby recalled that "we thought it was all pretty weird. We all thought, 'Wow, that's creepy.'"[361] Many recall the sinister role played by the mentally troubled dry drunk George W. Bush as the Nietzschean Blonde Beast, acting as kingpin for a gang of neocons in starting the Afghanistan and Iraq wars, which have caused the deaths of millions. Would Romney the sadistic prankster assume the same role in the midst of his own gaggle of angry neocons? The danger is severe, especially since Bishop Romney has been imbued with the antinomian spirit which pervades the entire history of Mormondom from 1830 to the present day. This antinomianism is closely related to the Nietzschean slogan of "everything is permitted," which the neocons have taken over. This will make for an explosive combination.

How explosive can perhaps be seen from the nominee's October 8, 2012 foreign policy speech to the Virginia Military Institute. This speech promised a return to all the bluster, bellicosity, bombing, and boots on the ground of the tragic Bush-Cheney era. In particular, Romney harped on the attack on the US Consulate in Benghazi, Libya, on September 11, 2012, which killed Ambassador Chris Stevens and three others. Romney's tirade was especially duplicitous, for two sets of reasons.

CIA MORMON MAFIA PRIME SUSPECTS
IN DEATH OF AMBASSADOR STEVENS

The anti-Moslem film which figured prominently in demonstrations in Egypt, Pakistan, and two dozen other countries across the world has been blamed on the hapless ex-convict and apparent patsy Nakoula Basseley Nakoula, aka Sam Bacile, but a key player in this project would appear according to published accounts to have been Joseph Nasralla Abdelmasih of Media for Christ, a Coptic Christian born in Egypt. Nasralla was a speaker at a rally organized by Pamela Geller and her Islamophobia Network near the site of the World Trade Center in New York City on September 11, 2010, for the purpose of protesting against plans to build a mosque and Islamic community center in the financial district. Another speaker at that conference was former State Department official John Bolton, who made a videotaped address. John Bolton is known to be one of the principal foreign policy advisers to Romney, and has been mentioned as a possible future Secretary of State in a Romney administration. Through the close connection between the Islamophobic network on the one hand and the Romney campaign on the

---

[361] Joe Conason, "Did Young Mitt Romney Impersonates a Police Officer? Another Witness Says Yes," The NationalMemo, June 6, 2012; see also Kranish and Helman.

other, we are justified in remarking that the Romney campaign is the prime suspect in the creation of this anti-Islamic film. It is not surprising that Romney wants to minimize the importance of this film as much as possible. This film and the violence it provoked may represent one of the most ambitious dirty tricks ever launched by a US presidential campaign in search of an October surprise in the service of their own candidate.

Romney obviously blames Obama personally, and not even Hillary Clinton's State Department, for the deaths of Ambassador Stevens and his associates. But here again, we may be dealing with a case of consummate lying. As US intelligence sources told Fox News on September 20, 2012, all signs suggest that the attack on the US Consulate in Benghazi and the murder of Ambassador Stevens were carried out by forces under the command of Sufyan Ben Qumu (or Kumu), a noted terrorist leader of the Libyan Islamic Fighting Group, an affiliate of Al Qaeda.[362] Qumu is a native of Derna, Libya, the city which US Army files suggest has produced more violent terrorists per capita than any other in the world. The US government knows everything about Qumu, who spent about five years as a prisoner in detention at Guantánamo Bay, Cuba. Qumu was then sent back to Libya in September 2007, where he was set free by Gaddafi in an amnesty in 2010.

Qumu illustrates the important fact that the Guantánamo prison camp is not just a place of confinement, but also of training and instruction for terrorists about to be sent forth into the world on missions assigned to them by the United States government. It is clear that the only way someone like Qumu could ever get out of Guantánamo would be by agreeing to serve for the rest of his natural life as a CIA double agent in service of the United States – assuming that he was not one already. Qumu appears to have been sent back to Libya for the purpose of preparing the civil war which, supplemented by NATO bombing, succeeded in overthrowing and killing Colonel Gaddafi in 2011. The State Department and Ambassador Stevens knew all about Qumu, with whom they may have negotiated to procure levies of terrorist fighters to be sent into Syria to wage civil war against President Assad and the Baathist party government.

The security for the US Consulate in Benghazi was provided by Libyan nationals working for Blue Mountain, a British private military firm on contract for the State Department. Even more disturbing, backup security in case of an attack was supposed to be provided by the February 17 Martyrs Brigade, a terrorist group which had taken part in the overthrow of Gaddafi. This backup security never materialized. The February 17 Martyrs Brigade is also generally considered guilty of the murder of General Abdel Fattah Younes (or Younis) and his staff in the spring of 2011. Younes was at that time the main military commander of the Libyan rebel forces opposing Gaddafi in eastern Libya. The death of Younes was especially advantageous to Khalifa Hifter (or Hiftar), the main rival of Younis.

Khalifa Hifter defected from the Gaddafi regime and created his own militia with money from the CIA, according to his own 2001 book *Manipulations africaines*, published by

---

[362] "Al Qaeda, Ex-Gitmo Detainee Involved in Consulate Attack, Intelligence Sources Say," Fox News, September 20, 2012.

Le Monde Diplomatique.[363] Hifter came to the United States and lived for about 20 years in Vienna, Virginia, only 5 miles from CIA headquarters. Hifter was shipped back to Libya in the spring of 2011, with the obvious intention of becoming the commander of all rebel forces. In the process, he collided with Younes, who was then eliminated by the February 17 Martyrs Brigade. From this we can assume that the February 17 Martyrs Brigade is also not lacking in contacts with the CIA.

The question is therefore, why would the CIA asset Qumu be sent to assassinate Ambassador Stevens of the State Department?

As this book has stressed, a Mormon Mafia has established itself across the entire US intelligence, diplomatic, and security community. The existence of this CIA Mormon Mafia is a well-known fact of life in Washington, DC. Even the mainstream *Washington Post* has noted "the influx of Mormons into positions in government, the military and the CIA."[364] The last time the United States had a president explicitly supported by the CIA, it was George H. W. Bush, who with the help of his National Security Adviser, the Mormon Brent Scowcroft, launched the United States on the current cycle of never-ending wars in the Middle East. Obama has been a terrible president, but he has not been able to rely on a dedicated network of hard-core backers across the main national security agencies. In the case of Romney, we have a presidential candidate who would receive the unquestioning support of the CIA Mormon Mafia. This could give Romney a greater unchecked power to do evil than many of his predecessors.

ROMNEY A BIGGER MISER THAN EBENEZER SCROOGE

On the domestic side, anyone who currently relies on a federal government program or might conceivably have to do so in the near future should be aware that Bishop Romney is a miser and skinflint so extreme as to make Ebenezer Scrooge look like the last of the big spenders. In contrast to other Republicans, Romney chose a shabby third-floor walk-up for his campaign headquarters, and furnished it with second-hand items from the General Services Administration. Although his personal net worth is about $250 million, Romney insisted on flying coach during his presidential campaign, and refused to pay $10 for early boarding. He insists on carrying his own suitcases because he is too cheap to tip a bellboy, and washes and irons his own dress shirts in his hotel room. When Romney's Massachusetts home needed repairs, the Bishop insisted on doing the work himself to save money. Romney has been known to buy mineral water from a nearby Seven-Eleven to save money while dining at an outdoor café. Those who know Romney comment that "He respects money very much ... He is frugal in the extreme," and reporters note that "Mitt Romney always seems to have kept score with dollar signs."[365]

---

[363] See Wikipedia article on Hifter.

[364] Diane Winston, "The Faith That Fills the Romney Soul," *Washington Post*, March 11, 2012.

[365] Ann Gerhart and Philip Rucker, "Romney's Money Trap: A Frugal Man Who Saw Wealth as a Path to Public Service is Now Paying the Price with Voters," *Washington Post*, September 30, 2012.

Romney's obsession with money as the measure of all things points to severe psychological alienation, which blinds him to the fact that human productive activity, and not money in any form, is the source of all wealth. Romney qualifies as a money fetishist, from whom the victims of his austerity measures can expect no mercy.

CONCLUSION: THE DANGER OF PERMANENT PLUTOCRATIC RULE

The danger represented by Bishop Romney's possible entry into the White House is that of permanent plutocratic rule, complicated by increased foreign adventurism, and by savage austerity verging on genocide against the American people. The 2012 election may represent a critical turning point in this regard.

From a demographic point of view, the current reactionary Republican Party, dominated by its racist, anti-immigrant and xenophobic Tea Party wing, is doomed to dwindle in importance over the coming decades, as the white population of the United States declines relative to Latinos and other new immigrant groups. At the same time, while the US ruling class is aware of Obama's valuable services as strike-breaker over recent years, the Republican Party offers a better prospect for imposing a permanent austerity dictatorship. This is because the Democratic Party will always have to offer some slight symbolic concessions to labor, blacks, Latinos, women, city dwellers, and the elderly. The Democratic Party is more a confederation of interest groups, while the Republican Party is animated by a unifying ideology of oligarchical privilege.

Therefore, according to some analyses, 2012 may represent a last chance for the Republicans to seize and hold power in the form of a permanent austerity dictatorship.

ROMNEY AS ARCHITECT OF PERMANENT AUSTERITY DICTATORSHIP?

As we have shown, a Romney presidency would be very narrow in its representation, with neocons taking control of foreign policy and Mormons dominating the domestic side. The neocons in question are still angry and humiliated because they were so roundly repudiated by the American people in 2008, when the popularity of the George W. Bush regime sank to just over 20%. The neocons want to vindicate themselves and their methods, and the only way they can imagine doing this is by successful wars of conquest, in contrast to the failed military adventures of the Bush-Cheney era. At the same time, Wall Street demands nothing less than genocidal austerity against the American people, with comprehensive attacks on Medicare, Medicaid, Social Security, unemployment compensation, Head Start, WIC, food stamps, and the other remaining elements of the social safety net. Over the long term, the Republican Party might be better able to deliver on this set of foreign and domestic policies.

The Republican recipe for a permanent austerity dictatorship or plutocracy begins with disenfranchising large parts of the US electorate through voter suppression and related methods. More stringent voter identification laws, based on the nonexistent threat of "voter fraud" (as distinct from vote fraud as favored by Karl Rove and his minions) function like a modern poll tax in making it more difficult for the poor, the elderly, Hispanics, blacks, and working people in general to cast a ballot. At the same time,

Republican governors are hiring corrupt contractors to remove hundreds of thousands of probable Democratic voters from the voting rolls, with the pretext that these people are felons, deceased, no longer residents, etc. In addition, reactionary Republicans are making it more difficult to vote early or to obtain an absentee ballot.

In the wake of the Citizens United Supreme Court Decision, sponsored principally by the RATS cabal (Roberts, Alito, Thomas, and Scalia), billions of dollars are being mobilized to support reactionary candidates at all levels of government. Labor unions, which might have countered this tendency with money contributions and campaign volunteers, have been under heavy attack by reactionary Republican governors in states like Wisconsin, Ohio, Indiana, Maine, Florida – and also New York and California. The expansion of the so-called "right to work laws" for union-busting has weakened the labor organizations which have traditionally constituted one of the most effective forms of resistance against totalitarianism and oppression.

Given the structure of the US electorate, it is likely that a Romney-Ryan victory in November 2012 would be accompanied by reactionary Republican majorities in the House and Senate as well. The last time the United States suffered such a catastrophe of one-party rule was under Bush and Cheney, and the tragic consequences of that are still with us. If Republicans can control the entire federal government, they will attempt to radically narrow the franchise in such a way as to make it almost impossible to dislodge them from power during the years ahead.

Because the creation and consolidation of a permanent plutocracy or austerity dictatorship must, under current US conditions, entail a policy of severe repression against blacks, Hispanics, and working people in general, Romney appears as a much more suitable candidate than Obama to lead such a regime. Obama is notoriously timid, diffident, cautious, cowardly, and weak. Romney has brazenly proclaimed his scorn and contempt for poor people, working people, and the 47%, as this book has documented, Romney brings with him an ingrained Mormon theological hostility to black people, brown people, poor people, and to the American people in general. Romney has a mean and cruel streak which may make him indifferent to the suffering he causes, as during his years as an asset stripper at Bain Capital. Romney's servile devotion to Netanyahu of Israel, and his venom against Putin and Russia, complete this picture of the grim future which lies before the United States in 2012.

Once again, you have been warned.

JOSEPH SMITH AS PHYLLIS GREENACRE'S "IMPOSTOR"[366]

Fawn Brodie, in her biography of the Mormon Prophet Joseph Smith, suggests that one important tool for understanding the psychology and the demagogic appeal of the founder of the Latter-day Saints can be found in the psychological disorder of *pseudologia fantastica*, whose victims or practitioners are often referred to as impostors. Brodie preferred the notion of impostor to literary historian Bernard DeVoto's classification of Joseph Smith as a "paranoid," or Kimball Young's labeling of the Prophet as a "parapath," that is to say as someone unable to separate fantasy and reality.

MULTIPLE PERSONALITY *ORDER*

In the experience of the present author, the notions of the imposter and of *pseudologia fantastica* might well be expanded to include greater emphasis on the question of multiple personalities and multiple personality disorder. This insight derives from my own observation over a number of years of a charismatic political leader with strong tendencies toward the creation of a personality cult, somewhat on the model of Joseph Smith. The individual in question is Lyndon H. LaRouche. In the 1960s and 1970s, LaRouche was remarkable for his intelligence overview and programmatic orientation, which tended more and more to be overshadowed by a crude demand for adulation and unquestioning obedience, precisely along the lines of a personality cult. Over time, one got the impression that LaRouche had several distinct personalities – one perceptive and insightful, one raging, narcissistic, and vindictive, and yet another whimsical and nostalgic. Needless to say, it was the insistent and vindictive personality which employed the other selves to recruit a following and then impose on them the yoke of his personality cult. In this process, he exhibited moments of charismatic rhetorical appeal, and other moments of the most primitive infantilism. He also neglected the most elementary precautions. On the one hand, he launched campaigns of exposure and denunciation against Henry Kissinger, Jimmy Carter, Nelson Rockefeller, and other public figures of some power, while at the same time he refused to submit yearly federal income tax returns. It was this latter failing which helped to put him in jail for five years. On at least one known occasion, LaRouche reportedly boasted of his multiple personalities, while claiming that he had the ability to shift at will from one personality to another, according to his own psychological needs. LaRouche called this his "multiple personality *order*." The parallels of this syndrome to the case of Joseph Smith are evident.

In her discussion of the impostor, Phyllis Greenacre also cites the case of Titus Oates (1649-1705), who was the great protagonist of the fictitious "Popish Plot" during the reign of Charles II Stuart of England. This plot was supposedly aiming at a Catholic takeover of England with the help of the Stuarts. Fictitious though this report turned out to be, its political effects were most welcome to the pro-Venetian Whig party of the

---

[366] Phyllis Greenacre, "The Impostor," *Psychoanalytic Quarterly* XXVII (1958), pp. 359-82.

English aristocracy. Without intelligence networks interested in promoting Titus Oates' story, he might have been relegated to total obscurity. Oates was a mythomaniac, recounting wild inventions he knew his listeners wanted to hear, all in a desperate bid to attract attention. But there were powerful political forces who found his hallucinations advantageous. This reminds us once again, as in the case of Joseph Smith, to always look for the interaction between the individual impostor and the organized networks which constitute and assemble the audience which the impostor so urgently desires. Some key excerpts from Greenacre:

> "An impostor is not only a liar, but a very special type of liar who *imposes* on others fabrications of his attainments, position, or worldly possessions. This he may do through misrepresentations of his official (statistical) identity, by presenting himself with a fictitious name, history, and other items of personal identity, either borrowed from some other actual person or fabricated according to some imaginative conception of himself. There are similar falsifications on that part of his identity belonging to his accomplishments, a plagiarizing on a grand scale, or making claims which are grossly implausible. Imposture appears to contain the hope of getting something material, or some other worldly advantage. While the reverse certainly exists among the distinguished, wealthy, and competent persons who lose themselves in cloaks of obscurity and assumed mediocrity, these come less frequently into sharp focus in the public eye. One suspects, however, that some "hysterical" amnesia is, and dual or multiple personalities are conditions related to imposturous characters. The contrast between the original and the assumed identities may sometimes be not so great in the matter of worldly position, and consequently does not lend itself so readily to the superficial explanation that it has been achieved for direct and material gain. The investigation of even a few instances of imposture – if one has not become emotionally involved in the deception – is sufficient to show how crude though clever many impostors are, how very faulty any scheming is, and how often, in fact, the element of shrewdness is lacking. Rather a quality of showmanship is involved, with its reliance all on the response of an audience to illusions.

> "In some of the most celebrated instances of imposture, it indeed appears that the fraud was successful only because many others as well as the perpetrator had a hunger to believe in the fraud, and that any success of such fraudulence depended in fact on strong social as well as individual factors and especial receptivity to the trickery. To this extent those on whom the fraudulence is imposed are not only victims but unconscious conspirators. Its success too is partly a matter of timing. Such combinations of imposturous talent and a peculiar susceptibility of the times to believe in the swindler, who presents the deceptive means of salvation, may account for the great impostures of history. There are, however, instances of the repeated perpetration of frauds under circumstances which give evidence of a precise content that may seem independent of social factors....

"It is the extraordinary and continued pressure in the impostor to live out his fantasy that demands explanation, a living out which has the force of a delusion, (and in the psychotic may actually appear in that form), but it is ordinarily associated with the 'formal' awareness that the claims are false. The sense of reality is characterized by a peculiarly sharp, quick perceptiveness, extraordinarily immediate keenness and responsiveness, especially in the area of the imposture. The over-all utility of the sense of reality is, however, impaired. What is striking in many impostors is that, although they are quick to pick up details and nuances in the lives and activities of those whom they simulate and can sometimes utilize these with great adroitness, they are frequently so utterly obtuse to many ordinary considerations of fact that they give the impression of mere brazenness or stupidity in many aspects of their life peripheral to their impostures....

"The impostor has, then, a specially sharpened sensitivity within the area of his fraud, and identity toward the assumption of which he has a powerful unconscious pressure, beside which his conscious wish, although recognizable, is relatively slight. The unconscious drive heightens his perceptions in a focused area and permits him to ignore or deny other elements of reality which would ordinarily be considered matters of common sense. It is this discrepancy in abilities which makes some impostors such puzzling individuals. Skill and persuasiveness are combined with utter foolishness and stupidity.

"In well-structured impostures this may be described as a struggle between two dominant identities in the individual: the temporarily focused and strongly assertive imposturous one, and the frequently amazingly crude and poorly knit one from which the impostor has emerged. In some instances, however, it is also probable that the imposture cannot be sustained unless there is emotional support from someone who especially believes in and nourishes it. The need for self-betrayal may then he one part of the tendency to revert to a less demanding, more easily sustainable personality, particularly if support is withdrawn.

"The impostor seems to flourish on the success of his exhibitionism. Enjoyment of the limelight and inner triumph of 'putting something over' seems inherent, and bespeak the closeness of imposture to voyeurism. Both aspects are represented: pleasure in watching while the voyeur himself is invisible; exultation in being admired and observed as a spectacle. It seems as if the impostor becomes temporarily convinced of the rightness of his assumed character in proportion to the amount of attention he is able to gain from it.

"In the lives of impostors there are circumscribed areas of reaction which approach the delusional. These are clung to when the other elements of the imposture have been relinquished....

"Once an imposturous goal has been glimpsed, the individual seems to behave without need for consistency, but to strive rather for the supremacy of the gains from what can be acted out with sufficient immediate gratification to convince others. For the typical impostor, an audience is absolutely essential. It is from the confirming reaction of his audience that the impostor gets a 'realistic' sense of self, a value greater than anything he can otherwise achieve. It is the demand for an audience in which the (false) self is reflected that causes impostures often to become of social significance. Both reality and identity seem to the impostor to be strengthened rather than diminished by the success of the fraudulence of his claims....

"The impostor seems to be repeatedly seeking confirmation of his assumed identity to overcome his sense of helplessness or incompleteness. It is my impression that this is the secret of his appeal to others, and that often especially conscientious people are 'taken in' and other impostors as well attracted because of the longing to return to that happy state of omnipotence which adults have had to relinquish....

APPENDIX B

JOHN C. BENNETT'S 1842 ACCOUNT OF JOSEPH SMITH'S PLAN FOR A WESTERN EMPIRE

John Cook Bennett became, between 1840 and 1842, one of the top two or three associates of Joseph Smith. Bennett, a medical doctor, was apparently attracted to Mormonism because he was interested in the carnal benefits of polygamy. Once he had joined Joseph Smith's entourage, he became embroiled in intrigues and rivalries with other leading Mormons. Sometimes these clashes involved conflicts over women. He claimed to be in the possession of abortifacients, and he would sometimes cite this as a talking point with his potential conquests. The beginning of the end of Bennett's status as the leading protégé of Joseph Smith came when the two became rivals for the affection of 19-year-old Nancy Rigdon, the daughter of Sidney Rigdon, who – on paper at least – was the number two in the entire Mormon hierarchy.

The separation of John C. Bennett from the community of Saints in Nauvoo, Illinois was a complicated, month-long process. He was finally publicly excommunicated on June 23, 1842. Bennett retaliated against the man he called "Holy Joe" and his armed retainers, the brotherhood of Dan or Danites, with a series of articles that were published starting on July 8, 1842 in the *Sangamo Journal* of Springfield, Illinois. Bennett started his series with a melodramatic report: "I write you now from the Mormon Zion, the city of the Saints, where I am threatened death by Holy Joe, and his Danite band of murderers."[367] These articles were immediately reprinted in the leading newspapers of the United States, including the *New York Herald*. Bennett's animus against Joe Smith is clear, but his accusations were not simply manufactured out of whole cloth. Bennett embroidered his account, but in many cases he started from actual events. Bennett's observations were collected in book form as *The History of the Saints, or an Exposé of Joe Smith and Mormonism* (Boston: Leland and Whiting, 1842).

An important revelation provided by Bennett is that Joseph Smith was planning the secession of numerous states along the frontier of that time. In this, the Prophet was following in the footsteps of the infamous arch-traitor Aaron Burr, who had attempted a similar project decades before. Here are some relevant passages:

"My attention had been long turned toward the movements and designs of the Mormons, with whom I had become pretty well acquainted, years before, in the state of Ohio; and after the formation of their establishment at Nauvoo in 1839, the facts and reports respecting them, which I continually heard, led me to suspect, and, indeed, believe, that their leaders had formed, and were preparing to execute, a daring and colossal scheme of rebellion and usurpation throughout the North-Western States of the Union. It was to me evident that temporal, as well as spiritual, empire was the aim and expectation of the Prophet and his cabinet. The documents that will hereafter be introduced, will clearly show the existence of a vast and deep laid scheme, upon their part, for conquering the states of Ohio, Indiana, Illinois, Iowa, and Missouri, and of erecting upon the ruin of their

---

[367] Brodie, p. 314.

present governments a despotic military and religious empire, the head of which, as Emperor and Pope, was to be Joseph Smith, the Prophet of the Lord, and his ministers and viceroys, the apostles, high priests, elders, and bishops, of the Mormon Church.

"The fruition of this hopeful project would, of course, have been preceded by plunder, devastation, and bloodshed, and by all the countless horrors which invariably accompany civil war. American citizens could not be expected to stand quietly by, and suffer their governments to be overthrown, their religion subverted, their wives and children converted into instruments for a despot's lust and ambition, and their property forcibly appropriated to the use and furtherance of a base imposture. The Mormons would, of course, meet with resistance as soon as their intentions became evident; and so great was already their power, and so rapidly did their numbers increase, that the most frightful consequences might naturally be expected to ensue, from an armed collision between them and the citizens who still remained faithful to the God and the laws of their fathers...."[368] [...]

CONTEMPLATED MORMON EMPIRE

"In illustration of the plans and proceedings of Joe Smith and the Mormons, it may not be amiss to give some descriptive remarks upon the states which he designed as the seat of his empire and dominion, and where he had begun to establish his devoted followers, the destined instruments of his treason and ambition.

"According to the Mormon prophets, the whole region of the country between the Rocky Mountains and the Alleghenies was, at a period about 1,300 years ago, densely peopled by nations descended from a Jewish family, who emigrated from Jerusalem in the time of the Prophet Jeremiah, some six or 700 years before Christ. Immense cities were founded, and sumptuous edifices reared, and the whole land overspread with the results of a high and extensive civilization. The *Book of Mormon* speaks of cities with stupendous stone walls, and of battles in which hundreds of thousands of men were slain! The land afterwards became a waste, howling wilderness, traversed by a few straggling bands of tribes of savages, descended from a branch of the aforesaid Jewish family, who, in consequence of their wickedness, had their complexion changed from white to black, or rather dark red; but the emigrants from Europe, and their descendents, having filled the land, and God having been pleased to grant the revelation by which is made known the true history of the past in America, and the events which are about to take place, he had also commended the Saints of the Latter-day to assemble themselves together there and occupy the land which was once held by the members of the true Church, The States of Missouri, and Illinois, and the Territory of Iowa other regions to which the Prophet has hitherto directed his schemes of aggrandizement, and which were to form the NUCLEUS of the great MORMON EMPIRE. The remaining states were to be licked up like salt,

---

[368] John C. Bennett, *The History of the Saints, or an Exposé of Joe Smith and Mormonism* (Boston: Leland and Whiting, 1842; reprinted, Andrew F. Smith ed. (Urbana: University of Illinois Press, 2000), pp. 5-6.

and fall into the immense labyrinth of glorious prophetic dominion, like the defenseless lamb before the mighty king of the forest....[369] [...]

"If this Mormon villain is suffered to carry out his plans, I warn the people of these United States, that in less than 20 years we will see them involved in the civil war of the most formidable character. They will have to encounter a numerous and ferocious enemy, excited to the utmost by fanaticism and by pretended revelations from God, and led on by reckless, ambitious, and, in some respects, evil scoundrels, who will not pause in the execution of their projects, even though to accomplish them they should deluge this fair land with the blood of her sons, and exterminate the result of the toil and the civilization of more than two centuries. I *know* that these things are so. I know that the Mormon leaders entertain these designs, and I know the strength and the force that a few more years of impunity will enable them to bring to the accomplishment of their treasonable projects."[370]

---

[369] Bennett, p. 293.
[370] Bennett, p. 306.

THOMAS CARLYLE'S 1854 DRAFT ESSAY ON THE MORMONS[371]

January 9, 1854

An article on the Mormons? It were well worth writing, had one heart for it. Mormonism is a gross physical form of Calvinism; gross, physical and in many ways very base; but in this one point incommensurably (transcendently) superior to all other forms of religion now extant. That it is believed, that it is practically acted upon from day to day and from hour to hour; taken as a very fact, the neglect or contradiction of which will vitiate and ruin all other facts of the day and of the hour. That is its immeasurable superiority; in virtue of that it has still a root in this feracious Earth, and prospers as we see.

Beneficent Nature is tolerant of much rubbish […] but there is one thing which the Earth will not grow: […] the thing called Hypocrisy; the generally respectable but thrice and four times accursed thing. […]

From this curse of curses, which indeed is an almost quite unadulterated curse, Mormonism is free: and that is an immense point. […]

Mormonism illustrates: 1° The value of sincerity towards one's convictions (as above); 2° It offers a good illustration of the mixture of Despotism and Liberty, – indicates, in dim rude outline, what the perfect Form of Government may be which men are so universally groping after at present. Here, sure enough, is Liberty: all these people are free citizens, to begin with; members of the model republic: entitled to the ballot box, caucus, free press, open vestry, open congress, fourth estate and every form of opposition, conceivable by the human mind. – nothing to limit whatever mutiny may be in them except the universal parish-constable, speaking symbolically. "Hands *not* in each other's pockets; hands off each other's skins!" To this degree of liberty, unsurpassable even by fancy they were all born; to this any time they can appeal, and practically return, with themselves and all their interests. But the curious point is to see Despotism withal. No Czar of Russia is so absolute as Joseph Smith's successor. Foul drains, with the means of cleaning them apparent to everybody, are not probable under his government; ill will it fare in the Mormon City with any vested interest that grounds itself on fomenting mud and the poison of the citizens' blood. Dirty water, so soon as there is money and strength to produce clean, Joseph Smith's successor is not likely to continue drinking. What is wrong he *can* put right. Intolerable nuisance losses and abominations, admitted to be such by all reasonable man, need not there continue because there is not somewhere "power" to clear them out of the man's sight. Here then is a "beneficent

[371] Clyde de L. Ryals, "Thomas Carlyle on the Mormons: an Unpublished Essay, *Carlyle Studies Annual* (XV) 1995, pp. 49-54.

Despotism": a thing much in request with some among us, but impossible to discover hitherto by any hustings manipulation, or other constitutional apparatus. The question. How it is got there, is very well worth meditating, and will lead a man's thoughts into many reflections not quite common to the general mind at present.

How is J. Smith's successor got elected? I suppose there is voting, even universal voting, concerned in it; all the people, no doubt, some way or other give their votes; signify their willingness; nay it is their loyal choice, and express relation and appointments that can alone be conceived to bring about the result. Voting enough: and yet I suppose, there is a good deal of "usurpation" in it too. Joseph Smith's successor first of all, as I cannot but conclude, gives a plumper [a direct and blunt solicitation] in behalf of himself; passes an act of legislature within his own head that he is successor; the fittest man. The worthiest about him have perhaps still earlier seen this; these and he control the others by superiority of insight; force them to vote voluntarily to the same effect. I can fancy the process, which were long to describe. Some way or other the result is brought about: this all men can see, and the most salutary results it is for the Mormon Community. (By no Contrivance in the fashion or handling of this ballot box, – ah no; by far other means and methods, little known to *us* at present, the approximately Best of Mormons is got sifted and hustled out, and raised to the top of the Mormon Community with a power to remove nuisances, to promote cooperations, repress contradictions and superfluities and increase the general amount of wisdom and therefore of success in the Society's operations, to a really surprising degree. [...]

But alas the Mormons have several advantages in choosing their King, in which we European men are still sadly behind them. First they had the conviction that wisdom is necessary; that it will be a sin, nay the chief fountain of sins, if the Fittest Mormon is not got to the top of Mormonism: sin which God will assuredly punish; – and indeed it is too plain to me that the very laws of Nature, as we call them, do protest daily and hourly against any other than the Fittest being put to the top in anything whatever, especially in Society which is the summary of things. [...]

Being in earnest about this preliminary part is probably the chief secret of the Mormon success in getting their Fittest Man. And a second head of advantage to them, their getting a beneficent despot in their Fittest follows out of this first one, or is almost only the first one over again. The Mormon Government is supreme in Mormon Conviction; what he does and orders is what every good Mormon is longing to see done. That is the secret of just despotism, of a Despotism which can be called beneficent. The few wise are all for it; None but the insincere and unwise are against it – and these are not so given up to their many insincerities and cowardices and unwisdoms as not to be amenable when better is shown to them. Joseph Smith's successor as his Council of Elders, Inspectors, Deacons etc. etc. – an actual Aristocracy sufficient for the nonce. All proceeding from sincerity on the part of his people. A Government that fills us with envy.

APPENDIX D

BRIGHAM YOUNG'S UTAH SECESSION DECREE

PROCLAMATION BY THE GOVERNOR [BRIGHAM YOUNG][372]

September 15, 1857

CITIZENS OF UTAH:

We are invaded by hostile forces, who are evidently assailing us to accomplish our overthrow and destruction.

For the last twenty-five years we have trusted officials of the government, from Constables and Justices to Judges, Governors and Presidents, only to be scorned, held in derision, insulted and betrayed. Our houses have been plundered and then burned; our fields laid waste, our principal men butchered while under the pledged faith of the Government for their safety, and our families driven from their homes to find that shelter in the barren wilderness, and that protection among hostile savages, which were denied them in the boasted abodes of Christianity and civilization.
The constitution of our common country guarantees unto us all that we do now or ever claimed.
If the constitutional rights, which pertain unto us as American citizens, were extended to Utah, according to the spirit and meaning thereof, and fairly and impartially administered, it is all that we could ask.

Our opponents have availed themselves of prejudices existing against us, because of our religious faith, to send out a formidable host to accomplish our destruction. We have had no privilege, no opportunity of defending ourselves from the false, foul and unjust aspersions against us before the Nation. The Government has not condescended to cause an investigating committee or other person to be sent to inquire into and ascertain the truth, as is customary in such cases. We know those aspersions to be false, but that avails us nothing. We are condemned unheard, and forced to an issue with an armed mercenary mob, which has been sent against us at the instigation of anonymous letter writers, ashamed to father the base, slanderous falsehoods which they have given to the public; of corrupt officials who have brought false accusations against us, to screen themselves in their own infamy; and of hireling priests and howling editors, who prostitute the truth for filthy lucre's sake.

The issue which has been thus forced upon us compels us to resort to the great first law of self preservation, and stand in our own defense, a right guaranteed unto us by the genius of the institutions of our country, and upon which the Government is based.

---

[354] Douglas O. Linder, "Mountain Meadows Massacre (1875-76)," *Famous Trials*, University of Missouri-Kansas City (UMKC) School of Law, 2012, online at umkc.edu.

Our duty to our families requires us not to tamely submit to be driven and slain without an attempt to preserve ourselves. Our duty to our country, our holy religion, our God, to freedom and liberty, requires that we should not quietly stand still and see those fetters forging around, which are calculated to enslave and bring us into subjection to an unlawful military despotism, such as can only emanate (in a country of constitutional law) from usurpation, tyranny and oppression.

Therefore, I, Brigham Young, Governor and Superintendent of Indian Affairs for the Territory of Utah, in the name of the people or the United States in the Territory of Utah,

First - Forbid all armed forces of every description from coming into this Territory, under any pretense whatever.

Second - That all the forces in said Territory hold themselves in readiness to march at a moment's notice, to repel any and all such invasion

Third - Martial law is hereby declared to exist in this Territory, from and after the publication of this Proclamation; and no person shall be allowed to pass or repass, into or through, or from this Territory without a permit from the proper officer.

Given under my hand and seal at Great Salt Lake City, Territory of Utah, this fifteenth day of September, A.D. eighteen hundred and fifty seven, and of the Independence of the United States of America, the eighty-second.

(Signed) BRIGHAM YOUNG

APPENDIX E

"A STRANGE SYSTEM OF TERRORISM"
PRESIDENT JAMES BUCHANAN'S PROCLAMATION ON THE MORMON
REBELLION IN THE UTAH TERRITORY, APRIL 6, 1858

BY THE PRESIDENT OF THE UNITED STATES OF AMERICA
A PROCLAMATION[373]

Whereas the Territory of Utah was settled by certain emigrants from the States and from foreign countries who have for several years past manifested a spirit of insubordination to the Constitution and laws of the United States. The great mass of those settlers, acting under the influence of leaders to whom they seem to have surrendered their judgment, refuse to be controlled by any other authority. They have been often advised to obedience, and these friendly counsels have been answered with defiance. The officers of the Federal Government have been driven from the Territory for no offense but an effort to do their sworn duty; others have been prevented from going there by threats of assassination; judges have been violently interrupted in the performance of their functions, and the records of the courts have been seized and destroyed or concealed. Many other acts of unlawful violence have been perpetrated, and the right to repeat them has been openly claimed by the leading inhabitants, with at least the silent acquiescence of nearly all the others. Their hostility to the lawful government of the country has at length become so violent that no officer bearing a commission from the Chief Magistrate of the Union can enter the Territory or remain there with safety, and all those officers recently appointed have been unable to go to Salt Lake or anywhere else in Utah beyond the immediate power of the Army. Indeed, such is believed to be the condition to which a strange system of terrorism has brought the inhabitants of that region that no one among them could express an opinion favorable to this Government, or even propose to obey its laws, without exposing his life and property to peril.

After carefully considering this state of affairs and maturely weighing the obligation I was under to see the laws faithfully executed, it seemed to me right and proper that I should make such use of the military force at my disposal as might be necessary to protect the Federal officers in going into the Territory of Utah and in performing their duties after arriving there. I accordingly ordered a detachment of the Army to march for the city of Salt Lake, or within reach of that place, and to act in case of need as a posse for the enforcement of the laws. But in the meantime the hatred of that misguided people for the just and legal authority of the Government had become so intense that they resolved to measure their military strength with that of the Union. They have organized an armed force far from contemptible in point of numbers and trained it, if not with skill, at least with great assiduity and perseverance. While the troops of the United States were on their march a train of baggage wagons, which happened to be unprotected, was attacked and destroyed by a portion of the Mormon forces and the provisions and stores

---

[373] James Buchanan: "Proclamation - Rebellion in the Territory of Utah," April 6, 1858. Online text posted by Gerhard Peters and John T. Woolley, The American Presidency Project, http://www.presidency.ucsb.edu/ws/?pid=68308.

with which the train was laden were wantonly burnt. In short, their present attitude is one of decided and unreserved enmity to the United States and to all their loyal citizens. Their determination to oppose the authority of the Government by military force has not only been expressed in words, but manifested in overt acts of the most unequivocal character.

Fellow-citizens of Utah, this is rebellion against the Government to which you owe allegiance; it is levying war against the United States, and involves you in the guilt of treason. Persistence in it will bring you to condign punishment, to ruin, and to shame; for it is mere madness to suppose that with your limited resources you can successfully resist the force of this great and powerful nation.

If you have calculated upon the forbearance of the United States, if you have permitted yourselves to suppose that this Government will fail to put forth its strength and bring you to submission, you have fallen into a grave mistake. You have settled upon territory which lies, geographically, in the heart of the Union. The land you live upon was purchased by the United States and paid for out of their Treasury; the proprietary right and title to it is in them, and not in you. Utah is bounded on every side by States and Territories whose people are true to the Union. It is absurd to believe that they will or can permit you to erect in their very midst a government of your own, not only independent of the authority which they all acknowledge, but hostile to them and their interests.

Do not deceive yourselves nor try to mislead others by propagating the idea that this is a crusade against your religion. The Constitution and laws of this country can take no notice of your creed, whether it be true or false. That is a question between your God and yourselves, in which I disclaim all right to interfere. If you obey the laws, keep the peace, and respect the just rights of others, you will be perfectly secure, and may live on in your present faith or change it for another at your pleasure. Every intelligent man among you knows very well that this Government has never, directly or indirectly, sought to molest you in your worship, to control you in your ecclesiastical affairs, or even to influence you in your religious opinions.

This rebellion is not merely a violation of your legal duty; it is without just cause, without reason, without excuse. You never made a complaint that was not listened to with patience; you never exhibited a real grievance that was not redressed as promptly as it could be. The laws and regulations enacted for your government by Congress have been equal and just, and their enforcement was manifestly necessary for your own welfare and happiness. You have never asked their repeal. They are similar in every material respect to the laws which have been passed for the other Territories of the Union, and which everywhere else (with one partial exception) have been cheerfully obeyed. No people ever lived who were freer from unnecessary legal restraints than you. Human wisdom never devised a political system which bestowed more blessings or imposed lighter burdens than the Government of the United States in its operation upon the Territories.

But being anxious to save the effusion of blood and to avoid the indiscriminate punishment of a whole people for crimes of which it is not probable that all are equally guilty, I offer now a free and full pardon to all who will submit themselves to the just authority of the Federal Government. If you refuse to accept it, let the consequences fall upon your own heads. But I conjure you to pause deliberately and reflect well before you reject this tender of peace and good will.

Now, therefore, I, James Buchanan, President of the United States, have thought proper to issue this my proclamation, enjoining upon all public officers in the Territory of Utah to be diligent and faithful, to the full extent of their power, in the execution of the laws; commanding all citizens of the United States in said Territory to aid and assist the officers in the performance of their duties; offering to the inhabitants of Utah who shall submit to the laws a free pardon for the seditions and treasons heretofore by them committed; warning those who shall persist, after notice of this proclamation, in the present rebellion against the United States that they must expect no further lenity, but look to be rigorously dealt with according to their deserts; and declaring that the military forces now in Utah and hereafter to be sent there will not be withdrawn until the inhabitants of that Territory shall manifest a proper sense of the duty which they owe to this Government.

In testimony whereof I have hereunto set my hand and caused the seal of the United States to be affixed to these presents. Done at the city of Washington the 6th day of April, 1858, and of the Independence of the United States the eighty-second.

JAMES BUCHANAN.

By the President:

LEWIS CASS, *Secretary of State.*

DIVERGENCES OF MORMONISM FROM CHRISTIANITY: THE ANNOTATED CREED

Are Mormons Christians? One way to clarify this question is to compare basic Mormon beliefs to the Nicene-Constantinopolitan creed, which may be considered the most succinct summary of the main points of Christian belief. This creed or statement of faith was approved by the Council of Nicaea in 325 AD and then modified by the Council of Constantinople in 381 AD. Roman Catholics, Anglicans, Lutherans, Calvinists, Baptists, and other Protestant denominations accept this creed. The Greek, Russian, and other Eastern Orthodox churches accept the creed but not the sixth-century addition that specifies that the Holy Spirit also proceeds from the Son (*filioque*). The Oriental Orthodox churches (Armenians, Ethiopians, Copts, Syriacs, and others), sometimes called monophysites, profess the Nicene-Constantinopolitan Creed, but do not accept the other church councils starting with Chalcedon in 451 AD.

Some might argue that the Mormons represent a Christian heresy, not an entirely new religion. The question is where a series of divergences reach critical mass and turn into a totally new faith. The Mormons manage to combine the two heresies that received the most attention from the early church councils. The Mormons are Arians, meaning that they view Christ as created within time, and not on the same level as God the Father. Remarkably, they manage to simultaneously embrace Apollinarianism, the idea that Christ has divine soul in human flesh. Important is also Joseph Smith's testimony heavenly visitors told him all religions were corrupt, implying that a new one had to be founded. That is in fact what he did.

Here is the Christian Creed, with Mormon disagreements indicated in the notes.

I believe in one God,[374]
the Father Almighty,[375]
maker of heaven and earth,[376]
and of all things visible and invisible;[377]
And in one Lord Jesus Christ,[378]
the only begotten[379] Son of God,
begotten of his Father before all worlds,[380]

---

[374] Mormons are polytheists who believe in the existence of many gods, as in the pagan patheon.
[375] The Mormon god is not almighty, but more of a president or coordinator. The Mormon article of faith, "As man is, God once was. As God is, man may become," shows God as a being emerging within time whom humans may successfully imitate and match.
[376] Mormonism regards the universe as existing prior to God.
[377] The world of matter antedates the Mormon god.
[378] The Mormon Christ is only a superior god among other gods.
[379] Begotten in Mormonism means created by biological generation.
[380] Mormons see Christ as created within time.

God of God, Light of Light,
very God of very God,[381]
begotten,[382] not made,
being of one substance with the Father;[383]
by whom all things were made;[384]
who for us men and for our salvation
came down from heaven,[385]
and was incarnate by the Holy Ghost[386]
of the Virgin Mary,
and was made man;
and was crucified also for us under Pontius Pilate;
he suffered and was buried;
and the third day he rose again
according to the Scriptures,
and ascended into heaven,[387]
and sitteth on the right hand of the Father;[388]
and he shall come again, with glory,

---

[381] These two lines are thoroughly diluted and relativized in Mormonism.

[382] Again, "begotten" in Mormonism means created by biological generation.

[383] Mormonism explodes the Trinity and sees rather three separate persons working for similar goals.

[384] The Mormon God did not create the universe, but came into it.

[385] Mormonism posits a general desire by pre-existing spirits to acquire bodies and enter the material world.

[386] Mormonism seems to regard the Annunciation as a physical act by Elohim, rather than the action of the Holy Spirit.

[387] For Mormons, heaven is supposed to have three levels: "telestial," terrestrial, and celestial.

[388] Mormonism would add that Christ returned after the Ascension, specifically to preach in the western hemisphere.

to judge both the quick and the dead;[389]
whose kingdom shall have no end.[390]
And I believe in the Holy Ghost the Lord, and Giver of Life,
who proceedeth from the Father [and the Son];[391]
who with the Father and the Son together
is worshipped and glorified;
who spake by the Prophets.
And I believe one holy Catholic and Apostolic Church;[392]
I acknowledge one baptism for the remission of sins;
and I look for the resurrection of the dead,
and the life of the world to come.[393]
AMEN.

---

[389] Mormonism envisions a final judgment by Elohim, the Mormon Jesus, and Joseph Smith. Joseph Smith in particular holds the keys to salvation.

[390] The Mormon Heaven is the scene of eternal progression, including married life and family life.

[391] The procession of the Holy Spirit from the Father and the Son is at best murky in Mormonism.

[392] Mormonism holds that all other churches are fallen, and only the LDS offers salvation.

[393] For successful Mormon patriarchs, this means progressing to divinity and acquiring a planet to rule over, accompanied by a harem of spirit wives and spirit children.

SELECT BIBLIOGRAPHY

Ahlstrom, Sydney E. *A Religious History of the American People*. New Haven, Connecticut: Yale University Press, 1972.

Anderson, Rodger I. *Joseph Smith's New York Reputation Reexamined.* Salt Lake City, Utah: Signature Books, Inc., 1990.

Armstrong, Gregory K., Grow, Matthew J., and Siler, Dennis J. eds. *Parley P. Pratt and the Making of Mormonism.* Oklahoma, Arthur H. Clark Company, 2011.

Arrington, Leonard J. *Brigham Young, American Moses.* New York: Alfred A. Knopf, 1985.

Bagley, Will. *Blood of the Prophets: Brigham Young and the Massacre at Mountain Meadows.* Norman, Oklahoma: University of Oklahoma, 2002.

Bennett, John C. *The History of the Saints: or, An Exposé of Joe Smith and Mormonism.* Third Edition. Chicago, Illinois: University of Illinois Press, 2000.

Bigler, David L. and Bagley, Will. *The Mormon Rebellion: America's First Civil War, 1857 – 1858.* Norman, Oklahoma: University of Oklahoma Press, 2011.

Bringhurst, Newell G., ed. *Reconsidering No Man Knows My History: Fawn M. Brodie and Joseph Smith in Retrospect.* Logan, Utah: Utah State University Press, 1996.

Brodie, Fawn M. *No Man Knows My History: The Life of Joseph Smith the Mormon Prophet.* Second Edition. New York: Alfred A. Knopf, 1971.

Buerger, David John. *The Mysteries of Godliness: a History of Mormon Temple Worship.* San Francisco: Smith Research Associates, 1994.

Bushman, Richard L. *Joseph Smith and the Beginnings of Mormonism.* Chicago, Illinois: University of Illinois Press, 1984.

Bushman, Richard Lyman and Woodworth, Jed. *Joseph Smith: Rough Stone Rolling.* New York: Alfred A. Knopf, 2005.

Cannon, Hamlin M. *The Mormon War: A Study in Territorial Rebellion.* MA Thesis. Columbia University, 1938.

Carlyle, Thomas. *Reminiscences.* New York: Charles Scribner's Sons, 1881.

Dallimore, Arnold. *Forerunner of the Charismatic Movement: The Life of Edward Irving*. Chicago: The Moody Bible Institute, 1983.

Dickens, Charles. *The Uncommercial Traveller and Reprinted Pieces Etc*. New York: Oxford University Press, 1996.

Flegg, Columba G. *'Gathered Under Apostles:' A Study of the Catholic Apostolic Church*. New York: Oxford University Press, 1992.

Givens, Terryl L. and Grow, Matthew J. *Parley P. Pratt: The Apostle Paul of Mormonism*. New York: Oxford University Press, 2011.

Green, N. W. *Mormonism: Its Rise, Progress, and Present Condition*. Hartford, Connecticut: Belknap & Bliss, 1870. Reprinted New York: AMS Press, 1971.

Hewitt, Hugh. *A Mormon in the White House? 10 Things Every American Should Know About Mitt Romney*. Washington, DC: Regnery Publishing, Inc., 2007.

Hirshson, Stanley P. *The Lion of the Lord: A Biography of Brigham Young*. New York: Alfred A. Knopf, 1969.

Kranish, Michael and Helman, Scott. *The Real Romney*. New York: HarperCollins, 2012.

Lee, John D. *Mormonism Unveiled*. Albuquerque, New Mexico: Fierra Blanca Publications, 2001.

LeSuer, Stephen C. *The 1838 Mormon War in Missouri*. Columbia, Missouri: University of Missouri Press, 1987.

Long, E. B. *The Saints and the Union*. Chicago, Illinois: University of Illinois Press, 1981.

Madsen, Brigham D. *Glory Hunter: A Biography of Patrick Edward Connor*. Salt Lake City, Utah: University of Utah Press, 1990.

Millet, Robert L., ed. *Joseph Smith: Selected Sermons and Writings*. New York: Paulist Press, 1989.

Oliphant, Margaret. *The Life of Edward Irving, Minister of the National Scotch Church, London*. London: Hurst and Blackett, 1864.

Romney, Mitt. *No Apology: The Case for American Greatness*. New York: St. Martin's Press, 2010.

Romney, Mitt with Robinson, Timothy. *Turnaround: Crisis, Leadership and the Olympic Games*. Washington, DC: Regnery Publishing, 2004.

Romney, Thomas Cottam. *Life Story of Miles P. Romney.* Missouri: Zion's Printing and Publishing, 1948.

Sandeen, Ernest, R. *The Roots of Fundamentalism: British and American Millenarianism 1800-1930.* Chicago: The University of Chicago Press, 1970.

Taves, Ernest H. *Trouble Enough: Joseph Smith and the Book of Mormon.* New York: Prometheus Books, 1984.

Werner, Morris R. *Brigham Young.* New York: Harcourt, Brace and Company, 1925.

Wicks, Roberts S. and Foister, Fred R. *Junius and Joseph: Presidential Politics and the Assassination of the First Mormon Prophet.* Logan, Utah: Utah State University Press, 2005.

Romney's

Famous

Flip

Flops

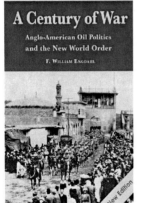

Two by Henry Makow

Illuminati: Cult that Hijacked the World tackles taboos like Zionism, British Empire, Holocaust denial. How international bankers stole a monopoly on government credit, and took over the world. They run it all: wars, schools, media. 249 pp, $19.95.

Illuminati 2: Deception & Seduction , more hidden history. 285 pp. $19.95

Four by Michel Chossudovsky

Towards a World War III Scenario: The Dangers of Nuclear War. The Pentagon is preparing a first-strike nuclear attack. on Iran. 103 pp, $15.95.

The Global Economic Crisis: The Great Depression of the XXI Century. by Prof. Chossudovsky with a dozen other experts. 416 pp, $25.95.

The Globalization of Poverty and the New World Order. Brilliant analysis how corporatism feeds on poverty, destroying the environment, apartheid, racism, sexism, and ethnic strife. 401 pp, $27.95.

America's "War on Terrorism" Concise, wide-reaching, hard-hitting study on 9/11 in geopolitical context. 387 pp, $22.95.

History

Two by George Seldes: *1,000 Americans Who Rule the USA* (1947, 324 pp, $18.95) and *Facts and Fascism* (1943, 292 pp., $15.95) by the great muckraking journalist, whistleblower on the plutocrats who keep the media in lockstep, and finance fascism.

Afghanistan: A Window on the Tragedy. 98 black and white photos, steeped in the pathos and predicament of the Afghan people. 110 pp, $3.99.

Enemies by Design: Inventing the War on Terrorism. A century of imperialism in the Middle East. Bio of Osama bin Ladeen; Zionization of America; PNAC, Afghanistan, Palestine, Iraq; 416 pp, $17.95.

Global Predator: US Wars for Empire. A damning account of the atrocities committed by US armed forces over two centuries. Also by Stewart H. Ross:

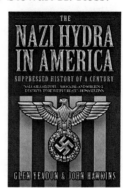

Propaganda for War: How the US was Conditioned to Fight the Great War Propaganda by Britain and her agents like Teddy Roosevelt sucked the USA into the war to smash the old world order. 350 pp and $18.95 each.

Inside the Gestapo: Hitler's Shadow over the World. Intimate, fascinating Nazi defector's tale of ruthlessness, intrigue, and geopolitics. 287 pp, $17.95.

The Nazi Hydra in America: Suppressed History of a Century by Glen Yeadon. US plutocrats launched Hitler, then recouped Nazi assets to erect today's police state. Fascists won WWII because they ran both sides. "The story is shocking and sobering and deserves to be widely read." – Howard Zinn. 700 pp, $19.95.

Sunk: The Story of the Japanese Submarine Fleet, 1941-1945. The bravery of doomed men in a lost cause, against impossible odds. 300 pp, $15.95.

Terrorism and the Illuminati, A 3000-Year History.
"Islamic" terrorists are tentacles of western imperialism—
the Illuminati. 332 pp, $16.95.

Witness in Palestine: *A Jewish-American Woman in the*
Occupied Territories. The nuts and bolts of everyday
oppression. Color photos. 400 pp, $28.95.

Psychology: Brainwashing

The Manipulated Mind. Why is it so hard to get people to see the truth? What
is brainwashing? It's the manipulation of influences that act on us all the time,
like emotional dependency. Can some traits help us resist? Self-directedness,
sense of purpose, loved ones... Hardback, no dustjacket, 217 pp, $14.95.
The Rape of the Mind: The Psychology of Thought Control, Menticide and
Brainwashing. Conditioning in open and closed societies; tools for self-
defense against torture or social pressure. 320 pp, $16.95.
The Telescreen: An Empirical Study of the Destruction of Consciousness,
by Prof. Jeffrey Grupp. How mass media brainwash us with consumerism and
war propaganda. Fake history, news, issues, and reality steal our souls.
199 pp, $14.95. Also by Grupp: ***Telementation: Cosmic Feeling and the Law***
of Attraction. Deep feeling rather than thought or faith is our secret nature and
key to self-realization. 124 pp, $12.95.

Conspiracy, NWO

Corporatism: the Secret Government of the New World Order by Prof.
Jeffrey Grupp. Corporations control all world resources. Their New World
Order is the "prison planet" that Hitler aimed for. 408 pp, $16.95.
Descent into Slavery by Des Griffin. How the banksters took over America
and the world. Covers the Founding Fathers, Rothschilds, the Crown and the
City, the world wars, and globalization. 310 pp, $16.
Dope Inc.: Britain's Opium War against the United States. "The Book that
Drove Kissinger Crazy." Underground Classic, new edition. 320 pp, $12.95.
Final Warning: A History of the New World Order by D. A. Rivera. Classic,
in-depth research into the Great Conspiracy: the Fed, the CFR, Trilateral
Commission, Illuminati. 360 pp, $14.95.
How the World Really Works by A.B. Jones. Crash course in conspiracy
offers digests of 11 classics like *Tragedy and Hope, Creature from Jekyll*
Island. 336 pp, $15.
The Triumph of Consciousness by Chris Clark. The real Global Warming
and Greening agenda: more hegemony by the NWO. 347 pp, $14.95.

Conspiracy: False Flag Operations

9/11 on Trial: The W T C Collapse. 20 closely argued proofs the World Trade
Center was destroyed by controlled demolition. 192 pp, $12.95.
9/11 Truth Novel ***Instruments of the State*** by Dave Aossey. 550 pp, $14.95.
Conspiracies, Conspiracy Theories and the Secrets of 9/11, German best-
seller explores conspiracy in history, before tackling 9/11. 274 pp, $14.95.

Enigma of Gunpowder Plot 1605*: The Third Solution.* The authoritative work showing Guy Fawkes was a patsy in a state-sponsored false-flag terror scheme that was the foundation of the British empire. 528 pp, sale price: $55.

Gladio, NATO's Dagger at the Heart of Europe: *The Pentagon-Mafia-Nazi Terror Axis.* The blood-red thread of terror by NATO death squads across Europe, from WW2 right up to 2012. 484 pp, $16.95.

Subverting Syria*: How CIA Contra Gangs and NGO's Manufacture, Mislabel and Market Mass Murder.* The Syrian "uprising" is a cynical US plot using provocateurs, mercenaries, and Wahhabi fanatics. 116 pp, $10.00

Terror on the Tube: Behind the Veil of 7/7, an Investigation, by Nick Kollerstrom. The only book with the glaring evidence that all four Muslim scapegoats were completely innocent. 3rd ed, 322 pp, $17.77.

The War on Freedom. The seminal exposé of 9/11. "Far and away the best and most balanced analysis of September 11th." – Gore Vidal. 400 pp, $16.95.

Truth Jihad*: My Epic Struggle Against the 9/11 Big Lie.* Kevin Barrett's outrageously humorous autobiographical testament. 224 pp, $9.95.

Coming Soon

Just Too Weird*: Bishop Romney and the Mormon Takeover of America; Polygamy, Theocracy, and Subversion*, by Webster Griffin Tarpley.

The Real Pearl Harbor Conspiracy, by Webster Tarpley. Japanese aggression was part of British empire scheme to conquer the US. Crypto-fascists, not FDR, let Pearl Harbor be attacked.

The Money Power: Empire of the City and Pawns in the Game. Two classic geopolitics books in one. The illuminist Three World Wars conspiracy.

In Search of the Truth: *An Exposure of the Conspiracy,* by Azar Mirza-Beg. A portrait of our times, society and religion, and the threat that faces us.

George Washington*: The Scoundrel and his Misdeeds.* He was a British spy who assassinated the French ambassador, starting the French & Indian War.

Twin Towers of Terror*: 9/11 and the Media Cover-Up,* by Geoffrey H. Smith

Troublesome Country. A history of the USA in light of failure to live up to its guiding democratic creed.

E-Books
9/11 Synthetic Terror: Made in USA
Barack Obama, the Unauthorized Biography.
Gladio, NATO's Dagger at the Heart of Europe
The Nazi Hydra in America
Subverting Syria

ProgRESSive Independent Media.
ProgressivePress.com

CPSIA information can be obtained at www.ICGtesting.com
Printed in the USA
BVOW060439151012

302920BV00004B/2/P